Almanac of World War I

Almanac of

David F. Burg
and
L. Edward Purcell

World War I

Introduction by
William Manchester

THE UNIVERSITY PRESS OF KENTUCKY

Publication of this volume was made possible in part
by a grant from the National Endowment for the Humanities.

Editorial and Sales Offices: The University Press of Kentucky
663 South Limestone Street, Lexington, Kentucky 40508-4008
www.kentuckypress.com

07 06 05 04   5 4 3 2 1

Library of Congress Cataloging-in-Publication Data

Burg, David F.
    Almanac of World War I / David F. Burg and L. Edward Purcell ;
  introduction by William Manchester
       p.   cm.
  Includes bibliographical references and index.
  ISBN 0-8131-2072-1 (cloth : acid-free paper)
  ISBN 0-8131-9087-8 (paper : acid-free paper)
    1. World War, 1914-1918—chronology. 2. Military biography.
  3. World War, 1914-1918—Biography. I. Purcell, L. Edward.
  II. Title.
  D522.5.B87   1998
  940.3'02'02—dc21   98-26625

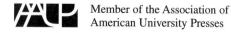

Member of the Association of
American University Presses

Contents

Maps and Sidebars

Maps

Sidebars

Acknowledgments

We owe an immense debt to the legions of historians, biographers, and memoirists who have written about World War I. We were assisted in our search for information by the unusually competent reference staff of the Margaret I. King Library at the University of Kentucky, and we gratefully acknowledge their help. We are also grateful for assistance from the staff of the Prints and Photographs Division of the Library of Congress and especially to Peter Harrington, curator of the Anne S.K. Brown Military Collection at Brown University. We also much appreciate the assent of Academy Chicago Publishers for permission to reproduce the maps.

As is ever the case, we could not function without the loving support of our families, for which we can express only our pitifully inadequate thanks.

The Great War — An Introduction

William Manchester

Few men, including most of those who were to die in it, knew precisely how World War I started. They can hardly be blamed. The explanation was not only complicated; it didn't even make sense. The immediate reason for the conflict was a murder in the Balkans. On Sunday, June 28, 1914, a Serb fanatic, armed with a revolver, assassinated Franz Ferdinand, Archduke of the Austro-Hungarian Empire, while he was riding through the Bosnian capital of Sarajevo.

That was the small crime. The greater crime, which followed it, grew out of commitments made by generations of diplomats. The great European powers had joined alliances binding them to fight for one another. Thus, the slaying of the Archduke by a Serb, followed by an Austrian decision to attack the little kingdom of Serbia, set off a chain of events that arose inexorably from those diplomatic pledges.

But not at once. Everything moved more slowly then, including vengeance. It took the Austrians a full month to declare war on Serbia. Then the czar of Russia, Serbia's ally, ordered his generals to begin mobilization. Berlin was alarmed. The Russians would require a long time to call their men up, but then their army would be enormous. Therefore, Germany, Austria's ally, declared war on Russia. Next, France, bound to the Russians by treaty, declared war on the Germans.

Great Britain had reached an understanding—an entente—with the French. They were not obliged to fight, but their sympathies were obvious. In addition, they were worried about the safety of little Belgium, which was situated in harm's way. Therefore, Whitehall asked Berlin to guarantee Belgian neutrality. Berlin refused. On August 4, Britain's declaration of war on Germany expanded the growing holocaust. Nearly three weeks later, the Japanese, who had allied themselves with the English, followed suit. Italy and the United States announced that they would remain neutral; but in 1916, the Italians became belligerent, and so, the following year, did the Americans.

Europe's last general war had ended at Waterloo ninety-nine years earlier. In 1914, men marched gaily away, unaware of how terrible fighting could be. In that high summer, 6 million men sprang to arms with medieval ardor, and a month passed before anyone knew what had happened to them. The chief sources of confusion, it turned out, were the meticulous war plans that had been drawn up by the various general staffs. Their elaborate battle scenarios had long lain in vaults, awaiting the call to glory. To their authors, they seemed perfect, but as the curtain rose on the Great War, events revealed that all shared the same crippling flaw. Each had assumed that the enemy would do what the planners expected, and now, to their exasperation, their enemies were doing the unexpected.

France's plan—Plan 17—was the worst. It called for *l'offensive à outrance,* carried out with *toujours l'audace* by gallant men crying *"En avant! A la baionette!"* In general headquarters, French generals spoke glowingly of the natural elan of the *poilu.* They had never stopped dreaming of Murat and Ney and the glint of Austerlitz moonlight on the lances of the emperor's cavalry, never lost their yearning for *la gloire,* and never paused to ponder the changes in warfare wrought by technology: automatic weapons, heavy steel artillery, barbed wire—all of which should have been obvious to European observers of the Russo-Japanese War ten years earlier. The result was the Great War's first engagement, the four-day Battle of the Frontiers. Bayonets fixed, an army of young Frenchmen lunged into Lorraine in a mindless *attaque brusque.* The Germans, dug in and prepared, drove the invaders out and slaughtered 140,000 of them. The French generals, their confidence intact, vowed that every fallen *poilu* would be avenged, thereby ending any possibility of a negotiated peace.

The kaiser's *Offizierkorps* had a better plan, and it almost worked. The gray tide of the German right wing, a million *Soldaten* strong, swept down through Belgium like a swinging scythe, cutting a swath seventy-five miles wide and enveloping France's extreme left flank. The French fell back again and again but finally rallied on the Marne, where, after a seven-day battle involving more than 2 million men, the enemy wave recoiled and receded to the Loire.

Then the sidestepping began, the lines of the opposing armies extending westward and then northward as each tried to outflank the other in what was called a "race to the sea." The possibility that eventually they would run out of land seems never to have occurred to them. However, that is what happened. The last chance for a short war had vanished. By the end of September, the French, joined by the British, were defending a snakelike chain of trenches that began on the Swiss border and ended 466 miles away on the Channel at Nieuport, just below Ostend. Because the armies on both sides were enormous, the density of human concentration was unprecedented; there was one soldier for every four inches of front. Mobility and the opportunity for maneuver were gone. The stalemate was intolerable. Surely, people thought, an early breakthrough was inevitable. But it wasn't. It wasn't even possible, because offensive weapons were no match for the weapons available to defenders. And whenever a position was in peril, it could be swiftly reinforced. Troop trains could rocket to the tottering sector while the attacking infantrymen could plod no faster than soldiers in the Napoleonic wars.

Separated by the junkyard of no-man's-land, amid the stench of urine, feces, and decaying flesh, the great armies squatted on the Western Front for four gory years, living troglodytic lives in candlelit dugouts hewn from Fricourt chalk or La Bassée clay, or scooped from the porridge of swampy Flanders. The efficient Germans tacked up propaganda signs (*Gott strafe England; Frankreich, du bist betrogen*), then settled down to teach their language to French and Belgian children while the Allies furiously counterattacked.

The titanic struggles that followed were called battles, but although fought on a fantastic scale, with nearly 2 million soldiers killed at Verdun and on the

Somme, they were really siege assaults. Every Allied drive found the kaiser's defenses stronger. At dawn, *poilus* and Tommies would crawl over their parapets, lie down in front of jump-off tapes, and wait for their officers' zero-hour whistles. Then they would rise and hurtle forward toward as many as ten aprons of barbed wire with barbs as thick as a man's finger, backed by the pulsating Boche machine guns. A few trenches would be taken at a shocking cost—the price of seven hundred mutilated yards in one attack was twenty-six thousand men—and the beleaguerment would start again. Newspapers spoke of "hammer blows" and "the big push," but the men knew better. A soldier's mot had it that the war would last a hundred years, five years of fighting and ninety-five of winding up the barbed wire.

The war was a kind of cultural hinge—Lt. Col. Winston S. Churchill wrote afterward: "We seemed separated from the old life by a measureless gulf"—and to the most idealistic youth it came as a crisis of the spirit. At the outbreak of the war, Rupert Brooke had written: "Now God be thanked, Who has matched us with His hour, / And caught our youth, and wakened us from sleeping."

They had marched off to the lilt of "Tipperary," or "Die Wacht am Rhein," or "La Marseillaise," dreaming of braid and heroism. When they found that their generation was bleeding to death, with each casualty list redder than the last, the thoughtful among them fled to cynicism and despair. The composer of "Keep the Home Fires Burning" acquired an exemption from the draft and lolled around in a silk dressing gown, burning incense; thrice-wounded Harold Macmillan retreated to a study of Horace; Siegfried Sassoon flung his Military Cross into the sea and wrote bitterly: "Pray God that you may never know / The hell where youth and laughter go."

They were the sensitive. Most men fought stolidly. They had been bred to valor, taught fealty to the tribal deities of God or *Gott,* or *Dieu,* or *Dio,* and they numbly sacrificed themselves to a civilization that was vanishing with them. They were the first men to be exposed to poison gas, massive fire from automatic weapons, heavy shrapnel, and strafing aircraft. It was a weird, grimy life, unlike anything in their Victorian upbringing except, perhaps, the stories of Jules Verne. There were a few poignant reminders of prewar days—the birds that caroled over the lunar landscape each gray and watery dawn; the big yellow poplar forests behind the lines—but most sounds and colors on the front were unearthly. Bullets cracked and ricochets sang with an iron ring; overhead shells warbled endlessly. There were spectacular red Very flares, saffron shrapnel puffs, and yellow mists of mustard gas souring the ground. Little foliage survived here. Draftees arriving from Britain ("The necessary supply of heroes must be maintained at all costs," said Lord Carson) were shipped up in boxcars built for *hommes* forty or *chevaux* eight and marched over duckboards to their new homes in the earth, where everything revolved around the trench. You had a trench knife, a trench cane, a rod-shaped trench periscope, and, if you were unlucky, trench foot, trench mouth, or trench fever.

In the course of an average day on the Western Front, 2,533 men were killed in action, 9,121 wounded, and 1,164 missing, which usually meant they had been blown apart and were therefore unidentifiable. Even in quiet sectors there was a steady toll of shellfire casualties. In London, the methodical War Office called it "normal wastage." The survivors were those who developed quick reactions to danger. An alert youth learned to sort out the artillery whines that threatened him, though after a few close ones, when his ears buzzed and everything turned scarlet, he realized that the time might come when ducking would do no good. If he was a machine gunner, he knew that his life expectancy in combat had been reckoned at about thirty minutes. In time, if a soldier survived, he became detached toward death and casual with its appliances. Enemy lines would be sprayed with belt after belt from water-cooled machine guns to heat water for soup. Hopes for victory diminished and then vanished. After one savage attempt at a breakthrough, Edmund Blunden wrote, "By the end of the day both sides had seen, in a sad scrawl of broken earth and murdered men, the answer to the question. No road. No thoroughfare. Neither race had won, or could win, the War. The War had won, and would go on winning."

In that remote day of derbies and ostrich-plumed bonnets, when, as Churchill wrote, "the world was fair to see," civilization was in the midst of a profound transition. Culturally, it remained gyved to the horsy Edwardian past, yet the machine age was coming, and coming fast. Europe lay half in one period, half in the other, but no profession was more wedded to the past than the armed forces. Their leaders were not remotely capable of understanding the new mechanized warfare. England's Colonel Blimps were convinced that a chap could smash through that barbed wire if he had enough sand. They strode about in gleaming field boots and jingling spurs or toured the lines in Rolls-Royces, cursing slack discipline. On the other side, the *Junkers* cherished their monocles, spotless white gloves, and black-and-silver saber knots. If a soldier looked even remotely disrespectful, they slapped him.

By the spring of 1917, when the United States entered the war, the more fantastic anachronisms had disappeared from field uniforms. The Germans had shed the impractical spikes on their helmets; the French and British, who had had no helmets at all in 1914, were now protected. French infantrymen had shed the scarlet trousers and blue coats that had made them such easy targets, and the British no longer required new subalterns to visit the armorer and have their swords sharpened, like Henry V, before sailing for France. But new officers were still reminded that they should keep servants (batmen) in the dugouts and that before going over the top they must check to be sure that the senior company was on the right. At rest camps, subalterns were actually required to attend riding school and learn polo. During the worst fighting on the Somme, ceremonial horse shows were held just behind the front.

Each year the industrial revolution had been clanking out new engines of death, but the graduates of Sandhurst and *Saint-Cyr-l'École* accepted them grudgingly if at all. Lord Kitchener dismissed the tank as a "toy." England's Sir Douglas Haig, the British commander, called the machine gun "a much overrated weapon" and added that it had "little stopping power against a horse." France's Ferdinand Foch ridiculed the idea of aircraft in wartime: "*Tout ça, c'est du sport; l'avion c'est zéro!*" "Papa" Joffre, the constable of France, refused to use a telephone, insisting that he did not understand it. The Stokes trench mortar was rejected twice by Britain's War Office and finally introduced by Prime Minister Lloyd George, who begged the money for it from an Indian maharajah and was, as a consequence, branded "ungentlemanly" by British officers. The epauletted marshals placed their main reliance in masses of cavalry—as late as 1918, America's Gen. John Pershing was cluttering up his supply lines with mountains of fodder for useless horses—and their staffs rarely visited the front. The general staffs of all powers insisted that no one should have a voice in prosecuting the war unless he had spent forty years in uniform. As Basil Liddell Hart acidly noted, this would have eliminated Alexander, Caesar, Cromwell, Marlborough, and Napoleon.

Blessed with interior lines, the Germans could strike anywhere by rescheduling a few trains. As the deadlock continued in the west, they crushed a weak eastern ally each autumn, thus releasing more troops to fight against France. In 1914, they mauled the Russians at Tannenberg; in 1915, Bulgaria joined them to crush Serbia. The following year, Romania, misled by temporary Russian gains, threw in her lot with the Allies. Fiasco was the result. German troops withdrawn from the Western Front swarmed up the Carpathian Mountains just before snow sealed the passes they broke through, and the Romanians quit. And in 1917, Erich Ludendorff, Germany's military genius, turned on Italy, a latecomer to the Allied cause, sending a phalanx of picked divisions against the Caporetto sector. When the Italians finally rallied, they had lost sixty thousand men and were back on the Piave. Even the most ardent disciple of *la gloire* agreed that it looked like a bad war.

Nor was that the worst. The French had replaced Joffre with a new swashbuckling commander, Robert Nivelle, who announced an "unlimited offensive," promising to end the war with a quick, easy triumph. Instead, the drive moved a few yards a day, "leaving the dead," F. Scott Fitzgerald wrote, "like a million bloody rags." Nivelle was forced to call it off, and when he did, his troops mutinied. On one front fifteen out of sixteen divisions joined the revolt. France had been virtually knocked out of the war. In desperation, the Allies turned to Britain's Haig; he responded by giving them the nightmare of Passchendaele, an offensive even more disastrous than Nivelle's. After three months of failure, his army was exhausted. They too had failed. In London, ambulance trains unloaded at night, out of consideration for civilian morale, and in Flanders fields the poppies grew between the crosses, row on row, that marked 150,000 fresh British graves.

In that same year, two dramatic developments altered the course of the struggle. Russia's tormented masses revolted in March, and in April, the United States declared war on Germany. Overnight it was a new war. The revolutionaries took Russia out of the war, freeing a million German troops—enough to give Ludendorff the whip hand on the Western Front, provided he struck before America's waxing strength eclipsed his edge. The test came in the spring of 1918. He prepared three mighty drives against the Allies. The first two drove the defenders back ten miles, a record on that front. They hung on grimly but disintegrated when the third attack hit them in late May. The road to Paris seemed open. No other Allied troops were available, so the high command sent in newly arrived, unbloodied Americans—a brigade of U.S. Marines. For five days, the Marines held fast against the solid gray columns that came lunging out of Belleau Wood. Then they fixed bayonets and counterattacked, routing troops who had never before known retreat.

It was the beginning of the end, although Ludendorff later called August 8 the *"schwartz Tag"* ("black day") of the war. The British massed nearly five hundred tanks, cracked the German line, and gained over eight miles. It was an omen. Ludendorff knew it. He had lost 688,000 men in his spring offensives. Now the momentum had shifted away from him. After three years of bickering, the Allies finally agreed upon an overall commander in chief, Marshal Foch of France. Foch ordered an "arpeggio" of offensives against the enemy, telling commanders: "Everyone is to attack as soon as they can, for as long as they can," and *"L'Edifice commence à craquer. Tout le monde à la bataille!"* The American army, now 1.2 million doughboys, smashed into the heavily fortified Argonne Forest. The Germans' last ragged ditches caved in, and four days later, they had no front at all. Reports from the Fatherland were appalling. Ludendorff had been sacked, there was revolution in the streets, the fleet had mutinied, and the kaiser was fleeing into Holland. The Eiffel Tower was beaming directions to German envoys. An armistice went into effect at 11:00 A.M. on November 11, 1918, which was, editorial writers somberly noted, the eleventh hour of the eleventh day of the eleventh month.

Soldiers agreed that, though generals might haggle over words, this was more than an armistice; it was a surrender. But for once the generals were right. It was to be a long truce, but it wouldn't be peace because more than the war was finished. An age had reached Journey's End. The door of history had closed on all the elegance and fanfaronade of that disciplined, secure world. The doughboys didn't know it; neither did the statesmen—and the hysterical crowds in Times Square, the Champs Élysée, and the Buckingham Palace grounds knew it least of all, though the English had a kind of sign. As they romped over the mall with firecrackers, the sky suddenly darkened. It began to rain, hard. Some Londoners sought refuge in the lap of Queen Victoria's statue, but after huddling there a few minutes, they climbed down. They had found little shelter there, and less comfort. The arms were stone cold.

The Prelude to Conflict

The mind recoils when asked to consider the facts of World War I. The death and destruction of the Great War, as it was known to those who fought it, were on a scale unimaginable at the time and still difficult to grasp: What is the reality of 6 million dead soldiers?

It heightens our distress to contemplate the so-called reasons for the war. The ill-defined goals of the belligerents in 1914 seem in retrospect to be so frivolous and naive as to defy understanding, and the narration of how millions of men were ordered to their deaths during the four years that followed is one of the most depressing tales of the twentieth century, rivaled perhaps only by the chilling facts of the Holocaust, which was in a perverse way itself a result of the follies of World War I.

In essence, the war had come about because a handful of politicians thought they could improve the lot of their nations by means of a short, decisive conflict. They had been persuaded in part by their military commanders that such would be the case and in part by a logic that said modern industrial nations could not finance anything but a short war.

At the center of affairs was the young nation of Germany, formed only a generation earlier from the small German states and principalities, and by 1914 the greatest economic and military power on the Continent. The Germans wanted to increase their influence among their neighbors, expand overseas to become a colonial power, and assure their national security. Perhaps most of all, the Germans wanted respect from the other, older great powers of the world, and believed that a quick, decisive war on the model of those fought against Austria and France in the late nineteenth century might achieve it.

The Austro-Hungarian Empire, a Habsburg relic from centuries past, wanted simply to continue to exist and to find a way to lessen the centrifugal pressures of nationalisms within the empire. If the empire could pick up a scrap of new territory here and there, so much the better, but the main goal was to sever dissident internal nationalist groups in the Balkans (much the same groups whose mutual antagonisms the world has come to know only too well in the last decade of the century) from outside support and to quell those bothersome influences, such as Serbia and Russia, who kept disturbing the imperial peace.

France wanted revenge, pure and simple. The breathtaking swiftness of her defeat in 1870-71 at the hands of the new Germany had never been accepted, and the loss of Alsace and Lorraine had never been reconciled. The opportunity to redress the bitterness would come sooner or later.

The Russian national interests in 1914—aside from the survival of the Romanov imperium—were to hold on to territorial gains and to expand at the expense of the tottering Turkish Empire. Posing as the champion of Slavic peoples might also allow Russia to regain some of the prestige lost in its ignominious defeat by the Japanese ten years earlier—a defeat that nearly brought down the shaky state apparatus then.

Italy was the most cynical of all. It would opt for whatever position on either side would give the most in the way of postwar territorial gain, and it waited and trimmed until the answer seemed clear.

Great Britain wanted only to have a peaceful equilibrium prevail in Europe so that it might be allowed to continue to exploit the vast overseas empire built up during the previous hundred years. A major dislocation of the balance of power—as represented by the rise of Germany—was to be avoided if at all possible, even at the cost of military involvement on the Continent.

The years immediately preceding the outbreak of World War I were deceptively quiet.

The only direct armed conflicts were in Africa, where Italy declared war on Turkey in 1911 and managed to separate Libya from the Turkish Empire, and in the Balkans, where a series of two wars were fought during 1912 and 1913. The first pitted the three Christian Balkan states of Serbia, Bulgaria, and Greece against the Turks and resulted in the cession of nearly all Turkish territory in Europe; the second posed Bulgaria against her Balkan neighbors in an unsuccessful attempt to increase her share of the booty from Turkey.

All of Europe, however, had been poised for war for many years, and it seemed only a matter of time until some single event or irreconcilable issue set it off.

The creation of Germany in 1871 had skewed the balance of power in Europe, and a system of alliances had made the diplomatic and military fortunes of the Great Powers so intertwined as to make avoiding a general conflict very difficult. In 1882, Germany and Austria bound themselves together in a Dual Alliance. They were soon joined by Italy to form a Triple Alliance, but the passage of time led most to believe that Italy was increasingly less than serious about membership in this club of central European powers.

Opposing the Triple Alliance were France and Russia, who were joined by a formal treaty in 1892 that called for mutual assistance in the case of aggression against either from Germany, Austria-Hungary, or Italy. In 1904, the British signaled their support of the Franco-Russian alliance, although they refused to sign a formal treaty to that effect. Nonetheless, the Entente, as it was called, set up a firm wall around the Triple Alliance.

This frangible situation weathered a series of crises in the ten years before 1914, two having to do with Morocco and Germany's ambitions as a colonial power. The Balkans, however, represented the touchiest situation. With the Turks gone from the scene, it was only a matter of time until one of the small nationalities began to batter excessively at the multinational Austro-Hungarian Empire.

The Austro-Hungarians had annexed Bosnia-Herzegovina in 1908, a move that Serbia resented. The large Serbian population in Bosnia provided the pretext for Serbia—emboldened by the results of the two Balkan wars—to assume a belligerent stance vis-à-vis Austria-Hungary. The possibilities for a general conflict were increased by Russia's view that she was the natural protector of all Slavic peoples, including the Serbs. Thus, agitation by Serbs to "free" Bosnia-Herzegovina, which developed by the summer of 1914 into state-sponsored terrorism, had the potential to set off a chain reaction. If Austria-Hungary came into conflict with Russia over Serbia and Bosnia-Herzegovina, then Germany and France would soon be dragged in and Great Britain could not be far behind.

Several of the principals were, in fact, eager for a pretext to begin hostilities. The German general staff had been planning and building for a generation to sweep through Belgium and smash the French yet again in a lightning strike. French generals planned an all-out offensive into Lorraine that would wipe out the disgrace of the French defeat of 1871.

As Laurence Lafore, a great historian of the causes of the conflict, has written, the war the diplomats and military chiefs anticipated in the summer of 1914 was not the war they got. If nothing else, World War I can be characterized as a war of complete illusion, both at the beginning and through to its end. The smug prewar policymakers of Germany, France, Austria-Hungary, Russia, Italy, and Great Britain saw war merely as one of the tools of statecraft—the most drastic tool, perhaps, but no more than that. They almost all believed that wars could be limited in scope and effect, and that modern industrial economics had rendered large-scale, prolonged war impossible. They were, of course, completely and disastrously wrong.

With the assassination of Austrian Archduke Franz Ferdinand and his wife, Sophie, at Sarajevo in late June, a sequence of events begins that leads to an exchange of diplomatic ultimatums and subsequent military mobilizations by Austria-Hungary, Germany, Russia, Serbia, France, and Great Britain. By the last days of July, the nations begin to declare war on one another, and armed conflict becomes inevitable.

Germany launches a massive right-wing attack through neutral Belgium (thus providing the pretext for Britain to declare war), planning to sweep around the French left wing and drive on Paris. The Germans bring up huge artillery pieces and batter the Belgian fortresses into surrender, then turn toward the heart of France. Meanwhile, the tiny British Expeditionary Force lands and unwittingly takes up a station in the path of the German juggernaut.

The French begin to execute their Plan 17, which calls for a spirited, all-out offensive toward what has become the German center and toward Lorraine and Alsace.

On the Eastern Front, the Russians begin a rapid advance into East Prussia that alarms the German high command, but the two halves of the Russian advance fail to coordinate. Hindenburg and Ludendorff are given command of German forces in the East. In late August, they decisively defeat the Russians at Tannenberg, following up with another huge victory at the Masurian Lakes.

The French offensive bogs down as it becomes apparent that the main German attack is from the north. The German right wing moves rapidly into France, brushes aside the British, and moves with great speed toward its goal of enveloping the French capital and armies. However, a gap opens between key elements of the German armies, and a fateful decision is made to turn the outermost elements inside Paris in order to trap and annihilate the main French forces in the field. Aided by troops sent from the Paris garrison, the French counterattack along the Marne River and halt the German advance. The German high command orders a fortification of existing lines.

Throughout the remaining weeks of the year, the two forces in France slide sideways toward the northern coast, each trying unsuccessfully to find the enemy's flank. By the end of 1914, a long fortified line is established from the sea to Switzerland, a line that is progressively dug in and made more defensively secure until the Western Front is one long system of opposed trenches and fortifications that will defy attack until the very last days of the war.

The conflict has meanwhile spread to Africa and the Pacific. Large numbers of Allied troops begin to chase a much smaller German force in the former, and a German flotilla enjoys initial success in the latter before being destroyed in December.

To the east, the Germans continue to smash the Russians and seize Galicia, but the Austrians alone cannot defeat the much-outnumbered Serbs.

28 June 1914

Sarajevo, Bosnia, Austria-Hungary. Celebrating Saint Vitus's Day commemorating the Serbians' rebellion and independence from Turkey, spectators line the streets awaiting the open car of Archduke Franz Ferdinand, heir apparent to the throne of Austria-Hungary, and his beloved wife, the Duchess Sophie of Hohenberg, who are accompanied by Gen. Oskar Potiorek, military governor of Bosnia, and Count von Harrach. It is the royal couple's fourteenth wedding anniversary. Among the onlookers lurk seven youthful Serbian nationalists, ostensibly associated with the Black Hand terrorist group, who are intent on assassinating the archduke in an effort to gain added recognition for Serbia, where he is considered a villain. As the archduke's car traverses the Cumuria Bridge one of the conspirators hurls a bomb. The driver, spotting the missile, speeds forward as the

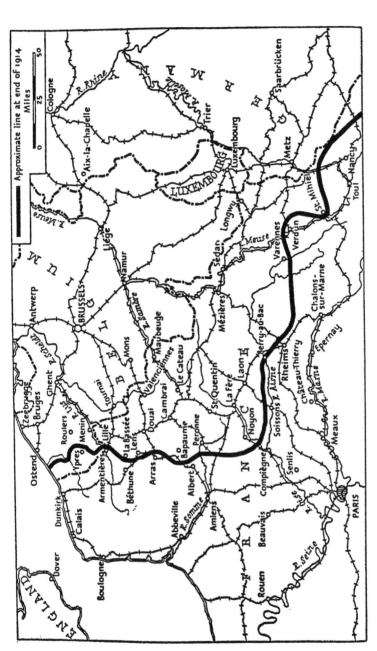

The Western Front. From *A History of the Great War, 1914-1918*, byt C.R.M.F. Cruttwell, published by Academy Chicago Publishers. All rights reserved.

archduke throws up his arm to protect his wife. The bomb bounces off the folded-back car roof to explode beneath the following car, wounding two officers and twenty spectators. After a brief pause, the procession moves on to City Hall. Here the archduke decides to alter the route, asserting it is his duty to visit the bomb victims at the hospital. The duchess insists on accompanying him despite his protestations of concern for her safety. En route their driver makes a wrong turn and brakes abruptly in order to turn around. In this instant one of the conspirators, Gavrilo Princip, steps to within a few feet of the car and fires two shots. One bullet pierces the archduke's neck; the other, the duchess's abdomen. Momentarily they appear to be unhurt. But suddenly blood spurts from the archduke's mouth, and Sophie collapses unconscious. Franz Ferdinand bends over his wife, pleading for her to survive. General Potiorek orders the driver to speed ahead. Count von Harrach asks the archduke if he is in pain. The archduke responds, "Es ist nichts"—his final words. It is now eleven o'clock in the morning.

Ischl, Austria-Hungary. The vacationing Emperor Franz Joseph is informed during the night that his nephew Franz Ferdinand and Sophie have been assassinated by a Serbian. Expressing no sense of outrage, the emperor declares calmly that the incident will probably serve to enhance order in his troubled and ethnically divided domain.

Kiel, Germany. Kaiser Wilhelm II is racing his yacht *Meteor* in Kiel Bay when a launch brings news of the assassination. He blanches but otherwise accepts the news undemonstratively.

29 June 1914

Belgrade, Serbia. An Austrian diplomat raises the possibility of Serbian complicity in the assassinations. For four hours mobs of Croats and Moslems riot in Sarajevo, attacking Serbians and their businesses, homes, and public institutions. Fifty people are wounded and one is killed. Other anti-Serbian riots erupt throughout Bosnia and in Vienna.

30 June 1914

Berlin. Foreign Secretary Gottlieb von Jagow receives word from his ambassador in Vienna that Count Leopold von Berchtold, the Austrian foreign minister, insists that Serbia is responsible for the assassinations.

4 July 1914

Arstetten, Austria. The archduke and the duchess are buried on their private estate.

5 July 1914

Sarajevo. The last of the conspirators is arrested.

Berlin. Count Alexander Hoyos, an envoy from Berchtold, arrives with a letter from Franz Joseph to the kaiser inquiring whether Austria can expect Germany's support if she mobilizes against Serbia. Austrian Ambassador Count Szogyeny lunches with Wilhelm II at Potsdam New Palace and receives the kaiser's assurances that Germany will stand by Austria, even if the result is war with Russia—a fateful commitment. Afterwards, Chancellor Theobald

The cover of sheet music for a patriotic song showing Kaiser Wilhelm and Austrian Emperor Franz Joseph "hand in hand" (Library of Congress)

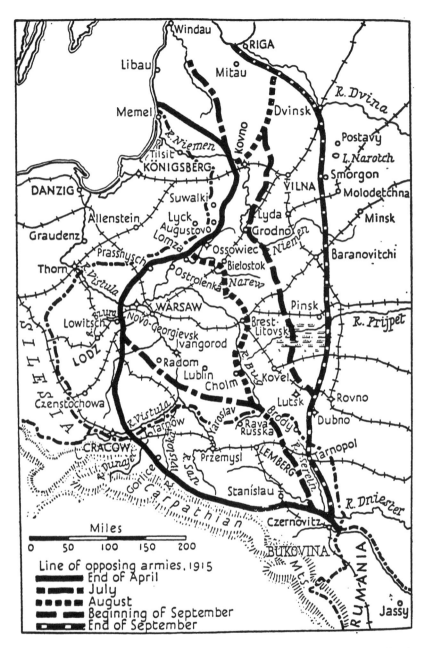

The Eastern Front. From *A History of the Great War, 1914-1918,* byt C.R.M.F. Cruttwell, published by Academy Chicago Publishers. All rights reserved.

von Bethmann Hollweg strolls with the kaiser and concurs with his answer to the Austrians. The kaiser and his minister anticipate no menacing eventualities, as threats have always achieved the desired results in the past.

6 July 1914
Kiel. Wilhelm II embarks aboard the royal yacht *Hohenzollern* for his annual holiday cruise in the waters off Norway.
Saint Petersburg. Foreign Minister Sergei Sazonov summons the Austrian chargé d'affaires, Count Ottokar von Czernin, and warns him that Russia will find objectionable any unreasonable Austrian demands upon Serbia.

7 July 1914
Vienna. Now assured of German backing, Berchtold pursues his devious scheme to punish Serbia. The Council of Ministers and chiefs of staff discuss responses to Serbia. Their meeting lasts seven hours. Count Istvan Tisza, prime minister of Hungary, is the sole but firm opponent of mobilizing and of sending to Serbia an ultimatum so worded that it cannot be accepted.

11 July 1914
Sarajevo. Baron Friedrich von Wiesner arrives from Vienna to review and report on the trial of the conspirators. He cables this message to Vienna: "There is nothing to indicate that the Serbian Government knew about the plot."

12 July 1914
Dunkirk, France. Pres. Raymond Poincaré and Prime Minister René Viviani embark aboard the new battleship *France* for a scheduled state visit to Russia.

14 July 1914
Vienna. Berchtold persuades Count Tisza to support the hard-liners' position by assuring him that Austria will make no territorial demands on Serbia—a deliberate lie. Subsequently, the Council of Ministers agrees on the policy of sending Serbia an ultimatum.

18 July 1914
Portsmouth, England. King George V reviews 260 ships of the Royal Navy at the navy's Spithead base. The naval reserves have been called up following orders from First Lord of the Admiralty Winston Churchill and his first sea lord, Vice Adm. Prince Louis of Battenberg.

19 July 1914
Vienna. The Council of Ministers holds a secret meeting at Berchtold's house, deciding that Serbia must be brought to heel. They approve the wording of an ultimatum to be delivered to the Serbian government on 23 July, the day President Poincaré is scheduled to depart from Russia.

Naval Strength at the Beginning of the War

Ships	England	France	Germany	Austria	Russia	USA	Japan
Dreadnought	24	14	13	3	4	10	4
Pre-Dreadnought	38	15	30	12	7	26	2
Battle Cruisers	10	0	6	0	1	0	2
Cruisers	47	19	14	3	8	21	9
Light Cruisers	61	6	35	4	5	11	15
Destroyers	225	81	152	14	106	50	56
Submarines	76	76	30	14	36	39	15

20 July 1914
Saint Petersburg. Czar Nicholas II welcomes Poincaré and Viviani at the Kronstadt naval base. He later hosts the French leaders at a banquet at Peterhof Palace.

21 July 1914
Saint Petersburg. Poincaré discusses the Serbian crisis with Russian officials and assures them that France will fulfill "all her obligations." Barricades block the streets of the capital city as strikers oppose police.

22 July 1914
Berlin. The Austrian ambassador, Count Szogyeny, shows a copy of the Austrian ultimatum to Foreign Minister Jagow, who approves the wording.
London. Foreign Minister Sir Edward Grey learns of the harshness of the Austrian ultimatum from the Austrian ambassador. Subsequently, Grey adjures the German ambassador, Prince Karl Marx Lichnowsky, that Germany should not support the ultimatum.

23 July 1914
Saint Petersburg. Poincaré and Viviani sail for France. Nicholas II has counseled them that war is unlikely; Russia has taken no steps toward mobilizing.
Belgrade. At 6:00 P.M., Austrian Ambassador Baron Vladimir von Giesl delivers his government's ultimatum to the Serbian foreign ministry. Among ten demands, Austria stresses prosecution of the conspirators, with Austrian officials heading the investigation, and condemnation of anti-Austrian propaganda, with Austrian agents allowed to operate with Serbian officials in Serbia to suppress such propaganda. These and other terms are not only humiliating, but also require the sacrifice of Serbian sovereignty. Austria gives Serbia forty-eight hours to accept.

24 July 1914
Belgrade. Premier Nicholas Pashich and other ministers hurry back to Sarajevo from electioneering trips in the countryside to address the crisis. Early in the year Nicholas II has told Pashich: "For Serbia, we shall

do everything." Now Pashich calls on Russia for guidance and is counseled to accede to all those Austrian demands that do not require relinquishing sovereignty.
London. Sir Edward Grey decries the Austrian ultimatum as "the most formidable document that was ever addressed from one state to another." He calls for mediation by Great Britain, France, Germany, and Italy.

25 July 1914
Belgrade. An emissary delivers the Serbian government's conciliatory response—accepting all the demands except having Austrian officials in Serbia—to Ambassador Giesl. This qualified response having been anticipated, Giesl has orders to break relations with Serbia. He and his staff, their bags already packed, board the 6:30 P.M. train for Vienna. The Serbian government orders mobilization and removes to Niš.
Vienna. Franz Joseph signs the order mobilizing Austria-Hungary's armies.
Berlin. Gen. Helmuth von Moltke, army chief of staff, and Adm. Alfred von Tirpitz, minister of the navy, return early from their summer holidays.
London. Churchill and Battenberg confer before the minister departs the city to join his wife at the seaside, leaving Battenberg in charge of the Admiralty. Other cabinet ministers have also gone off for weekend holidays.

26 July 1914
London. Battenberg, apprised of the increasing tensions between Austria and Serbia, in the evening issues orders for the naval reservists to remain on duty and for the fleets not to disperse following their review maneuvers. Churchill returns to London.

27 July 1914
Saint Petersburg. Nicholas II sends a cable to Pashich stating that if war comes Russia "would not remain indifferent to the fate of Serbia."
Berlin. Wilhelm II returns early from his holiday. He has not been told that his government has already rejected the British call for mediation.
Paris. The French government telegraphs

Gen. Louis Lyautey, proconsul of Morocco, to abandon the protectorate and send all his troops home. The general decides to retain some of his force to keep order in the protectorate's interior regions, but dispatches forty thousand troops to Bordeaux.

Moroccan cavalry (called *saphirs*) in France during 1915 (by Jean Berne-Bellecour, courtesy of the Anne S.K. Brown Military Collection, Brown University Library)

28 July 1914
Vienna. At noon, Franz Joseph signs Austria-Hungary's declaration of war against Serbia.
Saint Petersburg. The Council of Ministers orders partial mobilization of the Russian army near the Austrian border.
Berlin. Bethmann Hollweg telegraphs Berchtold: "Serbia has in fact met the Austrian demands in so wide-sweeping a manner that if the Austro-Hungarian government adopted a wholly uncompromising attitude, a gradual revulsion of public opinion against it in all of Europe would have to be reckoned with." Berchtold ignores the appeal.

29 July 1914
Berlin. Bethmann Hollweg telegraphs Berchtold that Germany must refuse to let herself be drawn into war since Austria "has ignored our advice." His protest is too

late. The German chancellor makes an offer to Sir Edward Grey: remain neutral and Germany will promise not to annex any of mainland France. He also warns Russia that its partial mobilization is inflammatory. The German navy begins to mobilize in the North Sea.
London. Churchill orders the Grand Fleet to proceed to its war anchorage at Scapa Flow in the Orkney Islands.
Paris. Poincaré and Viviani arrive back in the capital.
Belgrade. Austrian river monitors shell the Serbian capital—the first bombardment of the ensuing war.
Pola, Italy. The German battle cruiser SMS *Goeben* and her companion, the light cruiser *Breslau,* sail for Trieste. They are commanded by Rear Adm. Wilhelm Souchon and have been stationed in the Mediterranean since 1912.

30 July 1914
Saint Petersburg. Despite warnings from Austria and Germany, Sazonov concludes that Russia has no choice but intervention. After hearing his arguments, a reluctant Nicholas II orders total mobilization. The Russian navy begins mobilizing in the Baltic and Black Seas.

31 July 1914
Berlin. The government issues a midnight ultimatum to Russia: demobilize within twelve hours and make "a distinct declaration to that effect." Another ultimatum goes to the government at Paris, delivered by Ambassador Baron Wilhelm von Schoen, asking for a reply within eighteen hours to the question of whether France will remain neutral in the event of war between Germany and Russia.
Vienna. At the insistent urging of Field Marshal Count Conrad von Hötzendorf, the government orders full mobilization.
Constantinople. The government orders mobilization for 3 August.
Paris. Following the vociferous demands of commander in chief Marshal Joseph Joffre, the cabinet authorizes a general mobilization.
Malta. Adm. Sir Archibald Berkeley Milne, commander in chief of the British

Mediterranean fleet, receives a telegram from the Admiralty warning that war is possible and instructing him that, if war ensues, he is to aid transportation of French troops stationed in Africa by engaging individual German ships, especially the *Goeben,* that might interfere with the French transports. He is advised not to engage "superior forces."

London. Grey has rejected Bethmann Hollweg's offer concerning British neutrality—an offer he regards as "infamous"—but he continues to solicit Germany's help in resolving the dispute between Austria and Serbia. Grey also inquires of both France and Germany whether they will respect Belgium's neutrality. The French reply: "Certainly." The German reply: silence.

1 August 1914

Paris. The government orders a general mobilization.

Berlin. Having received no reply from Russia to its ultimatum, at 5:00 P.M. the government orders a general mobilization.

At the same moment, the Sixty-ninth Infantry Regiment stages a premature intrusion across the border at Ulflingen, Luxembourg, to capture railroad and telegraph junctions, while the kaiser sends a telegram ordering no frontier crossings. At a little after 7:00 P.M., the government declares war on Russia. At midnight, Moltke countermands the kaiser's earlier order.

London. Churchill orders that two dreadnoughts built for Turkey at a shipyard on the River Tyne be transferred to the British Fleet—an act that outrages the Turks, who had raised money by public subscription to pay for the ships.

Heligoland. German U-boat flotillas concentrate as the High Seas Fleet mobilizes at the Jade harbor.

Malta. The British Mediterranean Fleet assembles; the *Goeben* and the *Breslau* reach Brindisi.

Brussels. The government declares Belgium's determination to uphold its neutrality and independence, guaranteed by an international treaty signed by England, France, Russia, Prussia, and Austria in

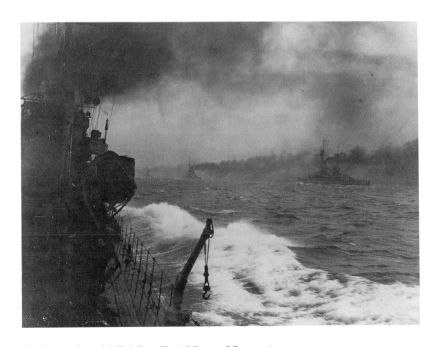

The German Imperial High Seas Fleet (Library of Congress)

1839 and upheld by the signatories ever since. Denmark and Norway declare their neutrality also. King Albert and his ministry have ordered a general mobilization to prepare for the defense of Belgium's borders.

2 August 1914
Brussels. German minister Herr von Below-Saleske opens a sealed envelope conveyed by courier from Berlin on 29 July after receiving a telegram instructing him to deliver the note it contains to the Belgian government by 8:00 P.M. and to demand a response within twelve hours. The note asserts that Germany has learned that France intends "to advance against Germany through Belgian territory." Stating Germany's need to anticipate this attack and therefore to traverse Belgian territory, the note advises that if Belgium will remain neutral, then Germany will evacuate at the conclusion of peace and pay for any damages incurred by the intrusion, while also guaranteeing Belgium's independence and sovereignty. If Belgium opposes German passage, then Germany would regard Belgium as an enemy to be attacked. The note is delivered by 7:00 P.M. The Council of State meets at 9:00 P.M. King Albert's opening statement is: "Our answer must be 'No,' whatever the consequences. Our duty is to defend our territorial integrity." The Council concurs.
London. The Admiralty orders mobilization of the British fleet.
Constantinople. The government receives from Berlin a signed mutual defense pact against Russia that Minister of War Enver Pasha had secretly proposed to the Germans on 27 July.

3 August 1914
Kalish, Poland. German troops invade, capturing Kalish, Chenstokhov, and Bendzin.
Brussels. At 7:00 A.M., a Foreign Office emissary delivers to the German ambassador Belgium's defiant rejection of Berlin's ultimatum. Later in the day, King Albert is made commander in chief of the Belgian army.
London. Parliament convenes at 3:00 P.M.

Grey advocates fulfilling Britain's obligation to sustain Belgian neutrality. He declares: "If . . . we run away from these obligations of honor and interest as regards the Belgian Treaty . . . I do not believe for a moment that, at the end of this war . . . we should be able . . . to prevent the whole of the West of Europe opposite us from falling under the domination of a single power . . . and we should, I believe, sacrifice our respect and good name and reputation before the world. . . ." When Grey concludes his speech, the members rise, cheering their support. Following the session of Parliament, Grey pledges military assistance to Belgium if Germany invades the neutral nation. As evening approaches Grey remarks to a friend: "The lamps are going out all over Europe; we shall not see them lit again in our lifetime."
Berlin. Within a few hours of the Parliament's meeting in London Germany declares war on France. A million and a half troops move into position to comprise seven field armies for the invasion of Belgium and France. Another half million troops assemble on the Eastern Front. Admiral von Tirpitz sends Admiral Souchon a telegram: "Alliance with Turkey concluded. Proceed at once to Constantinople."

4 August 1914
Berlin. In the early morning, Germany declares war on Belgium. After listening to the kaiser speak from his throne at Potsdam New Palace, deputies of the *Reichstag* reconvene at the *Reichstag* at 3:00 P.M. to hear Chancellor Bethmann Hollweg. They do not yet know that German forces have already invaded Belgium. Bethmann Hollweg announces that the troops are in Luxembourg and "perhaps" in Belgium. Acknowledging that France has pledged to support Belgian neutrality, he asserts, nevertheless, "We knew that France was standing ready to invade Belgium," and therefore a German invasion was a military necessity. And then, astoundingly, he adds: "Our invasion of Belgium is contrary to international law but the wrong—I speak openly—that we are committing we will make good as soon as our

Population and Military Strength at the Beginning of the War

	England	France	Germany	Austria	Russia	Serbia
Population (in millions)	46	39.6	65	49.9	167	5
Peacetime Army	255,000	823,250	880,000	480,000	1.4 mil.	30,000
Mobilization	700,000	4.5 mil.	5.7 mil.	2.3 mil.	5.3 mil.	459,000

A review of Russian troops in 1917 shows the one aspect of the Imperial Russian Army that scared the Central Powers, the seemingly unending supply of manpower. By this stage, however, the Russian officer corps and bureaucracy had managed to completely squander this advantage (Library of Congress)

military goal has been reached." The *Reichstag* deputies approve a war credit of five billion marks and dissolve for four months—presumed by one and all to be the duration of the war.

Gemmenich, Belgium. Shortly after 8:00 A.M., German troops sweep across the Belgian frontier along a fifteen-mile front. Six infantry brigades with accompanying artillery and three cavalry divisions, all under the command of Gen. Otto von Emmich, march to attack Liége, thirty miles distant. By nightfall, they reach the Meuse River at Visé. At noon, King Albert appeals for military support by the other nations that are guarantors of Belgian neutrality.

Vitry-le-François, France. General Joffre establishes his staff headquarters, Grand Quartier General (GQG) at this village on the Marne River halfway between Paris and Nancy.

London. Prime Minister Herbert Asquith abruptly recalls Lord Kitchener, the hero of Khartoum, to be war minister, and he designates Adm. Sir John Jellicoe as commander in chief of the Grand Fleet. Grey sends the German government an ultimatum: halt the invasion of Belgium or by midnight Great Britain will declare war. Bethmann Hollweg expresses astonishment to the British ambassador that Britain would go to war because of "a scrap of paper." The declaration of war follows at 11:00 P.M. At the same moment the Admiralty orders the fleet to "commence hostilities against Germany."

Malta. Adm. Sir Berkeley Milne wires the Admiralty that HMS *Indomitable* and HMS *Indefatigable* are tailing the *Goeben* and the *Breslau*.

Tsingtao, China. The German East Asiatic Squadron commanded by Adm. Count Maximilian von Spee leaves its base bound for the South Pacific.

5 August 1914

Liége, Belgium. Because the Belgian government has refused to allow German troops to pass freely through Liége, the Germans stage a surprise night attack against four of the city's eastern forts. They fail to capture these or any of Liége's twelve defensive forts despite recklessly sending waves of troops—successively slaughtered by Belgian rifle and machine-gun fire—into the assault that they had assumed would result in an easy victory. The German attack force comprises fifty thousand men; Liége is defended by twenty-five thousand Belgians commanded by Gen. Gérard Mathieu Leman, with orders from King Albert to "hold to the end."

Berlin. General von Moltke writes to his Austrian counterpart, commander in chief Field Marshal Franz Conrad von Hötzendorf: "The struggle that will decide the course of history for the next hundred years" has begun.

Vienna. At noon Austria-Hungary declares war on Russia.

Cetinje, Montenegro. The Montenegran government declares war on Austria-Hungary.

Harwich, England. Two British destroy-

Marshal Joseph Joffre (Library of Congress)

Infantry Tactics

Infantry tactics were shockingly deficient during World War I, especially along the trench lines of the Western Front. The powers of defense as embodied in the heavy artillery, the machine gun, and the well-fortified trench systems made nineteenth-century-style infantry tactics the same as suicide. But this did not prevent the armies from using the outmoded methods. Most infantry were equipped with bolt-action rifles and bayonets as their main armaments. In trench warfare conditions, they also had hand grenades and a series of often improvised specialty weapons. The main tactic of the Allied armies remained the same throughout the war: a frontal assault by troops going "over the top" into no-man's-land in an attempt to overrun the opponents' trenches. The foot assaults were usually preceded by massive bombardments of the opposing barbed wire and frontline trenches, a technique aimed at flattening the wire and destroying or weakening the human defenders. Seldom was this style of bombardment effective, especially in the later years of the conflict when both sides learned how to cope with pre-assault artillery barrages. The advancing infantry would often follow a "creeping" barrage that was designed to provide a curtain of precisely timed explosives that would lift and move forward to lead a line of infantry across to its objective. In practice, such barrages were difficult to time, and if anything went wrong with the infantry's advance, little could be done to alter the timing or movement of the barrage. Gas attacks, aimed at disabling defenders, worked sometimes, but capricious winds and improved gas protection made this weapon less and less effective as the war went on. In essence, the frontal assault was an outmoded tactic. Sending men into a no-man's-land defended by barbed wire, mines, and machine guns was tantamount to mass murder. Late in the war, the Russians and then the Germans developed alternative tactics that worked much better and at less cost to the attackers. Surprise replaced long preliminary bombardments, and specially trained troops were sent forward in sharply focused groups that bypassed strong points and tried to penetrate quickly to the rear of the first opposing trench lines. While these tactics achieved great local success, seldom were they followed up with consolidation of the initial gains, and eventually the British developed offsetting defense in depth tactics.

ers sink the German minelayer *Königin Luise,* named for the kaiser's wife, fifty miles off the coast of Suffolk.

Washington, D.C. Pres. Woodrow Wilson offers the United States' services as a neutral party to mediate the escalating conflict in Europe.

Messina, Sicily. The *Goeben* and the *Breslau* enter port to take on coal.

6 August 1914

Belgrade, Serbia. The government declares war on Germany.

Liége. Zeppelin *L-Z,* sent from Cologne, drops thirteen bombs on the city, killing nine civilians and inaugurating war from the air. Subsequently, Gen. Erich Ludendorff, commander of the German Fourteenth Brigade that now commands the heights on the right bank of the River Meuse, sends an emissary into the city under a flag of truce to try to persuade Gen. Gérard Leman to surrender. The effort fails, as does a ruse of sending six officers disguised as British, who kill Leman's aide, Major Marchand, and are themselves killed by the outraged members of Leman's staff. Leman, realizing that he cannot hold the city because German troops have moved in between two of its protective forts, escapes to Fort Loncin to continue the resistance and orders his Third Division to fall back to Louvain in order to keep his army intact. In Brussels, the citizenry celebrates their army's success in checking the German advance.

Longwy, France. German troops invest this city on the Luxembourg border, opening the Battle of the Frontiers.

Constantinople. The German ambassador delivers a letter to the Turkish government guaranteeing war compensations, including the awarding of the Aegean Islands if Greece enters the war and expansion of its borders with Russia.

Cape Ortegal. HMS *Vindictive* captures SS *Schlesien*. Elsewhere in the Atlantic, British ships seize four German merchant ships.

Southampton and Portsmouth, England. Following a decision of the War Council on the previous day, 80,000 troops of the British Expeditionary Force (BEF) under the command of Gen. Sir John French, along with 30,000 horses and 315 field guns, begin to assemble for disembarkation to France.

Heligoland. Ten U-boats commanded by Comdr. Hermann Bauer leave their base and head northward to search for British patrols.

Messina. As night begins to fall, the *Goeben* and the *Breslau* leave port, pass through the straits, and enter open water. They feign a northeast course toward the Adriatic, but before midnight they shift to head southeastward.

Ponape, Caroline Islands. Vice Adm. Count Maximilian von Spee, commander of the German East Asiatic Squadron, leaves port with three cruisers, the *Scharnhorst, Gneisenau,* and *Nürnberg.* His orders are to traverse the Pacific and menace British merchant shipping for as long as possible.

Little Popo (Anécho), Togoland, Africa. French troops, invading from Dahomey, capture this coastal border town—the first seizure of German territory by an Allied force since the beginning of the war.

Cameroons, Africa. A small French force from Brazzaville captures two small German outposts in the northeastern corner of the colony, an area France had unwillingly ceded to Germany only three years before.

7 August 1914

Liége. Following a full night of artillery shelling, Emmich and Ludendorff lead their troops into the city, occupying it without resistance.

Altkirch, Alsace. At 5:00 A.M., the French VIIth Corps led by General Bonneau descends the ridges of the Vosges range to launch a bayonet attack on Altkirch, the first stage of a drive toward Mulhouse. After a six-hour battle resulting in a hundred casualties, they are successful, but the cautious Bonneau decides not to continue on to Mulhouse.

Gulf of Kalamata. Capt. Howard Kelly of the *Gloucester,* trailing the *Goeben* and the *Breslau,* must turn away when the German ships begin firing, but he notes that the Germans are heading toward the Aegean and so informs Rear Adm. Sir Ernest Troubridge, Milne's second in command.

8 August 1914

Mulhouse, Alsace. Impelled by orders from an impatient GQG, Bonneau's VIIth Corps enters Mulhouse without a shot being fired—the German troops have withdrawn from the city to join defensive forces farther to the north.

Dar es Salaam, German East Africa. The British cruiser *Astraea* arrives off the colonial capital, lobs a few shells at the wireless station, and lands an armed party at the harbor. Subsequently, the ship's captain and local German authorities agree to a truce stipulating that the Royal Navy will not attack the city and in turn its inhabitants will remain peaceable throughout the war—an agreement neither of the warring European governments can accept. Dr. Heinrich Schnee, the governor of German East Africa, wants to maintain peace at any cost, outraging Lt. Col. Paul Emil von Lettow-Vorbeck, the colony's military commander, who had arrived in the colony in January. He encamps his troops inland at Pegu to prepare for war.

9 August 1914

Le Havre and Boulogne, France. Two corps of the British Expeditionary Force (BEF) land.

Mulhouse, Alsace. With reinforcements from Strasbourg, the Germans attack Bonneau's forces occupying the city.

Vienna. Austria-Hungary declares war on Montenegro.

North Sea. German U-boats out of Heligoland spot British ships. At the same time, Capt. Arthur Duff aboard the cruiser *Birmingham* sights the periscope of U-boat *15* and, with an abrupt maneuver, rams and sinks it, with all hands going to the bottom.

10 August 1914

Cape Helles, Dardanelles. Having hurriedly taken on coal at Denusa in the Aegean and sped toward the Dardanelles, Admiral Souchon's *Goeben* and *Breslau* arrive at the cape. He secures a pilot to guide his ships through the minefields and moves up the strait to Constantinople, escaping the pursuing British fleet.

Paris. France declares war on Austria-Hungary.

Mulhouse, Alsace. After twenty-four hours of battle, the French, fearing encirclement, withdraw and cede the city to the Germans.

11 August 1914

San Francisco, California. The *Leipzig,* belonging to Admiral von Spee's farflung squadron, anchors.

12 August 1914

Haelen, Belgium. Belgian riflemen cut down German cavalry under the command of Gen. Georg von der Marwitz during repeated saber charges. The Germans withdraw in defeat, creating a mistaken euphoria among Belgians.

Liége. The Germans move giant siege cannons into position to bombard the city's fortresses. At 6:30 P.M., the first shell explodes on target—Fort Pontisse—with frightful destructive force. Skoda 305s join in the bombardment.

Sabac, Serbia. Austrian troops cross the River Sava, capturing Sabac and nearby villages and inflicting carnage on the civilian populace.

Warsaw, Poland. Gen. Alexander Samsanov, commander of the Russian Second Army in East Prussia, arrives at headquarters.

Marggrabowa, East Prussia. Gen. Pavel K. Rennenkampf, commander of the Russian First Army, launches the invasion of East Prussia. A detachment of his army captures this town five miles inside the border.

London. Great Britain declares war on Austria-Hungary.

Malmedy, France. Obit Jahnow dies when his airplane crashes—the first German pilot killed on active duty in the war.

Lomé, Togoland. Two companies of the British Gold Coast Regiment led by Frederick Carkeet Bryant land at this capital and chief port of the German colony after local authorities refuse to surrender. They encounter no opposition.

13 August 1914

Liége. After twenty-four hours of shelling, Fort Pontisse falls to the Germans. Two other forts also surrender.

14 August 1914

Amiens, France. Sir John French, commander of the BEF, arrives. He is accompanied by Sir Archibald Murray, BEF chief of staff; Gen. Henry Hughes Wilson; and Colonel Huguet, the French liaison officer to the BEF.

Liége. All the forts to the east and north of the city have fallen to the Germans; the First Army, under command of Gen. Alexander von Kluck, begins the advance toward Brussels. The German siege cannons are moved forward to concentrate on pounding the forts to the west of the city.

Alsace and Lorraine. The French relaunch their Plan 17 attack against the German left and center, with the Army of Alsace under Gen. Paul Marie Pau moving against the Germans in Alsace while the First Army under Gen. Auguste Dubail and the Second Army under Gen. Édouard de Castelnau assault the Germans in Lorraine. Dubail's objective is Sarrebourg; Castelnau's, Morhange.

Boulogne. Sir John French arrives to command the BEF.

Sabac, Serbia. Austrian troops repulse a Serbian effort to retake the city. The Austrian XIIIth Corps captures Loznica.

Nigeria. Col. C.H.P. Carter, commandant

of the Nigeria Regiment, receives the British Ministry's permission to invade the Cameroons.

15 August 1914
London. British and French representatives agree to mount a joint attack on the Cameroons; surprisingly, the French accept having the force commanded by a British officer, Brig. Gen. Charles McPherson Dobell.
Liége. Eleven of the city's twelve forts have fallen to the Germans, but Fort Loncin holds out, as General Leman refuses to surrender.
Taveta, British East Africa. Sent out by Lt. Col. Paul von Lettow-Vorbeck, German and askari (native African) troops commanded by Tom von Prince capture this town near the southern slopes of Kilimanjaro only twenty-five miles from the German town of Moshi.
Tokyo, Japan. The government declares its support of the Allies (France, Great Britain, and Russia) in issuing an ultimatum to Germany to evacuate Tsingtao. Russia will now be free to move more troops to the Eastern Front. Yüan Shih-k'ai, president of China, predicts that Japan will take advantage of the war to secure control over China.

16 August 1914
Liége. A German shell lands in the magazine at Fort Loncin, destroying the fort. Occupying German troops discover General Leman trapped beneath fallen masonry and assume he is dead, but discover that the general is merely unconscious. They revive him and take him before General von Emmich to surrender. Leman passes his sword to Emmich, who, in honor of his opponent's courage, returns it to him. Liége is now in German hands.
Constantinople. The government announces that the *Goeben* and the *Breslau* have been renamed and transferred to the Turkish navy.
Belgrade. Gen. Radomir Putnik launches a Serbian army attack against the Austrians at a bend in the Drina-Sava River to the southwest of the capital. The Battle of the Jadar extends along a thirty-mile front tracing the Jadar River and results in Austrian defeat as the day ends.
Vienna. During the night, Field Marshal Franz Conrad von Hötzendorf departs for Przemysl, Galicia, the fortress that will be his headquarters for the Austrian salient against Russia.
Coblenz, Germany. The General Staff moves the *Oberste Heeresleitung* (OHL, or Supreme Headquarters) from Berlin to this city on the Rhine River to be closer to the Western Front.
Vitry-le-François, France. Sir John French visits Joffre at GQG. The French

Austrian commander Baron Conrad von Hötzendorf (center) with Archduke Frederic at the headquarters of the Hungarian army (Library of Congress)

commander urges him to send the BEF into action with Gen. Charles Lanrezac's troops on the Sambre River on 21 August. General French agrees to do his best to be in readiness by this date.

17 August 1914

Brussels. Following a conference between Premier de Broqueville and King Albert, the government begins to withdraw from the capital to remove to Antwerp.

Galicia. Field Marshal Conrad von Hötzendorf learns of the Austrian defeat at the Battle of the Jadar and orders Gen. Oskar Potiorek to send a corps from the Austrian Second Army to try to recoup the loss.

Liége. With the city occupied, the German Second and Third Armies begin their advance.

Marggrabowa, East Prussia. General Rennenkampf's First Army, comprising two hundred thousand troops, begins the advance into East Prussia. His goal is the Insterburg Gap, open land about thirty miles in width lying between Königsberg and the Masurian Lakes, some thirty-seven miles ahead—about a three-day march for his army. Rennenkampf anticipates joining General Samsanov's Second Army, moving up toward the Masurian Lakes from the south, and engaging the Germans in a common front near Allenstein.

Stalluponen, East Prussia. In defiance of the German strategy, devised by Col. Max Hoffmann and accepted by the Eastern Front commander, Lieutenant General von Prittwitz und Gaffron, to lure the Russians inland to Gumbinnen and thus strain their supply lines, Gen. Hermann von Francois engages the Russians at this town only five miles inside the border. He forces the Russians to retire to the frontier and reform, but he also withdraws his own troops toward Gumbinnen, acceding to orders from an angry Prittwitz.

18 August 1914

Louvain, Belgium. With Kluck's troops attacking Belgian front lines at the Gette River, only fifteen miles distant, and Maj. Gen. Karl Ulrich von Bülow's troops en route to Namur after crossing the bridge at Huy, King Albert orders a general retreat

from the Gette to Antwerp and moves his headquarters from Louvain to Malines.

Morhange, Lorraine. The XXth Corps of Castelnau's Second Army under the command of Gen. Ferdinand Foch captures Château Salins, placing the French within striking distance of Morhange.

Sabac, Serbia. In daylong waves of attacks and counterattacks, the Serbs stall the Austrians and inflict heavy losses.

Lomé, Togoland. The French force that seized Little Popo after invading from Dahomey on 6 August links with Byrant's Gold Coast Regiment force.

19 August 1914

Bartenstein, East Prussia. Having renewed his advance, Rennenkampf pauses in order not to outdistance his supply services, while General Francois urges Prittwitz, headquartered at Bartenstein, to order a counterattack before Samsonov completes the Russian pincers.

Aerschot, Belgium. After crossing the Gette River and finding the Belgian army has withdrawn, German troops, following Kluck's orders, inflict reprisals for Belgian sabotage of railroads, telephone and telegraph lines, and bridges and especially for the sniping of lone resisters. They burn houses and round up and shoot 150 civilian residents of this small village.

Louvain. German troops enter the city.

Serbia. The Austrian Fifth Army retreats toward the Drina River pursued by Serbian forces. At Lesnica the Austrians shoot 150 peasants.

Washington, D.C. Pres. Woodrow Wilson addresses the United States Senate, advocating American neutrality "in fact as well as in name" toward the European war.

20 August 1914

Gumbinnen, East Prussia. Deciding not to await a Russian attack, Prittwitz has authorized Generals Hermann von Francois, August von Mackensen, and Otto von Below to launch an offensive against Rennenkampf. Francois's heavy artillery bombards Rennenkampf's far right, and his troops sweep around to attack the Russian transports. But at his center and left, Rennenkampf forces Mackensen and Below to retreat. In the evening, desperate to save the Eighth Army, Prittwitz orders a general retreat to the Vistula River—much to Francois's dismay. Moltke is astounded when he receives the news at OHL. But Rennenkampf, though victorious, breaks off the attack, giving the Germans breathing time while Prittwitz's deputy chief of operations, Col. Max Hoffmann, argues strenuously against retreat.

Belgrade. Serbian troops inflict a final defeat on the Austrians as the Battle of the Jadar concludes, with Austrian troops fleeing toward the Drina River amidst exploding Serbian artillery shells. General Potiorek orders the Austrian Second Army to fall back across the Sava River.

Brussels. German troops occupy the city following the Belgian army's withdrawal to Antwerp. Kluck parades his troops in seemingly endless ranks through the streets, an imposing sight for the subdued residents, and installs a governor-general to take control.

Morhange, Lorraine. Castelnau's Second Army attacks the German lines but is badly mauled by a counterattack directed by Prince Rupprecht of Bavaria, whose artillery and Bavarian troops inflict heavy casualties. Dubail's First Army has made some headway in advancing against the Germans, but both French commanders are ordered to withdraw by Joffre, thus ending the opening engagement of the Battle of the Frontiers that rages not only in Lorraine, but simultaneously at the Ardennes, Charleroi, and Mons. Castelnau and Dubail establish defensive positions on the Grand Couronné.

Sambre River. General Lanrezac's Fifth Army reaches the river and prepares to launch a counteroffensive the following day to coordinate with the French offensive in Lorraine.

21 August 1914

Charleroi, Belgium. Bülow's troops smash across the Sambre and drive back Lanrezac, whose British ally, General French, is a day's march behind, too far away to join the fray. Lanrezac sends troops to reinforce the defense of Namur, suffering heavy bombardment by German siege guns.

Coblenz. Fearful that the Eastern Front is in danger of collapse, the OHL dismisses Prittwitz; recalls from retirement Gen. Paul von Beneckendorff und Hindenburg to become commander of the Eighth Army in East Prussia; and names Gen. Erich Ludendorff, conqueror of Liége, to be his chief of staff.

22 August 1914

Mons, Belgium. Advancing toward Mons, a British cavalry squadron happens upon German cavalrymen, gives chase, and inflicts three deaths in an ensuing skirmish with swords—the BEF's first engagement of the war.

Charleroi. Lanrezac and Bülow resume the battle. Densely formed German attacks, aided by artillery barrages directed to targets by airplane spotters flying over the French lines, inflict especially heavy losses on Lanrezac's left, forcing him once again to fall back by the end of the day. During

A British infantryman strikes a theatrical pose (by Jean Berne-Bellecour, courtesy of the Anne S.K. Brown Military Collection, Brown University Library)

the night, Gen. Max Klemens von Hausen, commander of the German Third Army, moves four corps of fresh troops, with 340 artillery pieces, into position on the Meuse and gains some bridgeheads across the river, further menacing Lanrezac.

Namur, Belgium. With three major forts destroyed by the German cannonade, the Belgian garrison escapes and flees southward toward the French lines.

Lorraine. German troops occupy Lunéville.

Hanover, Germany. Hindenburg and Ludendorff meet at the railroad station and embark for East Prussia as Samsonov's army is capturing Soldau and Neidenburg.

Vienna. The Austrian government declares war on Belgium.

Nuatja, Togoland. Capt. Frederick Bryant's mixed force of British, French, and African troops attacks German police and volunteers dug in on the north bank of the Chra River. Fighting in dense bush, the Allies lose sight of each other and suffer seventy-three casualties, including twenty-three dead, at the hands of the defenders, who slip away to safety during the night.

Saint Petersburg. By imperial decree the government prohibits the sale of alcoholic beverages for the duration of the war.

23 August 1914

Charleroi. Standing outside his headquarters at Philippeville, twenty miles from the front, Lanrezac watches in silence as Belgian refugees stream by, clogging the roads. At noon he learns that Belgian troops are evacuating Namur. Receiving no guidance from GQG, he rejects his staff's urgings that he order a counterattack by General Louis Franchet d'Esperey. In late afternoon, Lanrezac learns from Gen. Fernand de Langle de Cary that the Fourth Army has been forced into retreat in the Ardennes battle, exposing Lanrezac's right flank. At the same time, Gen. Max Klemens von Hausen's troops have increased their bridgehead at Onhaye near Dinant. Surmising that the French armies are in general retreat along their entire line between the Vosges range and the Sambre River and fearful that his Fifth Army will be encircled and destroyed, the French general, without consulting GQG, orders a general retreat. His reasoning is that, although the French have suffered a major defeat, "As long as the Fifth Army lives, France is not lost." But the general retreat means the collapse of any hope of achieving the grand strategy of swift victory and a quick end to the war. Plan 17 has failed.

Mons, Belgium. The BEF, totaling seventy thousand troops with three hundred pieces of artillery, holds positions to the east and west of the city. The western position, under command of Gen. Sir Horace Smith-Dorrien, stands in the direct line of Kluck's advance. Kluck has twice the British strength, with four corps of 160,000 men and 700 cannons, but nearly half his force is held far back in reserve, as ordered by Bülow. As a result, Kluck is unable to outflank Smith-Dorrien and attacks head-on against stubborn British resistance. After heavy bombardment and repeated assaults, the British are forced to withdraw. During the night, Sir John French learns that Lanrezac has been forced to disengage at Charleroi and retreat behind the line the BEF holds, thus increasing the peril for the British forces at Mons. Near midnight French orders a retreat.

Marienburg, East Prussia. Hindenburg and Ludendorff arrive at the headquarters of the Eighth Army. They discover that Col. Max Hoffmann, now head of the Operations Department and the General Staff's Russian specialist, has managed to stop the German retreat and has also devised a strategy to defeat the Russians. Ludendorff adopts it wholesale as it coincides with the thinking of OHL.

Tokyo. Japan declares war on Germany.

Dinant, Belgium. General von Hausen, supposedly upset by what he regards as "perfidious" behavior by local civilians, has his troops round up men, women, and children and hold them captive in the city's main square. At evening the troops line up the captives at opposite edges of the square, men facing women. Firing squads at the center of the square execute them. The Germans' victims total 612, including some infants.

24 August 1914

Mons. During the early morning hours, the

BEF falls back toward Sir John French's headquarters at Le Cateau.

Vitry-le-François. General Joffre, accepting the current reality, sends a report to Minister of War Adolphe Messimy stating that the French army is "condemned to a defensive attitude." Joffre blames his field commanders for the catastrophe, and the ministry backs his policy of removing them, authorizing him to "eliminate the old fossils without pity." Joffre anticipates forming a defensive line along the Somme River and from there launching offensives against the Germans.

Morhange, Lorraine. The XXth Corps of the French Second Army led by Gen. Ferdinand Foch counterattacks, driving the Germans back two miles and blocking them east of Nancy.

Sabac, Serbia. Serbian troops recapture the city; the Austrians withdraw across the Serbian border.

Frankenau, East Prussia. Samsanov's troops force General Scholtz's XXth Corps to fall back ten miles but suffer heavy losses.

Marienburg, East Prussia. Having intercepted orders transmitted to General Samsanov concerning his troop movements on 25 August, German Eighth Army headquarters sends orders to Mackensen and Below to march south to confront Samsanov's advance.

Nigeria. Col. C.H.P. Carter orders the invasion of the Cameroons, with attacks on Mora, Garua, and Nsanakang.

25 August 1914

Vitry-le-François. General Joffre orders a general retreat and secretly has troops withdrawn from Mulhouse, Alsace.

Namur, Belgium. German headquarters announces capture of the city and five thousand prisoners, setting the stage for invasion of northern France.

Louvain, Belgium. A sudden Belgian army sortie out of Malines drives Kluck's rear guard back into Louvain. The Germans claim they were fired on by Belgian civilians and begin to burn the city in reprisal.

Mulhouse. German troops occupy the city.

Sedan, Lorraine. German troops capture the city.

Krasnik, Poland. Austrian troops are victorious and take six thousand prisoners. They begin to advance toward Lublin.

Mora, Cameroons. The British force sent by Colonel Carter attacks a German force occupying an impregnable stronghold.

26 August 1914

Tannenberg, East Prussia. The German plan, based on orders sent out before midnight on the twenty-fifth, is to envelop and destroy Samsanov's army. Mackensen's corps will attack Samsanov's right; Scholtz's corps, the center; and Francois's, the left. Ludendorff receives a call from OHL in Coblenz, apprising him that Moltke has authorized sending him three corps and a cavalry detachment from the Western Front as reinforcements. Ludendorff, among others, believes their removal to the East will jeopardize the invasion of France, but he has no choice—on Moltke's orders the reinforcements are being sent from Namur. As Mackensen launches his attack against Samsanov's left (the VIth Corps), the Russians assume that his troops are retreating before Rennenkampf's advance, giving the Germans an advantage. By the end of the day, Mackensen has succeeded, and while Francois has hesitated, Scholtz has driven back Samsanov's center. The Russian commander perceives that his army is in imminent danger of being enveloped.

Baltic Sea. The German cruiser *Magdeburg* runs aground in the Gulf of Finland.

Paris. Gen. Joseph-Simon Galliéni, a veteran of the 1870 Franco-Prussian War and now sixty-five years old, has been strenuously advocating the defense of Paris with little success. Now, in the aftermath of German success in the Battle of the Frontiers, Minister of War Messimy appoints Galliéni military governor of the city. The question is how to talk Joffre out of troops for the city's defense.

Le Cateau, Belgium. The British IInd Corps, commanded by General Smith-Dorrien, has become separated from Lieutenant General Haig's Ist Corps during the retreat from Mons and has paused in exhaustion. Beginning at 6:00 A.M., a superior force of German artillery bombards them for seven hours; the outgunned British artillery replies effectively. Shortly after one o'clock, the Germans attack into a deadly British cannonade. Though greatly outnumbered and with some units completely surrounded, the British troops hold their ground, temporarily halting Kluck's advance into France.

Lemberg, Galicia. Conrad von Hötzendorf has been advancing his Austro-Hungarian First and Fourth Armies commanded by Generals Dankl and Auffenberg northward, anticipating a major battle with the Russians above Lemberg and meeting slight resistance. Unaware of this advance, Grand Duke Nicholas has sent the Russian Fifth Army under General Plehve westward across Auffenberg's path. The armies have joined in battle without knowing each other's strength. At the same time, the Russian Third Army has routed the Austrian Third Army twelve miles to the south but comes to a halt.

Lomé, Togoland. Accepting that there is no alternative, Major von Doring, the acting German governor, surrenders the province unconditionally to Capt. Frederick Bryant.

27 August 1914

Lille, France. Having declared Lille an open city on 24 August, the French now abandon it before the German advance.

Tannenberg, East Prussia. At 4:00 A.M., Francois's artillery unleashes a massive bombardment of the Russian Ist Corps. Unable to withstand the punishment, the Ist Corps abandons the field of battle by 11:00 A.M. Francois succeeds without committing a single German soldier to the attack.

Tsingtao, China. Japanese and British ships begin a blockade of Kiaochow Bay.

Paris. After Messimy's refusal to resign forces resignation of the entire government, Viviani reshuffles his cabinet, replacing five ministers. Étienne-Alexandre Millerand takes Messimy's place as minister of war. Messimy assumes his rank as major and joins Dubail's army at the front.

Heligoland Island, North Sea. The British navy has been eager to engage the Germans at sea, and Commodores Reginald

Tyrwhitt and Roger Keyes have devised a plan to lure German destroyer patrols into an attack by Tyrwhitt's two light cruisers and two destroyer flotillas and Keyes's submarines. Unknown to the commanders, Adm. David Beatty, commander of the Grand Fleet's Battle Cruiser Squadron, has received Jellicoe's permission to join them with the First Light Cruiser Squadron. The Germans have learned of the operation and lure Tyrwhitt into confrontation with a fleet of cruisers at Heligoland Bight. Tyrwhitt calls for assistance and is amazed when Beatty's force comes to the rescue. The combined British force achieves victory, sinking three German light cruisers and a destroyer; severely damaging three other light cruisers; and killing, wounding, or capturing a total of twelve hundred German seamen. The Battle of Heligoland Bight evokes joy within the Royal Navy but also apprises the Admiralty of weaknesses in planning, communication, and organization.

28 August 1914

Tannenberg. Once again General von Francois begins the day with a huge artillery barrage. Ignoring Ludendorff's orders to relieve Scholtz's troops engaged at the center of the battle, Francois pushes straight eastward against Samsanov's left. By afternoon Mackensen's force drives hard against Samsanov's right, and Below leads a force into a gap at Allenstein to join the attack on Samsanov's center. With his flanks turned and sensing disaster, Samsanov telegraphs General Jilinsky, commander of the Northwest Army Group, that he is taking personal command of the battle. He and seven of his staff mount horses and ride to the front.

Louvain. Hugh Gibson, first secretary of the American Legation to Belgium, and his counterparts from Sweden and Mexico visit the city after three days of barbarous havoc inflicted by German soldiers. They find smoldering buildings and streets strewn with dead horses, executed Belgians, and wreckage. The visitors are appalled.

Nancy, France. Having helped to forestall the German advance toward the Grand

Marshal Ferdinand Foch (Library of Congress)

Couronné and the Trouée de Charmes during three days of fierce battle in Lorraine, General Foch receives orders to take command of a special army of three corps taken from the Third Army and the Fourth Army and to join de Langle in defense of the Meuse River line near Sedan. The detachment will be known as the Ninth Army. Foch also receives news that his only son and his son-in-law have both been killed at the Battle of the Meuse.

Amiens. Sir John French abandons his forward base and orders that ammunition and other items be discarded from transport wagons so that they can carry soldiers and thus hasten the British retreat to Compiègne.

29 August 1914

Compiègne. Joffre visits Sir John French, urging him to come to Lanrezac's assistance by rejoining the battle, but Sir John refuses, insisting that his men need several days' rest.

Guise, France. German forces hurl back Lanrezac's Fifth Army attack at Saint-Quentin, and Bülow's troops move against

Lanrezac's right. The French commander fears being outflanked by Kluck and Hausen. He concentrates his energies at Guise, where the Fifth Army not only halts the German advance but launches a successful counterattack, forcing Bülow's troops to withdraw. Nevertheless, Lanrezac remains in peril because the BEF and the French Fourth Army are already a day's march to his rear, exposing his flanks. At 10:00 P.M., Joffre sends him orders to blow up the bridges across the Oise River and withdraw.

30 August 1914

Louvain. Perhaps as a result of widespread outrage following reports of the atrocities in worldwide newspapers, the Germans end the destruction at Louvain but continue to blame the victims.

Tannenberg. After Below breaks through at Allenstein, the Russian army is virtually surrounded. Some corps flounder, lost in forests and marshes. General Samsanov, also lost and realizing his army has suffered disaster, moves off alone into a pine thicket and shoots himself. The Germans have captured ninety-two thousand prisoners and half of the Second Army's cannons.

Luxembourg City. OHL moves from Coblenz to this city only ten miles from the French border.

Paris. Galliéni warns the French government to leave the capital as soon as possible because "Paris cannot hold out." In the afternoon a German pilot flying a Taube drops three bombs on the Quai de Valmy and leaflets urging Parisians to surrender. The bombs take two lives.

Cameroons. One of the three columns of Carter's invasion force captures Nsanakang, but a German counterattack damages the British force, inflicting nearly a hundred deaths and driving the survivors into the bush.

Galicia. The Austrians lose twenty thousand men and are forced into retreat by a Russian attack at the Gnila Lipa River.

31 August 1914

Neidenburg, Prussia. The Germans retake the city, captured a second time by Russian troops under General Sirelius the day before. The Battle of Tannenberg ends with the Germans securing "one of the great victories in history," Max Hoffmann writes in his diary. Now Ludendorff can move against Rennenkampf's army.

Amiens. Kluck's First Army pivots to the southeast and begins to march toward the River Oise and Compiègne to join Bülow in fighting d'Esperey.

London. Alarmed by a letter from Sir John French that suggests the British commander is abandoning the French, Kitchener asks Asquith to call a cabinet meeting. The cabinet, perplexed by Sir John's letter, decides to send Kitchener to meet with him and urge his accession to the wishes of General Joffre. Kitchener boards the train for Paris at two-thirty in the afternoon.

Cameroons. Carter's column from Yola captures Garua but is forced to withdraw after suffering heavy losses.

1 September 1914

Saint Petersburg. The city is renamed Petrograd, eliminating the Germanic ending.

Paris. Kitchener meets at the British Embassy with Sir John French, Viviani, Millerand, and officers sent by Joffre. After a testy discussion, Kitchener takes French alone into a private room and orders him to position his troops in accord with the French line of battle and withdrawal. At the urging of Galliéni that he provide troops for the defense of Paris, Joffre places Galliéni in command of Gen. Michel-Joseph Maunoury's Sixth Army, which is retreating toward Paris before the onrushing Kluck.

Compiègne. Kluck's First Army has crossed the Oise and passed Compiègne, and now engages rear-guard units of the French Sixth Army and the BEF only thirty miles from Paris. The British troops fight gamely, stalling Kluck's advance and gaining time for the main BEF force to retreat unscathed.

2 September 1914

Paris. The government leaves the capital, moving to Bordeaux following a request from Joffre.

Lemberg (Lvov), Galicia. Russian troops

commanded by Gen. Aleksey Brusilov have pushed back the badly outnumbered Austrian right flank and surrounded the city of Lemberg, a communications center of the Empire. The Austrians, having suffered 130,000 losses, abandon the city.

Laon, France. Bülow's troops capture Laon and push to the banks of the Aisne River.

Tsingtao, China. The first of nearly 24,000 Japanese troops land on the Shantung Peninsula 150 miles northeast of the city.

Lublin, Poland. The Russian Fourth and Ninth Armies stop the Austrian Fourth Army.

3 September 1914

Lemberg. Russian troops occupy the city.

Lagny, France. The BEF escapes to safety across the Marne River as Kluck, his troops now exhausted from forced marching in pursuit of the British, abandons the chase and turns farther east to engage the French Fifth Army.

Sézanne, France. Joffre visits the Fifth Army headquarters to relieve Lanrezac of command—someone has to take the blame for the failure of Plan 17. Joffre chooses Gen. Franchet d'Esperey as Lanrezac's replacement.

4 September 1914

Nancy. Frustrated at being stymied by the French in the continuing Battle of Grand Couronné and thus unable to break through at the Trouée de Charmes, the Sixth Army, commanded by Crown Prince Rupprecht of Bavaria, now launches a furious artillery barrage and assault against the fortifications protecting Nancy.

Dammartin. With the Sixth Army now reinforced by other units to form a larger Army of Paris and concentrated at this site twenty miles northeast of the city, Galliéni sees an opportunity. Kluck's right flank is dangerously exposed and, in addition, his troops are enervated and well ahead of their supply lines, so Galliéni urges Joffre to authorize an attack by the Army of Paris on Kluck's right. Galliéni has been apprised by French aviators flying reconnaissance over the German lines that it is "vital to act quickly."

5 September 1914
Châtillon-sur-Seine, France. The French high command falls back thirty miles to the south and reestablishes headquarters here.

Claye, France. Troops from Kluck's army reach this town, only ten miles from Paris.

Rebais, France. Kluck receives orders at 7:00 A.M. from Moltke, who is deeply concerned that German forces are dangerously overextended, that he should turn to the west and protect his flank. But believing communiques that the German armies are "advancing victoriously along the whole front," Kluck chooses to advance, reaching this site near the Grand Morin River only five miles from French Fifth Army and BEF outposts. In the evening Moltke's chief of intelligence, Colonel Hentsch, appears, sent from OHL. Hentsch informs Kluck that Prince Rupprecht's Sixth and Seventh Armies are stalled at Nancy and Crown Prince Friedrich Wilhelm's Fifth Army troops are halted at Verdun. Kluck's new orders are to begin withdrawing north of the Marne.

Monthyon, France. Kluck sends troops under General von Gronau to check on his right flank; they are surprised to discover the superior force of Maunoury's Army of Paris. The ensuing Battle of the Ourcq is the first encounter in the Battle of the Marne. During the night Gronau withdraws six miles.

Masurian Lakes, East Prussia. German troops commanded by General Francois move against Rennenkampf's First Army, opening the Battle of the Masurian Lakes, with the intent of driving the Russians back across the border.

Firth of Forth, North Sea. The German U-boat *U-21* sinks *Pathfinder,* the lead ship of the Grand Fleet flotilla.

London. Representatives of the Allies sign a pact that binds them "not to conclude any separate peace in the course of the present war." The poster "Your Country Needs You" first appears in *London Opinion.*

6 September 1914
Meaux, France. At dawn, Maunoury's troops join battle with troops of Kluck's First Army commanded by General von Linsingen. Kluck begins withdrawing corps from his center to reinforce his left defense against Maunoury. Near Esternay and Sézanne, troops under Generals d'Esperey and Foch attack Bülow's Second Army.

7 September 1914
Rebais. Kluck withdraws his IIIrd and IXth Corps from deployment with Bülow to reinforce his right, thus opening a gap of nearly thirty miles between his army and Bülow's.

Maubeuge, France. German troops capture the city after heavy shelling, taking forty thousand prisoners.

Christmas Island, Pacific Ocean. Count von Spee's flotilla arrives.

8 September 1914
Crépy-en-Valois, France. Hoping to break the deadlock of battle, Maunoury tries to move above and behind the German flank but is stopped by the just-arrived IIIrd and IXth Corps. Maunoury seeks help from Galliéni, who rounds up six thousand reserves in Paris and hastens them to the front in six hundred of the city's taxis. To the east of the Marne front, BEF troops and d'Esperey's troops cross the Petit Morin River and attack Bülow's center, forcing him to abandon Montmirail, while his left under General Hausen manages to push Foch back with vigorous counterattacks. Now, however, there is no hope of closing the gap between Kluck's and Bülow's armies.

A ruined French village after the war had passed through in 1914 (by Reni-Mel, courtesy of the Anne S.K. Brown Military Collection, Brown University Library)

Indian Ocean. The cruiser *Emden* from Spee's fleet begins raids on Allied merchant ships while fourteen Allied warships join in trying to hunt her down.

9 September 1914
Château-Thierry, France. The BEF crosses the Marne. The British advance validates orders brought from OHL Colonel Hentsch to Bülow and Kluck—the Germans must retreat in coordination to the Aisne River or risk envelopment. To effect this end, Bülow receives command of the First Army as well as the Second.

10 September 1914
Lötzen, East Prussia. General Francois, following a rapid march, cuts off part of Rennenkampf's First Russian Army, taking five thousand prisoners.
Châtillon-sur-Seine. Joffre sends orders for the combined BEF and Fifth Army troops to pursue Kluck as rapidly as possible during his retreat.
Insterburg, East Prussia. Rennenkampf abandons his forward camp and retreats toward Russia, delaying the German pursuit with counterattacks.
Krasnik, Poland. Russian troops defeat the Austrian First Army commanded by Gen. Baron Viktor von Dankl and rout the Austrians at Rava Russka, Galicia, thirty miles northwest of Lemberg. The three Austrian armies are forced into retreat.

11 September 1914
Compiègne. With the Battle of the Marne decided in the Allies' favor, Maunoury reaches Compiègne while Foch advances to Châlons-sur-Marne, as the German First and Second Armies retreat to the Aisne River.

12 September 1914
Compiègne. Between here and Berry-au-Bac, the German First and Second Armies halt and make their stand on the north bank of the Aisne River while the French retake Rheims.
Grodek, Galicia. The city falls to the advancing Russians as the Austrian armies retreat beyond the San River.
North Sea. British Lt. Comdr. Max Horton

in submarine *E-9* fires two torpedoes into the German cruiser *Hela*—Britain's first destruction of an enemy ship by a submarine.

13 September 1914
Aisne River. The main body of BEF troops and units from the French Fifth and Sixth Armies cross the river and advance several miles, but German corps moved from Maubeuge and Alsace block their chance of moving between Kluck's and Bülow's armies. The Germans retain control of that part of France that provides 80 percent of the Allied nation's coal and contains nearly all of its iron reserves. French troops recapture Soissons and Amiens.

14 September 1914
Luxembourg. General von Moltke resigns as chief of staff and is replaced by Gen. Erich von Falkenhayn, who immediately moves high command headquarters forward to Charleville on the Meuse River.
Pacific Ocean. Spee arrives at Samoa but finds no ships in the harbor.

15 September 1914
Aisne River. German troops, now occupying trenches, successfully repulse French and BEF attacks.

French infantry in a frontline trench (by A. Barrere, courtesy of the Anne S.K. Brown Military Collection, Brown University Library)

Masurian Lakes, East Prussia. The battle ends with Rennenkampf withdrawing across the Niemen River, where he establishes defensive positions.

16 September 1914
Aisne River. Sir John French issues orders for the BEF to build trenches.
Cameroons. Germans unsuccessfully at-

tack the gunboat *Dwarf* in the estuary of the Cameroon and Dibamba (Lungasi) Rivers with a torpedo mounted on a launch.
Washington, D.C. President Wilson receives the Belgian mission.

17 September 1914
Antwerp. The Belgian army falls back to the temporary capital.
East Prussia. The Russian command dismisses Jilinsky, replacing him with Gen. N.V. Russki.
Aisne River. The French Sixth Army advances four miles between Soissons and Compiègne.
Cameroons. The German steamer *Nachtigal* rams the *Dwarf,* creating reparable damage, but then explodes.

18 September 1914
Aisne River. Joffre orders Maunoury to halt at Soissons-Bailly, and the Allied advance peters out.
Tsingtao. The Japanese land troops without opposition at Lao-shan Bay, thirty miles to the east of the port.

19 September 1914
German South-West Africa. Commanded by Col. P.S. Beves, 1,824 South African troops land at Luderitzbucht.

20 September 1914
Metz. Crown Prince Wilhelm launches a thrust toward Saint-Mihiel, gaining ground along a twelve-mile front, but the French stop him at Fort Troyon.
East Africa. The German cruiser *Königsberg* steams into the harbor at Zanzibar, where HMS *Pegasus,* commanded by Capt. J.A. Inglis, has docked for repairs. Capt. Max Loof raises his battle flags and begins firing on the *Pegasus,* ending with broadside shellings that set the British ship afire and silence her guns. Thirty-one crew members die and fifty fall wounded, while the Germans suffer not a single casualty. Steaming back out of the harbor, Loof fires three shells into the picket ship *Helmut,* posted at the harbor's entrance. The *Helmut,* which had failed to spot the *Königsberg,* explodes.

21 September 1914
Noyon. French troops retake the city, while Gen. Maurice Sarrail stalls the German advance on Saint-Mihiel.
East Prussia. The German Eighth Army reaches the Niemen River and forces Rennenkampf's troops to cross over.

22 September 1914
Poland. The German Ninth Army, formed the week before and comprising 250,000 troops, arrives north of Cracow.
North Sea. During the early morning, U-boat *U-9,* commanded by Captain Weddingen, torpedoes and sinks the British cruiser *Aboukir,* on patrol with her sister cruisers, *Hogue* and *Cressy.* As the *Hogue* picks up survivors, it is hit by two torpedoes. The ship sinks within ten minutes. The *Cressy,* hit twice, capsizes while all her boats are on the water picking up survivors. The British lose fourteen hundred seamen.
Indian Ocean. The *Emden* shells the facilities of Burmah Oil Company at Madras, India, destroying fifty thousand tons of oil.
Cologne and Dusseldorf, Germany. British planes bomb the Zeppelin sheds located in these cities.

23 September 1914
Halifax, Canada. A division of the Canadian Expeditionary Force (CEF) embarks for Great Britain.
Tsingtao. Over thirteen hundred British troops land at Lao-shan to support the Japanese.
Cameroons. The cruiser HMS *Challenger,* part of a squadron under Capt. Cyril T.M. Fuller's command, arrives in the Cameroons estuary along with six transports carrying Brig. Gen. Charles McPherson Dobell and the British troop contingent for the combined French-British Cameroons Expeditionary Force.

24 September 1914
Cameroons. The French contingent of the Cameroons Force arrives. Dobell now has under his command over 4,900 soldiers, including 154 British officers, 54 French officers, and 4,319 askaris, supported by over 4,300 carriers.

25 September 1914
Aisne River. German troops recapture Noyon.

26 September 1914
Antwerp. Alarmed by the prospect that British forces may come to the rescue of Belgium—two thousand British marines had landed at Ostend early in the month— Falkenhayn has authorized besieging the fortress at Antwerp, protected by sixty-five thousand regular Belgian army troops and eighty thousand second-line troops. With 173 heavy guns in place, the Germans begin an artillery barrage of the fortress.
Sandfontein, German South-West Africa. Capt. E.J. Welby and his 120-man South African patrol, attacked the day before by Germans, receive reinforcements under Lt. Col. R.C. Grant sent from Raman's Drift, occupied two days earlier by a force of nearly twenty-five hundred men commanded by Brig. Gen. Henry T. Lukin. Grant's squadron brings two thirteen-pound cannons and a machine gun, but two German columns approach before they can position themselves. The Germans, who have cut the telephone wires to Raman's Drift, begin a cannonade at 8:00 A.M. By midmorning, a direct hit destroys one of the South African cannons and kills or wounds all the gunners. In the early afternoon, the German commander, Colonel von Heydebreck, launches an infantry attack, but the South Africans, though outgunned and perhaps outmanned by ten to one, wage a furious defense. At six o'clock, badly wounded and finally accepting the inevitable, Colonel Grant surrenders. After the firing stops, thirsty men from both sides run to the nearby wells and mingle together drinking water as if nothing had happened. The South Africans have suffered sixty-seven casualties, including sixteen dead, while inflicting sixty casualties on the Germans, including fourteen dead. But the Battle of Sandfontein marks the end of any hope of a South African invasion of German South-West Africa, as they must divert their attention to a rebellion of Afrikaners that has begun in the Orange River and Transvaal provinces.
Meuse River. French troops stymie an attempted German crossing of the river at Saint-Mihiel.

27 September 1914
Constantinople. Gen. Liman von Sanders, head of the German Military Mission in Turkey, orders Enver Pasha to close the Dardanelles to shipping to and from Russia, a mortally crippling blow to that Allied nation's ability to sustain its economy and therefore its war effort.
Tsingtao. Japanese troops attack the city's outer defenses.
Cameroons. Planning a direct assault on Douala, General Dobell and Gen. Edmund H. Gorges, commander of the British land forces, board the Nigerian yacht *Ivy* for reconnaissance of a suitable landing site. While they watch, explosions rock the city and destroy the wireless station. White flags appear above Government House and other buildings, and at 11:00 A.M., a German official comes aboard the *Ivy* and unconditionally surrenders both Douala and Bonaberi.

28 September 1914
Malines, Belgium. German troops capture Malines, midway between Brussels and Antwerp, where the artillery barrage continues.
Poland. To relieve pressure on the Austrians, Hindenburg begins an advance by the Ninth Army on a wide front between Cracow and Czenstochowa.

29 September 1914
Tsingtao. Japanese drive German troops from the protective forts on the city's outskirts.

30 September 1914
Antwerp. After three days of German bombardment, with one-ton shells hurtling down on the city's perimeter forts, King Albert requests aid from the Allies.
Cameroons. A flotilla with 150 men from the West African Regiment leaves Douala and attacks German troops at Tiko, driving them off and killing their commander.

1 October 1914
Aisne River. With Joffre having acceded

to his request to transfer the BEF to Flanders, Sir John French begins to move his troops north to occupy a line from Bethune to Hazebrouck south of Ypres.

East Prussia. At the Augustów Forest, the Russian Tenth Army under Rennenkampf pushes back the German Eighth Army and follows after the retreating German troops.

Antwerp. German troops occupy the city's perimeter forts and the trenches stretching between them. They are still too distant to shell the city itself.

Berlin. *Kriegsbrot,* "war bread" made with artificial ingredients, is introduced.

3 October 1914

Antwerp. Dispatched by the British cabinet, Winston Churchill arrives in the beleaguered city with promises of aid and persuades King Albert not to withdraw the Belgian government and troops.

4 October 1914

Belgium. Pursuing their "race to the sea," German troops advance, capturing Lens and other towns and beginning a bombardment of Lille.

Cameroons. Pushing inland, the Allied force advances nearly to Yabassi, about fifty miles north of Douala.

Indian Ocean. The *Emden* arrives at Diego Garcia, where the British subjects do not yet even know of the outbreak of war, and begins cleaning and coaling.

5 October 1914

Duffel, Belgium. German troops cross the Nethe River.

6 October 1914

Antwerp. The Belgian army begins to withdraw from the city, and the government moves to Ostend. Nearly a quarter of a million residents flee toward Holland and France.

Cameroons. A French contingent of the Cameroons Expeditionary Force, four hundred *tirailleurs* with artillery carried upriver by Captain Fuller's British cruisers, the *Cumberland* and the *Challenger,* and deployed at the Yapona railway bridge over the Dibamba River, succeed in securing the wrecked bridge, crossing the river,

and driving off the Germans, ending the threat of an attack on Douala from the east and creating the possibility of an Allied attack on Edea.

7 October 1914

Antwerp. German artillery begins to bombard the city. Too late to assist in the city's defense, a corps of British troops commanded by Gen. Sir Henry Rawlinson disembarks at Ostend and Zeebrugge. German troops cross the Scheldt River and menace the retiring Belgian army.

8 October 1914

Doullens, France. Under orders from Joffre, Foch takes command of the Allied armies defending Flanders. Sir John French confers with him and subsequently establishes BEF headquarters at Abbeville.

Cameroons. An expedition sent out by Dobell and commanded by Brig. Gen. E.H. Gorges fails in an attack against the Germans near Yabassi.

9 October 1914

Antwerp. The mayor surrenders the city. Occupying German troops capture 936 members of a British naval brigade there to help defend the city. The Belgians' lengthy resistance has cost the Germans precious time, diverting their forces away from the "race to the sea." But final German success allows Falkenhayn to transfer four corps and the artillery used in the Antwerp siege to the offensive against the Allied forces in Flanders at Ypres.

Flanders. From Abbeville, four hundred French buses transport ten thousand British troops to Saint-Pol.

Poland. The Austrian offensive, coordinated with the German advance to the north against Rennenkampf, captures Jaroslaw on the San River in Galicia but comes to a halt.

Upington, South Africa. Col. Salomon Gerhardus Maritz declares himself in support of the Afrikaner rebels and tells his troops that they have one minute to decide whether to join with him or accept arrest. Sixty troops who decide to remain loyal to Great Britain are arrested and turned over to the Germans. Elsewhere, two of the great leaders of the Boers, Louis Botha and Jan Smuts, have remained loyal, with Botha having become commander in chief in the colony on 22 September.

10 October 1914
Antwerp. The Belgian commander, Deguise, surrenders his sword as the Germans complete the occupation of the city. The Belgian army manages to hold the pursuing Germans near Ghent.
Poland. A corps of Mackensen's Ninth Army defeats Russian troops at Grojec to the south of Warsaw.

11 October 1914
Bruges, Belgium. The Belgian army begins to establish a defensive line along the Yser River.
Poland. Mackensen's troops capture Sochaczew, advancing to within thirty miles of Warsaw, while the Russian Fourth, Fifth, and Ninth Armies fail in their effort to cross the Vistula River to the south defended by the Germans.

12 October 1914
Poland. Mackensen's army advances to within seven miles of Warsaw but is ordered by Ludendorff to halt and entrench.
Sarajevo. The trial of Gavrilo Princip and his co-conspirators begins.
Belgium. Allied troops evacuate Ostend and Zeebrugge as the BEF and the Belgian army move to Roulers.

13 October 1914
Belgium. The Belgian government withdraws from Ostend to relocate at Le Havre, while British troops occupy Ypres. German troops occupy Ghent and Lille.

14 October 1914
Belgium. German troops occupy Bruges.
Plymouth, England. The first contingent of the Canadian Expeditionary Force arrives in England.
Pacific Ocean. Japanese troops occupy the Mariana Islands and the Marshall Islands, both German colonies.

15 October, 1914
Belgium. German troops occupy Ostend

and Zeebrugge as the Belgian army completes digging in on the Yser River.
Poland. Mackensen's Ninth Army begins a final offensive to drive the Russians across the Vistula, attacking near Jozefow and Warsaw, where preparations begin for evacuating the city.
Washington, D.C. The State Department takes the position that American firms have the right to sell "any article of commerce" to any of the belligerents involved in the war.

16 October 1914
Belgium. The Germans attack at Dixmude.
Wellington, New Zealand. The first contingent of the New Zealand Expeditionary Force, 8,574 men, sails for France.

17 October 1914
Albany, Australia. The first contingent of the Australian Expeditionary Force, 20,226 men, embarks for France.

18 October 1914
Poland. After four days of incessant rain and futile battle, stymied and driven back by a counteroffensive launched by Grand Duke Nicholas, Mackensen realizes he cannot succeed, especially as no relief can be forthcoming from the Austrian army, now being driven back at the San River front in Galicia. Ludendorff orders Mackensen to begin retreating.
Easter Island. With his *Scharnhorst* and *Gneisenau* having been reinforced by the arrival of the *Dresden* and the *Leipzig* during the preceding week, Count von Spee sails toward Chile. The Admiralty has ordered a squadron out of the Falkland Islands to hunt him down. The squadron, commanded by Rear Adm. Christopher Cradock, consists of two armored cruisers, *Good Hope* and *Monmouth,* with six-inch guns, representing about half the firing power of the German cruisers; the light cruiser *Glasgow;* and the converted liner *Otranto.* Cradock is supposed to be reinforced by the old battleship *Canopus,* with twelve-inch guns, and the armored cruiser *Defence* en route from the Mediterranean. But on this day at Port Stanley, Cradock receives a message from the *Canopus* that

the slow-going battleship will be a week late in joining him.

19 October 1914
Flanders. Battle rages along the entire front from the English Channel to Armentières as German troops mass for an attack against the BEF at Ypres, a vital communications center and transportation link to the Channel. Falkenhayn's objective is capture of the port cities of Dunkirk, Calais, and Boulogne.

20 October 1914
North Sea. Fourteen miles off the Norwegian coast, the German U-boat *U-17,* commanded by Lieutenant Commander Feldkircher, overtakes the British merchant steamer SS *Glitra.* The Germans board the ship, allowing the *Glitra*'s crew to lower and board their boats in accord with international law, and then open the ship's sea cocks, sending her to the bottom. The *Glitra* thus becomes the first merchantman ever sunk by a submarine.
Flanders. On the very day that the British Ist Corps, commanded by Sir Douglas Haig, arrives at Ypres, joining the Cavalry Corps commanded by Gen. Edmund Allenby, the Germans launch an offensive along the entire Flanders front from the La Bassée Canal to the sea, with the Fourth Army attempting to defeat the BEF near Ypres and pour through their line for a flanking movement against Foch's troops. Simultaneously, the Allies launch offensives between Givenchy and Ypres.
Poland. Mackensen begins a measured withdrawal from engagement with the Russians near Warsaw.
Cameroons. Dobell launches an expedition to travel up the Nyong River to Dehane, from which he will march overland to attack Edea.

21 October 1914
Flanders. A reinspirited Sir John French sends Haig's corps along with two French divisions into battle north of Ypres, intending to break through to the coast.

22 October 1914
Flanders. A German counterattack stymies

Haig's advance. In their offensive against the Belgian army, German troops expand their bridgehead, slogging through swampy terrain and crossing the Yser near Tervaete.
Cameroons. Dobell's expedition against Edea reaches Dehane.

23 October 1914
Poland. Russian troops advance along their entire front; in Galicia they recapture Jaroslaw.

25 October 1914
Flanders. After several days of attacks and counterattacks, neither side has gained an advantage, although the Belgian army seems in a desperate spot after suffering huge casualties in its ardent resistance. At Foch's suggestion, they attempt to stop the German advance by opening the sluice gates of the coastal dikes to flood the area between the Yser and the railway embankment extending from Dixmude to Nieuport.

26 October 1914
Poland. Mackensen's Ninth Army completes a sixty-mile, six-day retreat. During their withdrawal the Germans have destroyed all bridges, roads, and rail lines, leaving all the villages intact, in order to impose a limit on the Grand Duke's supply lines and force the Russians to halt—a successful strategy, though the Germans have suffered forty thousand casualties.
Sarajevo. The court accepts guilty pleas from all the assassination defendants except Princip and sentences those under the age of twenty to twenty years' imprisonment and the others to death.
Cameroons. The Anglo-French expedition sent out by Dobell captures Edea.
South Africa. Louis Botha assembles artillery and six thousand cavalrymen at Vereeniging and sets out on a march to capture the rebel leader Christiaan De Wet, who he learns is in Mushroom Valley.
Pacific Ocean. Count von Spee's flotilla anchors off the island of Más Afuera, about five hundred miles from the coast of Chile.

27 October 1914
Atlantic Ocean. Great Britain's Second Battle Squadron, composed of eight super-

dreadnoughts, heads out to sea for firing practice. When twenty miles out from Tory Island (northeast Irish coast) the dreadnought *Audacious* hits a mine. Efforts to tow the ship to safety, observed by picture-snapping American tourists aboard the White Star liner *Olympic,* fail. In the evening, she blows up and sinks, leaving the Grand Fleet with nineteen dreadnoughts against the High Seas Fleet's sixteen.

28 October 1914
Poland. Russian troops recapture Lodz and Radon.
Indian Ocean. The *Emden* raids Penang, Malaya, entering the harbor and sinking the Russian cruiser *Zemtchug.* Emerging from the harbor, the *Emden* spots the French destroyer *Mousquet* and destroys it with shelling but rescues some of the crew members.
Pacific Ocean. Cradock, now off of Coronel, Chile, has realized from intercepted German signals that he is near Spee's squadron. On 26 October, he had sent a signal to the *Defence* to join him, but Churchill now sends word that he has ordered the *Defence* to remain in the Atlantic off the East Coast of South America. Undeterred, Cradock signals to his squadron: "Spread twenty miles apart and look for the enemy." He dispatches the *Glasgow* to Coronel to send a telegram to the Admiralty outlining his intent and deployment.

29 October 1914
Black Sea. The *Goeben* and the *Breslau* (now given Turkish names) and a third Turkish ship stage a surprise raid in the Black Sea, sinking the Russian gunboat *Donetz* at Odessa and other vessels at smaller ports.
Tsingtao. Japanese siege guns begin bombarding the port's small garrison.

30 October 1914
Flanders. The waters unleashed by opening the sluice gates of the coastal dikes finally reach a flood stage of three to four feet in depth and two miles in width between Dixmude and Nieuport, forcing the Germans to withdraw and thus allowing the embattled Belgian army and King Albert to retain control over a portion of the kingdom.
London. Savaged by detractors in the Royal Navy, defamed for his German back-

A triumphant German army enters the key Polish city of Lodz (Library of Congress)

ground, and victimized by the general unease in the government over the navy's thus far unprepossessing performance, Prince Louis of Battenberg resigns as first sea lord. He is immediately replaced by Sir John Fisher, former first sea lord, architect of the navy's reformation and dreadnought building program, and now Churchill's first choice as partner at the Admiralty.

31 October 1914
Flanders. In what seems a turning point in the First Battle of Ypres, the Germans capture Gheluvelt at noon, breaking the BEF's line and creating the possibility for a crippling flank attack. But a counterattack sweeps the Germans back and reestablishes the British line.
Berlin. Ludendorff visits Falkenhayn to argue that Germany should assume a defensive posture on the Western Front so that troops may be diverted to Prussia for an offensive that will knock the Russians out of the war, after which troops on the Eastern Front can be transferred back to the West for a decisive blow against the French. Falkenhayn is obdurate, insisting that capture of the Channel ports is the greater goal.
Mombasa, British East Africa. The first contingent of Indian Expeditionary Force B, commanded by Maj. Gen. Arthur E. Aitken, arrives. Comprising about eight thousand mostly poorly trained sepoys, the force's orders are "to bring the whole of German East Africa under British authority."

1 November 1914
Flanders. German troops capture the strategic ridges at Messines and Wytschaete. Kitchener confers with Joffre and Foch at Dunkirk, promising to send a million men to France within eighteen months.
East Prussia. Hindenburg becomes commander in chief of all the German armies on the Eastern Front, establishes his headquarters at Posen, and begins to prepare a major new offensive in northern Poland.
Constantinople. Turkey declares war on the Allies.
Pacific Ocean. Learning that the *Glasgow* has been in Coronel, Spee speeds south in hopes of isolating and destroying her be-

fore she can rejoin Cradock, while Cradock moves north hoping to inflict the same fate on the *Leipzig,* Spee's slowest ship, whose wireless messages Capt. John Luce aboard the *Glasgow* has intercepted and reported to Cradock. At four-thirty in the afternoon, Spee, aboard the *Gneisenau* about fifty miles out from Coronel, sights smoke from Cradock's squadron. He tightens the formation of his squadron and speeds toward the enemy. Spee maneuvers his ships so that, as the sun sets at seven o'clock, Cradock's ships will be silhouetted in a line along the horizon. At twelve thousand yards, Spee opens fire on the *Good Hope,* Cradock's flagship, destroying one of her two big guns and setting her on fire. Then the *Monmouth* takes a hit and bursts into flames. The *Otranto,* not equipped for such battle, withdraws, as Spee's light cruisers zero in on the *Glasgow.* Captain Luce's ship, though hit five times, suffers only minor damage and is able to flee, sending a warning by wireless to the *Canopus,* nearly three hundred miles to the south. The *Good Hope* and the *Monmouth* sink. Spee sets out for Valparaiso, leaving two cruisers behind to search for survivors. There are none.

2 November 1914
Flanders. Ceding the Messines and Wytschaete Ridges to the Germans, BEF and French forces now concentrate on the defense of Ypres. The Germans withdraw from most of their positions on the Yser.
Tanga, German East Africa. HMS *Fox,* commanded by Capt. F.W. Cauldfield, arrives outside the harbor in advance of the convoy transporting Major General Aitken's Indian Expeditionary Force B south for the invasion of German East Africa. The local German commissioner, Herr Auracher, comes aboard and is informed by Cauldfield that the neutrality agreement protecting Tanga and Dar es Salaam is now abrogated and that Tanga must be surrendered or be shelled by the *Fox.* Cauldfield asks whether the harbor is mined. Auracher asserts that it is and requests an hour's grace period to discuss Cauldfield's ultimatum with his superiors. He returns to shore; joins Lt. F.B. Adler, who had directed the

artillery at Sandfontein; and sends word to Lettow-Vorbeck. Since he has been kept well informed of Aitken's expedition—surprisingly, there was no effort to keep it secret—Lettow-Vorbeck has been expecting an attack at Tanga. Although Governor Schnee has ordered him not to defend Tanga, Lettow-Vorbeck ignores the governor's wishes and rushes his askaris by rail to the town, while Cauldfield sends the *Helmuth* to sweep the harbor for mines—there are none. During the late hours of the night, Aitken begins to land troops at a site on Manza Bay, two miles above the city.

4 November 1914
Tanga. Having landed the last of his troops without opposition the night before, Aitken is ready to advance to Tanga, where Lettow-Vorbeck and reinforcements have arrived at 3:00 A.M. Although confusion reigns during the day's battle, including shells fired from the *Fox* falling among British troops, Aitken's men manage to drive back the German askaris and enter Tanga. But Lettow-Vorbeck's redoubtable friend Tom von Prince arrives with reinforcements to repulse the British. At one point, troops on both sides of the battle flee before the anger of bees enraged by bullets hitting their hives. Though outnumbered eight to one, Lettow-Vorbeck stages a counterattack after the arrival of his Fourth Field Company, whose withering machine-gun fire sends the British force into chaotic flight.
Longido, German East Africa. An Anglo-Indian force of fifteen hundred men that has marched from Namanga across the border advances against Longido, situated on the northern slopes of Kilimanjaro. Maj. Georg Kraut, who has been aware of the British advance, unleashes his force of eighty Germans and six hundred askaris in a series of punishing attacks that generate fifty-two casualties and a British retreat.

5 November 1914
Cyprus. Declaring war on Turkey, Great Britain annexes Cyprus.
Tanga. Giving orders to leave behind all arms, ammunition, and supplies on the shore, Aitken begins to evacuate his troops and wounded—some being treated in the German hospital that had been hit by a shell from the *Fox* during the battle—to their transport vessels. They embark at night for Mombasa, leaving Lettow-Vorbeck a huge supply of matériel, including modern rifles, six hundred thousand rounds of ammunition, and sixteen machine guns. Aitken's expeditionary force has suffered 817 casualties, including 360 dead. The German defenders report only 148 casualties, but among their dead is Tom von Prince, mortally wounded by a stray bullet. During the night Aitken cables his battle report to London. News of the debacle is not released to the public.

6 November 1914
Serbia. General Potiorek, having massed a force of 119 Austrian battalions, launches a major offensive against a much smaller Serbian army on the Drina River front.

7 November 1914
Tsingtao. Following Japanese assaults on Forts Bismarck and Moltke, the German governor surrenders the city.

8 November 1914
London. Having received at the end of October a copy of the German navy's cipher signal books recovered from a corpse by the Russians after they sank the *Magdeburg,* and also possessing recovered German operational charts of the North Sea, the Admiralty decides to capitalize on these advantages by setting up a secret decoding department known as "Room 40." Sir Alfred Ewing heads the department.
Atlantic Ocean. Capt. John Luce's *Glasgow,* joined by the *Canopus,* arrives at Port Stanley, Falkland Islands.

9 November 1914
Serbia. The Austrians cross the Sava River east of Belgrade but are stopped by the Serbs.
Indian Ocean. After three months of raids resulting in the sinking of seventeen merchantmen and a paralysis of shipping in Indian Ocean waters, the *Emden* arrives at

Cocos Island with the intent of destroying the wireless station there and refueling. The wireless operators spot her despite the camouflage of a false funnel and signal an Anzac convoy moving westward only fifty-five miles distant. The Australian light cruiser *Sydney* steams off to investigate. After ramming the wireless station and sending a landing party ashore to finish the job, the *Emden* awaits the collier's arrival. Mistaking the *Sydney* for the collier, the *Emden* falls victim to the larger, faster, more heavily armed Australian cruiser; she ends up a flaming ruin on the island's reef.

11 November 1914
Flanders. After several days of thrusts and counterthrusts, the Germans send thirteen divisions into a massive, densely formed attack along a nine-mile front spread from Messines to the Menin Road amid heavy rain and wind. They manage to drive forward a thousand yards in a breakthrough that promises victory. But the British press into battle every possible man, including sappers, cooks, servants, engineers, and transport drivers; and at Nun's Woods (Nonne Boschen) the Oxfordshire Light Infantry hurls the Germans back. As the battle dies down the Germans begin shelling Ypres.
Poland. After transferring most of General Mackensen's Ninth Army to join the Eighth Army south of Torun—a huge undertaking that uses over eight hundred trains—for an offensive designed by Ludendorff, the Germans launch an advance along the Vistula River toward Warsaw and Lodz.

12 November 1914
Mushroom Valley, South Africa. Botha arrives at De Wet's rebel encampment and begins shelling in the early morning. De Wet stems the panic among his men to muster a strong resistance, but as Botha's force steps up the attack, the rebels flee into the mountains. De Wet, with a small group of his followers, escapes into the Kalahari Desert. Botha sends Col. Coenraad Brits, one of his ablest officers, in pursuit.

13 November 1914
Flanders. The German thrust diminishes as the First Battle of Ypres winds down.

15 November 1914
Flanders. The First Battle of Ypres draws to a close after generating enormous costs to both sides—German casualties reach 130,000; British, over 58,000, with perhaps an equal number of French casualties. The armies on both sides are now ensconced in trenches along nearly their entire shared front as harsh winter weather settles in.

French trench works in the Lorraine (by A. Barrere, courtesy of the Anne S.K. Brown Military Collection, Brown University Library)

16 November 1914
Poland. After fierce fighting at Vlotsavek and Kutno, German troops force the Russians back to assume a defensive position at Lodz.

17 November 1914
Mesopotamia. British troops rout a Turkish force at Fort Sahil, taking 150 prisoners.
East Africa. German troops withdraw from Longido, allowing a British force commanded by Gen. James Stewart to occupy the town without opposition.

18 November 1914
Paris. The French government returns from Bordeaux.

20 November 1914
Poland. German troops maintain the offensive southwest of Warsaw and at Lodz.

21 November 1914
Mesopotamia. British forces occupy Basra, believed by British strategists to be

crucial to securing the Shatt-al-Arab, the combined Tigris and Euphrates Rivers flowing into the Persian Gulf southeast of the city, and also to aligning the Arabs with the British cause.

22 November 1914

Poland. Mackensen's troops, their ammunition now running low, approach Lodz. General Ivanov's troops defeat the Austrians near Cracow, taking six thousand prisoners.

25 November 1914

Lodz, Poland. Although encircled by Rennenkampf's First Army—the Russians anticipate a major victory—General von Schaffer seizes an advantage when Rennenkampf fails to seal off the Germans' possibility of escape to the north, turns the tables by smashing the hold of a Siberian division, and extricates his force from entrapment while capturing ten thousand prisoners and sixty guns.

Mesopotamia and Persia. From *A History of the Great War, 1914-1918,* byt C.R.M.F. Cruttwell, published by Academy Chicago Publishers. All rights reserved.

26 November 1914
Flanders. A German assault on the Yser canal gets nowhere.

27 November 1914
Posen, East Prussia. Hindenburg gains the rank of field marshal as General Litvinov becomes commander of the Russian First Army, replacing Rennenkampf, who had fallen from grace because of his failure at Lodz.

28 November 1914
Poland. After a week of unsuccessful fighting in Galicia, the Austrians retreat to the east of Cracow, while Conrad von Hötzendorf withdraws his Fourth Austrian Army south of the Vistula River. Grand Duke Nicholas meets with his commanders at Siedice to plan a Russian offensive at Cracow.
German East Africa. Adm. Herbert King-Hall, commander at the Cape station, has sent the cruiser *Fox,* the battleship *Goliath,* and the tug *Helmuth* to Dar es Salaam. When officers from two of the British ships inspect purported German civilian liners, German troops open fire and eventually capture the *Goliath's* doctor. Comdr. Henry P. Ritchie of the *Goliath* suffers eight wounds and is later awarded the Victoria Cross—the first naval award of the medal during the war.

29 November 1914
Serbia. Serbian troops begin the evacuation of Belgrade.

30 November 1914
Poland. Mackensen's Ninth Army and Litvinov's First Army commence battle at Lowicz-Sanniki.

1 December 1914
Flanders. King George V visits hospitals and troops near the front.
Serbia. The Austrian Fifth Army occupies Belgrade.
South Africa. De Wet and the remnants of his rebel force surrender to Colonel Brits.

2 December 1914
Atlantic Ocean. After a perilous passage,

Count von Spee's squadron emerges from the waters off Cape Horn and captures a four-masted barque flying the British flag and carrying three thousand tons of coal—enough to replace the coal the Germans had to throw overboard to escape capsizing in the Straits of Magellan and the Cape waters.

3 December 1914
Serbia. The Serbian First Army, commanded by Gen. Radomir Putnik, regroups and launches an unexpected counterattack in the Battle of the Ridges, surprising Potiorek's Sixth Army.

6 December 1914
Poland. Russian troops evacuate Lodz and begin retreating thirty miles to a line along the Rawka and Bzura Rivers, where they create formidable entrenchments.
Serbia. After three days of battle, the Austrians break and retreat headlong toward the Kolubara River. The Serbs capture forty thousand prisoners and large quantities of guns and ammunition.

7 December 1914
South Africa. Botha's troops smash rebels led by Christiaan Frederik Beyers, former commander of the nation's Defence Force. Beyers drowns while trying to escape across the Vaal River.
Falkland Islands. Capt. Heathcoat Grant, following his orders from the Admiralty and on his own initiative, has mired his *Canopus* in mud at a concealed site in Port Stanley harbor, transformed his twelve-pound guns into shore batteries, placed mines across the harbor entrance, and set up observation stations, while Captain Luce sailed the *Glasgow* to rendezvous at Montevideo with a flotilla sent out from England by the Admiralty to hunt down Spee. The flotilla, including battle cruisers *Invincible* and *Inflexible*, four armored cruisers, and two light cruisers, accompanied by the *Glasgow,* arrives at Port Stanley under the command of Vice Adm. Sir Frederick Doveton Sturdee in the *Invincible.*

8 December 1914
Falkland Islands. At 7:30 A.M., an ob-

server spots the approach of Count von Spee's squadron, come to raid Port Stanley before proceeding to the Plate River, New York, and home. Though news of Sturdee's mission has been wired to Valparaiso, operators there have been unable to reach Spee, who has rejected the counsel of his subordinates to save supplies and ammunition, reduced by half during the Battle of Coronel, for the trip home—Spee believes raiding Port Stanley will demoralize the British. As they move in to bombard Port Stanley, the *Gneisenau* and *Nürnberg* sight the British ships in harbor. The concealed *Canopus* opens fire, hitting a funnel on the *Gneisenau.* Spee orders the two ships to withdraw at top speed. Because the *Invincible* and other ships in Sturdee's flotilla are taking on coal, it is two hours before they can get up steam and give chase, but Spee in the meantime fails to take advantage of their vulnerability. He could have moved in and shelled them like sitting ducks but chooses instead to speed off. The faster British ships quickly close on Spee, who divides his squadron to do battle. For a time his maneuvers succeed, as firing from the *Invincible* goes astray— the result of both poor shooting and obscuring clouds of smoke. The Germans' firing is accurate but has little effect on the heavy armor of the British battle cruisers. Now, at closer range, British shelling finds its target—Spee's flagship *Scharnhorst* takes over forty hits. Spee sends a final message to Captain Maerker, who had opposed the Falklands raid, aboard the *Gneisenau:* "You were right after all." The *Scharnhorst* sinks with all hands. The *Invincible* and the *Inflexible* turn their guns full on the *Gneisenau.* After a tremendous pounding, she goes to the bottom just after 6:00 P.M., but the British lower boats and rescue two hundred survivors, including Comdr. Hans Pochhammer. Elsewhere, the *Kent* dispatches the *Nürnberg,* while the *Glasgow* and the *Cornwall* sink the *Leipzig;* but the *Dresden* escapes, steaming southwest over the horizon. The Battle of the Falklands, costing four ships and twenty-two hundred dead, is a disaster for Germany and a blow to national morale and pride. It also means the oceans are freed for unhindered Allied commerce and troop transportation and that Sturdee's ships can rejoin the Grand Fleet.

9 December 1914
Serbia. Serbian troops recapture Lazarevac and Uzice. General Potiorek orders a general retreat.

12 December 1914
Serbia. The Austrian Sixth Army recrosses the Sava River near Sabac.

13 December 1914
Turkey. British Lt. Norman Holbrook pilots his *B-11* submarine through the Narrows at the Dardanelles, skirting five rows of mines, and enters the straits as dawn breaks. Sighting the Turkish battleship *Messudieh* anchored in Sari Sigla Bay, he fires a torpedo from six hundred yards, ascertains that the ship is destroyed, dives quickly, and scuttles back out through the Narrows, sometimes touching bottom. His reward is the Victoria Cross.

15 December 1914
Serbia. As the retreating Austrians had recrossed the Sava River at Belgrade the day before, Serbian troops reoccupy the city, bringing to an end the third Austrian invasion of Serbia.

16 December 1914
North Sea. Having received reports on 14 December from Sir Alfred Ewing's Room 40 decoders that the Germans plan to send a scouting squadron of five battle cruisers commanded by Admiral Franz von Hipper for raids at Harwich and the Humber River, Jellicoe has deployed six super-dreadnoughts, four battle cruisers, and squadrons of destroyers and light cruisers to intercept and destroy the German ships. Hipper's ships shell Scarborough, Hartlepool, and Whitby. Although close to engagement, the British commanders botch signals, and the weather minimizes visibility, allowing Hipper to return safely to harbor. Both sides missed opportunities for decisive victory, to the disgust of both the Admiralty and the German navy. The British public is outraged, as the German vio-

lation of the Hague Agreement has generated 86 dead and 424 wounded in Scarborough.

20 December 1914
Champagne, France. After three weeks of seesaw battles along the Flanders front, with little gained or lost by either side, Joffre, now determined to pursue a policy of attrition, launches the Fourth Army into battle in Champagne.

21 December 1914
England. Following a German bombing raid at Dover, Lord Kitchener orders a doubling of expansion plans for the Royal Flying Corps.

23 December 1914
Austria-Hungary. Archduke Eugen replaces General Potiorek as commander in chief of Austrian forces in the Balkans.

25 December 1914
Flanders. An unofficial "Christmas truce" prevails in many of the war's sectors. On the Ypres front at dawn, British soldiers hear carols floating across no-man's-land from the German trenches. The Germans hoist Christmas trees with lighted candles above the parapets and then walk halfway into no-man's-land, shouting greetings and proffering cigars and schnapps. British officers and troops join them, and they mingle between the opposing trenches, chatting, exchanging cigarettes, and playing soccer.

Neither side will acknowledge the stalemate along the trench lines of the Western Front, and they continue to send forth offensive after offensive in vain attempts to break through and regain the power of maneuver. The efforts founder because of the ability of the machine gun to stop advancing troops and the power of artillery to weaken assaults even before they begin. A basic pattern develops whereby major assaults consume huge numbers of men and vast amounts of matériel but usually fail to penetrate far into the defenses. Even if a strong offensive pushes through, it is impossible to follow up rapidly enough to force a breakout. "Battles" last for weeks and months and exact tens of thousands of casualties on both sides. Even the use of poison gas by the Germans at Ypres in April fails to achieve a permanent advance.

The British Grand Fleet begins a blockade of Germany that is intended to starve the opponent. The huge German High Seas Fleet is kept in port, since the Germans are afraid to risk its destruction. Only German submarines break into open waters, where they begin to ravage commerce. After sinking the *Lusitania,* however, the Germans are brought up short by American protests, and they moderate the use of U-boats against defenseless merchant ships.

The Italians enter the war in May on the side of the Allies and begin a series of offensives along the Isonzo River, a natural line of defense held by the Austrians. Repeated and expensive attacks continue for month after month, to no avail.

The British and the French launch an expedition to seize the Dardanelles from the Turks, but the first all-naval attacks fail and the follow-up amphibious assault is crushed and pinned to the beaches by the stout Turkish defenders. The entire campaign is a bloody disaster for the Allies, and they begin to evacuate their forces at the end of the year.

On the Eastern Front, the Germans continue to defeat the Russians but have to divert troops to aid their allies, the Austri-

ans. Serbia finally falls to a combined force under German leadership. By the autumn of the year, the Germans call a halt to further advances against Russia in order to bring more troops to the Western Front.

After initial successes against the Turks in the Persian Gulf, a British force made up of Indian troops is trapped and besieged.

1 January 1915

Berlin. Falkenhayn, Ludendorff, and Conrad von Hötzendorf confer.

British Channel. The German submarine *U-24* torpedoes and sinks the unescorted British battleship *Formidable.* The Germans rescue 201 survivors, but 547 seamen die.

German East Africa. SMS *Königsberg,* bane of the *Pegasus* at Zanzibar on 20 September and now secreted and camouflaged in the Rufiji River, receives greetings from HMS *Fox* over the wireless: "A Happy New Year. Expect to have the pleasure of seeing you soon. British cruiser." German Capt. Max Loof replies: "Many thanks. Same to you. If you want to see us we are always at home. *Königsberg.*"

2 January 1915

London. Churchill has long been interested in a British operation on the Baltic front—he first raised the possibility of an Anglo-Russian joint effort on 14 August 1914 in a message to Grand Duke Nicholas—as a means of increasing pressure on the Germans, but his attention has shifted to the Balkans as a strategically better alternative, especially as the war on the Western Front has bogged down. Now the War Council, having received a request from Russia for help in relieving Turkish pressure in the Caucasus, takes up discussion of a possible land and sea operation at Gallipoli, first suggested to the Council by Churchill on 25 November.

Cameroons. Brig. Gen. Edmund H. Gorges has marched his Allied detachment relentlessly inland to reach Dschang, which surrenders after his artillery opens a bom-

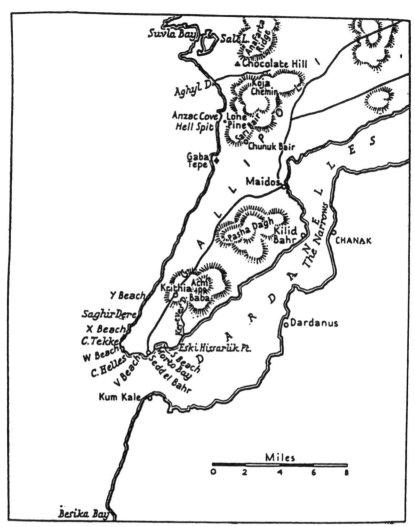

Gallipoili. From *A History of the Great War, 1914-1918*, by C.R.M.F. Cruttwell, published by Academy Chicago Publishers. All rights reserved.

bardment. Gorges destroys the fort at Dschang and heads back to the railhead.

3 January 1915
London. In a letter to Churchill, Kitchener states: "The only place that a demonstration might have some effect in stopping reinforcements going east would be the Dardanelles. Particularly if . . . reports could be spread at the same time that Constantinople was being threatened." First Sea Lord Sir John Fisher and Maurice Hankey, secretary of the Committee of Imperial Defence (CID), present a joint plan to Churchill for an attack on Gallipoli by a force composed of seventy-five thousand British troops from France augmented by Indian, Greek, and Bulgarian troops. They assume that still-neutral Greece and Bulgaria would want to take part. Fisher is enthusiastic about an attack at the Dardanelles, "But only if it's immediate!" Kitchener insists that no troops are currently available, most certainly not from France. Churchill, dubious about the complications of an army operation, opts for the final suggestion of a purely naval operation: a bombardment from the sea followed by ships steaming through the straits and on to Constantinople. He sends a telegram to the navy commander in the area, Vice Adm. Sackville H. Carden, asking whether the commander deems such an operation feasible. At the same time, the Foreign Office sends a telegram to Grand Duke Nicholas assuring him that there will be some sort of move against Turkey by the British.

4 January 1915
Armenia. After a week and a half of fighting, the Russians finally destroy the Turkish IXth Corps at Sarikamish, relieving the threat on their Caucasus front. For some reason the Russians do not relay word of this victory to the other Allies—the news might possibly have obviated the Gallipoli campaign. The Turks also suppress news of the loss, but for their own reasons: only twelve thousand of the ninety thousand troops sent into the campaign return home, a disastrous outcome for Turkish Minister of War Enver Pasha.

5 January 1915
France. The French continue their thrusts in the Argonne and Alsace following successful, though modest, Allied advances during the previous week, including recapture of Steinbach.
London. Churchill receives a response from Carden: "I do not consider Dardanelles can be rushed. They might be forced by extended operations with large number of ships." After consulting with military advisers, Churchill telegraphs back: "Your view is agreed to by high authorities here. Please telegraph in detail what you think could be done by extended operations, what force would be needed, and how you consider it should be used."
Cameroons. German troops attack vigorously at Edea, hoping to recapture the town, but the French garrison holds fast and the Germans withdraw.

8 January 1915
France. The French continue their incremental advances against the Germans in the Argonne near Verdun and in Alsace, temporarily capturing Burnhaupt-le-Haut.
Aisne River. Gen. Michel Maunoury's Sixth French Army launches an assault on German hill positions near Soissons.

9 January 1915
Aisne River. German troops commanded by General von Lochow retaliate at Soissons, shelling the city's cathedral and counterattacking Maunoury's troops.
Berlin. Pressure has been building to send airships to bomb England, and since the German air fleet has now expanded sufficiently to allow for both scouting and raiding, Adm. Paul Behncke, chief of the naval staff who favors bombing London docks and military installations, finally succeeds in persuading Bethmann Hollweg and Kaiser Wilhelm II to agree. But the kaiser insists that only military targets may be bombed, not London itself.

11 January 1915
Aisne River. After bringing up reinforcements, Lochow resumes his counterattack, which was checked by the French on the ninth.

London. Churchill receives Admiral Carden's plan for a naval operation at the Dardanelles. It entails using a massive force of twelve battleships, three battle cruisers, three light cruisers, sixteen destroyers, six submarines, four seaplanes, twelve minesweepers, one flotilla leader, and twenty other diverse vessels. Carden envisions a long-range bombardment followed by the flotilla's thrust up the straits preceded by the minesweepers, with the ships' guns destroying the Turkish artillery positions sequentially. Simultaneous diversionary bombardments would attack the base of Gallipoli Peninsula and at Gaba Tepe. After the flotilla entered the Sea of Marmara, patrols would keep the straits clear. Carden concludes: "Might do it all in a month about."

12 January 1915

German East Africa. The Germans control Mafia Island, twenty-two miles off the coast, which provides them an observation post for tracking British naval movements. Only twelve Europeans and forty askaris make up the German garrison. The British have transported soldiers from Zanzibar who successfully landed on the island and occupy it while the *Fox*, the ship that had shelled Tanga and Dar es Salaam in November, provides them a protective bombardment.

13 January 1915

Vienna. At the urging of Count Tisza, who regards Count Berchtold as indecisive, Emperor Franz Joseph removes Berchtold as foreign minister, replacing him with Baron Burian.

London. Churchill, now an enthusiastic supporter of Carden's proposal, presents the plan and advocates its adoption at a meeting of the War Council attended by Kitchener, Fisher, Hankey, Sir Edward Grey, Prime Minister Asquith, Chancellor of the Exchequer Lloyd George, Adm. Sir Arthur Wilson, and others. Churchill's enthusiasm prevails. Hankey, secretary for the council, writes: "The whole atmosphere changed." Kitchener, Hankey's minutes say, "thought the plan worth trying. We could leave off the bombardment if it did

not prove effective." And so the War Council unanimously decides "that the Admiralty should prepare for a naval expedition in February to bombard and take the Gallipoli Peninsula with Constantinople as its objective."

14 January 1915

Aisne River. Although floodwaters on the Aisne have washed out some of the bridges, General von Lochow launches a final successful assault against French lines on the north bank of the river near Soissons. The Germans capture fifty-two hundred prisoners and fourteen guns while inflicting over twelve thousand casualties.

15 January 1915

Perthes, Champagne. After two months of attacks and counterattacks, French forces have managed to advance only a thousand yards.

18 January 1915

German East Africa. After the failure of a surprise attack six days earlier to recapture Jassin (Yasini), taken by the British on 25 December and garrisoned by Indian troops commanded by Col. Rahbir Singh, Lettow-Vorbeck personally directs an attack on the garrison. The Indians hold him at bay, with his askaris miserably ensconced in the swampy terrain.

Norfolk, England. Three Zeppelins (*L-3, L-4,* and *L-6*) set out across the North Sea for a night raid on England. Although *L-6* has to turn back with engine trouble, the others succeed. *L-3* drops bombs at Yarmouth, killing two people and injuring thirteen. *L-4* bombs at King's Lynn, also killing two people while damaging several houses. Both Zeppelins return safely to their base at Fuhlsbuttel, leaving the British with a sense of consternation and dismay that the Germans have been able to bomb with impunity.

23 January 1915

British East Africa. Although Europeans' fears that fighting between whites may inspire uprisings among native Africans have proved groundless, John Chilembwe, an African educated at an American university, has been advocating in Nyasaland a religion he calls "Ethiopianism" that espouses African nationalism and death to the whites. His followers attack an estate owned by the grandson of Dr. David Livingstone, killing three men and carrying off three women and five children. British volunteers and regulars rush to the area to rescue the captives and put down the uprising.

24 January 1915
Dogger Bank, North Sea. Having received news the previous day that a German flotilla commanded by Adm. Franz von Hipper is again venturing into the North Sea, Churchill has sent orders to Adm. David Beatty at Rosyth, Scotland, to race toward confrontation with Hipper with all available battle cruisers, light cruisers, and destroyers. Later Churchill also orders Adm. Sir John Jellicoe to sea to support Beatty. This time Hipper has only four battle cruisers—*Seydlitz, Moltke, Derfflinger,* and *Blücher.* At 7:00 A.M. Beatty, three hours in advance of Jellicoe, meets Commodore Reginald Tyrwhitt's squadron of light cruisers and destroyers out of Harwich. As the sun rises, they spot Hipper's flotilla, already exchanging fire with HMS *Aurora* but fleeing back to home waters. Beatty gives chase at full speed. At about nine o'clock, Beatty opens fire, although at the extraordinary range of twenty thousand yards. Hipper returns the fire, with the *Seydlitz* and the *Derfflinger* concentrating on the *Lion,* Beatty's flagship. By eleven o'clock, severely damaged by fifteen hits, the *Lion* has to abandon the battle. Beatty signals the *Tiger, Princess Royal,* and *New Zealand* to continue the chase—the slower *Indomitable* lags behind. Both the slow-going *Blücher* and the front-running *Seydlitz,* Hipper's flagship, are in flames and, although still sailing ahead, appear vulnerable. But Beatty sees the periscope of a German U-boat—or thinks he does—and, fearing Hipper has led him into a trap, making him easy prey for torpedoes or mines, he orders a ninety-degree turn. Although he intends for his sister ships to pursue Hipper, Beatty sends mixed signals, resulting in their concen-trating on the destruction of the hapless *Blücher,* which is left to its fate as the rest of Hipper's squadron hastens back to port. About 800 men go down with the *Blücher,* although the British rescue 234 survivors. Enraged by his failure, Beatty transfers to the *Princess Royal* and gives orders to tow the *Lion* back to base. His rage increases when he learns that Jellicoe is only 140 miles to the north and, had the Admiralty ordered him out sooner, could easily have been on hand to help inflict thorough destruction on Hipper's ships. The first large-scale clash of the navies disappoints both sides.

28 January 1915
London. Having totally changed his mind, Sir John Fisher has sent Churchill a message on 25 January opposing the Dardanelles operation, advocating a naval blockade of Germany centered at Zeebrugge, and submitting his resignation. Fearful that he cannot succeed without Fisher's support, Churchill persuades the admiral to consult with the prime minister before a War Council meeting. Asquith sides with Churchill. Still vehemently opposing the Dardanelles venture, Fisher abruptly leaves the conference table during the War Council meeting. Kitchener follows him and persuades Sir John to rejoin the discussion. Churchill finally wins over the admiral, who now becomes a devout convert.

29 January 1915
Argonne. Lt. Erwin Rommel earns an Iron Cross for leading his platoon in capturing four French blockhouses and successfully defeating a counterattack.

30 January 1915
New York City. Col. Edward M. House, President Wilson's closest adviser who, on behalf of the president, has been conducting discussions with the British and German ambassadors in Washington in an effort to arrange a peaceful resolution of the war, now sails for Liverpool aboard the *Lusitania* as Wilson's special envoy to pursue the peace discussions in Europe.

31 January 1915
Poland. Working on behalf of the ordnance

section of the German army, Walter Nernst, a professor of chemistry, has developed a gas-laden artillery shell. At Bolimow the Ninth Army launches eighteen thousand of the shells against Russian troops. But sub-zero temperatures neutralize the gas—an effect Ninth Army commanders did not know about—and easterly winds disperse it, with no harmful effects. Consequently, the Russians do not report this first use of poison gas in the war to the other Allies.

1 February 1915
Poland. Following the unsuccessful gas attack of the previous day, Mackensen sends the Ninth Army into a sweeping attack at Bolimow that advances the German line six miles. But a Russian counterattack recaptures the lost geography, restoring equilibrium along the front. The battle costs both sides heavily—twenty thousand losses for the Germans out of a force of one hundred thousand; forty thousand losses for the Russians.

3 February 1915
Suez Canal. British and Egyptian troops defeat a Turkish effort to seize the canal, destroying the only groups that manage to reach the west bank and driving the others off to reoccupy their own trenches on the east bank. Although hardly a major battle—the British have 130 wounded and 32 dead; the Turks, perhaps 2,000 casualties, including 716 taken prisoner—the victory preserves the canal for British shipping and discourages any threat of uprising in Egypt.

4 February 1915
Berlin. Following approval by Chancellor Bethmann Hollweg, Germany publicly declares a war zone encircling the British Isles wherein all merchant ships may be sunk by submarines without warning. Bethmann Hollweg had opposed such a policy on the grounds that unrestricted submarine warfare would alienate the neutral nations, in particular Italy and the United States, but he has acceded to the admirals' insistence. Germany's broadcast excuse for the new policy is that Great Britain has violated international law by ending the distinction between conditional and absolute contraband—that is, any goods, in-

Russian troops collect a dead comrade on the Eastern Front, 1915 (Library of Congress)

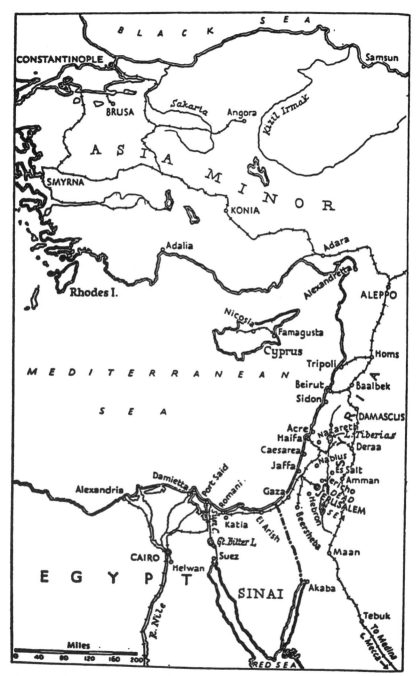

Egypt, Palestine, and Syria. From A History of the Great War, 1914-1918, by C.R.M.F Cruttwell, published by Academy Chicago Publishers. All rights reserved.

cluding food, shipped from a neutral nation that could be proved destined for Germany or Austria could be seized by the Allies. The Germans condemn this contraband policy with the term "hunger blockade," but the fact is that foodstuffs continue to enter Germany from Holland and the Scandinavian countries.

5 February 1915
France. French pilot Adolphe Pegoud, a pioneer of aviation and the first to parachute from an airplane, flies his Morane "L" above the Western Front and shoots down two German planes and forces a third to land.

7 February 1915
East Prussia. Hindenburg, now headquartered at Insterburg, commences the Winter Battle of Masuria, with the Tenth Army succeeding in capturing Johannisburg. But in the Carpathians the Russians hold fast to the passes, thwarting German efforts to push the second half of the pincer up from the south. Blizzards impede the Tenth Army's further advancement.

9 February 1915
Meuse River. French troops take Saint-Rémy, while in the Vosges region heavy snowfall deters action. The entire Western

Trench Warfare

It came as a shocking surprise to the generals on both sides to discover by the late fall of 1914 that the Western Front had become an immobile fortified system of trenches virtually from the North Sea to Switzerland. The failures of the German Schlieffen Plan and the French Plan 17 to produce a quick victory of open maneuver led to the long, undulating line of dug-in defenses, a situation neither planned for nor accepted by the military masterminds. The nature of the trenches differed dramatically from place to place. In some parts of the northern end in Flanders it was impossible to dig more than a few feet below the surface due to high groundwater; in other places across the front, the soil allowed for elaborate and deep workings, with huge underground galleries excavated to protect frontline troops from artillery bombardments. In essence the trench system resulted from the natural inclination of infantry to protect itself in the face of fire. Digging was the obvious response. After the first crude shelters were scratched from the soil, engineers and sappers began to devise careful schemes of entrenchment wherever conditions would allow. For the most part, the trench system was a refinement of the siege trench tactics that had been known and used in European warfare for several centuries, but instead of leading up to a fortified city or castle, the trenches led only to opposing trenches. The basic configuration was a line of frontline trenches facing each other with a no-man's-land in between. The lines were angled and zig-zagged to prevent enfilading fire by assaults from the other side, and there was usually a system of communication and supply trenches set at further angles that led to the rear. The forward approaches were likely to be covered by artillery and machine-gun fire and further made difficult by barbed wire and minefields. Wherever possible, the trenches were dug deeply enough to protect defenders from all but the most direct artillery fire, with parapets, firing steps, and advance listening posts provided as defensive positions. Life in the trenches was—obviously—difficult, uncomfortable, unhealthy, and dangerous. In addition to the constant danger from enemy fire or attack, trench troops had to endure cold, wet, disease, and vermin. In many places on the Western Front, life in the trenches was a figurative hell although in others it was comparatively quiet and comfortable except during rare periods of activity. Not until the very final weeks of the war was there a significant change in the mutual siege of the trench lines in the West, and trench warfare came to be remembered as the characteristic condition of World War I.

Front has settled into the near-stasis of "trench warfare," with inconsequential movements forward and back. The front trenches, excavated by shovel in the late weeks of 1914, are ragged ditches with holes carved in their sides to provide shelter.

11 February 1915
German South-West Africa. Louis Botha arrives at the coastal village of Swakopmund with his staff and a hundred-man force of bodyguards. His plan is to advance inland from Swakopmund for an assault on Windhoek, the capital of the German colony, 175 miles distant.

15 February 1915
Poland. German troops under the command of Gen. Max von Gallwitz capture Plozk on the Vistula River, while the XXIst Corps marches twenty-two miles in an effort to encircle a Russian force in the forest at Augustów.

17 February 1915
Poland. The German XXIst Corps succeeds in enveloping a Russian force of seventy thousand men in the Augustów Forest.
France. The French achieve slight gains near Verdun on the Meuse River and in the Artois, Champagne, and Vosges sectors—nearly the length of their line on the Western Front. The Germans, who have begun to counterattack during the night, retaliate after dark at Champagne.
Skagerrak Channel, Denmark. Heavy winds force down the two Zeppelins that bombed Norfolk on 19 January and have now been sent here on a scouting mission. Four members of one of the crews lose their lives; the rest are interned. Both airships are destroyed.

19 February 1915
Dardanelles. The Gallipoli Anglo-French naval expedition, the most powerful fleet ever assembled to date in the Mediterranean, has established its base at Mudros Bay in Lemnos, made available to the Allies by Greek Premier Eleutherios Venizelos. The French have committed four old battleships; the British, fourteen battleships. The British ships include two semi-

dreadnoughts, the *Lord Nelson* and the *Agamemnon,* and the battle cruiser *Inflexible,* which was victorious at the Battle of the Falklands. But the jewel of the fleet is the super-dreadnought *Queen Elizabeth,* Britain's newest, largest, and fastest battleship mounted with fifteen-inch guns, the most powerful in the world. Churchill has commandeered her for this mission, much to the chagrin of Admiral Jellicoe, who anticipated adding her to the Grand Fleet. Accompanying this mighty armada are numerous cruisers, minesweepers, and other vessels, including the *Ark Royal,* Great Britain's only seaplane carrier, sent along by Churchill with six planes for reconnaissance flights. In command of the fleet is Admiral Carden, aboard the *Queen Elizabeth.* Carden's plan is to bombard the Turkish forts in three stages, the first being from long range beyond reach of the Turkish guns—perhaps twelve thousand yards—to be followed by second and third stages successively closer in. The first-stage bombardment begins at 9:51 A.M. and continues through the morning. The Turkish forts make no response. In the afternoon, Carden sends some of his ships closer, to within six thousand yards, and their shelling draws fire from two of the forts. As darkness approaches, the ships withdraw. Since the British firing has proved inaccurate or inconclusive, it is now clear that the ships will have to move in close and take out the forts one at a time.

21 February 1915
Poland. Having failed to break out of the German encirclement at Augustów Forest, the Russians surrender.

22 February 1915
East Prussia. The Winter Battle of Masuria ends in German victory and the reported capture of one hundred thousand Russian prisoners and three hundred guns. General von Gallwitz attacks at Przasnysz.

25 February 1915
Dardanelles. Stormy weather and turbulent seas have forced a five-day hiatus in the British naval bombardment, but the weather moderates, allowing renewal of the

attack. The *Vengeance,* commanded by Vice Adm. Sir John de Robeck, leads a fleet of seven ships, including the *Queen Elizabeth,* up to the mouth of the straits to shell the outermost Turkish and German artillery sites. Unable to withstand the barrage, the defenders abandon the sites and withdraw northward.

26 February 1915
Dardanelles. Marines and sailors land at Sedd el Bahr to destroy guns, searchlights, and their emplacements at the tip of the peninsula evacuated by the Turks.

28 February 1915
London. Having received a telegram the day before from Grand Duke Nicholas promising to unleash the Black Seas Fleet and an army to attack Constantinople once the naval expedition enters the Sea of Marmara, Churchill anticipates early and complete success in the Dardanelles. He writes to Sir Edward Grey: "Should we get through the Dardanelles as is now likely, we cannot be content with anything less than the surrender of everything Turkish in Europe." He advises that he will order an attack on the Bosporus after destruction of the Turkish fleet, forcing Turkey's capitulation, and he outlines terms for an armistice.

1 March 1915
London. Retaliating for the German policy of a U-boat blockade announced on 4 February and begun on 22 February, the British government announces a total blockade on merchant shipping to and from Germany. Fearful of alienating the neutral nations, however, the government chooses to ignore continuing shipments to Germany by way of Holland and the Scandinavian nations.

2 March 1915
Dardanelles. As the landing parties continue to destroy Turkish gun emplacements near Sedd el Bahr, Admiral Carden telegraphs a message to the Admiralty declaring that, if the weather cooperates, he hopes to reach Constantinople in about a fortnight.

Turkish machine gunners near the Dardanelles. The Turks proved to be superb fighters during the Allied attempt to gain a foothold along the Turkish coast. Time after time, Turkish soldiers such as these, often commanded by German officers, repulsed the British and Commonwealth armies. (Library of Congress)

4 March 1915
Dardanelles. Carden's ships resume shelling the forts, but Turkish troops drive off the British landing parties and begin to re-establish artillery emplacements at Kum Kale and Cape Helles.

6 March 1915
Athens, Greece. King Constantine dismisses Prime Minister Eleutherios Venizelos. The king disagrees with Venizelos's policy of allowing Anglo-French troops to land at Salonika and disapproves of his intention to send Greek troops to join the Allies at the Dardanelles.
East Prussia. German Tenth Army troops, pursued by the Russians, withdraw from positions at Augustów Forest.

8 March 1915
Dardanelles. Defying Carden's plans, the weather turns bad, making it impossible to use seaplanes for spotting or minesweepers to clear the channel. Until the minesweepers can do their job, the fleet cannot advance through the straits.

10 March 1915
Flanders. The BEF, augmented by the First Canadian Division on 3 March, launches a new offensive at Neuve-Chapelle. (Joffre has changed his mind about making this a joint operation, as originally planned, because of his need to maintain troop commitments at the Champagne front.) Commanded by Sir Douglas Haig, the offensive's limited objectives are to penetrate the German line to take the Aubers Ridge and to menace the Germans at Lille. A thirty-five-minute artillery bombardment precedes the attack. Total surprise and a vastly superior force give the British an advantage.
London. Churchill's optimism about the outcome of the Dardanelles operation suffuses the members of the War Council—they discuss plans for the aftermath of Constantinople's fall.
Dardanelles. At the suggestion of his chief of staff, Comdr. Roger Keyes, Carden reluctantly approves sending seven minesweepers into the straits at night trailed by the battleship *Canopus*. But the tactic fails

as the Turks' searchlights splay the flotilla with light and their howitzers open fire. "We were fired at from all directions," Keyes says. In the resulting confusion of their escape, the minesweepers never lower their kites, and one hits a mine and explodes. But the *Canopus* escapes harm, and the flotilla suffers only two men wounded.

11 March 1915
Dardanelles. Keyes makes a second effort, taking minesweepers into the straits without an accompanying ship in hopes that greater stealth will lead to success. But at the first sound of artillery fire, the minesweepers flee to safety, much to Keyes's disgust.
London. Beginning to feel some impatience, Churchill telegraphs Carden that the goals to be attained at the Dardanelles "justify loss of ships and men if success cannot be obtained without. The turning of the corner at Chanak may decide the whole operation." He pressures Carden to take decisive action.

12 March 1915
Flanders. At dawn, the Germans counterattack boldly at Neuve-Chapelle, but the British hold fast. During the night, Haig has his men secure their initial advance—only twelve hundred yards along the two-thousand-yard front—with entrenchments.
London. Lord Kitchener calls in Gen. Sir Ian Hamilton and places him in command of troops—the Twenty-ninth Division and Anzac (Australian and New Zealand Corps) Division, totaling a corps of seventy thousand men—being assembled at Lemnos to support the Dardanelles campaign.

13 March 1915
Flanders. The Battle of Neuve-Chapelle ends with the British retaining possession of the village of Neuve-Chapelle while capturing sixteen hundred prisoners. Both sides suffer a roughly equal number of casualties—about thirteen thousand. But Haig's assault has consumed one hundred thousand artillery shells, 20 percent of the BEF's total supply, in achieving a most modest victory.

Dardanelles. With a fresh batch of volunteers aboard his flotilla of minesweepers, Keyes makes one more nighttime attempt to sweep the straits. Although once again the searchlights find the minesweepers and this time the Turks concentrate their shelling more effectively, the new crews hang on, succeeding in dislodging numerous mines, until all but three of the craft are too damaged to continue. With this success, Carden decides the sweeping will continue in the daytime.

14 March 1915

Pacific Ocean. The British cruisers *Kent, Orama,* and *Glasgow*—veteran of the Battle of the Falklands—trap SMS *Dresden* (sole survivor of Spee's squadron destroyed in that battle) while the German ship is anchored at Juan Fernandez Island. The Germans blow up the ship and accept internment in Chile.

Champagne. French troops capture most of the Sabot Woods and repulse German counterattacks. Joffre announces plans for a major offensive at the Meuse River and Argonne fronts.

15 March 1915

Aisne River. Gen. Michel-Joseph Maunoury, commander of the Sixth Army that defended Paris, suffers a severe wound, causing partial blindness, and retires from active duty.

17 March 1915

Dardanelles. Admiral Carden, pleading illness—he verges on having a nervous breakdown—has resigned his command the day before. Churchill designates Adm. John de Robeck to succeed him. Churchill sends a message to de Robeck that the first lord assumes the admiral believes the major operations about to commence are "wise and practicable. If not, do not hesitate to say so. If so, execute them without delay. . . . All good fortune attend you." De Robeck responds that, if the weather allows, he will execute the planned main attack the next day.

18 March 1915

Poland. Grand Duke Nicholas orders that hereafter all offensive operations will center on the southern fronts, in particular in the Carpathians.

North Sea. During exercises off the Pentland Firth, the Fourth Battle Squadron of the Greta Fleet spots an enemy submarine. HMS *Dreadnought,* commanded by Adm. Doveton Sturdee, rams and sinks the submarine, revealed to be *U-12,* which had sunk the *Aboukir,* the *Hogue,* and the *Cressy.*

Dardanelles. De Robeck sends his ships to the attack in three divisions, the first composed of the *Queen Elizabeth, Agamemnon, Lord Nelson,* and *Inflexible* flanked to each side by the *Prince George* and *Triumph.* Following a mile behind is the French division of four ships also flanked by two British battleships. The third grouping of the remaining six battleships and the destroyers and minesweepers wait outside the straits. At 10:30 A.M., the first division steams up the straits. Within an hour they reach their targets, and the *Queen Elizabeth*'s fifteen-inch guns rain shells on the forts at Chanak, while her sister ships fire on the forts at Kilid Bahr across the straits. Turkish howitzers on both banks bombard the ships but cause only minor damage to their superstructures. Just after noon, de Robeck, aboard the *Queen Elizabeth,* decides it's time to move nearer and signals Admiral Guepratte to come on with the French division. The ships unleash a ferocious shelling for about three-quarters of an hour, but Turkish shells breach holes in the hulls of *Gaulois* and *Inflexible.* The Turkish barrage subsides as the forts suffer enormous damage. De Robeck decides to send the French division back and order up the third division. Just before two o'clock, the *Suffren* begins to lead the second division out. Suddenly her trailing ship, the *Bouvet,* rocked by a mighty explosion, heels over and in less than two minutes disappears, taking 640 men to their deaths. The Turks resume their fire; the ships respond. After two hours, the Turkish shelling again subsides, and de Robeck orders in the minesweepers. But after finding and blowing up three mines, the minesweepers abruptly leave their work and hasten back out the straits. The *Inflex-*

ible hits a mine and limps off in danger of sinking—miraculously her crew gets her to Tenedos. Another explosion rips the *Irresistible,* leaving her powerless and adrift. The *Wear* removes six hundred of the ship's crew, along with wounded and dead sailors. De Robeck terminates the day's action and sends Keyes aboard the *Wear* to try to salvage the *Irresistible* with the aid of the *Ocean* and the *Swiftsure.* Now the *Ocean* suffers an explosion, and a damaged steering gear sets her revolving. Upon reporting to de Robeck, Keyes discovers that the officers of both ships have been removed to the *Queen Elizabeth,* now safely out of the straits. Returning after dark to search for the two drifting ships, Keyes finds nothing.

19 March 1915
Dardanelles. Although the British shelling has done its job—Chanak and its forts are abandoned and in ruins, and the Turkish defenders have consumed half their ammunition—de Robeck does not know of his enemy's vulnerability. He and Keyes decide, nevertheless, to sweep the straits once more to remove mines and to resume the attack. But Ian Hamilton reaches a different conclusion: that the battleships cannot do the job alone. He telegraphs to Kitchener: "It must be a deliberate and prepared military operation, carried out at full strength, so as to open a passage for the Navy." Kitchener concurs.

21 March 1915
Paris. Three German Zeppelins fly over the city. One, hit by fire, returns home. The other two drop high explosive and incendiary bombs on the city and its suburbs, killing one person and injuring eight.

22 March 1915
Galicia. Russian troops capture Przemysl, taking nearly 120,000 German prisoners and 700 guns.
Dardanelles. After conferring with Hamilton aboard the *Queen Elizabeth* at Lemnos, de Robeck changes his mind about resuming the naval attack—he will not continue until the army joins in, and he so informs Churchill. Hamilton esti-

mates that his troops can be assembled and ready for landing operations on Gallipoli by mid-April.

24 March 1915
Constantinople. Enver Pasha offers Liman von Sanders command of the Turkish Fifth Army defending Gallipoli. He accepts.

25 March 1915
Dardanelles. Sanders leaves to assume command at Gallipoli as Ian Hamilton arrives in Alexandria, Egypt, to regroup his forces for the land operation.

28 March 1915
Irish Sea. German submarine *U-28* sinks the British steamer *Falaba,* causing 104 fatalities, including one American, resulting in a flap with the United States government.

30 March 1915
London. After Lloyd George denounces drinking as an enemy of the war effort, George V declares the royal household's willingness to abstain from consumption of alcoholic beverages for the duration of the war.

1 April 1915
Dixmude, Belgium. Lt. Roland Garros, the first French pilot to outfit his plane (a Morane scout) with one of Raymond Saulnier's forward-firing machine guns, shoots down his first victim, an Albatros, over the Western Front. The "dogfight" era begins, as the front-mounted machine gun with an interrupter gear, plus propellers with deflector plates, opens up aerial combat to planes with lone pilots. When the war began in August 1914, the Germans had only twenty antiaircraft guns; the Allies, none. Now, as the fighter plane emerges as a new weapon—not just a means of reconnaissance or a vehicle from which to launch bombs by hand—the Germans have 138 antiaircraft guns.

4 April 1915
Flanders. Gen. Karl von Bülow, commander of the Second Army, suffers a stroke and is retired from service, suc-

ceeded in command by Gen. Fritz von Below. Gen. Alexander von Kluck, having been badly wounded by an exploding French shell on 28 March, is also retired as commander of the First Army.

Carpathians. General Brusilov, who has been advancing against the Austrians for nearly two weeks and has captured over eleven thousand prisoners, reaches Sztropko. He is now fifteen miles inside Austria-Hungary.

6 April 1915
Carpathians. A German corps (*Beskidencorps*), formed on 28 March under the command of Gen. Georg von der Marwitz to relieve pressure on the Austrians, successfully attacks the Russians near Kosziowa, taking six thousand prisoners.

7 April 1915
Alexandria, Egypt. The first Anzac units assembled by Hamilton sail for the Dardanelles, while the general leaves for Lemnos.

8 April 1915
Turkey. The Turkish government, persuaded that the Armenians, who are Christian, are disloyal and have supported the Russians in the Caucasus fighting, launches the Turkish army on an operation to deport or exterminate the entire populace of about 2 million. They begin the months-long process by requisitioning the Armenians' belongings purposefully to generate resistance that can be suppressed; then follows rape, torture, execution, and forced exile of thousands to Mesopotamia.

Rome. The Italian government, under pressure from both sides in the war, makes demands on Austria-Hungary in return for continued neutrality: its neighbor must cede to Italy Trentino, Gorizia, Gardisca, and the islands off Dalmatia and also grant Italy primacy in Albania.

9 April 1915
Berlin. Falkenhayn, though wanting to launch a decisive blow on the Western Front, recognizes that the threat to Turkey and Austria-Hungary is too pressing. In response to urgings from Conrad von

Hötzendorf, who believes a successful campaign against Russia by the Central Powers may persuade Romania and Italy to join them (both commanders are convinced Italy plans to join the Allies), decides to divert eight of his fourteen divisions to the Eastern Front for a major spring offensive against the Russians. He places Mackensen in charge of the new Eleventh Army.

Indian Ocean. The *Kronborg,* formerly the British steamer *Rubens,* arrives at Aldabra Island carrying guns and supplies for the *Königsberg,* which has been making its way toward the delta of the Rufiji River to make a break for the open sea and escape from its relentless British pursuers.

11 April 1915
Mesopotamia. Qurna, located at the juncture of the Euphrates River and a branch of the Tigris, is shelled by the Turks, who lost the village to the British on 8 December. After garrisoning Qurna and driving the Turks out of Ruta to the north, the British had thought themselves safely ensconced at Qurna.

12 April 1915
Mesopotamia. Turkish and Arabian troops—six thousand of each—under Suleiman Askeri open fire on the British garrison at Shaiba, across the flooded Euphrates River from Basra. Gen. Sir John Nixon, sent to Basra with orders to organize an expedition to seize all of the Basra province and to plan an attack on Baghdad, must send Indian troops across in canoe-like Arab boats to mount a counterattack.

14 April 1915
Mesopotamia. After three days of intense fighting at Shaiba, the combined force of fifty-three hundred British and Indian troops, without water and low on ammunition, drives off the Turkish and Arabian attackers. Both sides have suffered heavy casualties: a 20 percent loss for the victors and an estimated 50 percent loss for the losers. The Turks also cease operations at Qurna, leaving the British free to develop this site as a base for possible future expeditions up the Tigris River.

A native lancer of the British Indian Army, in this case on duty on the Western Front, although many Indians fought in Mesopotamia (by Jean Berne-Bellecour, courtesy of the Anne S.K. Brown Military Collection, Brown University Library)

Indian Ocean. Signals between the *Königsberg* and the *Kronborg* have been intercepted by the British, and their rendezvous in the open sea aborts. The *Kronborg* is intercepted and destroyed by HMS *Hyacinth,* commanded by Adm. Herbert King-Hall, but the Germans salvage the supplies.

Flanders. While the French and British plan for a major offensive in May, the Germans prepare a surprise. A prisoner taken by the French recounts that cylinders of gas are stockpiled opposite Langemarck on the Ypres front defended by the French. In fact, the cylinders have been in place at the front since 8 April, and Falkenhayn has issued the orders for the attack. Significantly, the prisoner is revealingly equipped with a respirator.

15 April 1915

Flanders. Not only the German prisoner captured the day before, but also other prisoners and French agents provide reports that the Germans are preparing to use gas. Nevertheless, Gen. Sir Horace Smith-Dorrien, commander of the Second Army, writes in his diary: "The details given are so voluminous and exact that I am sure they are untrue. The prisoners described how they had arranged in their trenches batteries of enormous tubes of asphyxiating gas, and how, at a given signal, when the wind was in the right direction, all these tubes were to be opened and after a decent pause to allow our men to become insensible in the trenches, the Germans were to charge forward and mop them up." As a precaution, Smith-Dorrien passes the information on to Sir John French and his fellow commanders.

Berlin. Falkenhayn issues orders to transport eight divisions to the Carpathian front in Galicia. Thus the German Supreme Command commits Germany to switching its focus to the Eastern Front. For the duration of the Austro-German offensive in the Carpathians, Austrian commander Conrad von Hötzendorf has ceded overall command to the Germans.

17 April 1915

Dardanelles. The British submarine *E-15,* commanded by Theodore Brodie, attempts to move down the center of the straits (while seaplanes distract the Turks) and then make its way into the Sea of Marmara. But the effort is foiled by a violent current that drives the *E-15* aground. The Turks shell the foundering submarine, killing Brodie and several of his crew. Before abandoning the vessel, the British destroy it to prevent the Turks from capturing it.

Flanders. The Germans accuse the BEF of using gas during an attack near Saint Eloi, another clue that they are preparing to use gas, as they could claim a right to retaliate. But General Smith-Dorrien and Sir John French remain skeptical, as no German gas attack has yet been forthcoming and nothing suspicious has been discerned by air reconnaissance missions. General French adamantly denies the German accusation.

19 April 1915

Courtrai, Belgium. German ground fire forces down Lt. Roland Garros's Morane airplane behind lines, where he has been strafing a column of German infantry. Garros tries to destroy his plane to prevent the Germans from capturing the bullet-deflecting device. He fails, and the Germans immediately go to work on adapting the device for their planes. Garros claims to have shot down five German planes during the previous two weeks, a record for any pilot to date.

Dardanelles. Two spotters in a balloon attached by cable to the British kite-balloon ship *Manica* sight a Turkish encampment, fix its position on their map, and telephone the information to the *Manica*, which relays it to the cruiser *Bacchante*, hidden over the horizon. Shells from this unseen source rain down on the encampment, generating chaos among the amazed Turkish troops.

22 April 1915

Ypres. Having waited several days for suitable wind conditions, Gen. Duke Albrecht von Württemberg, commander of the Fourth Army, and his subordinates vacillate as the day progresses, until at five o'clock they order release of the gas. Totally surprised French colonial troops—the Algerian division and three battalions of Zouaves—panic and run, choking and gasping. Many collapse convulsively and die in their attempted flight. The Germans advance to their immediate objective, the Pilckem Ridge, in only half an hour and consolidate there. They have captured a sizable number of French artillery weapons and have opened a five-mile fissure in the British-French line; Ypres appears vulnerable before them. If they take Ypres, Brussels will be secure from Allied attack, and the BEF flank will be in peril. General Smith-Dorrien advises Sir John French that the situation is grave and recommends that Foch send reinforcements. The Second Battle of Ypres is under way with the Germans holding a strong initial advantage, although one they could have exploited more fully, given the element of surprise and panic their gas attack achieved.

23 April 1915

Ypres. Awaiting the resumption of the German advance, Allied troops, hastily strung along the new front, have been told to hold wet cloths over their noses and mouths, as the gas used has been identified as chlorine, a water-soluble gas. Reinforcements augment the line as the Germans pause. At Cassel General French vis-

Algerian troops in the service of France on the Western Front, 1916 (by Jean Berne-Bellecour, courtesy of the Anne S.K. Brown Military Collection, Brown University Library)

its Foch, who assures him that more reinforcements are en route. Artillery support, however, is limited because of the French losses the previous day. Unapprised of this circumstance, General French agrees to launch a British attack. It commences at 4:15 P.M. but is quickly stalled by German machine-gun fire that inflicts horrendous casualties.

Dardanelles. Sub. Lt. Rupert Brooke, the twenty-seven-year-old English poet whose poems have sung the glories of the Gallipoli campaign and his own exhilaration in the anticipation of combat, dies on this Saint George's Day of blood poisoning aboard a French hospital ship at Skyros—denied any experience of the invasion and battle he foresaw with relish.

Poison Gas

The most horrifying weapon of World War I was gas, first used by the French in August 1914. The immense frustration of stagnant trench warfare thereafter prompted military strategists on both sides of the war to contemplate the widespread use of gas as yet another promising breakthrough weapon that might restore the sort of open warfare they understood. The result, however, was merely to kill and wound thousands and thousands of men with seldom a measurable gain. Like the machine gun, poison gas proved to be a weapon capable of massive destruction but not of changing the war. The earliest French experiments centered on small grenades filled with a nontoxic gas that caused tearing (similar to modern police tear gas), but neither the gas nor the delivery system worked in the open air of the battlefield. The Germans in 1914 developed an artillery shell, filled partially with explosive and partially with an irritant gas, that they fired against the British in late October but with no effect. A more advanced German shell was used against the Russians on the Eastern Front in late January 1915, but cold temperatures inhibited the vaporization of the chemical agent and the Russians scarcely noticed the attack, despite the eighteen thousand shells fired. The first effective gas attack came near Ypres in April 1915. The Germans decided to use commercial gas cylinders to release a large amount of deadly chlorine against the opposing trenches. The idea was to kill or disable the defenders and then to rush forward and seize the empty trenches as soon as the volatile gas dissipated. The biggest problem facing the Germans was the prevailing west-to-east wind—they could attack westward only during a reversal of the usual weather patterns. The massed cylinders were crude devices at best, and the attackers had no control over the path the gas clouds might take once released. The winds favored the attackers on the evening of 22 April, and the Germans spewed chlorine into trenches held by French territorial and Algerian troops. The results were dramatic—the French were killed, incapacitated, or driven choking from their trenches. The Germans (who clutched makeshift wads of soaked cotton to their faces) rushed forward and penetrated four and a half miles, but as in nearly all such cases on the Western Front, the attackers could not permanently exploit the breach in the defenses. Renewed gas attacks did nothing more than produce new casualties, once the element of surprise was gone. Despite the limited results of these first gas attacks, both sides moved to develop new forms of toxic chemical agents and new ways to deliver them. Throughout the rest of the war, the Germans held a decisive lead in technology, far outstripping the Allies. The British favored using gas but were very slow to advance beyond the rather crude method of massing cylinders opposite specific targets, waiting for a good breeze, and loosing a cloud of gas in hope it would kill or drive away the opposition. The Germans, however, rapidly developed effective gas artillery shells, which allowed them to overcome the problem of prevailing winds and ultimately to devise tactics of surprise and harassment. A sudden gas bombardment could silence opposing artillery or clear sections of enemy trenches or fortifications (the Germans used such tactics in the attacks on the fortresses of Verdun in 1916). Even more devastating was the German use of so-called "mustard" gas—not really a gas but rather a vapor of a deadly blister-producing liquid toxic agent—that persisted in the attacked area for as long as a week. The French never developed an effective gas or an effective delivery system. By the end of the war, poison gases and other toxic chemical agents were regular features of the Western battlefields. Protective devices in the form of crude gas masks to some degree nullified the tactical effectiveness of chemical warfare, but the horror of being "gassed" was one of the worst experiences of the conflict for the individual soldier.

24 April 1915
Ypres. The German Fourth Army's Forty-sixth and Fifty-first Divisions resume the assault at Lizerne and Saint-Julien. Before dawn, a cloud of chlorine gas floats over the trenches held by Franco-Belgian and Canadian troops. Though some collapse, the vast majority hold the line, delivering a withering fire against the advancing Germans, who manage to capture Saint-Julien but fall back before a Canadian counterattack at Lizerne. The Germans, holding artillery superiority along the entire salient, thwart the attempted Canadian counterattack at Saint-Julien.

Dardanelles. Following a successful naval bombardment against Maidos on 23 April coordinated from the air by telephone-equipped planes, the Allied fleet of two hundred ships carrying the invasion force sets out from Mudros Harbor at Lemnos with troops headed to three destinations: the Royal Naval Division to the Gulf of Saros, the Anzac force to Imbros, and the British and French troops to Tenedos. The Gallipoli invasion is set for the following day. The lengthy delay of the planned invasion, however, has given Liman von Sanders time to gather his forces and to build defensive fortifications in anticipation of the landing. Believing that the most likely spot for a landing is the south bank of the straits, he posts two divisions near Troy. Regarding Bulair as another likely spot for a landing, he also places two divisions there. At Cape Helles he places a single division. He keeps another division in reserve at Maidos under command of Mustapha Kemal with the intent of sending it to whichever Allied beachhead seems most menacing as the landing unfolds.

25 April 1915
Dardanelles. The Allied landing on Gallipoli begins at dawn. Gen. Ian Hamilton remains aboard the *Queen Elizabeth,* only remotely in touch with events. Part of the fleet enters the Gulf of Saros and opens fire on the Turkish defenses at Bulair. Receiving reports at his headquarters in the town of Gallipoli, Liman von Sanders assumes that the main point of the invasion

must be Bulair, and he heads there. French troops land at Kum Kale on the Asian mainland across from Cape Helles and capture the fortress there. First ashore on the peninsula, the Anzac troops under command of Gen. Sir William Birdwood land at Gaba Tepe—or what they think is Gaba Tepe. A current has driven their landing craft to the north, where they disembark onto a small cove. They succeed in putting to flight the Turk defenders but quickly confront the cliffs of the Sari Bair range. Some Australian troops ascend the ridges and push inland after the scattering Turks. But Mustapha Kemal appears on the scene, rallies the retreating soldiers, and sends his own battalion to thwart the Australians' advance, depriving the Anzacs of a victory and keeping command of the heights in Turkish hands. British troops commanded by Maj. Gen. Sir Aylmer Hunter-Weston attempt to land at Cape Helles near Sedd el Bahr after British ships shell the Turkish defenses for over an hour. But the Turks weather the bombardment and reemerge from their trenches to fire on the British troops before they can disembark from their landing boats launched from the River Clyde. Though some of the troops manage to wade ashore and reach the safety of a hidden beach, the carnage is frightful. Air Comdr. C.R. Samson, flying reconnaissance overhead, reports the sea "absolutely red with blood." The Turks' relentless fire ends this landing attempt; only two hundred British soldiers are on shore. Elsewhere at two sites on the point, landings succeed, with British troops creating a base near Tekke Burnu and scaling the high ground at Eski Hissarik Point to establish a base on the heights above. A third force of two thousand (equal to the entire Turkish defense force at the point) lands unopposed at "Y" beach, four miles up the western coast. They could march to the rescue at Sedd el Bahr, but they have no way of knowing what is happening with the other landing parties and so sit tight awaiting orders to advance. Hunter-Weston never responds to their messages. Both Birdwood and Hunter-Weston, like their commander in chief, remain aboard ships, so none of the main commanders is in direct contact with these events. And as the brigade commanders have been wounded or killed, there is no senior officer on shore to give direction.

Ypres. German troops retake Lizerne.

German East Africa. Flight Lt. John Tullock Cull photographs the *Königsberg* from a reconnaissance plane.

26 April 1915

Gallipoli. After suffering seven hundred casualties during the night, the force at "Y" beach evacuates. Nevertheless, in the darkness of the late night and early morning hours, other Anzac troops have landed on the point, bringing their total to fifteen thousand. But the Anzac beachhead is only two miles long and less than a mile deep. After dark, Lt. Comdr. Edward Boyle pilots his submarine *E-14* past Cape Helles, dives as the Turkish searchlights threaten, and maneuvers underwater for six hours, passing Chanak and entering the Sea of Marmara—coming to the surface only once to torpedo and sink a Turkish gunboat.

Ypres. Reinforced by the Lahore Division, Sir Herbert Plumer's troops advance at Hilltop Ridge in the afternoon in coordination with a French attack to the north, but a German gas cloud disperses the Indian troops and German artillery fire stymies the British advance, inflicting two thousand casualties. Sir John French visits Foch and later in the day records in his diary that he "complained of the delay the French were making in their forward movement to retake the line. I warned Foch that unless a substantial advance was immediately made it would be necessary for me to withdraw from the forward line."

German South-West Africa. After two days of fighting, the Southern Force commanded by Gen. Jan Smuts defeats German troops at Gibeon. At Trekkopjes a column of South Africans and Rhodesians commanded by Col. P.C.B. Skinner defeats a German force with the aid of armored cars equipped with machine guns that are sent against the German flanks. The five-hour battle costs the Germans fourteen dead, fourteen wounded, and thirteen captives. Skinner's force suffers eight dead and thirty-four wounded.

London. After three days of negotiations, Italian diplomats join the Allies in signing the Treaty of London. By its terms, the Italians agree to declare war on Germany and her allies within a month. In exchange, the Allies promise to cede to Italy the South Tyrol, including the Brenner Pass, Gorizia, Istria, and most of Dalmatia once victory is secured.

27 April 1915

Ypres. In response to a letter General Smith-Dorrien has sent to Gen. Sir William Robertson, Sir John French's chief of staff, expressing his view that he sees little reason to continue the offensive "unless the French do something really big" and that it "will be very difficult to hold" the area east of Ypres, Sir John has Robertson reply: "He wishes you to act vigorously with the full means available in co-operating with and assisting the French attack . . . the combined attack should be simultaneous." In the evening a second message comes indicating Sir John's displeasure: "Chief directs you to hand over forthwith to General Plumer the command of all troops engaged in the present operations about Ypres." Sir John writes in his diary that Smith-Dorrien's "pessimistic attitude has the worst effect on his commanders" and that his letter to Robertson, advocating the very position French had pressed upon Foch on the same day (twenty-sixth), "was full of contradictions and altogether bewildering."

Adriatic Sea. A successful French naval blockade of the Adriatic, designed to prevent Austrian ships from entering the Mediterranean through the forty-five-mile-wide Straits of Otranto, suffers a menacing loss when the Austrian submarine *U-5*, commanded by Lt. Georg Ritter von Trapp, torpedoes the cruiser *Leon Gambetta*, sending 547 officers and crewmen to their deaths.

Gallipoli. At the Anzac beachheads, the *Queen Elizabeth* and two other battleships shell the Turks, who nevertheless maintain relentless firing on the boats attempting to land more troops and supplies on the beaches. Guided by spotters in kite balloons, the *Queen Elizabeth* lofts a shell that

The British land a 155 mm field howitzer at Sedd el Bahr during the Gallipoli campaign (Library of Congress)

luckily destroys a Turkish freighter seven miles distant in the narrows. At night both sides, exhausted by hand-to-hand combat, slow the fighting and draw back to rest. In three days the invaders have made no significant advance.

28 April 1915
Gallipoli. With Sedd el Bahr captured, Hamilton, eager to push inland before Liman von Sanders moves in reinforcements from the north, sends British and French troops into a general advance. They gain two miles but, meeting resistance, give in to fatigue. Continuing Turkish shelling renders the beaches chaotic, preventing or hindering resupply of these frontline troops. Hamilton's goal eludes him.

29 April 1915
Sussex Coast, England. The army Zeppelin *LZ-38,* first of Germany's new line of these 1-million-cubic-feet ships, bombs Ipswich and Bury Saint Edmunds.

30 April 1915
Gallipoli. Hamilton transfers from the *Queen Elizabeth* to the *Arcadian* and brings

his command staff together on board. Allied casualties now number about eleven thousand, double the War Office's original estimate for the campaign. And Liman von Sanders has brought three divisions of reinforcements to the front—he has seventy-five battalions to Hamilton's fifty seven—with orders from Enver Pasha to launch a full attack at Cape Helles and "drive the invaders into the sea."
Galicia. The Central Powers' forces, comprising the German Eleventh Army and the Austrian Third and Fourth Armies, have completed their buildup at Gorlice for the offensive against the Russians. Gen. August von Mackensen, commander of the Eleventh Army, is in charge. He has under his command twenty-two infantry divisions and one cavalry division against the Russians' fourteen infantry and five cavalry divisions. He also has vast artillery superiority, with 732 guns of varied calibers and 70 mortars. For the attack, the Eleventh Army will occupy the center, with the Austrian armies protecting its flanks.

1 May 1915
Ypres. After four days of stalling, the

French launch an attack in the late morning with British artillery support. The attack founders amid heavy losses. Apprised of the failure, Sir John French sends orders to General Plumer to begin withdrawing his troops "on the eastern part of the salient."

Gallipoli. Lieutenant Commander Boyle's *E-14* sinks a Turkish gunboat and a Turkish troopship in the Sea of Marmara. At Cape Helles, the Turks unleash their artillery at 10:00 P.M., following up with an infantry assault, but the invaders hold fast.

New York City. Passengers board the Cunard liner *Lusitania,* departing for Liverpool despite warnings published by the Imperial German Embassy in New York newspapers. These warnings, which were frequently adjacent to announcements of liner departures, stated that "vessels flying the flag of Great Britain, or of any of her allies, are liable to destruction" in the waters off the British Isles and that travelers sailing on such ships "do so at their own risk."

2 May 1915

Galicia. After firing intermittently during the night, the German artillery opens up at 6:00 A.M. with a full-scale bombardment along the entire nineteen-mile-long front near Gorlice. It lasts four hours. Under cover of the bombardment, Mackensen's troops move forward close to the Russian front positions. The Russian Third Army falls back before the ensuing Austro-German assault. The Eleventh Army takes Gorlice, now largely in ruins.

3 May 1915

Galicia. Mackensen's Eleventh Army smashes Gen. V.V. Sakharov's Xth Corps, pushing ahead eight miles and opening a twelve-mile gap in the Russian front line, as the Austrian armies move against the Russians from the north and south.

4 May 1915

Ypres. Following the Germans' second use of gas and an attack thwarted by French artillery, General Plumer completes the withdrawal of his troops, ending the Battle of Saint-Julien. Once aware that the Brit-

ish have withdrawn, the Germans occupy their vacated positions. Describing the effects of the gas, a German officer writes: "The whole countryside is yellow. . . . A curious, sour, heavy, penetrating smell strikes one."

Silesia. German headquarters (GHQ) moves to Pless.

5 May 1915

Ypres. Following another gas attack, the Germans take Hill 60 from the British. Otherwise both sides spend their time digging in.

German East Africa. Lt. H.E. Watkins and his observer are shot down while flying reconnaissance at the Simba Uranga mouth in the Rufiji River delta, but they are rescued and have spotted the *Königsberg.*

6 May 1915

Ypres. Sir John French dismisses Gen. Horace Dorrien-Smith, the British army's senior general. French's chief of staff, Gen. William Robertson, telephones Smith-Dorrien and declares: "'Orace—you're for 'ome."

Galicia. The Austrian Fourth Army captures Tarnow, inflicting heavy losses on the Russians and taking thirty thousand prisoners. General Radko-Dmitriev advises the Russian Supreme Command that his Third Army will have no choice but to retreat beyond the Vistula River.

German South-West Africa. Gen. Louis Botha and his Rand Rifles arrive at Karibib, occupied without opposition the day before by the South African Irish. The German force stationed there has withdrawn to Windhoek.

7 May 1915

Irish Sea. The Cunard liner *Lusitania* is about fifteen miles off of Old Head of Kinsale, Ireland, when at 2:10 P.M. the second officer calls out to Captain Turner: "There is a torpedo coming, sir." Almost immediately the torpedo, followed by a second, explodes in the ship's starboard hull. Passengers race to don life jackets and climb into lifeboats. Believing that the *Lusitania* is in no danger, officers shout orders not to lower the boats and for passengers and crewmen to vacate them. As the liner begins to sink, confusion mounts. Many of the lifeboats remain unlowered. Within twenty minutes, the *Lusitania* goes down; 1,198 people die, among them 128 Americans. After learning of the disaster, Col. Edward M. House, still in London on negotiations, says to Walter Hines Page, American ambassador to the Court of Saint James: "We shall be at war within a month." Page telegraphs President Wilson: "The United States must declare war or forfeit European respect."

Galicia. Gen. Otto von Emmich's troops drive toward Rymanow, joining forces with the Austrian Third Army.

8 May 1915

Ypres. At 5:30 A.M., German artillery begins shelling along the entire front, with especially heavy fire at the Frezenberg Ridge. Despite the merciless pounding, British troops on the ridge stop two German infantry assaults. The Germans step up the artillery bombardment, followed by a third assault that succeeds. The severely battered British have no choice but withdrawal. The Germans then attack along the entire front. Although repulsed in most sectors, they annihilate the British Eighty-fourth Brigade to the north, opening a two-mile-wide gap in the British line.

Galicia. Mackensen's Eleventh Army crosses the Wisla River and pressures the Russians along the San River.

Gallipoli. After three days of desperate seesaw fighting, the British hold fast at Cape Helles but are deprived of any gains. General Hamilton has lost sixty-five hundred men there, nearly a third of his force, and on all the fronts his losses exceed twenty thousand. He wires Lord Kitchener requesting "two fresh divisions."

9 May 1915

Ypres. The Germans renew the attack, concentrating on the British defenses on the Menin Road.

Neuve-Chapelle. In order to assist the major new French offensive on the Artois front, the British launch simultaneous offensives ordered by Sir John French and intended to capture Aubers Ridge. The ef-fort is doomed by inferior artillery and overconfidence and by the Germans' exceptional defenses. Following a brief and ineffective artillery barrage, at 5:30 A.M. Gen. Douglas Haig sends units of his First Army into no-man's-land for the assault. The German Sixth Army's machine gunners slaughter them. In the afternoon, Haig launches a second attack, also quickly smashed. By the end of the day, Haig loses 458 officers and 11,161 lower ranks with nothing gained.

Artois. The long-anticipated French offensive opens. Elaborate preparations, including digging forward trenches only one hundred or two hundred yards from the German lines and laying underground communication cables, precede the offensive. Based on plans conceived by General Foch, Gen. Victor d'Urbal's Tenth Army attacks the Germans at three points: the River Scarpe east of Arras, Lorette, and Vimy Ridge, with the latter as the major objective, as possession of the ridge provides the Germans a vantage point from which to view areas behind the Allied lines and thus most effectively direct artillery fire. The attack begins at 10:00 A.M., following five days of artillery bombardments of the German defenses. The attack succeeds initially—the French reach the incline of Vimy Ridge and capture La Targette and Aux Rietz, but they stall at Clarency and the Labyrinth. Crown Prince Rupprecht of Bavaria asks GHQ to let him send units of his Sixth Army to reinforce the thinly stretched German lines.

Gallipoli. All of the admirals involved in the campaign meet in de Robeck's stateroom aboard the *Queen Elizabeth*. They agree to try another major naval attack, though conceding that it will likely entail heavy losses, and they wire the Admiralty for permission to proceed.

10 May 1915

Washington, D.C. Speaking to a group of recently naturalized citizens, President Wilson states his position on the appropriate American response to the sinking of the *Lusitania:* "Americans must have a consciousness different from the consciousness of every other nation in the world. The example of America must be the example not merely of peace because it will not fight, but of peace because peace is the healing and elevating influence of the world and strife is not. There is such a thing as a man being too proud to fight. There is such a thing as a nation being so right that it does not need to convince others by force that it is right."

Neuve-Chapelle. Accepting reality, Haig terminates the offensive against the German Sixth Army, but with the consent of Sir John French he plans a less ambitious attack at Festubert in order to help the French Tenth Army's efforts at Vimy Ridge.

Galicia. After three days of counterattacks and strenuous resistance to the German advance near Besko and severe losses in battle at Sanok, the Russian Third and Eighth Armies crack. General Radko-Dmitriev reports to Supreme Headquarters that the Third Army has been "bled to death." The Supreme Command decides to retreat from the Carpathians, and Grand Duke Nicholas requests that the British and French launch another offensive on the Western Front to divert the Germans from concentrating on the Eastern Front and to prod Italy toward joining the Allied cause.

London. The Zeppelin *LZ-38* returns to England and, despite having been damaged by antiaircraft fire, bombs Southend.

11 May 1915
Galicia. The Russian Third and Eighth Armies begin a full-scale retreat along the entire nearly two-hundred-mile front, retiring north toward the Vistula River.

12 May 1915
Artois. The Seventieth Division of d'Urbal's army takes Clarency, capturing a thousand prisoners.

Gallipoli. In the darkness of early morning, a Turkish destroyer commanded by a German lieutenant sails out of the straits and approaches the battleship *Goliath,* berthed a hundred yards from shore in Morto Bay. The destroyer slams three torpedoes into the *Goliath*, which sinks so rapidly—in only two minutes—that five hundred crewmen drown despite the short

distance to shore. Alarmed by the report of the sinking sent to London, Adm. Sir John Fisher orders the *Queen Elizabeth* to leave the Dardanelles and return to the Grand Fleet to secure her from potential menace. Fisher and Churchill disagree on the next move at Gallipoli, as Fisher is totally opposed to the new naval assault proposed by de Robeck.

German South-West Africa. Louis Botha and his Rand Rifles occupy Windhoek. The German government and the *Schutztruppe* have abandoned the town of eight thousand, leaving behind several thousand women and children. Botha and Theodor Seitz, governor of the colony, have agreed by telephone the day before to a forty-eight-hour armistice to begin on 20 May while they discuss terms for ending hostilities at a meeting in Giftkop.

13 May 1915
London. The government decides to intern all aliens of military service age from enemy countries.

14 May 1915
London. The War Council heatedly debates the next move in the Gallipoli campaign. Lord Kitchener vents anger and dismay over the failure to date, while

Captured German officers under the guard of a French soldier, 1915, by Jean Berne-Bellecour, courtesy of the Anne S.K. Brown Military Collection, Brown University Library)

Churchill advocates sending reinforcements to Hamilton as the only viable option at the moment.

15 May 1915

Neuve-Chapelle. At a half hour before midnight, General Haig sends two of his divisions into battle at Festubert, the BEF's first major night battle. Their purpose is to achieve a modest salient of only a thousand yards. The Second Division scores initial success, but the Germans chew up the Seventh Division.

London. Although he has resigned or threatened to resign several times before, this time Adm. Sir John Fisher means it. Unable to continue any show of support for the Gallipoli campaign, the first sea lord sends a letter of resignation to Churchill at 5:00 A.M. and then immediately goes to ground in the Charing Cross Hotel. Discovered there, he agrees to talk with Lloyd George and Asquith, but to no avail. Later, in a rage, Fisher sends a final note to Churchill: "You are bent on forcing the Dardanelles and nothing will turn you from it—nothing. . . . You will remain and I shall go—it is better so." Prime Minister Asquith rejects Fisher's petulant demand that he be given total control over the Royal Navy and Churchill be sacked by instead accepting his resignation. During the night Fisher leaves for Scotland.

16 May 1915

Neuve-Chapelle. Haig's troops continue the Battle of Festubert in the early morning hours but make little progress, stymied by German counterattacks.

Galicia. Units of Mackensen's Eleventh Army reach the San River at Jaroslaw.

17 May 1915

Neuve-Chapelle. In the early morning, Haig's artillery launches a barrage of such surprising accuracy that it sends German troops racing toward British lines for safety—450 surrender even before the infantry attack begins. Sir John French's current objective is La Bassée. He hopes the First Army can cross to the south side of the canal there and thus relieve the pressure on the French forces at the Artois front.

But rain, water-filled dikes, and stiffening German resistance slow the British advance.

18 May 1915

Galicia. The Austrian Third Army crosses the San River and captures Sieniawa, as Mackensen's Eleventh Army establishes a bridgehead at Jaroslaw.

Neuve-Chapelle. Deeply concerned by reports of disorderliness among troops facing the British, the German command has rushed reinforcements to the Festubert front and now has doubled the size of its force there as Haig renews his assault in the afternoon. As a result, the British effort fails. Haig begins withdrawing his tired Second and Seventh Divisions during the night, replacing them with fresh troops, including the Canadian Division.

19 May 1915

Neuve-Chapelle. The Battle of Festubert degenerates into inconclusive local actions.

Galicia. Mackensen's army smashes a Russian salient on the west side of the San River and turns his artillery loose on Przemysl.

Gallipoli. The Turks continue their attack on the Anzac positions. Though outnumbered by over two to one, the seventeen thousand Anzacs again hold fast. Hamilton receives a gloomy dispatch from Kitchener, expressing his disappointment over the continuing failure at Gallipoli and his concern "whether we can long support two fields of operation draining on our resources." Kitchener encourages Hamilton to bring the campaign to a conclusion before the possibility of withdrawal comes up for discussion.

20 May 1915

German South-West Africa. Following arrangement of a two-day ceasefire on May 19, General Botha and Gov. Theodor Seitz meet at Giftkop to discuss terms for ending the fighting. The talks fail, and both men return to their bases to prepare for renewed hostilities.

21 May 1915

London. Pressured by Andrew Bonar Law, leader of the Conservative Party, and other members of the opposition after Fisher's resignation and amid an emerging scandal over inadequate production of munitions leading to shortages, Asquith agrees to remove Churchill as first lord of the admiralty and to form a coalition government.

23 May 1915
Rome. The Italian government declares war on Austria-Hungary but defers any declaration regarding Germany. Ostensibly, the Italians' objective is territorial annexations, but by not declaring war on Germany or Turkey, they violate the terms of the Treaty of London agreed to on 26 April.
Gallipoli. During the night the *E-11*, commanded by Lt. Comdr. Martin Nasmith, enters the narrows to make its way to the Sea of Marmara bound upon a daring attack on Constantinople.

24 May 1915
Ypres. After a relatively quiet interim of two weeks, the German Fourth Army returns to the offensive in the early morning releasing a cloud of gas against British troops holding the Bellewaarde Ridge. Though some of the defenders are overcome by the gas, they manage to hold most of their line but give up some positions both at the north end of the line and to the south around Bellewaarde Lake. General Plumer concedes that a counterattack is doomed

without heavy artillery support, but the British are nearly out of shells both here and to the south at Neuve-Chapelle.
Galicia. After a week of counterattacks achieving only temporary relief from the Austro-German onslaught at various points on the front, the Russians fall back again. Mackensen's army destroys the Fifth Caucasus Corps, takes twenty-one thousand prisoners, and advances eleven miles to the east of the San River.
Gallipoli. After several days of slaughter and two days of both impromptu and formal meetings between officers on both sides, the Anzac and Turkish opponents stage a nine-hour truce to allow for the burial of the dead. Lt. Col. Aubrey Herbert, poet, former member of Parliament, and now Hamilton's intelligence officer, crosses to the Turkish lines to observe and ensure Turkish compliance with terms of the truce. Traversing the battle scene, Herbert says: "The fearful smell of death began as we came upon scattered bodies. We mounted over a plateau and down through gullies filled with thyme, where there lay about 4,000 Turkish dead. It was indescribable. One was grateful for the rain and the grey sky." By 4:00 P.M., the grisly work is done, and the burial teams have returned to their lines. At four-forty-five, the shooting begins again.

The ghastly remains of war in the trenches. The dead were often left to rot in the open when combat prevented burial (Library of Congress)

Machine Guns

The machine gun was one of the significant nineteenth-century developments in weapons technology that deeply affected the course of World War I. It was essentially a marriage of the traditional infantry small-bore weapon with the technical advantages of the industrial machine age. The result was a weapon of awesome destruction when employed in the defense of a well-designed and well-constructed trench system. The basic machine gun of World War I was of light caliber, similar in projectile to the basic issue rifle carried by infantrymen on both sides; however, the machine gun was not a single-shot weapon but a technical marvel that was self-powered and needed only a reasonably attentive mechanic in order to indefinitely spew a veritable storm of bullets against which no soldiers—no matter how brave or foolhardy—could stand. Thus, when placed efficiently to cover interlocking fields of fire in front of defensive trenches, machine guns virtually assured that advancing attackers would never make it to the defenders in sufficient numbers to be a threat. If the attackers had to cross open ground (and defenses were usually contrived to make this so) against well-sited and well-served machine guns, an assault was nothing more than suicide. The machine gun had been developed almost exclusively by Americans, although the American army had failed to adopt the weapon and was equipped with inferior French-designed weapons when it finally took the field in France in 1917. Richard Gatling had introduced a rapid-fire, multi-barrel gun during the American Civil War. The first true machine gun was perfected by Hiram Maxim in 1885 (Maxim became a British subject and was knighted shortly after the turn of the century). Maxim's design harnessed the recoil of each round to reload, recock, and fire the next shell—thus he created a self-perpetuating mechanism of death that continued to operate so long as it was fed with ammunition. John Browning invented a gas-powered mechanism a few years later. The majority of machine guns used in the war by both sides were patterned after the Maxim, although the lightweight Lewis gun, first designed for use on aircraft, was also common. One machine gun was fully capable of firing at a rate equal to forty or fifty infantrymen, and thus a single crew could dominate the entire stretch of no-man's-land in front of their position. The only tasks were to pull the trigger and then keep the machine supplied with belts of cartridges and cooling liquid. The gunner usually set up the weapon to fire at a certain height across the ground in front of the position and then slowly traversed his fire back and forth by gently tapping the breech of the gun from side to side. The only defense against the machine gun was to kill the gunners or to completely destroy the weapon's emplacement before launching an open-field attack, and both sides developed great skill at surviving even prolonged pre-attack bombardments. On battlefield after battlefield, machine gunners killed opposing infantry in rows as they came dumbly forward.

A French machine-gun emplacement of the sort that made assaults across trench lines tantamount to suicide (Library of Congress)

25 May 1915
Ypres. The Second Battle of Ypres winds down. Both sides lack artillery ammunition. Sir John French advises General Haig that munitions stocks are low, the Germans have restored their defensive line, and he thinks it "improbable" that Haig's First Army's offensive can succeed because of the difficult terrain and the German defenses. At a terrible cost—over fifty-nine thousand casualties, with seventeen thousand dead in the battles at Aubers Ridge and Festubert—the British front line has barely moved from where it rested before the battles. The Germans have suffered nearly thirty-five thousand casualties, but their defenses hold.

London. Asquith announces his coalition government. Arthur James Balfour replaces Churchill at the Admiralty, with Adm. Sir Henry Jackson as first sea lord. David Lloyd George heads the new Ministry of Munitions formed to mobilize British industry.

Gallipoli. Warned by the *Vengeance* that a torpedo crossed her bow, de Robeck transfers his flag from the *Lord Nelson* to the yacht *Triad* and orders his best battleships and transports to withdraw to safety at Mudros. The torpedo was launched from the German submarine *U-21,* which had slipped out of Ems bound for the Mediterranean on 25 April under the command of Lt. Comdr. Otto Hersing. Around noon, Hersing slams a torpedo into the twelve-year-old battleship *Triumph,* which lists heavily, throwing men on deck overboard, and then capsizes with seventy-one men below decks. De Robeck orders other ships to Mudros, leaving behind only one battleship, the *Majestic,* standing off Cape Helles with an accompaniment of destroyers. At the same time, Nasmith's *E-11,* which sank the ammunition carrier *Nagara* on 23 May, surfaces at the Golden Horn and torpedoes the freighter *Stamboul,* berthed at the arsenal in Constantinople. As the Turkish ship sinks, Nasmith dives and speeds into the Bosporus.

26 May 1915
London. The Zeppelin *LZ-38* makes a third attack, dropping grenades and incen-

diaries on Southend that kill three and wound three.

Ludwigshafen, Germany. In retaliation for the German poison gas attack of 22 April, eighteen Voisin airplanes from Malzeville near Nancy bomb the chlorine gas and acid factories at Ludwigshafen near Mannheim. The resulting explosions send clouds of gas wafting over the lower section of Mannheim. One airplane, flown by the commander of the mission, Commandant Goys, develops ignition problems and is forced to land.

27 May 1915
Ypres. Sir John French halts further operations by Haig's First Army at Festubert. He then telegraphs London, stating that there will be no more attacks until artillery ammunition is replenished. Unknown to him, Gen. Duke Albrecht von Württemberg, commanding the Fourth Army, sends the same message to German headquarters.

Gallipoli. Imperiled by the currents in the Bosporus, Nasmith pilots the *E-11* back past Constantinople and resumes sinking ships that approach the port, creating widespread fear in the city.

Isonzo River, Italy. The Italian-Austrian frontier extends four hundred miles from the Isonzo River where it enters the Adriatic Sea to the west of Duino, northwestward through the rugged Alps Mountains, and on to the Dreilanderspitze. Although not certain where the Italians will attack, the Austrians concentrate the newly constituted million-man Fifth Army in the Isonzo River valley since they wish to retain control of the Adriatic. In this sector the Italians have two objectives: Trieste and Gorizia (Görz). Gen. Svetozar Boroevic von Bojna, a Croatian officer called away from Przemysl, now takes command of the Fifth Army. Confronting the Austrian Fifth Army at the Isonzo are the one million troops of the Italian Second and Third Armies, organized by Count Luigi Cadorna, chief of the General Staff, who has placed Gen. Pietro Frugoni in charge of the Second Army and Gen. Vittorio Emanuele, Duke of Aosta, in charge of the Third Army. General Boroevic issues utterly simple orders to his troops: "Construct positions, place obstacles in front of them and remain there." The Austrians had begun building their Isonzo defenses a month earlier. Italian troops in the Carniche Alps sector have already secured several peaks, among them the Great Pal and the Small Pal, at the Plocken Pass, giving them a commanding view of the Austrian positions there; nevertheless, they sit tight.

29 May 1915
English Channel. The German minelayer *UC-11,* the first of its class out of Zeebrugge, lays twelve mines off the coast at The Downs.

31 May 1915
Mesopotamia. With the oilfields now secure, Gen. Sir John Nixon begins to advance up the Tigris River, with Al 'Amarah, eighty-seven miles above Qurna, as the objective. But to reach this goal the British first must rout the Turks from their defensive positions only a few thousands yards from Qurna on both sides of the river. General Nixon decides on an amphibious operation, using gunboats and troops poling their way forward through the shallower waters in small boats. The operation, commanded by Maj. Gen. C.V.F. Townshend, begins at 5:00 A.M. with two gunboats and two launches moving upstream in advance. Shelling of the Turkish positions sends the defenders into flight, as Indian and British troops capture four abandoned hills. This first phase of the attack ends by noon, as intense heat and weariness force a halt.
Isonzo River. Following several days of Italian artillery bombardments during which the fort at Lusern nearly surrenders, the Austrians manage to hang on to four of their forts defending the Isonzo front. The Bavarian elite *Alpenkorps* arrives in Trentino to reinforce the Austrian First Army.

1 June 1915
Gallipoli. General Hamilton disembarks from the *Arcadian* to establish his headquarters on shore on the island of Imbros.
Mesopotamia. An attack on Abu Aran scheduled to begin at dawn proves unnecessary since the Turkish defenders have withdrawn following a British artillery bombardment. In fact, the Turks are in flight up the Tigris. Townshend and some of his staff board the *Espeigle* and hasten after them accompanied by the British flotilla, leaving behind most of their troops. Navigating through totally unfamiliar waters, "Townshend's Regatta" catches up with the gunboats *Marmaris* and *Mosul* towing barges filled with Turkish troops. The gunboats hastily cast off the barges, which, along with sailboats also carrying troops, make for shore. HMS *Odin* veers off to capture the fleeing Turks while the rest of the "Regatta" continues the pursuit until darkness forces them to stop.

2 June 1915
Mesopotamia. "Townshend's Regatta" sweeps down on the *Marmaris,* now run aground and on fire, and the *Mosul,* which surrenders. Al 'Amarah, still fifty miles distant, beckons, but Townshend's larger ships draw too great a draft to continue upriver, and the body of his troops remains fifty miles behind. Townshend, however, inspired by the Turks' headlong flight, decides to maintain the pursuit. He transfers to the *Comet* and, with a handful of troops, heads for Al 'Amarah. Reaching Qal'at Salih, Townshend sends into flight some Turkish cavalrymen and infantrymen with a round or two of shelling; the village surrenders. Townshend moves on, stopping at dusk a little over halfway to his destination.

3 June 1915
Galicia. Falkenhayn and Conrad von Hötzendorf order their combined offensive to continue pushing against the Russians east of the San River. They reorganize the Austrian Second and Fourth Armies and the German Eleventh Army as Army Group Mackensen, redeploying much of the Austrian Third Army to the Italian front. The combined armies recapture Przemysl.
German East Africa. The British monitors *Severn* and *Mersey* reach Mafia Island opposite the mouth of the Rufiji River and prepare for a mission against the *Königsberg.*

Mesopotamia. As Townshend progresses upriver, he sees nothing but white flags raised in surrender. He sends the launch *Shaitan* ahead to ascertain whether Al 'Amarah is fortified. As it nears the town of twenty thousand, the *Shaitan* sights a barge loading troops and fires a shot. The troops and others coming down to the river disperse. The rest of "Townshend's Regatta" approaches. Although he has only a hundred sailors and soldiers in his company and is vastly outnumbered, Townshend bluffs. The town and a battalion of Turkish troops stationed there surrender, thinking that Townshend's army is fast approaching.

4 June 1915

Gallipoli. The Anzacs attack at Cape Helles along a one-mile front, gaining a few hundred yards but suffering sixty-five hundred casualties in doing so. Turkish casualties number nine thousand. The same kind of trench warfare—with attacks and counterattacks achieving meaningless gains—that prevails at the Western Front in Europe settles upon the Gallipoli confrontation.

Mesopotamia. Townshend's troops arrive in Al 'Amarah in the nick of time. Without suffering a single casualty, Townshend has captured two thousand Turkish prisoners and confiscated large stores of booty.

5 June 1915

Isonzo River. After unsuccessful attacks at Monte Sabotino, Gorizia (Görz), and Krn, the Italians stage more determined assaults at Gorizia, Monte Kuk, and on the Doberdo Plateau, again without success.

Gallipoli. Since a defect has shown up in one of *E-11*'s motors and the submarine's supply of torpedoes is nearly exhausted, Lieutenant Commander Nasmith decides to leave the Aegean Sea after his successful raids at the Golden Horn. On its way out through the narrows, the submarine snags a mine but proceeds for an hour until reaching open waters, where Nasmith orders full speed astern, and the mine breaks loose and floats away. Nasmith heads the *E-11* toward Malta for repairs.

6 June 1915

England. Of three Belgian-based Zeppelins sent to raid France and England, *LZ-38,* whose target is London, turns back with engine trouble and is destroyed in her shed by bombs dropped from Royal Navy Farmans flying out of Dunkirk. Another, *LZ-37,* whose target is Calais, goes down in flames after being bombed over Belgium by Flight Sub. Lt. R.A.J. Warneford, who receives the Victoria Cross for his success. The commander of *LZ-37* and seven members of his crew perish in the flames, but quite miraculously one member of the crew hurtles from the Zeppelin as it crashes over a convent at Ghent, falls into a bed, and survives. The third Zeppelin, *LZ-39,* though also attacked by a British airplane, succeeds in bombing Harwich.

Berlin. The government orders U-boat commanders not to torpedo large passenger ships.

7 June 1915

Cameroons. Following Lt. Col. Austin Haywood's capture of Ngwe, So Dibanga, and Wum Biagas and French conquest of Eseka during May (both Allied forces suffered costly casualties because of stubborn German resistance), the two forces have combined under French leadership at Wum Biagas. Accepting the vicissitudes of murderous jungle terrain and torrential rains, and because of an inability to supply them, Brig. Gen. Charles Dobell orders a retreat. The Germans harass the Allied force so relentlessly that Dobell must send reinforcements.

8 June 1915

Washington, D.C. Secretary of State William Jennings Bryan, who has loyally supported President Wilson, resigns as an act of conscience. He objects to what he regards as a confrontational tone in Wilson's protest notes to Germany over the sinking of the *Lusitania.* Bryan believes that Americans have no moral right to endanger their nation's peaceful stance by becoming passengers on ships operated by the belligerent nations that are known to be transporting munitions. Wilson appoints Robert Lansing to succeed Bryan.

11 June 1915
Isonzo River. Italian troops launch an attack against the Austrian position at Hill 383 near Plava in hopes of establishing a bridgehead between Gorizia (Görz) and Tolmino.

12 June 1915
Carnishe Alps. The Italians capture two mountain passes and fend off Austrian efforts to oust them.

13 June 1915
Galicia. Having advanced across the San and Lubaszowka Rivers and moved into position the day before, Army Group Mackensen launches a new offensive along a thirty-one-mile front. Gen. Nikolai Ivanov's troops strenuously resist the advance—a near miracle, given their status. Many of his men lack rifles and ammunition and must wait to grab the weapons of their dead or wounded comrades as they fall. Official Russian estimates place their losses in the South-Western Front during May at 412,000 men, either killed, wounded, or captured. The Third Army endured one-third of these horrendous losses, and the hapless remnants of this force occupy the center of the resistance. General Ivanov insists on holding the line against impossible odds. At 4:00 A.M., seven hundred German artillery weapons of varied calibers open up, shelling the Russian positions for an hour and a half. Then the German troops push forward.

15 June 1915
Galicia. At Lubaczow, Army Group Mackensen smashes through the Third Army and pierces the front lines of the Eighth Army at Mosciska, establishing a new front along a line extending from Zolkiev through Rava-Russka to Lemberg.

16 June 1915
Artois. After weeks of sallies, General d'Urbal's French Tenth Army has taken Ablain, the Loretto Woods, and the Labyrinth. Now reinforced with three added divisions for a total of eighteen divisions, it begins a second general offensive with Vimy Ridge as the first objective. But Crown Prince Rupprecht of Bavaria's German Sixth Army has also been reinforced with the addition of 5 divisions and over 130 artillery pieces. As the day begins, the French artillery fires at the German lines, but the shells fall mostly in no-man's-land and on their own front lines. The only real successes of the day occur when the Moroccan Division of Pétain's XXXIIIrd Corps reaches the crest of Vimy Ridge.

17 June 1915
Isonzo River. Despite a ferocious effort, the Italian assault on Hill 383 comes to naught after a week of fighting.
Galicia. The Russian Supreme Command, meeting at Cholm, decides to order a withdrawal, though a fighting one, if Lemberg falls. Near Lemberg the Austrian Fourth Army drives the Russians back, while to the north the German Eleventh Army reaches Magierow, as Army Group Mackensen relentlessly advances.

18 June 1915
Artois. Toughened German resistance and counterattacks have thwarted the French offensive, and General Foch realizes that the fighting must stop, as the German defenses are too strong to be breached. At a cost of an estimated hundred thousand casualties, including thirty-five thousand dead, the French offensives have conquered about five square miles, but only the Loretto heights have real value. Relations between the Allies are strained because the BEF has foundered at Aubers Ridge and Festubert, where it was supposed to help the Artois cause by diverting German troops. Now the Germans, following their success in Galicia, are moving troops from the Eastern Front to bolster their forces on the Western Front.

20 June 1915
German South-West Africa. Louis Botha's troops capture Omaruru, abandoned by the German government.

21 June 1915
Gallipoli. French troops attack at Kereves Dere, gaining two hundred yards but sustaining twenty-five hundred casualties. The Turks' casualties number six thousand.

22 June 1915

Galicia. Austrian troops penetrate the fortifications circling Lemberg. General Brusilov has ordered abandonment of the city, which falls to the Austrians. The Russian Eighth and Eleventh Armies have been ordered to retreat. Falkenhayn and Conrad von Hötzendorf mean to continue Army Group Mackensen's offensive, thrusting against the Russians along the Vistula and Bug Rivers.

German East Africa. Brig. Gen. James M. Stewart, with a combined force of British, Punjabi, and African troops, raids Bukoba, a small port located on the eastern shore of Lake Victoria. After disembarking at daybreak from their ships and landing at the foot of a steep cliff three miles outside the town, Stewart's troops meet heavy German resistance and manage to advance only two miles by dusk.

23 June 1915

Isonzo River. Following several days of attacks to gain staging areas, the Italian Third Army launches a major battle along a twenty-one-mile front stretching from the Adriatic to Monte Santo. Here on the Karst Plateau they have significant advantages over the Austrians: 75 battalions to the Austrians' 40, and 530 light and heavy guns to the Austrians' 242. The battle opens with a heavy artillery bombardment that the Italians plan to maintain for seven days.

German East Africa. In the morning, fighting resumes at Bukoba, terminating in the early afternoon with a German retreat. The British blow up the German arsenal and the wireless station tower. Brig. Gen. James M. Stewart grants his troops permission to loot Bukoba. The men, joined by their officers, go on a shameless, drunken orgy of vandalism, rape, and pillage. The scene appalls intelligence officer Capt. Richard Meinertzhagen. His view of Stewart is succinct: "A great gentleman, great charm, but a hopeless, rotten soldier."

26 June 1915

Galicia. Mackensen's army advances to the Bug River.

Saint Petersburg. The indolent and self-indulgent Minister of War Gen. V. Sukho-

A member of the Austrian field artillery, 1915 (by B. Berg, courtesy of the Anne S.K. Brown Military Collection, Brown University Library)

milov, whose administration has left the Russian army so badly undersupplied, resigns from office after scandalized members of the Duma pressure Nicholas II to sack him. Sukhomilov is placed under arrest for suspicion of being involved in the gross corruption that afflicts the entire Russian armaments production and supply system. The czar appoints Gen. A.A. Polivanov as his replacement.

28 June 1915

Gallipoli. The British attack at Gully Spur, gaining half a mile while suffering thirty-eight hundred casualties.

Cameroons. During a tornado, a column of the Nigeria Regiment led by Lt. Col. W.I. Webb-Bowen attacks and routs surprised German outposts at Ngaundere and occupies the town.

29 June 1915

Galicia. Mackensen's army continues its advance, reaching Tomaszow.

Building German trenches on the Western Front during 1915 (Library of Congress)

30 June 1915
Isonzo River. After their seven-day artillery bombardment of Austrian positions, the Italians attack along the twenty-one-mile front. Their objective is Gorizia (Görz).
Argonne. Although not a scene of major fighting, the Argonne is one of the sectors on the front where both sides try to deplete the other's resources of men and matériel by means of small-scale attacks and counterattacks. On the heels of an artillery pounding, Lt. Erwin Rommel leads his regiment forward near Labordaire. They secure their salient by entrenching immediately.

1 July 1915
Poland. Mackensen's army occupies the fortress at Zamosc, but the Austrian Fourth Army fails at Krasnik.

2 July 1915
Posen (Poznan), Germany. At a war council with his generals, Kaiser Wilhelm II

decides the Eastern Front offensives must continue. The Twelfth Army will push toward the Narew River; the Ninth Army, toward the Vistula River; and Mackensen's army will swing northward and clear the Russians from the territory between the Vistula and Bug Rivers. Ludendorff and Hindenburg prefer the idea of enveloping all of Grand Duke Nicholas's forces, but Falkenhayn advocates the adopted plan and has persuaded the kaiser. Falkenhayn, however, has rejected an important part of the plan originated by Mackensen's chief of staff, Hans von Seeckt, that would have had the Austrian Second Army join the offensive by traversing the Pripet Marshes and outflanking the Russians' southern flank to the east of the Bug River. Falkenhayn mistakenly believes that the marshes are impassable. Falkenhayn has also chosen to attack at the Narew River rather than make the attack north of the Niemen River favored by Ludendorff and Hindenburg.
London. Parliament passes the important Munitions of War Act, introduced for con-

Life in the German trenches on the Western Front, summer 1915 (Library of Congress)

The embodiment of the German Imperial state and the war effort: Kaiser Wilhelm (center), flanked by Hindenburg (to the kaiser's right) and Ludendorff (to his left) (Library of Congress)

sideration on 23 June, that organizes British industry for war. It mandates compulsory arbitration of labor disputes, largely bans strikes or lockouts, limits profits, authorizes the Minister of Munitions to declare any plant "a controlled operation" and

Propaganda

World War I was not the first conflict that saw government-sponsored propaganda play a role, and the pitch and scope of propaganda never approached the level that was achieved during the later global war of the 1940s. Nevertheless, propaganda was important in shaping attitudes and actions, especially among civilian populations. As the war developed into a long-term conflict of attrition that called on nearly all the reserves of the belligerent nations, it became more and more important for governments to control images of the enemy and exhort everyone to throw full support to the war. The most effective propaganda was seen in Great Britain. The country fought during the first years with a volunteer army, so it was crucial to inculcate a fever pitch of enthusiasm for the war among the general population as the basis for recruiting. The main technique was to vilify the enemy, transforming the Germans into barbaric Huns that must be suppressed at all costs to the British nation. The Germans played into the hands of British propagandists early in the war by showing little regard for niceties while marching through Belgium. A relatively few cases of brutality, however, were transformed by the British into powerful stories and images of atrocities against innocent people. As the war progressed, the British gained sophistication in the techniques of large-scale propaganda, using the press as the primary tool. They not only endeavored to keep domestic support for the war at the highest level, but the British enjoyed considerable success in influencing the coverage of the war in America, so that when the time was ripe, the people of the United States were converted to the same simplistic view of Germany as had been spread earlier in the British Isles.

to approve all wage changes, and places other restrictions on both employers and wage earners.

4 July 1915
Gallipoli. Commander Otto Hersing's *U-21* slips out through the narrows into the Aegean and torpedoes the French troop transport *Carthage* off Cape Helles, killing six men.
German South-West Africa. While Botha and the Germans have agreed to a truce at Otavi, troops under Martinus W. Myburgh, unaware of the truce, have pushed on to capture Gaub, and now they force the surrender of Tsumeb. They confiscate huge stores of arms, ammunition, and equipment brought here to be distributed to the rebels in South Africa. Tsumeb is also the site of a prisoner-of-war camp. Myburgh sets free the six hundred inmates.

5 July 1915
Isonzo River. Although five days of spirited attacks against an enemy outnumbered six to one in some areas of the front have netted the Italians nothing more than a slight salient on the river at Sagrado and some positions on the Karst Plateau allowing an overlook of Monte San Michele, General Cadorna remains obdurate. He orders the entire Second Army into the assault at Görz. At 6:00 P.M., the Italians attack along a line from Podgora to Doberdo, but General Boroevic's troops, reinforced by small reserves, hold fast and inflict four thousand casualties. The Austrian defense during the entire First Battle of the Isonzo has cost 8,800 casualties and 1,150 taken prisoner; but the Italians have experienced 13,411 casualties, including 1,916 dead and 1,500 captured. Görz eludes General Cadorna. He now realizes that any future hope of advancing to Trieste depends upon capturing Monte San Michele.
Mesopotamia. With his current objective An Nasiriya, potential base of an attack against Basra and control point for com-

munications between the Tigris and Euphrates Rivers, General Nixon sends a force commanded by Maj. Gen. Sir George Gorringe to drive the Turks out of this key town on the Euphrates.

6 July 1915
German East Africa. In the darkness of 4:00 A.M., the British monitors *Severn* and *Mersey* move into the delta of the Rufiji River to attack the *Königsberg.* The monitors withstand the fire from the shore batteries, blow up a torpedo launched by the Germans, and by 6:30 A.M. anchor and open fire. Return fire from the *Königsberg* finds the range and slams two shells into the *Mersey,* killing four seamen and wounding four others. The exchange of fire continues into the afternoon, with the monitors expending 635 shells, four of which hit the *Königsberg,* killing four seamen and opening a hole in her hull. With their guns overheated and their men weary, the monitors head back down the river past the German gauntlet and return to the safety of the delta at four-thirty.

9 July 1915
German South-West Africa. Governor Theodor Seitz concedes defeat, and the Germans surrender unconditionally. Botha allows the officers to retain their arms but no ammunition. Reservists are allowed to retain both because they "should have the means of self-protection against the natives." Botha heads back to Cape Town.

10 July 1915
Armenia. Turkish troops massacre Armenians in villages near Mush.

11 July 1915
Frévent, France. Joffre, after assessing the offensive at Artois, concludes that its failure resulted from attacking on only a single and too-narrow front. Consequently, he decides that the autumn offensive of the British and French forces, now augmented with new armies, must be more extensive. The main French attack will occur in the Champagne Plain, with a secondary attack at Artois and a renewed effort by Foch at

the Vimy Ridge. Haig's BEF troops will attack on a line from Lens to the La Bassée Canal. Sir John French had agreed to the Lens-Loos offensive but then became reluctant to commit the British to anything but artillery bombardments without infantry attacks. He even suggested to Joffre that the entire offensive be postponed into 1916. The two now meet at Frévent, and Joffre insists that Sir John accept Joffre's plan. Sir John acquiesces.
German East Africa. At 10:30 A.M., the *Severn* and the *Mersey* again enter the Rufiji estuary and renew the attack. At 1:16 P.M., explosions rock the *Königsberg.* The *Mersey* moves closer and fires more rounds into the wounded ship, setting it ablaze from stern to bow. The British monitors withdraw, and the Germans abandon ship. The *Königsberg*'s 255-day saga comes to an end.

13 July 1915
Flanders. The newly formed British Third Army, commanded by Gen. Sir Charles Monro, takes over from the French a fifteen-mile stretch of the front between Arras and the Somme. The BEF now has twenty-one divisions in France, six of them in Monro's force.
Poland. The Twelfth Army, with units of the Eighth Army at its left flank, all under the command of Gen. Max von Gallwitz, begins the drive to the Narew River.

18 July 1915
Poland. The Russians stage a general retreat after three days of fighting with Mackensen's forces, which take Krasnostav.
Isonzo River. The Italian Third Army opens the Second Battle of the Isonzo with a cannonade in the early afternoon. The objective is again the Karst Plateau, but Gen. Vittorio Emmanuel's troops make little headway because General Boroevic has used the battle hiatus to construct better trenches and to replace the soldiers wearied from the first battle.

20 July 1915
Isonzo River. Having gained little on the second day of the offensive, Gen. Vittorio

Part of the battlefield near Arras held by the British. The scene includes infantry, field artillery, a tank, and even cavalry in the distance (Library of Congress)

Emmanuel switches tactics and sends the Third Army to storm and capture Monte San Michele.

21 July 1915
Isonzo River. The Austrians counterattack and retake Monte San Michele as fighting rages along the entire front.

23 July 1915
Poland. Gen. Max von Gallwitz's troops attack Rozan and Pultusk.

24 July 1915
Mesopotamia. Although the Turks have fought fiercely, finally engaging General Gorringe's men in hand-to-hand combat, the British succeed in capturing An Nasiriya. The campaign cost the Turks 500 dead and 950 prisoners; British casualties number 533. The victory encourages Lord Hardinge, Viceroy of India and General Nixon's commander, to decide that Nixon should now move against Kut, one more step toward Baghdad.

25 July 1915
Isonzo River. Though reinforced for a fresh assault along the entire front that be-

gan 23 July, the Italian Third Army remains frustrated in its efforts to capture the Karst Plateau. The Austrians, also reinforced, hold their lines.
Poland. Gallwitz's advancing army crosses the Narew River.

30 July 1915
Flanders. Using six flamethrowers, the Germans spew liquid fire over the British trenches at Hooge and follow up with a barrage of small-arms fire and an infantry attack. The surprised British—those who survive—fall back, and the advancing Germans easily capture the so-called Hooge crater, a great hole 120 feet across and 20 feet deep created by a British mine explosion. Though the Germans have used flamethrowers before, this marks the new weapon's first real success, owing to the exceptionally short expanse of no-man's-land (only fifteen yards) where the attack is focused.
Cape Province, South Africa. Louis Botha arrives back in Cape Town to a hero's welcome—but a hero of the British, not the Afrikaners. He has helped to secure the Union and the sea lanes between England and India for the British.

1 August 1915
Arras. French Voisins equipped with machine guns have controlled the skies over the Western Front and have bombed and strafed in Germany with impunity, but a dramatic change occurs as Lt. Max Immelmann, flying a Fokker E-1 monoplane, wounds the pilot of a British BE2c with a burst from his machine gun and forces the plane down at Douai. Eleven German pilots have taken to the air in these new planes designed by Dutch engineer Anthony Fokker, who has adapted what he learned from the Roland Garros Morane-Saulnier captured by the Germans in April. With the new plane, the Germans can fight back in the air. The "Fokker Scourge" has arrived.

3 August 1915
Poland. Spurred by the success of the German offensive, the Austrian Fourth Army now begins pressing northward along the course of the Vistula River to Ivangorod, already menaced by German troops under Gen. Remus von Woyrsch. Farther north, the Ninth Army smashes through the fortifications south of Warsaw.

4 August 1915
Poland. The Russians evacuate the major part of Warsaw but occupy the suburban areas on the north side of the Vistula.
Brussels. Officers of the Secret Police appear at the clinic run by English nurse Edith Cavell and her second in command, Sister

Airplanes

The airplane made its debut as a weapon during World War I and underwent rapid and significant development. The technology of flight was still in its infant stages when the war began. The Wright brothers' first flight occurred scarcely more than a decade before the opening guns on the Western Front, but the two intrepid inventors had sold their machines and ideas to European military establishments soon after setting up the first airplane manufacturing company (their own native American army had initially turned down the chance to develop the plane as a weapon). In 1914, the plane was still a crude piece of machinery, barely able to perform its main function of taking men aloft on a routine basis; yet, by the end of the war four years later, airplanes had improved dramatically in speed, range, altitude, and reliability. The rapid strides came as the result of practical experimentation during the conflict after the military discovered the efficacy of airborne reconnaissance. Despite the glamour and publicity that eventually accrued to single-plane combat and the cult of the "ace" fighter pilot, the true value of the plane during the war was in giving a clear and hitherto unparalleled view of the enemy. Reconnaissance by aerial photography meant that planners on either side could know the exact disposition of the opposition. Much of the early aerial combat developed in response to the need to destroy or inhibit the enemy's flying reconnaissance. Gradually, more and more single-plane combat took place, especially after both sides learned how to mount forward-firing machine guns on fast, maneuverable planes. The result was the development of the romantic figure of the fighter pilot—men such as the famed "Red Baron," Manfred von Richthofen, and American Ace Eddie Rickenbacker, a former race car champion—who took to the skies day after day to seek out enemy fliers and engage in dogfights above the lines. In an otherwise static war, such encounters took on psychological importance far beyond their military significance. The fact was that airplanes could not carry enough weaponry to do much damage to troops or installations on the ground. Not even the giant German Gothas and British Handley-Paige twin-engine machines developed late in the war were capable of much more than morale-damaging raids because they carried such a light bomb load as to be practically worthless as strategic weapons.

A night attack with phosphorous bombs near Goudrecourt on the Western Front, August 1915 (Library of Congress)

Wilkins, and arrest them both. They are charged with helping at least two hundred Allied servicemen escape to their own lines.

5 August 1915
Poland. The Ninth Army enters Warsaw. The Tenth Army attacks at Kovno.
Paris. The government appoints Gen. Maurice Sarrail, dismissed by Joffre in July, as commander in chief of the French Army of the Orient, which does not yet exist. Sarrail has solid political support in the Chamber of Deputies.

6 August 1915
Gallipoli. Although the fighting has continued through July, neither side has achieved any meaningful gain, but Lord Kitchener, grown sympathetic to Hamilton's position, has provided five new divisions, raising the number of troops under Hamilton's command to 110,000. Hamilton is now headquartered at Imbros, from which he can communicate by telephone (the cables are under water) with Cape Helles and Anzac Cove. He has planned a major new assault with the intent of capturing a new objective—the heights of Sari Bair Ridge. The force at Anzac Cove, now reinforced to a total of thirty-seven thousand with the addition of twenty thousand fresh troops, will make the assault along with twenty-five thousand troops at a new beachhead at Suvla Bay. To aid in this campaign, Hamilton requested that Kitchener send him Gen. Sir Henry Rawlinson or Gen. Sir Julian Byng from France, but instead Kitchener has sent the elderly and inexperienced Gen. Sir Frederick Stopford. Diversionary actions in the afternoon at Cape Helles and in the evening at Anzac Cove draw the Turks' attention while the British troops unload at Suvla for a nighttime launch of the combined assault from Anzac and Suvla. Although the Turks have been expecting a new offensive and Mustapha Kemal supposedly has warned

that Suvla may be Hamilton's staging area, Liman von Sanders, also forewarned by German intelligence, has only ninety-five thousand troops under his command, and they cannot be everywhere on the peninsula. He has deployed forty thousand of his troops at Cape Helles and another thirty thousand at Anzac Cove. The rest are stationed at Bulair. The British offensive begins in the afternoon at Cape Helles and results in seventy-five hundred Turkish dead and thirty-five hundred British casualties, but again without any meaningful gain. The afternoon offensive at Anzac Cove, however, boasts some success, aided by dispersing the troops from tunnels that the commander, Gen. Sir William Birdwood, ordered built under no-man's-land so that his troops could emerge close to the Turkish front lines. Even so the Turks and the Australians between them suffer ten thousand casualties here. By 10:00 P.M., the first units of the twenty thousand British troops destined for Suvla Cove have landed and begun to move inland unopposed, although an outpost of Turkish troops at Lala Baba has spotted the incoming troop carriers.

7 August 1915
Gallipoli. By 1:30 A.M., troops advancing from Anzac Cove have captured several positions on the heights leading to Chunuk Bair. By dawn, they are within a thousand yards of Chunuk Bair. But their commander, disregarding his orders, calls a fateful two-hour halt. During the night, Liman von Sanders has detached his reserves from Bulair and sent them quick-marching to the defense of this position and the plain at Suvla, and at 7:00 A.M. he sends still more troops to these sites. By the time the Anzacs begin their attack on the summit at Chunuk Bair, the Turkish troops are in place and their machine guns thwart the advance—the moment has been lost. Lack of support from Chunuk Bair dooms the other Anzac assaults at Nek, Pope's, and Quinn's. Meanwhile at Suvla Cove, where the twenty thousand assembling troops vastly outnumber the fifteen hundred Turkish defenders, General Stopford, aboard the *Jonquil* and cut off

from direct communication with the beachhead, allows his troops to stand pat through the day—again, the opportunity is wasted.

8 August 1915
Gallipoli. Lt. Comdr. Martin Nasmith has held the *E-11* lying in wait at the narrows, anticipating that the Turkish battleship *Barbarossa Harradin* will appear to participate in the unfolding battle. The battleship does arrive at dawn, and Nasmith sends it to its grave with a torpedo. The ship capsizes and sinks in less than fifteen minutes. Nasmith proceeds to Constantinople, where he sinks a collier, just arrived from the Black Sea. In the fighting on land, British and New Zealand troops briefly occupy the heights at Chunuk Bair, but Turkish attacks force them to withdraw to their positions of the previous day. At Suvla, the troops still remain poised, resting in preparation for action. Dismayed that his troops have not seized the advantage, Hamilton visits Stopford in the evening and then lands at Suvla and insists that securing the heights is imperative before the Turks mount a defense. But the subsequent attack is too late, and the Turks thwart the too-long-delayed nighttime assault. The hoped-for British victory at Gallipoli fades, though the struggle continues.
Constantinople. Having learned of the truth of the Turkish brutality against the Armenians, the German ambassador, Baron von Wangenheim, protests to Minister of the Interior Talaat Bey (Mehmet Talaat Pasha), but to no avail.

10 August 1915
Gallipoli. Mustapha Kemal arrives at Sari Bair to inspire the beleaguered defenders. Against all odds, he impetuously decides to attack along the front at Chunuk Bair, the Rhododendron Ridge, and "The Farm" on the heights above Anzac Cove. His troops smash ahead, even mounting a bayonet attack, against the surprised Anzacs, capturing Chunuk Bair and "The Farm" and pushing on until machine-gun fire finally stops them at the Rhododendron Ridge. They have inflicted twelve thousand casualties on the British and Anzac forces. British hopes of success at Sari Bair col-

lapse, though Hamilton persists in thinking otherwise.

13 August 1915
Poland. As the German advance continues, all of their armies are now in contact and moving along a continuous front, but the Russian retreat has been so orderly and resistant that no hope remains of squeezing the Russians in a pincers movement and destroying their flanks. As the Russians retreat, they burn and lay waste, destroying crops, farmhouses, and entire villages in an effort to deny the Germans any hope of sustenance from the conquered land. But the Germans have their own well-run supply system, so it is the Poles who suffer from the losses. Tens of thousands of Polish refugees stream eastward into Russia.
Gallipoli. The British complete removal of their sick and wounded—some twenty-two thousand men—to hospitals in Egypt and Malta.

14 August 1915
Gallipoli. At the suggestion of Lord Kitchener, General Hamilton removes Stopford from his command. Kitchener chooses Lt. Gen. Julian Byng, one of Hamilton's original choices to head the offensive, to replace Stopford.

15 August 1915
Gallipoli. Hamilton places Gen. Sir B. de Lisle in charge of Stopford's troops at Suvla. The Turks defeat a British attack on Tekke Tepe launched from Suvla.
Compiègne. Lord Kitchener arrives at GQG for a series of discussions with Joffre, who is displeased with Sir John French's reluctance to have the BEF participate fully in a new offensive. They also discuss the worrisome developments on the Eastern Front, where the Russian defeat may free German units for service on the Western Front.

18 August 1915
Poland. The German Tenth Army takes Kovno.

19 August 1915
Poland. The Germans capture Novo-Georgiewsk (Modlin), with the surrender

German infantry fires on advancing French troops in August 1915 (Library of Congress)

of ninety thousand Russian prisoners and sixteen hundred guns.

Baltic Sea. In support of the German infantry offensive in Poland, cruisers from the High Seas Fleet have been trying to bottle up Russian ships in the gulf at Riga. The battleships *Posen* and *Nassau* along with three cruisers—*Seydlitz, Moltke,* and *Von der Tann*—enter the gulf for an attack on the Russian ships and on Riga itself. But the British submarine *E-1,* commanded by Noel Laurence, fires a torpedo into the *Moltke.* The German ships open fire and set ablaze two Russian gunboats but then steam out of the gulf.

20 August 1915
Rome. The Italian government declares war on Turkey.

21 August 1915
Gallipoli. British troops attack Scimitar Hill but are repulsed after suffering heavy casualties. The story is the same at W Hills, attacked by a combined British and Anzac force.

23 August 1915
Gallipoli. After refusing to serve under General de Lisle, Gen. Bryan Mahon has been sent to Lemnos. General Stopford is on his way back to England, and General Hammersley collapses and must be removed from the peninsula. The August offensive, now at a standstill, has cost the British forty thousand casualties, including men fallen to sickness.

Compiègne. Sir John French bows to the will of Joffre, who receives a battle plan from the British commander that agrees with Joffre's entirely. French's agreement results from a message sent from London the day before apprising him that Kitchener and the cabinet support Joffre's plan. The British First Army will attack in conjunction with the French on whatever date Joffre sets.

26 August 1915
Poland. German troops—called the Bug Army because fighting follows the Bug River—commanded by Gen. Alexander von Linsingen capture Brest-Litovsk.

27 August 1915
Poland. General Max von Gallwitz's army takes Bialystok. Despite the opposition of Hindenburg and Ludendorff, who would like to strengthen the armies in the East in hopes of annihilating the main Russian forces, Falkenhayn orders redeployment of one of the divisions in Mackensen's army to the Danube River front. He plans further such redeployments from the Eastern Front. Falkenhayn believes that a major Allied offensive in France is planned for September. He also believes that the Russians, having lost a million men and great quantities of war matériel, have no hope of mounting an offensive in the near future.

29 August 1915
Mesopotamia. With Baghdad as his final goal, Gen. Sir John Nixon has concentrated his forces at Al 'Amarah under the command of Maj. Gen. Sir Charles Townshend. Now Townshend receives his orders. They direct him to "destroy and disperse the enemy, and to occupy Kut, thereby consolidating our control of the Basra vilayet."

30 August 1915
Berlin. The government orders U-boats not to sink merchant ships or passenger liners without first giving warning and providing time for the crews and passengers to disembark.

31 August 1915
Poland. The Austrian First Army captures Lutsk, pushing Gen. Aleksey Brusilov's army back.

Belfort, France. French flying ace Adolphe Pegoud is shot down and killed.

1 September 1915
Russia. The German Eighth Army attacks Grodno.

Cameroons. Col. Frederick Hugh Cunliffe opens a determined assault on the fort at Mora, where the Germans refuse to surrender. A formidable target, the fort stands atop a mountain that rises steeply to a height of seventeen hundred feet.

2 September 1915
Poland. The Eighth Army captures

Grodno. The Tenth Army attacks at Vilna, where Hindenburg hopes for a breakthrough that may still allow destruction of the Russians' northern flank.

Gallipoli. At Imbros, General Hamilton receives word from London that the French have agreed to send six divisions commanded by Gen. Maurice Sarrail to support the Allied invasion of the peninsula. Hamilton is much heartened.

5 September 1915

Petrograd. Court intrigue finally takes its toll. Though the Duma has supported the war effort, while criticizing its administration, Nicholas II has prorogued the parliament against the advice of his Council of Ministers. He now takes a further step at the urging of the Czarina Alexandra: he removes Grand Duke Nicholas from command and himself assumes the role of commander in chief. The czarina has fallen under the spell of the compelling monk Rasputin, who thereby holds enormous influence at the court and with the czar. The czarina intensely dislikes Grand Duke Nicholas, who detests Rasputin and has reputedly said he would hang the monk if he ever appeared at the front. The czar's actions raise grave concern among Russian patriots, who regard Alexandra as pro-German—she is the daughter of the Grand Duke of Hesse but is also the granddaughter of Queen Victoria. Czar Nicholas arrives at the Russian headquarters, Stavka, at Mogilev and assumes command. Nicholas's army order states: "Today I have taken supreme command of all forces of the sea and land armies operating in the theatre of war. We shall fulfill our sacred duty to defend our country to the last. We will not dishonor the Russian land." Nicholas's newly appointed chief of staff, Gen. Mikhail Alexeyev, has proved an effective commander during the Russian retreat from Poland.

6 September 1915

Pless, Germany. Falkenhayn, General Conrad von Hötzendorf, and Lt. Col. Peter Ganchev, the latter representing Bulgaria, sign a military agreement committing Bulgaria to enter the war on the side of the Central Powers. The Bulgarians agree to send four divisions against Serbia and another against Serbian-controlled Macedonia. In exchange, Bulgaria receives territorial concessions: Macedonia, or most of it; a port on the Adriatic Sea; and territory along both sides of the Maritsa River ceded by Turkey. Both sides in the war have wooed the neutral Balkan states, which have held out for territorial gains, but the Central Powers have enjoyed some advantage with Bulgaria, whose King Ferdinand has been staunchly pro-German. Strategically located and referred to as "the Prussia of the Balkans," Bulgaria brings to the Central Powers the largest army in the Balkans, 517,000 men, and the ability to mobilize over 300,000 more out of a total population of 6 million.

8 September 1915

Cameroons. After a week of repeated but failed attacks on Mora, Colonel Cunliffe gives up. The Germans will not be dislodged.

Russia. Grand Duke Nicholas arrives in Tiflis to assume his duties as Viceroy of the Caucasus, the post Nicholas II appointed him to after dismissing him as commander.

9 September 1915

Russia. With the reluctant acceptance of Falkenhayn but no reinforcements, Hindenburg and Ludendorff begin a new major offensive aimed at Vilna (Vilnyus). They still hope for a massive victory. Once again their idea is to capture the Russian troops in a mighty pincer, with Gen. Otto von Below leading one army against them from the northeast and Gen. Hermann von Eichorn leading another from a southeasterly angle.

12 September 1915

Mesopotamia. Townshend has assembled his force—nearly eleven thousand troops and thirty guns—at Ali al Gharbi for the advance on Kut. This launch point is in the domain of the Ben Lam tribe led by a chief named Gazban. Townshend has decided to attack along the left bank of the Tigris. The march toward Kut begins in temperatures ranging between 110 and 120 degrees Fahrenheit.

16 September 1915
Russia. The Bug Army captures Pinsk.
Mesopotamia. Townshend's force reaches the Chahela mounds and bivouacs there to await artillery being brought upriver by boats. Four of the airplanes that had been involved in the *Königsberg*'s demise arrived in Basra on 5 September, and Townshend sends them aloft to fly reconnaissance.

18 September 1915
Russia. The German Tenth Army under General Eichhorn captures Vilna (Vilnyus) but at great expense: fifty thousand casualties.
Berlin. Responding to American protests over U-boat attacks on neutral shipping, German Grand Adm. Henning von Holtzendorf, chief of the Naval Staff, reluctantly orders their withdrawal from the English Channel, confining their continuing operations largely to the Mediterranean Sea.

19 September 1915
Russia. Falkenhayn orders Hindenburg and Ludendorff to release five divisions for redeployment to the Western Front.

20 September 1915
Hungary. General Mackensen, commanding troops deployed from Russia for a prospective invasion of Serbia, sets up his headquarters at Timisoara. The German intent is to push through Serbia in order to establish a connection with Turkey while discouraging other Balkan states from siding with the Allies.
German East Africa. Lt. Col. Francis Jollie attacks Longido with a mixed force of Indian and other troops, including the Third King's African Rifles (KAR), which suffers forty-one casualties in the abortive raid.

21 September 1915
Champagne. Preparations are complete for Joffre's planned "great attack," with fresh reinforcements brought in, supply dumps built, telephone wires laid, and new

trenches dug. The French have stockpiled twelve hundred rounds each for their field guns and a total of eight hundred thousand rounds for their heavy artillery. Their forces outnumber the Germans' by eighteen divisions to seven divisions along the Champagne front, and by sixteen to six on the Artois front. The French artillery bombardment preparatory to launching the infantry attack begins. Summoned by Kaiser Wilhelm II, Falkenhayn leaves Belgium and travels to Pless to visit the kaiser.

22 September 1915
Sofia, Bulgaria. King Ferdinand orders the mobilization of the Bulgarian army.

23 September 1915
France. A combined squadron from the Royal Flying Corps and the Aeronautique Militaire begins five days of bombing sorties against railroad installations in an area bounded by Lille, Douai, and Valenciennes—another prelude to Joffre's autumn offensive.

25 September 1915
Russia. Hindenburg and Ludendorff receive orders from Falkenhayn to terminate their offensive. The commander in chief wishes to consolidate German positions behind their front lines before winter weather sets in along the Eastern Front. The Germans have gained no significant advantage from the September offensive.
Champagne. At 9:15 A.M., French troops go over the top along the twenty-mile Champagne front. Shortly after noon, their cohorts at the Artois front, which is also twenty miles long, join them. Visiting his armies with the kaiser, Falkenhayn reaches the Fifth Army's headquarters at midday and receives alarming reports of British gains at Loos and French gains at Souchez near the Vimy Ridge. He orders reinforcements forward and heads for OHL. Souchez culminates the French troops' gain, however, as the German defenders halt, turn, and destroy them. Elsewhere the French secure a small salient against the German Third Army at Perthes Woods after a ferocious battle, including being mistakenly bombarded by their own artillery. But the

A German machine-gun position in the trenches on the Eastern Front, opposite the Russians (Library of Congress)

greater danger for Falkenhayn occurs at Loos. Here six divisions of Haig's First Army assault a single division of the Sixth Army. Preceding the assault, the BEF releases 150 tons of chlorine gas before 7:00 A.M., but the Germans have expected the cloud and don their masks. Unfortunately for the advancing British, their artillery fire has failed to destroy German barbed wire in many places. British troops succeed in pushing the Germans back to secondary positions east of Loos, but they suffer appalling losses in the process.

26 September 1915

Champagne. The Germans have had time during the night to reinforce their lines at Loos and Hulluch, where the BEF troops must advance over open countryside into devastating machine-gun and artillery fire. The British, augmented by reinforcements from Kitchener's New Army, advance gamely, but German counterattacks open gaps in their lines. Joffre continues the attack at Vimy.

28 September 1915
Champagne. At the insistence of Joffre, the Allied offensive has continued at Champagne and Loos, with slight back-and-forth gains and losses by both sides. Foch's troops from the Tenth Army support the British right flank, and at Vimy Ridge the French briefly penetrate the German second line.

Mesopotamia. Townshend has positioned his troops at Kut after a night march on 26 September and a feint to draw off the Turks on the right bank at Es Sinn. The British march to battle in the darkness of early morning, divided into two columns. The Turkish frontline trenches quickly fall, but thirst and exhaustion force a halt in the British advance. During the afternoon and night, the Turks withdraw, managing to haul away their artillery from the right-bank positions.

29 September 1915
Mesopotamia. Townshend captures Kut. His strategy has worked. The British success costs 1,229 casualties, but they inflict 1,700 casualties on the Turks and take nearly 1,300 prisoners and 17 guns in addition to their objective.

30 September 1915
Champagne. After five days of unsuccessful attacks, Joffre calls a temporary halt at both the Champagne and Artois fronts.

5 October 1915
Sofia, Bulgaria. The Allies sever diplomatic relations.

Salonika, Greece. Although Greece remains neutral, Prime Minister Eleutherios Venizelos favors the Allies. As France and Great Britain are guaranteed by international law the right to intervene in the Balkans via Greece in the event of some upheaval in the Balkans, Venizelos has suggested to them that they send a force to Salonika with the intent of coming to Serbia's aid. The Allies had considered such a move as early as December 1914,

but now the stalemate at Gallipoli and the Russian retreat on the Eastern Front have lent urgency to the plan. The first 13,000 troops of a planned 185,000-man Anglo-French force arrive.

Athens. King Constantine, displeased with Venizelos's policy of involving Greece in the war by supporting the Allies' use of Salonika, forces the premier to resign and names A. Zaimis as his replacement.

6 October 1915
Champagne. Joffre attempts a resumption of the offensive at Champagne and persuades Sir John French to do likewise at Loos, beginning on 11 October.

7 October 1915
Serbia. Mackensen's army begins the invasion of Serbia. Mackensen sends in the Eleventh Army, commanded by Gen. Max von Gallwitz, along the Danube River to the east of Belgrade and directs the Austrian Third Army, intended to occupy Belgrade itself, to approach from the north and northwest. The Serbians confront this combined force of 180 battalions and 900 guns with 120 battalions and 330 guns. This is the army that inflicted defeat on the Austrian army in December 1914 through the strategy of Marshal Radomir Putnik, who is still in command. In addition, Mackensen's force must first cross the broad sweep of the Danube and Sava Rivers. The German troops struggle across in the morning darkness, but with great difficulty, in many cases losing their boats to Serbian fire. The Austrians reach Belgrade and encounter street fighting.

8 October 1915
Serbia. The street fighting continues in Belgrade.

9 October 1915
Serbia. The Austrians capture Belgrade, but the Serbians hold the ridges to the south of the city. The German Eleventh Army has succeeded in crossing the river at Ram and establishes bridgeheads near Semendria and Valiko Gradiste. The fighting has cost the Austrians seven thousand men and the Germans three thousand.

Loos. Viscount Richard Haldane, secretary for war in the British cabinet, visits Haig at his headquarters. The general complains bitterly of Sir John French's conduct of the battle, especially his reluctance to commit the reserve troops. Lord Haldane will convey Haig's statements to George V.

11 October 1915
Serbia. Aided by their heavy artillery, the Germans capture Semendria and Pozarevac.
London. The Dardanelles Committee asks Lord Kitchener to report on the possibility of withdrawal from Gallipoli, and he responds that abandoning the campaign "would be the most disastrous event in the history of the Empire." Nevertheless, he sends a cable to Hamilton requesting an estimate of the costs of withdrawal. Because he believes that evacuation is "unthinkable," Hamilton responds that half of his troops and all of the equipment would be lost.

12 October 1915
Brussels. German authorities have allowed Edith Cavell's colleague, Sister Wilkins, who admitted nothing, to return to the clinic; but Edith Cavell has freely confessed her deeds and faces execution. The guards come for her at 6:00 A.M. They tie her to a post alongside Philippe Baucq, an architect who had assisted her efforts to save Allied troops. Two shots end their lives.
Salonika. Gen. Maurice Sarrail arrives.

14 October 1915
London. In a meeting of the Dardanelles Committee, Lloyd George rallies the opposition to Gen. Ian Hamilton and, along with Bonar Law, threatens to resign. Kitchener must fire Hamilton. He chooses Gen. Charles Monro as Hamilton's successor. Now serving on the Western Front, Monro has never been a supporter of the Gallipoli adventure.
Serbia. Bulgaria declares war on Serbia, and the Bulgarian army joins the invasion, driving from the east toward Zajecar and Pirot. Farther south their so-called Macedonian Legion, mostly volunteers from the Bulgarian province seized by Serbia in 1913, invades Macedonia, intent on capturing the province and severing its railway links to Salonika.

15 October 1915
London. Great Britain declares war on Bulgaria.
Cetinje, Montenegro. The government declares war on Bulgaria. The Montenegran population, related to the Serbians, approaches three hundred thousand; their army numbers forty thousand.

16 October 1915
Serbia. Handicapped by poor supply conditions, with floats unable to cross the river and equipment mired in the bogs on its north bank, General von Gallwitz's troops have managed to advance only eight miles along a forty-mile-wide front. Their casualties number five thousand. The Serbs resist steadfastly.
Paris. France declares war on Bulgaria.

17 October 1915
Serbia. The Austrian assault at Belgrade has been slowed by their inability to transport their heavy guns across the Danube because their bridges cannot hold the weight. They finally take the Serbian positions south of the city at Avala.

18 October 1915
Isonzo River. Cadorna resumes the offensive along the entire front, as his armies open up with an artillery barrage.

19 October 1915
Rome. Italy declares war on Bulgaria.
Petrograd. Russia declares war on Bulgaria.

21 October 1915
Isonzo River. After three days of artillery bombardment of the Austrian lines, the Italian Second and Third Armies plunge into the attack, but once again their gains are minuscule.
Bulgaria. French troops sent from Salonika by General Sarrail engage Bulgarian troops in battle near Strumica, drive them

off, and proceed along the railway to Negotino, where they encounter the Bulgarian Second Army. The British troops, on orders from London, remain confined largely to Salonika—they are not allowed to cross the Serbian border. They are under the command of a frustrated Lt. Gen. Sir Bryan Mahon, transferred from the Gallipoli campaign.

22 October 1915

Serbia. Still impaired by poor supply conditions and running low on munitions, General von Gallwitz's advance comes to a halt. But the Bulgarians have pushed sixty miles into Macedonia, reaching Kumanova and Stip and severing Serbia's railway and other contacts with the Allies.

Belgian Congo. The British launch probably the most ambitious and flamboyant enterprise of the war in Africa, an expedition devised by African big-game hunter John R. Lee to transport a gunboat from England to Cape Town and from there to Lake Tanganyika via railway, ox-drawn trailer, and traction engines. The Admiralty approved the venture, added a second gunboat, placed Adm. Sir David Gamble in charge, and on 26 April appointed the capricious, formerly deskbound Lt. Comdr. Geoffrey B. Spicer-Simson to serve as the expedition's naval officer. He has christened his vessels *Mimi* and *Toutou.*

24 October 1915

Constantinople. Baron von Wangenheim, German ambassador to Turkey and an architect of the German-led defense of Gallipoli, dies following a stroke.

25 October 1915

Isonzo River. The Italians broaden their offensive to include the front at Gorizia (Görz), pushing hard against the Austrian Fifth Army.

27 October 1915

Champagne. King George V visits the French armies at the front after talking with Sir John French's chief of staff, William Robertson, who advises him that French must be replaced as commander in chief and recommends Haig for the post.

28 October 1915

Serbia. Mackensen's Eleventh Army has advanced to within fifteen miles of Kragujevac. The commander's plan has been to envelop the Serbians here, but his troops have been unable to roll up the Serbian flanks.

Belgian Congo. The British launch *Mimi* and *Toutou* on Lake Tanganyika.

Paris. Premier René Viviani resigns, a political victim of Joffre's failed autumn offensive and the failure to win Bulgaria's commitment to the Allies. Aristede Briand replaces him.

31 October 1915

Serbia. Putnik stages a successful retreat into Kragujevac.

Gallipoli. General Monro, who arrived at Imbros to take command of the campaign on the twenty-eighth, has toured Anzac Cove, Suvla Bay, and Cape Helles on the thirtieth, hearing discouraging accounts from all the commanders. He has also read the General Staff's report stating that to succeed at Gallipoli will require 400,000 troops in a new campaign that cannot begin until the spring and that to evacuate will cost half of the current force of 134,000 men and two-thirds of the 400 guns on the peninsula. Monro cables a message to Kitchener recommending evacuating the peninsula and estimating that the withdrawal will cost forty thousand men.

2 November 1915

Paris. As Briand has appointed Gen. Joseph Galliéni to the post of War Minister, Gen. Joseph Maunoury succeeds him as military governor of Paris.

3 November 1915

Athens. Prime Minister Zaimis resigns. S. Skuludis, a neutralist who threatens to attack the Allied force at Salonika, succeeds him.

4 November 1915

Champagne. Joffre's "great attack" at the Artois and Champagne fronts finally plays out. The Allies claim to be victorious, but it's clearly a Pyrrhic victory. At Artois they

Artillery

If a single type of weapon could be said to have transformed the conditions of war between 1914 and 1918, it was artillery. Military planners had long had evidence that modern artillery placed in sound defensive positions made offensive frontal assaults impossible—the American Civil War and the Russo-Japanese war had demonstrated this beyond any rational doubt—but somehow the lessons refused to penetrate, and planners expected to win by the offensive. Thus, both sides before the war planned for artillery to be mobile. The classic field gun was the French 75 mm, a relatively powerful cannon capable of rapid fire due to a revolutionary recoil system. The Germans developed huge guns specifically to reduce the Belgian forts during the first weeks of the war, but otherwise neither the Central Powers nor the Allies anticipated the need for large amounts of munitions and many, many large caliber guns. After the stalemate settled on the Western Front, it slowly became the practice to amass the largest possible number of heavy guns in an attempt to pound the opposing defensive trench lines into submission. The Germans developed large guns more rapidly than did the Allies, and they produced munitions to supply the guns more efficiently. The British suffered from scandalous shortages of shells and from severe mismanagement. By mid-war, artillery bombardments of gigantic proportions were used as the preliminary to a foot assault by infantry. For example, the British fired twenty-one thousand tons of shells over a seven-day period as the prelude to the first day's battle on the Somme in June 1916. They discharged nearly a million and a half shells, hitting a relatively small area of German defenses with the average of thirty shells for every thousand square yards. (Modern French and Belgian demolition teams in the 1990s still unearthed tons of unexploded World War I shells annually.) Such massive bombardments usually failed to destroy the defenders or even the barbed wire approaches, but they did create a completely devastated landscape that became symbolic of the war in the West. Late in the war, the Germans demonstrated their technical acumen by developing the specialized ultra-long range "Big Bertha" which they used to shell Paris from a distance of seventy-five miles, although they accomplished little serious harm. Artillery proved to be much less of a factor in creating successful offensives than it was in stifling all serious attempts to break the opposing line. By the end of the war, as many as one-fourth of all the men on active duty were artillerymen, and nearly six out of ten casualties were caused by artillery fire.

A French artilleryman, circa 1918 (by Reni-Mel, courtesy of the Anne S.K. Brown Military Collection, Brown University Library)

have suffered 47,000 casualties; at Champagne, 144,000. The German casualties number eighty-five thousand. The Allies have learned a great deal about conducting trench warfare, but a major part of that lesson is that the Germans can beat them at it.

Isonzo River. The Third Battle of the Isonzo ends, with the Austrians still holding their positions. The offensive has cost the Italians sixty-seven thousand losses, including nearly eleven thousand dead; the Austro-Hungarian losses total forty-two thousand.

London. General Monro has an opponent in Adm. Sir Roger Keyes, who arrived in London from Gallipoli at the same time Monro arrived at Imbros and staunchly supports the campaign in discussions at the Admiralty, persuading First Sea Lord Henry Jackson. He meets with Lord Kitchener and effectively advocates his plan for a new naval attack involving sending ships into the Sea of Marmara. On the other side, the coalition government favors giving up the Gallipoli campaign in order to send more troops to Salonika, and Joffre, of course, emphasizes the Western Front, demanding the influx of 150,000 new British troops. A perplexed Kitchener, who wants to pursue the Gallipoli venture, stalls and dissembles.

5 November 1915
Serbia. Bulgarian troops capture Niš.

Cameroons. After two days of fierce defense, bombarding the slowly climbing attack force sent by Lt. Col. Frederick Cunliffe, the German defenders of the mountaintop bastion of Banyo surrender.

6 November 1915
Serbia. Mackensen's troops take Krusvac.

7 November 1915
Serbia. In taking Aleksinac, the Germans also capture a major part of the Serbian army's artillery. Giving up the fight, many of the Serbian troops return to their farms, but the army as a whole manages to retreat toward the "Field of Blackbirds" and Pristina, heading for the mountains of Albania. Mackensen and the German high command regard the campaign as a suc-

cess. Not wanting to aggravate Greece by pursuing the campaign, Falkenhayn decides to redeploy five of the Eleventh Army's divisions to the Western Front, a move Conrad von Hötzendorf vigorously protests. He also dislikes the idea that the Bulgarians, gratified with their acquisition of Macedonia, may absorb still more territory. The resulting discord among the three allies leads Falkenhayn to allow two of the divisions he had planned to remove to remain at the Serbian front.

10 November 1915
Isonzo River. After reinforcing his troops and adopting advice from the French about artillery tactics, Cadorna resumes the battle on an abbreviated front extending between Plava and Doberdo.

11 November 1915
Mesopotamia. Having received clearance from London, Townshend begins the advance to Baghdad, occupying Zor. His force comprises 13,700 men and 29 guns, but he is well extended from his supply base at Basra, over 300 miles distant.

London. The War Council (formerly the Dardanelles Committee) reforms with five members: Asquith, Bonar Law, Balfour, Lloyd George, and Reginald McKenna, Chancellor of the Exchequer. Churchill resigns from the cabinet.

14 November 1915
Gallipoli. Lord Kitchener arrives at Mudros to visit the beachheads and make a personal assessment of the campaign.

17 November 1915
Salonika. Kitchener visits General Sarrail.
Gallipoli. Fierce storms churn waves that smash the piers at Cape Helles and Anzac Cove.
Isonzo River. After dropping warning leaflets from airplanes over Gorizia (Görz), the Italians begin an artillery bombardment of the city, intending to raze it totally.

18 November 1915
Flanders. Winston Churchill joins the Grenadier Guards unit at the front as a major in the BEF.

19 November 1915
Serbia. After ten days of retreating, Putnik begins concentrating his troops near Pristina for the purpose of securing access to the plateau at Gnjilane known as the "Field of Blackbirds" so that some of his troops can move through the Karadag Pass and on to Skopje to link up with Sarrail's Armee d'Orient out of Salonika. The Battle of the "Field of Blackbirds" begins.
Mesopotamia. Townshend's force reaches Zor, where HMS *Firefly*, the first of a group of new river gunboats expressly designed for operations in Mesopotamia, joins the flotilla.

20 November 1915
Salonika. Concerned that his force may be overextended along the Crna River, General de Lardemelle, without Sarrail's approval, orders a retreat.
Mesopotamia. Townshend reaches Lajj.

21 November 1915
Serbia. Putnik issues orders for the retreat into Albania. French troops withdraw south of the Crna River, heading for Salonika.

22 November 1915
Mesopotamia. In the early morning mists, Townshend's troops, divided into four columns, advance to attack the Turkish entrenchments at Ctesiphon. The high riverbanks minimize the effects of supportive firing from the flotilla. And since the Turks shot down the reconnaissance plane Townshend had sent out the day before, he does not know that the enemy's lines have been reinforced. Thinking the Turks are retreating, Townshend violates his own plan to hold off a major attack until some mounds marking the Turk's front line have been taken. He had wanted all four of his columns to converge for the attack but sends two of them ahead. The British manage to take the Turkish frontlines, but they can advance no farther and have paid a heavy price of four thousand casualties to get this far. Townshend's campaign begins to unravel as the night progresses.
Gallipoli. Kitchener sends an equivocating message to London, recommending that the troops be evacuated from Suvla Bay and Anzac Cove but that Cape Helles be held. Gen. Sir William Birdwood will be in charge of the evacuation, while General Monro remains at Lemnos as commander in chief of the Eastern Mediterranean forces—that is, at Gallipoli and Salonika.

23 November 1915
Serbia. The Germans triumph at Pristina and Mitrovica against Putnik's troops and claim seventeen thousand prisoners. The Bulgarians have won at the "Field of Blackbirds," closing this escape route. The Serbians' long retreat over the mountains and into Albania begins. Two hundred thousand troops and refugees hope to escape Mackensen's pursuing army.

24 November 1915
Gallipoli. Kitchener sails for England.

25 November 1915
Gallipoli. Admiral de Robeck sails for England on sick leave. Adm. Sir Rosslyn Wemyss takes his place.
Mesopotamia. After two days of futile efforts to dislodge the Turks at Ctesiphon, Townshend concedes failure and orders a withdrawal to Lajj. His total casualties number nearly forty-six hundred; the Turks, nearly sixty-two hundred. But the Turks have achieved a "strategic defeat with far-reaching results." Nixon has overreached in his desire to capture Baghdad, only twenty miles distant from Ctesiphon yet now beyond all hope. Urged on by his second in command, Kalil Bey, the Turkish commander, General Nur-ud-Din, decides to push the advantage and pursue the retiring British force.

30 November 1915
Gallipoli. After a murderous thunderstorm with hurricane-force winds on 27 November, followed by two days of plummeting temperatures, snow, and sleet, the Allied commanders assess the damage—two hundred men drowned, five thousand suffering from frostbite, another five thousand casualties to other maladies.

3 December 1915
Mesopotamia. Plagued by problems with

the flotilla, Townshend's retreating force finally reaches Kut.

6 December 1915
Chantilly, France. The Allied War Conference, moved here from Calais, where Asquith advocated withdrawing the Anglo-French force of 150,000 from Salonika, concludes that the Salonika front should remain active. The commanders and government officials also agree that there should be a coordinated offensive in the summer of 1916 on the Anglo-French front, the Russian front, and the Italian front—all the other fronts being of only secondary import.

7 December 1915
Albania. Gen. Radomir Putnik, along with the Russian ambassador to Serbia, King Peter, and some staff officers, arrives at Skadar (Scutari) following a strenuous transmountain flight. Putnik, for a while near death and litterbound, resigns his command, citing his ill health.
Serbia. The Austrian Third Army, pursuing the retreating Serbian army, captures Pec.
Mesopotamia. The Turks have surrounded Kut and begin a siege of the town. Townshend has ten thousand men (two thousand are ill or wounded) and thirty-five hundred noncombatant Indians under his command. The Arab inhabitants number about seven thousand.

8 December 1915
Gallipoli. Preliminary stages of the evacuation of Suvla Bay and Anzac Cove begin. Everything must be done at night with utmost secrecy in order to successfully remove the eighty thousand men, five thousand animals (horses and mules), two thousand vehicles, and two hundred guns. The commanders estimate that before its completion the evacuation may result in twenty-five thousand casualties. First to be removed are the sick and wounded and the prisoners and then, slowly over time, the infantrymen.

11 December 1915
Egypt. Diplomacy and bribery have failed to woo the Senussi tribesmen from siding with the Turks, who have plied them with gold, machine guns, and other gifts brought to the Libyan coast in German submarines. The Grand Senussi, Sayed Ahmed, placed Nuri Bey, half brother of Enver Pasha, in charge of his troops. They have captured 120 miles of British territory along the Egyptian coast during November, forcing Lt. Gen. Sir John Maxwell, British commander in charge in Egypt, to form the Western Frontier Force, comprised of territorial battalions, at Marsa Matruh. They attack a Senussi encampment at Wadi Senab, south of Matruh, and drive them off, killing eighty while suffering sixteen dead.

15 December 1915
Albania. Most of the retreating Serbian army units have reached refuge in Skadar and other Albanian towns, though some have remained in the mountains to form resistance groups and a few have linked with Sarrail's army. Although their pursuers have now called a halt to their advance, Serbian losses tell a woeful story. They have suffered 94,000 casualties, 120,000 men lost to the Germans and Austrians as prisoners, and 50,000 to the Bulgarians—well over half of the Serbian army. The Serbian troops feel betrayed by the Allies.
Flanders. Sir John French, apprised on 4 December that he must resign, now does so. General Haig takes his place.

19 December 1915
Gallipoli. Through a variety of ruses, such

Field Marshall Sir Douglas Haig (Library of Congress)

as rigging rifles in the front trenches to fire on their own, firing artillery at intervals, rebuilding defenses, and leaving empty tents standing, the British have successfully completed the preliminary evacuation of Suvla and Anzac Cove, silently removing half of the eighty thousand troops to the ships in small boats during the dark hours. Now the final evacuation occurs. During the night, the small boats return again and again to carry off twenty thousand of the remaining troops.

Flanders. The Germans use phosgene gas for the first time in a battle north of Ypres, killing 120 British soldiers but instigating no panic and gaining no advantage, even though phosgene is ten times as toxic as chlorine.

20 December 1915

Gallipoli. During the early morning darkness, the last of the twenty thousand troops to leave Anzac Cove and Suvla ferry out to the ships. The British have mined the dumps of ammunition and supplies left behind on shore, and as the last of the small boats carry the troops to safety, the mines go off, detonating huge explosions and fires. The Turks open fire, but they are too late. The British ruses and stealthy tactics succeed—the evacuation of Suvla and Anzac Cove concludes without the loss of a single life.

Potsdam. General Falkenhayn proposes to an enthusiastic Kaiser Wilhelm II that in the coming year the Germans concentrate on a battle of attrition at Verdun, with the objective of compelling the French commanders "to throw in every man they have. If they do so, the forces of France will bleed to death—as there can be no question of a voluntary withdrawal—whether we reach our goal or not. If they do not do so, and we reach our objectives, the moral effect on France will be enormous." He labels this policy "*Gericht*"; in effect, a judgment imposing punishment. While returning by train to GHQ at Mézières, Falkenhayn outlines the offensive for General Schmidt von Knobelsdorf, chief of staff of the Fifth Army, to relay to Crown Prince Wilhelm, the Fifth Army commander at Verdun. The Crown Prince is "disquieted" by what he hears.

21 December 1915

London. Gen. Sir William Robertson becomes chief of the Imperial General Staff following Gen. Sir Archibald Murray's resignation. Robertson concurs with General Haig that all British forces should be concentrated on the Western Front for a war of attrition.

22 December 1915

Egypt. Gen. Sir Archibald Murray replaces Lt. Gen. Sir John Maxwell as commander of British troops in Egypt.

23 December 1915

Lake Tanganyika. Now out of hiding, *Mimi* joins *Toutou* for test runs on the lake.

25 December 1915

Egypt. The Western Frontier Force moves out of Matruh once again, traverses the Kedival Road westward, and engages the Senussi in a major skirmish at Wadi Medwa. The British kill three hundred Senussi; their own losses number thirteen dead and fifty-one wounded.

27 December 1915

London. After more days of temporizing, the cabinet decides that the troops remaining on Cape Helles at Gallipoli should also be evacuated. De Robeck will return to Gallipoli, while Monro is assigned command of the First Army in France (Haig's former command), and Admiral Wemyss goes to the East Indies.

Bukovina. General Ivanov launches an offensive against the Austrian Seventh Army on a front that extends ninety miles between the Prut River and the Dneister River.

30 December 1915

Salonika. A base with two hundred thousand civilians of varied nationalities, numerous spies, and a daily train that transports diplomatic mail, Salonika generated problems for Sarrail. To alleviate the problems, the commander arrests staff members of the consulates of the four Central Powers and expels them from Greece, effectively assuming dictatorial control of Salonika despite protests by Premier Zaimis's government in Athens.

Both fronts in Europe continue to be vast killing grounds during the year. Literally millions of casualties result from a series of huge, prolonged offensives, launched by both the Central Powers and the Allies. The so-called "battles" last for month after month until all available men have been consumed, but almost no advantage is gained anywhere by either side of the conflict.

On the Western Front, the German high command decides early in the year on a campaign of massive attrition that will bleed the French army to death. The weakly held fortresses at Verdun are attacked in late February by overwhelming numbers of German troops and with incredible artillery bombardments. The French have withdrawn much of the fortress line's armament and men, but cannot now face the loss of the important symbols, so they throw everything they can into a belated defense. The Germans score many initial successes, taking several of the forts from the brave but overpowered French defenders. The aggressors, however, cannot quite completely break the line, despite fierce fighting into April. A shuffle of French command puts the resolute Pétain in charge, and he organizes a line of supply and defense to save Verdun. Huge casualty lists begin to pile up—one hundred thousand on each side by April, perhaps a quarter million each by July—and exhaustion begins to set in. The back-and-forth offensives are halted by the end of the year, after nearly eleven months of fighting. Both German and French armies are nearly destroyed by the effort.

On the final day of May, the two great surface fleets meet off Jutland in the only large naval engagement of the war. The Germans sink more tonnage than their opponents, but turn and flee back to the safety of port, leaving the British still in control of the North Sea and the approaches to the Continent.

In July, the British launch a major attack along the Somme River as a way to take pressure off the French at Verdun. The initial assault is one of the greatest disasters in British military history, with nearly sixty thousand casualties the first day, many from deadly machine gunnery. Despite the carnage and lack of advance, the British keep attacking until November, losing over a million casualties before calling an end. The British government falls as a result of the debacle.

Russia's position worsens early in the year as the defeats on the Eastern Front sap economic energy and manpower while government corruption and incompetence at home negate the sacrifices of the army. Her fortunes in the field are revived in the summer by a great offensive by Brusilov—he smashes through and advances at a breakneck pace. However, the Russian supply and transportation systems are totally inadequate to sustain the advance, and it grinds to a halt and is slowly reversed. By August, the offensive is back where it began at the cost of a total of a million and a quarter casualties.

Early in the year, the Austrians mount an offensive campaign against the Italians in the Trentino, but progress is slight and the offensive must be weakened to turn and counter Brusilov to the east. In August, the Italians begin a long series of brutal but unrewarding offensives along the line of the Isonzo River.

The Romanians enter the war on the side of the Allies but are smashed by a mixed army of the Central Powers. An Allied army operating from Salonika takes control of Greece and makes a campaign against Bulgaria.

In Mesopotamia, the British try futilely to succor the surrounded army at Kut, losing twice as many casualties as the numbers they seek to rescue, and the besieged army is forced to surrender in April.

1 January 1916

Cameroons. British troops, the Fourth Nigerians, capture Yaounda and free the British and French prisoners held there. Governor Ebermaier has already fled the day before, heading for Rio Muni, a neutral Spanish colony.

2 January 1916
Gallipoli. With General Monro having sailed for Egypt on New Year's Day, the British now end their submarine campaign, recalling *E-2*.

4 January 1916
Mesopotamia. General Nixon has placed Lt. Gen. F.J. Aylmer in charge of an advance up the Tigris River to relieve the besieged Townshend at Kut. The initial advance, with Aylmer sending sixteen infantry battalions and seventeen squadrons of cavalry along with forty-two guns and four gunboats under the command of Gen. Sir G. Younghusband, sets out from Ali al Gharbi toward Sheikh Saad, held by an estimated ten thousand Turkish troops.

6 January 1916
Mesopotamia. After an early morning mist that might have concealed their advance burns off, Younghusband's troops attack the Turkish positions on both banks of the Tigris several miles out from Sheikh Saad but with no success. Receiving reports from Younghusband in the evening, Aylmer orders him not to renew the attack the next morning as planned but to wait until Aylmer sends further orders.

7 January 1916
Gallipoli. The British ruses used at Anzac Cove and Suvla Cove have worked once again at Cape Helles, as the bewildered Turks have hesitated to act. The French troops have been evacuated first, followed by nightly streams of British troops. With the remaining garrison now down to nineteen thousand men, Liman von Sanders at last sends his troops to the attack in the early afternoon, opening up with a four-and-a-half-hour artillery bombardment. But the Turks have to cross at least one hundred yards before reaching the British trenches, and British fire is so deadly that the Turkish soldiers end their advance, refusing to carry out their officers' orders.
Mesopotamia. Under Aylmer's orders,

Younghusband's troops begin a full frontal attack shortly before noon. British troops fight off a menacing Turkish cavalry flanking effort and, elsewhere on the line, manage to capture the Turk's forward positions but at a cost of four thousand casualties.

8 January 1916
Gallipoli. The British mine their stores of ammunition and supplies, anticipating the final evacuation of Cape Helles during the night, but heavy winds collapse the pier twice, causing unnerving delays.
Montenegro. The war comes home for this little Balkan state of 250,000 people ruled by King Nikita. It had joined Serbia in declaring war on Austria-Hungary in August 1914. In the first months of the war, Montenegro's forty-five-thousand-man army had captured a few sites on the Adriatic Sea and had invaded Bosnia, but an Austrian counterattack on 14 October 1914 had forced their withdrawal, followed by inactivity through 1915. But with the success of the combined Austrian-German invasion of Serbia, the Austrians have poised a fifty-thousand-man army at Mount Lovcen in preparation for an attack on Cattaro, the Adriatic port the mountain guards. At dawn, five hundred Austrian artillery, backed by the guns of an Austrian naval squadron at the entrance to the Bay of Cattaro, begin a barrage of the Montenegrin defenses. The Austrians' initial goal is the fort at Kouk, over three thousand feet up on the side of Mount Lovcen.
Cameroons. Troops led by Lt. Col. Austin H.W. Haywood engage the fleeing German rear guard in battle at the Nyong River, but the Germans hold, buying enough time for 832 German troops and 6,000 askaris to reach safety in Rio Muni, from which the Germans will be sent to Spain for internment until the war ends. The Allies now control all of the Cameroons except Mora.

9 January 1916
Gallipoli. By 3:00 A.M., all but two hundred men have been evacuated. Commanded by General Maude, they make their way to Gully Beach on the west coast, where they discover the lighter sent to pick

Austrian field artillery on the Eastern front during 1916 (courtesy of the Anne S.K. Brown Military Collection, Brown University Library)

them up has run aground. They hasten to "W" Beach, two miles distant at the tip of the peninsula, but en route General Maude discovers that he has left his valise behind at Gully. He refuses to leave without it, and he and another officer head back. The troops arrive at "W" Beach, where they find the last remaining barge to carry them to the ships, and they wait for Maude. Just as the commander of the barge announces that he can wait no longer, Maude and his companion appear. Ten minutes after they push off, just before 4:00 A.M., the munitions and supply dumps explode, and the Turks follow up with a heavy shelling of the Cape Helles beaches. The British have miraculously escaped once more—over 35,000 troops and over 3,600 horses and mules, 127 guns, and 328 vehicles have been evacuated without a single casualty. But the escape is their only success. During the 259 days of the Gallipoli campaign, the British and French have suffered 252,000 casualties by official count, 47,000 of them French. The Turkish official estimate is 251,000 casualties. For both sides the total is staggering, but the Turks at least have the consolation of victory.

Galicia. General Ivanov's offensive along the Dniester River comes to an end, with only minuscule gains to show for his fifty thousand losses (including six thousand taken prisoner).

Mesopotamia. British cavalry patrols in the early morning discover that the Turks are withdrawing from their positions at Sheikh Saad. In the afternoon, Younghusband occupies the village. This small gain has cost him four thousand casualties. The Turks have lost the same number and have had 650 taken prisoner besides, but the major part of their force escapes intact and regroups along the Wadi River after their new commander, Kahlil Pasha, learns that the British have paused, exhausted.

10 January 1916
Montenegro. After two days of experiencing shelling and having bombs dropped from airplanes, demoralized Montenegrin troops abandon the fort at Kouk and retreat to Cetinje.

Russia. A Turkish offensive launched a year earlier against the Russians in the Caucasus—devised by Enver Pasha in defiance of Liman von Sanders's advice—

Despite the advent of the internal combustion engine, mule-drawn wagons remained one of the prevalent forms of transportation during the war (by F. Journey, courtesy of the Anne S.K. Brown Military Collection, Brown University Library)

has stalled. Concerned that the British evacuation of Gallipoli will free more Turkish troops for a renewal of the offensive, Gen. Nicolai Yudenich has persuaded Grand Duke Nicholas, viceroy and commander in chief in the Caucasus since his fall from grace at court, that now is the time to strike decisively against Enver Pasha's Third Army. He initiates the battle at Koprukoy to the surprise of the Turks, who have expected a lull in hostilities during the harsh winter. The Turks have sixty-five thousand men and one hundred guns at Koprukoy—the major part of their seventy-eight-thousand-man force is positioned on a line from Lake Van to the Russian border—to protect the routes to Erzerum, a major northern bastion. Yudenich opposes them with 130,000 infantry and 35,000 cavalry.

11 January 1916
Montenegro. The Austrians capture Cetinje. Remaining units of the Monte-negrin army concentrate near Pec.

Mexico. Whereas the Wilson administration had previously supported Francisco "Pancho" Villa's faction in the Constitutionalists' civil war in Mexico, Robert Lansing had instigated an about-face in the fall of 1915 out of concern over the machinations of the Germans, who he believes are trying to maneuver the United States into war with Mexico. Prodded by Lansing, Wilson had joined the leaders of six Latin American nations in October in recognizing the Constitutionalist government of Venustiano Carranza, Villa's former ally and current adversary. The policy angers Chief of Staff Gen. Hugh L. Scott, leader of the Villa supporters in Washington. Villa, of course, is also unhappy, and even though once again recognized by Carranza, begins a campaign to discredit the Mexican president, provoke American intervention, and regain power. At Santa Ysabel the Villistas stop a Mexico Northwestern train and seize seventeen Americans on board, forcing them off the train and shooting sixteen of them beside the tracks. Outraged by the massacre, members of the United States Congress call for sending troops to Mexico.

13 January 1916
Mesopotamia. Aylmer has planned for Younghusband's troops to encircle the Turkish positions at the Wadi River, but the effort fails. During the night, the Turks steal away to dig in again at the Hanna defile, three and a half miles distant. Another small advance costs the British sixteen hundred casualties.

15 January 1916
Washington. The Wilson administration and its supporters in Congress manage to block passage of a Congressional resolution authorizing the president to use force in Mexico in response to Villa's provocations, but the Senate does approve a resolution asking Secretary of State Lansing to report on how many Americans have been killed in Mexico since the beginning of the revolution there in February 1913.

17 January 1916
Montenegro. King Nikita has fled to Scutari and from there sailed to Brindisi. After three days of intense fighting at Mojkovac, the Montenegrin commander in chief, Gen. Radomir Vesovic, has sent his troops home. He now capitulates.
Russia. After a week of fighting in blizzards, General Yudenich's army captures Koprukoy, inflicting twenty-five thousand casualties and sending the remnants of the Turkish Third Army into retreat to Erzerum.

19 January 1916
Mesopotamia. Lt. Gen. Sir Percy Lake succeeds Nixon as commander in chief while General Aylmer has his men prepare for an advance against the Turks at the Hanna defile. The weather is a handicap, however, with heavy rains, flooding, and high winds resulting in the loss of his pontoon bridge, so his men can no longer maneuver back and forth across the river to secure potential advantages.

21 January 1916
Albania. Austrian troops, following after the Serbs, enter Scutari. But the surviving Serbian army has been moved down the coast to Durazzo and Valona and evacuated to Corfu, there to be reequipped by the Allies for future deployment at Salonika.
Mesopotamia. Aylmer has moved his front line to within five hundred yards of the Turkish trenches at the Hanna defile; but a bombardment on the previous day, including enfilading fire from the right bank of the Tigris, has proven ineffective, and the preliminary bombardment for today's frontal attack fares similarly. Aylmer's Black Watch battalion, attacking in heavy mud, reaches the Turkish forward position, but most of the battalion falls before the Turks' firing, and the survivors must retreat. Despite such grievous losses, Aylmer sends waves of men into the attack, until Younghusband accepts reality and orders a withdrawal. Of Aylmer's total force of 7,600 infantrymen, 2,741 are casualties, many of them left out in overnight torrential rains because they cannot be rescued.

23 January 1916
Egypt. A reconnaissance plane has spotted an encampment of six thousand Senussi, including the Grand Senussi, at Halazin, twenty-two miles southwest of Matruh. The Western Frontier Force, aided by artillery, attacks and defeats the Senussi in a pitched battle that costs the British 312 casualties, including 21 dead. The Senussi suffer seven hundred casualties, including two hundred dead. Following the skirmish, the British return to Matruh.

24 January 1916
North Sea. Vice Adm. Reinhard Scheer replaces Adm. Hugo von Pohl, stricken with cancer, as commander in chief of the High Seas Fleet. Scheer advocates bolder, though not audacious, operations by the fleet, and Kaiser Wilhelm II awards him greater freedom to act than his two predecessors enjoyed. Room 40's intelligence reports this information to the British Admiralty, where hopes rise that a major battle between the High Seas Fleet and the Grand Fleet may result.
Mesopotamia. General Lake sails to

Aylmer's headquarters at the Wadi River to evaluate the situation. He has learned from Townshend that the Kut garrison has enough supplies to hold out for eighty-four days—far longer than previously surmised—although Townshend proposes the possibility of breaking out of the siege, a possibility Lake does not preclude while still hoping to succeed in rescuing him.

27 January 1916
Berlin. Discontent arising from food shortages and other privations and from disillusionment over the government's failure to grant democratic reforms sunders the uneasy patriotic political truce known as the *Burgfrieden,* as revolutionaries form the Spartacus League, led by Rosa Luxemburg and Karl Liebknecht.

29 January 1916
Mesopotamia. After several days at the front, General Lake is less sanguine about prospects for relieving Kut. He has fourteen thousand troops and forty-six guns at hand, with another eleven thousand troops and twenty-eight guns in reserve as reinforcements if they reach the front. The Turks have ten thousand men on the right bank of the Tigris River and reserves in Shumran and elsewhere. They are well entrenched, and word has come from Constantinople that on 20 January thirty-six thousand troops left Gallipoli bound for Mesopotamia. Lake decides to pursue the campaign, bolstering Aylmer by appointing the able Maj. Gen. Sir George Gorringe as his chief of staff.
Paris. The Germans make a second and final Zeppelin bomb attack on the capital city, resulting in eighteen deaths and thirty-one people injured.

31 January 1916
England. Nine Zeppelins raid the English Midlands, their bombs inflicting 138 casualties but only minor destruction, as mists and fog obscure industrial targets, including Liverpool.

1 February 1916
Verdun. Major General Beeg, general officer commanding the artillery for the Fifth

Individual foxholes dug and manned by French infantry near Verdun, 1916 (by A. Barrere, courtesy of the Anne S.K. Brown Military Collection, Brown University Library)

Army, reports to Falkenhayn that he has 1,220 guns in position for the Verdun offensive, concentrated on an 8-mile front and scheduled to begin on 12 February. The guns vary in caliber from the thirteen 420 mm "Big Berthas," or "Gamma Guns," made by Krupp, to 77 mm field guns. To feed this array of weapons, the Germans have stockpiled 2.5 million shells, enough to last six days. Moving the shells to the Verdun front has required thirteen hundred trains. The German arsenal also includes flamethrowers. Remarkably, assembling this massive firepower and 140,000 troops for the assault has been achieved with utmost secrecy, including the construction of concrete underground bunkers along the entire front from which the troops will emerge.
Petrograd. Boris Sturmer, a tool of Rasputin, becomes prime minister, replacing Ivan Goremykin. By now Russia confronts catastrophe—25 percent of the working-age population is dead, captured, or in the army, and diminished 1915 harvests and food shortages have generated the worst black market and profiteering conditions ever. Food prices increase by an average of 114 percent, over twice the inflation rates in Great Britain and France. Crisis overtakes the entire economy.

2 February 1916
North Sea. The Zeppelin *L-19,* returning from the bombing of the English Midlands, is fired at by the Dutch and buffeted by winds. It loses its way and crashes 110 miles out from Flamborough Head. A

trawler out of Grimsby comes upon the downed aircraft in the water, but after talking with the Germans, the fishermen sail off, leaving the airmen to perish in the icy waters of the North Sea.

England. At Hatfield Park the team that has worked since the previous August on developing the prototype "tank"—so called for security purposes—demonstrate their creations for Kitchener, Lloyd George, and other officials, following a rehearsal demonstration for themselves on 29 January. Kitchener tells the team of designers that "the war would never be won by such machines."

6 February 1916

Cape Town, South Africa. Jan Smuts accepts command of an augmented British force, including the King's African Rifles, assigned to conquer German East Africa. Gen. Sir Horace Smith-Dorrien had been appointed to the post, but en route to Cape Town in late December, he fell ill with pneumonia and had to resign.

9 February 1916

Vienna. Angrily defying Gen. Erich von Falkenhayn, who for more than two months has strongly opposed a major new offensive against Italy as impractical, the Austrian commander Field Marshal Franz Conrad von Hötzendorf issues orders for the offensive to Archduke Eugen, commander of Austrian forces on the Southwestern Front. The offensive, he has argued in a letter to Falkenhayn on 18 December, is a "necessary prelude to the final and decisive victory. This victory must be gained in 1916; many reasons make success not merely necessary, but imperative for the survival of the Austro-Hungarian Empire." The secretive Falkenhayn, contemptuous of his ally and certainly undiplomatic, has told Conrad von Hötzendorf nothing about the scale and strategy of his own major offensive scheduled for Verdun. Conrad has assembled two armies composed of fourteen divisions for his planned Trentino offensive. The new Eleventh Army, created mostly from troops withdrawn from the Isonzo River front and commanded by Gen. Viktor Dankl, will execute the main attack. The Third Army, commanded by Gen. Hermann Kovess von Kovesshaza, will serve as a backup force. The Eleventh Army has 811 guns; the Third Army, 245. These forces begin to assemble in the Lessini Alps, most difficult terrain, where the Italian front is protected by a series of sturdily built fortresses.

Durazzo, Italy. The last of the Serbian troops are evacuated to Corfu.

Lake Tanganyika. The patched-up *Kingani* has been added to Spicer-Simon's force (rechristened as *Fifi*), and the Belgians have added three boats to expand the Allied fleet to six vessels. In the early morning, the *Hedwig von Wissmann* steams into view, and Spicer-Simson, aboard *Fifi,* accompanied by two other vessels, attacks. As he fires the last of his ammunition, one of his shells rips through the German boat's hull, detonating in the engine room and sending her to the bottom. The British rescue the survivors.

11 February 1916

Turkey. Having captured and fortified the Kargabazar Dag Ridge, which he sees as the key to advancing against the forts at Erzerum, Yudenich now begins the offensive, sending his men down the ridge to attack the forts.

12 February 1916

Western Front. The Germans stage diversionary attacks at the Champagne and Flanders sectors.

14 February 1916

Chantilly. Haig and Joffre meet to discuss tactics for the 1916 offensive. They agree on a plan that includes secondary attacks in late June to involve German reserve forces followed by a major offensive at the beginning of July on both sides of the Somme River. The French will field forty divisions for the offensive; the British, twenty.

15 February 1916

Turkey. Although some of his men have frozen to death during their descent from the Kargabazar Dag Ridge, Yudenich's army captures Erzerum.

Tanks

The tank was one of the few genuinely new modern weapons developed during the war—planes, machine guns, and submarines had been known before, but not the tank. The British invented the tank as a way to break the power of the defensive trench and restore the longed-for mobility in battle. Using secret navy funds provided by Winston Churchill, a British experimental unit modified the design of commercial tractors, fitting out a rectangular armored box with caterpillar tracks that the makers hoped would rumble across no-man's-land and climb over and through the trenches. The first models came in two versions, a "male" tank with two light naval cannon and four machine guns, and a "female" type with six machine guns. The first tanks' top speed across flat, firm terrain was about three and a half miles an hour (the slow speed made it possible to fire the guns with reasonable accuracy while underway), and with an experienced crew, the machines proved adept at crossing barbed wire and climbing right into the enemy's trenches. It was hard going for the tank crews, however. The crew compartment was nothing more than a large metal box, with the gasoline engine mounted inside to the forward and a gearbox and gas tank to the rear. The engine produced deafening noise, choking fumes, and intense heat. The guns were mounted in projecting sponsons on each side of the main compartment and filled the tank with smoke and shell casings when fired. The tanks were manned by a crew of eight: a commander and driver who both sat in the front of the crew compartment ahead of the engine, four gunners (two to a side), and two gearsmen, who sat to the rear and manually changed gears in response to hand signals from the driver. When grinding along under combat conditions, the tank was hell on wheels for its crew. However, it was even more fearsome for the Germans. When the first tanks appeared on the Somme in the fall of 1916, the Germans were completely helpless and were saved only by the mechanical fragility of the British weapons, most of which self-destructed before really entering the battle. A year later, the British had produced significant numbers of improved models and had developed sound tactics that combined tanks with infantry. At the Battle of Cambrai in November 1917, the British swept aside German resistance and penetrated five or six miles through the German lines. As was almost always the case during World War I, however, the logistical system was incapable of following up the breakthrough, and all the ground won with relative ease by the tankers was subsequently lost to German counterattacks. The inference was nonetheless clear: the tank bode well to return warfare to an affair of rapid maneuver. The Germans were very slow to react to the threat of the new weapon and produced almost no tanks of their own during the remainder of the war. In fact, the most effective German tank assaults were those using captured British machines. The French developed a couple of working models, and the Americans took over machines from their allies. The tank failed to turn the tide of the war, despite its proven effectiveness in the short run.

While the tank did not quite achieve the breakthrough hoped for by its British inventors, the clanking monsters did demonstrate in several battles the immense wartime potential of mobile armored vehicles (Library of Congress)

17 February 1916
Turkey. Yudenich's army captures Ilica, routing the Turks. The Russians have taken 12,000 prisoners and 327 guns, while suffering 10,000 casualties. Turkish losses exceed 15,000.

18 February 1916
Cameroons. After a long and successful defense of the fort at Mora, the German commander, accepting the hopelessness of his position and generous British terms, surrenders the Germans' last bastion. The entire Cameroons fall to the control of the British and French. The cost to the British is a total of 4,600 casualties, including 1,668 dead, mostly from disease. The French dead number 2,567, again mostly victims of disease.
Lake Tanganyika. Spicer-Simson leaves Lukuga, ostensibly to search for other vessels on the Congo River that might be added to the fleet. He leaves Lt. A.E. Wainwright in charge, ordering him not to attack the *Graf von Götzen* unless Lukuga is attacked.

19 February 1916
British East Africa. Jan Smuts arrives in Mombasa to take command, a week after a humiliating defeat suffered by Gen. Wilfrid Malleson's South African troops at Salaita, where a bayonet charge by Maj. Georg Kraut's askaris sent them into flight.

21 February 1916
Verdun. The offensive at Verdun, postponed by Crown Prince Wilhelm during a raging blizzard followed by rain and fog, finally begins. The delay has worked to the French defenders' advantage, as two divisions have arrived to augment the four divisions of Gen. A.P.A. Chretien's XXXth Corps, although their capability remains well below the prowess the Germans have amassed. In fact, Joffre, convinced that, if the Germans do attack, their offensive will center at either Champagne or Artois, has persistently rejected pleas for bolstering the defenses at Verdun and has even had guns removed from the forts there for use elsewhere. The forts alone, however, present the Crown Prince's Fifth Army with a for-midable obstacle. The troops must capture or neutralize four outer forts—Douaumont, Vaux, Tavannes, and Noulainville—then conquer Fort Souville and push on to take another chain of three forts—Belleville, Saint Michel, and Belrupt—before they reach Verdun itself. Douaumont is the farthest forward, largest, and strongest of these forts. Its inner walls and ceiling are built of eight feet of concrete alternating with sand, and earth several feet thick covers the ceiling concrete. Douaumont commands a height of twelve hundred feet overlooking the northeastern approaches to Verdun, and its turret guns have been left intact, unlike Vaux, which has been stripped of all its guns. At dawn, the German artillery begins a nearly continuous nine-hour bombardment that destroys the outer French trenches. The roar of the cannons can be heard a hundred miles away by soldiers on the Vosges front. Shells sever telephone lines so that no orders can be called to the front, and the bombardment closes down the railroad at Verdun so that no reinforcements can be sent in. At 4:00 P.M., the bombardment ceases—284 shells for every 6 feet of the front have saturated the battlefield. But instead of launching a massive attack, the Fifth Army sends out patrols to probe for gaps in the French lines, thus squandering the apparent opportunity to overwhelm the presumably shell-shocked defenders. One German corps pushes forward to capture the Bois d'Haumont, and some patrols spread panic with their flamethrowers. But destruction is not as great as anticipated, and the Germans are met with discouraging machine-gun and rifle fire. At the close of the day, impatient with the meager advance, the Crown Prince's chief of staff, General Schmidt von Knobelsdorf, orders a full-scale attack to be launched the next morning.

22 February 1916
Verdun. The French mount surprising, though weak, counterattacks. Their defense, however, thwarts the Germans throughout the day, especially at the Bois de Caures, where the redoubtable Lt. Col. Emile Driant, one of the ignored propo-

Typical desolation of a battlefield on the Western Front (by A. Barrere, courtesy of the Anne S.K. Brown Military Collection, Brown University Library)

nents of augmenting the defenses at Verdun, commands two battalions of Chasseurs, who hold out until encircled. German fire mows them down as they retreat—Driant falls dead, shot through the temple. The French left wing at Brabant on the Meuse River also holds, although the Germans manage to capture Haumont.

Persia. Another of Yudenich's armies, commanded by General Baratov, captures Kermanshah. Transported by ship, Baratov and his troops had landed at Bandar-e Pahlavi in November and in subsequent weeks had taken Qom and Hamadan. This final victory at Kermanshah ends any possibility that Persia will assist the Central Powers' war effort.

Petrograd. The Duma reconvenes, and Czar Nicholas II, at Rasputin's suggestion, appears in person to address the members and present a decoration to the president in an effort to assuage the growing hostility toward the monarchy resulting from the disastrous shuffling of officials.

23 February 1916

Verdun. The French defense depends upon the survivors of only the Fifty-first and Seventy-second Divisions, but they hold on and, once again, the Germans make only modest headway. The French relinquish Brabant but hold Beaumont, from which their machine-gun fire exacts a heavy toll upon the German XVIIIth Corps, which is punished also by its own artillery fire falling short into German lines. The Seventy-second Division holds fast to Samogneux into the night, when, believing the village is already lost to the Germans, French ar-

tillery opens up, destroying both the village and their own troops. The two defending French divisions, originally numbering 26,523, have been reduced by casualties to 10,299 men—a tragic harbinger of the slaughter to come for both sides.

24 February 1916

Verdun. The Germans smash through the French second-line positions, creating the opportunity for a major advance, but the opportunity is lost once again to overcautiousness. On the French side, Zouave and Moroccan troops have been rushed in, but they are unprepared for the harsh winter weather and break under the murderous German artillery bombardment. By the end of the day, French morale ebbs. During the night, Gen. Langle de Cary, commander of the Central Army Group, obtains Joffre's permission to withdraw troops from the Woevre Plain to the east of Verdun and redeploy them on the heights of the Meuse River east and southeast of the city. Joffre sends Gen. Édouard de Castelnau, who recently became his chief of staff, from Chantilly to Verdun to do whatever he deems necessary, which is a commitment at the eleventh hour to defend Verdun. The Germans' modest success moves them into positions from which to attack the first cordon of forts.

25 February 1916

Verdun. Castelnau arrives, tours the front, miraculously rekindles confidence in the men, determines that the right bank of the Meuse offers a defensible site, and telephones his findings to Joffre. The commander in chief has meanwhile designated General Pétain to take command of defending the left-bank positions on the Meuse, and Castelnau urges him to place Pétain in total command at Verdun. In appointing Pétain, Joffre seals the commitment to defending Verdun and thus unwittingly to suffering the "bleeding white" battle of attrition Falkenhayn has envisioned. While these decisions are being made, Douaumont falls to the Germans. Crown Prince Wilhelm assumes that the fort is damaged but well defended, and he sends a Brandenburg Regiment to assault the fort after a morning artillery shelling. With them go a group of pioneers whose job is to clear away barbed wire and other obstacles that might impede the advance. Some of these men, led by their sergeant, race ahead unopposed through the fort's outer defenses, enter a tunnel in the fort, and make their way into its interior, capturing many of the defenders. The Brandenburgers follow on their heels, entering a different way, and Douaumont quickly changes hands. Only fifty-six gunners and one officer defend the fort. The fall of Douaumont stuns the French and electrifies the Germans. Demoralized residents of Verdun begin evacuating the city. At midnight General Pétain assumes command. To Castelnau he asserts: "They shall not pass."

26 February 1916

Verdun. General Pétain has pneumonia, but his illness is kept secret. His presence restores confidence, and from his bed he issues orders to hold the line of forts still in French hands and to concentrate the artillery for greater effectiveness. Reinforcements arrive, with more en route. General Haig aids the effort by agreeing to relieve the French Tenth Army positioned between the British First and Third Armies near Arras. Since German artillery fire has rendered the railroad useless, Pétain's only supply route is the road from Bar-le-Duc—soon to be christened the "Sacred Way" by French political writer Maurice Barres. Pétain rounds up all available trucks from throughout France to keep the supplies flowing in.

Mesopotamia. General Aylmer sends Townshend a message outlining his plan for relieving Kut: a full-scale frontal assault against the Turkish positions on the right bank of the Tigris by the majority of Aylmer's force. Since the beginning of the month, the British artillery has kept up a steady barrage on the Turkish defenses at the Hanna defile, but to no avail. Aylmer schedules the new attack for 6 March.

Egypt. The Western Frontier Force has re-established its base forty-five miles west of Mutrah and is proceeding westward to

Tangled in the barbed wire and killed on the Western Front (by Reni-Mel, courtesy of the Anne S.K. Brown Military Collection, Brown University Library)

The road from Clermont-en Argonne to Verdun, clogged with supply traffic in April 1916 (by A. Barrere, courtesy of the Anne S.K. Brown Military Collection, Brown University Library)

recapture Sollum. They attack a Senussi camp fifteen miles southeast of Sidi Barrani. After three hours of fighting, the Senussi withdraw, trailed by the British, who finally sweep toward them in a daring cavalry charge. Nuri Bey is wounded but carried off by the retreating Senussi. The victorious have 184 casualties, including 47 dead.

28 February 1916
Verdun. A thaw transforms the battlefield and the road from Bar-le-Duc to mud, but the French spread gravel on the road and the trucks continue arriving. For some reason the Germans have never attempted to bomb them, though they have Zeppelins and other aircraft at the front. Pétain's decisiveness succeeds. With the addition of over 335 heavy guns to their original 164, his artillery punishes the German flanks with enfilading fire. The French lines hold. The German attack is "virtually brought to a standstill." But the battle of attrition will continue.

29 February 1916
Verdun. Falkenhayn accedes to the recommendations of Knobelsdorf and authorizes a renewed offensive aimed at the west bank of the Meuse River. The major German objective is capture of le Mort Homme in order to terminate the threat of flanking fire from the artillery Pétain has concentrated on the ridge at Bois Bourrus. Pétain, desiring to take control of the air over the Verdun front, issues the following orders to Maj. Tricornot de Rose, commander of

fifteen escadrilles that he has organized into fighter units, an innovation at Verdun already in effect with the German air force: "Offensive patrols will be carried out on a regular basis. . . . The mission of the escadrilles is to seek out the enemy, to fight him and to destroy him. They will patrol by escadrille or by demi-escadrille. They will adopt a formation that will place them in echelon in all three dimensions."

2 March 1916
Verdun. Several French efforts to recapture Douaumont have failed. Pétain's own Thirty-third Regiment makes one more effort and fails, sustaining heavy casualties. Among the wounded is Capt. Charles de Gaulle, taken prisoner by the Germans.
London. The government announces that all single men between the ages of eighteen and forty-one are liable for service in the armed forces.
Turkey. The IVth Caucasian Corps on the left wing of Gen. Nicolai Yudenich's army captures Bitlis near Lake Van in order to prevent the Turkish Second Army from moving freely into the area. At Erzerum, he re-forms his troops and improves the supply system preparatory to a renewed offensive to take Bayburt and Trebizond.

4 March 1916
Verdun. The Germans secure the fort at Douaumont and occupy the village.

5 March 1916
German East Africa. Jan Smuts begins an offensive in the Kilimanjaro region,

approaching from two directions. One column commanded by Gen. James Stewart moves out from Longido around the southeastern base of the mountain; a second column commanded by Brig. Gen. Michael J. Tighe approaches by way of Salaita and Taveta. Their major objective is Moshi, the end point of the Northern Railway, where they might be able to stop the retreat of the German force commanded by Maj. Georg Kraut. The army assembled under Smuts's command is the most diverse racially and nationally of modern times.

6 March 1916
Verdun. Anticipating a German offensive on the west bank of the Meuse, the French have not only added infantry reinforcements, but have also enhanced their air support, bringing in a group of fighter pilots known as "the Storks" that includes the famous aces Georges Guynemer and Charles Nungesser and increasing their aircraft numbers to 120. The Germans have 168 planes, 14 observation balloons, and 4 Zeppelins at the front, along with 2 of their greatest aces—Max Immelmann and Oswald Boelke. Verdun marks the largest use of aircraft in the war to date as an adjunct to the conduct of the artillery and infantry battle being waged on the land. The anticipated attack on the left bank begins with a monstrous artillery bombardment that replicates the one on the opening day of battle. Afterwards the advancing German troops capture Forges and Regneville and the northeastern slopes of le Morte Homme, but the defenders' firing stymies the German approach to the northern slopes.

7 March 1916
Mesopotamia. Stationing sixty-five hundred men and twenty-four guns to keep the Turks pinned down at the Hanna defile, Aylmer has twenty thousand troops assemble at the Pools of Siloam for a march in four columns to attack Turkish positions at the Dujaila Redoubt. Maj. Gen. G.V. Kemball commands the two spearhead columns for the attack. Maj. Gen. H. D'Urban Keary commands the other two columns, accompanied by Generals Aylmer and Gorringe.

Turkey. Using ships to land troops and guns and also to shell Turkish positions, General Lyakhov, commander of Yudenich's right wing, has advanced along the coast of the Black Sea to Rize, placing him within only thirty miles of Trebizond.

8 March 1916
Verdun. Employing a bayonet charge, the French stall the German advance on the northeast slopes of le Morte Homme, and the Germans' attempt to take Fort Vaux fails.
Mesopotamia. Reconnaissance confirms that the Turks at Dujaila Redoubt are totally unaware of the British force coming to attack, but instead of taking advantage of the great opportunity surprise offers, Kemball adheres to the original attack plan, which calls for a three-hour artillery bombardment before the troops assault the Turkish positions. The bombardment, of course, apprises the Turks of the British presence, and they rush in six thousand reinforcements. The now-prepared Turks handily defeat the British assault, inflicting heavy casualties. Once again the relief of Kut comes to a halt.
German East Africa. Two South African brigades—one mounted, the other infantry—that are part of Smuts's force and are commanded by Brig. Gen. Louis Jacob van Deventer occupy the Chala Heights and Salaita, abandoned by the Germans, who have gone to Taveta.

9 March 1916
Berlin. Angered that Portuguese authorities seized German ships in harbor at Lisbon, Germany declares war on Portugal. The British have been cultivating Portuguese support for the Allies. Portugal's goal is to preserve her colonies in Africa, which, somewhat ironically, the British and Germans had been negotiating to divide between them before the war began.
New Mexico. Continuing his efforts to provoke the Wilson government to intervene in Mexico, Francisco "Pancho" Villa raids Columbus with a force of five hundred men. They attack the U.S. Cavalry garrison, burn the town, and kill nineteen residents. The ensuing outcry in the United

States forces Wilson to send orders to the military commanders in Texas to put together an expeditionary force.

11 March 1916
German East Africa. Lettow-Vorbeck's troops occupying a strong defensive position at Latema-Reata defeat a British frontal attack, inflicting 270 casualties. The Germans quietly withdraw during the night.

12 March 1916
Berlin. After continuous wrangling over the role of U-boats—Chancellor Theobald von Bethmann Hollweg opposes their unrestricted use as a provocation to the Americans, while Adm. Alfred von Tirpitz advocates unrestricted submarine warfare—the kaiser sides with his chancellor. Wilhelm II had decided on 3 March against the resumption of unrestricted warfare, compounding the pressures on the old admiral. Accepting the kaiser's intent, Tirpitz resigns.

13 March 1916
German East Africa. Smuts reaches Moshi, but his plan to trap Lettow-Vorbeck's force through a pincers movement comes to naught. The German commander skillfully eludes major battles with Smuts's forces, while inflicting serious casualties as he retreats. His strategy forces the British to maintain the pursuit, occupying troops that might be used on other fronts against the Germans.

14 March 1916
Egypt. The Western Frontier Force enters Sollum unopposed, and its armored car unit, commanded by the Duke of Westminster, pursues the fleeing Senussi twenty-five miles into Libya.

15 March 1916
Mexico. Following the suggestion of Venustiano Carranza, Robert Lansing has negotiated an agreement with the Mexican ambassador in Washington that permits either nation to pursue bandits across their shared border. The American Punitive Expedition, commanded by Gen. John J. Pershing and eventually numbering ten thousand troops, crosses into Mexico in pursuit of Villa. Pershing's orders are to avoid any hostility with forces loyal to Carranza.

17 March 1916
Egypt. The Duke of Westminster's armored car unit of the Western Frontier Force drives 120 miles into Libya from Sollum to Bir Hakeim and rescues the 91 surviving crew members of the *Tara* and the *Moorina,* sunk by a German U-boat in November. The crewmen have been held prisoners by the Senussi.

18 March 1916
Russia. In order to assist the French effort at Verdun, Czar Nicholas II has agreed to mount an offensive three months before the Russian commanders anticipated being ready to resume the battle. The offensive centers at Lake Narotch, gateway to the railhead at Vilna (Vilnyus), with the Second Army commanded by General Ragoza as the spearhead and with secondary and diversionary assaults elsewhere. Although an unexpected thaw renders the lakes that the troops must cross unsafe and floods the swamps they will traverse with a foot of water, the battle begins. The 271 guns the Russians have assembled at the front shell the German positions for three hours, and then the infantry moves to the attack. But the Germans had learned of the Russian buildup at the front and, assuming an attack was planned, have reinforced their lines, so the attacking Russians encounter withering artillery and rifle fire that halts their advance. At the end of the day, the Russians have four thousand casualties; the Germans, two hundred.
German East Africa. General Stewart and General Tighe have resigned from Smuts's army, the former under fire for his fatal slowness, and have headed for India. Smuts sends van Deventer to attack Lettow-Vorbeck near the Ruvu River. Van Deventer catches up with the Germans at Kahe, but with the same results as before—Lettow-Vorbeck withdraws during the night. With the rainy season beginning, further pursuit must wait.

19 March 1916
Russia. General Ragoza resumes the offensive at Lake Narotch on a broader front, but not with success: the Germans hold.
Egypt. Gen. Sir Archibald Murray becomes commander in chief, assuming the duties formerly carried out by his co-commander Gen. Sir John Maxwell in Alexandria.

20 March 1916
Verdun. To secure any position at le Morte Homme, the Germans must capture a similar ridge to the west called Côte 304, from which French machine-gun fire can hit troops on their right flank. Forearmed with information about the defenses on Côte 304 given them by French deserters, the Germans capture a position at the ridge's base, but they thereby only expose themselves to still more machine-gun fire.
Russia. The Lake Narotch offensive resumes again, and again the Germans hold. During the night the temperature drops to thirteen degrees Fahrenheit, ending the thaw.

21 March 1916
Russia. At midnight on 20 March, Ragoza's artillery began a bombardment. At 3:30 A.M. his troops attack at two sites and succeed in taking the Germans' forward trenches. A German counterattack fails. The Russians capture a German position at Postavy as the Lake Narotch offensive continues.

22 March 1916
Russia. In the morning the Russians must free three hundred of their wounded from the ice of the frozen battlefield swamp. The Germans recapture the position at Postavy. The thaw resumes, turning the battlefield again into mud mixed with slush and water-filled shell holes.
Egypt. Capt. T.E. Lawrence leaves Cairo on a secret mission to Basra.
Peking, China. Yüan Shih-k'ai, the military overlord of China who has been obliged to grant the Japanese numerous concessions in the preceding two years, responds to opposition throughout China and from foreign governments—including

Japan's—by abjuring any effort to restore the monarchy. He had been chosen as emperor the previous November, although he has not yet been crowned.

24 March 1916
Russia. General Ragoza's week-long offensive has succeeded in capturing only two lines of German trenches stretching between Lake Narotch and Lake Vishniev, and now the thaw has left the swampy parts of the terrain impassable.
English Channel. The German submarine *U-29* torpedoes the French passenger ship *Sussex* as it sails from Dieppe to Folkestone. Several of the 380 passengers, including Americans, die, although the ship stays afloat. The Wilson administration sends a protest and an ultimatum: Germany must cease such submarine warfare or the United States will break off diplomatic relations.

25 March 1916
Petrograd. At the urging of his wife, Czar Nicholas II dismisses his minister of war, Gen. A.A. Polivanov, an opponent of Rasputin who has been responsible for greatly improving the systems of training and supplying the army. He appoints Gen. D.S. Shuvayev in Polivanov's place.

26 March 1916
Russia. The Russians attack once more at Lake Narotch without success. By now the entire battle area has become a virtual lake. General Ragoza begins withdrawing troops.

27 March 1916
Russia. Following another failed attack, the Russian offensive at Lake Narotch pauses.

31 March 1916
Verdun. The Germans capture Malancourt. But the grim weeks of seesaw battle over control of le Morte Homme have exacted a dreadful toll. French casualties at the Verdun front now total 89,000; German casualties, 81,607. Falkenhayn's plan to bleed the French white works, but his own army suffers the same fate. Along the "Sacred Way," six thousand trucks per day now

sustain the supply lifeline of the French troops, helping also to rotate them regularly from the front to rear positions for rest and to bring fresh troops.

3 April 1916
German East Africa. Under orders of Jan Smuts, Gen. Louis Jacob van Deventer leaves Arusha with the 1,200-man South African Mounted Brigade—the beginning of a laborious trek to Kondoa Irangi, 150 miles to the southeast of Moshi over difficult terrain.

4 April 1916
Russia. Gen. A.A. Brusilov, chosen by Commander in Chief Alexeyev, replaces General Ivanov as commander on the South-West Front, as the Russians begin planning an offensive to recapture Vilna.
German East Africa. Van Deventer's Mounted Brigade has traversed thirty-five miles but now confronts German Capt. Paul Rothert and his Twenty-eighth Field Company holding Lolkisale Hill. The South Africans charge up the hill. Their firing wounds Rothert so badly that his askaris abandon the fight, forcing the *Schutz-truppe*'s first surrender and defeat since the war began.

5 April 1916
Verdun. The Germans capture Haucourt as they push slowly but relentlessly forward on the left bank.
Mesopotamia. The third effort to relieve Kut begins, with Gorringe now serving as commanding officer. The British attack at Fallahiyeh and Sannaiyat at the Hanna defile after an artillery pounding. Surprise affords initial success; nevertheless, the Turks hold fast and inflict major casualties—thirty-six hundred for the Thirteenth Division alone.
Corfu. Allied ships complete the evacuation of Serbian troops to Corfu and other destinations. They have transported nearly 261,000 men, over 10,150 horses, and 68 guns without a single loss—the largest sea evacuation ever attempted to this time.

7 April 1916
Russia. General Ragoza's Second Army

renews the assault on the German positions at Lake Narotch; again, the Germans hold.

8 April 1916
Verdun. The Germans take Bethincourt.
Mexico. Pershing's Punitive Expedition has advanced over three hundred miles into Mexico in search of Villa. Carranza, who had expected the expedition to be small and of limited duration, finds its size and intrusion alarming.

9 April 1916
Verdun. Crown Prince Wilhelm has placed Gen. Bruno von Mudra from the Argonne campaign in command of his forces on the right bank of the Meuse River and Gen. Max von Gallwitz, veteran of the successful Balkans campaign, in command on the left bank. They coordinate a full-scale attack on the entire front on both banks of the Meuse, with a major thrust against French positions on both le Morte Homme and Côte 304, advancing to only a secondary summit on le Morte Homme—the French continue to hold the main summit a hundred feet higher still and several hundred yards farther on—while failing totally at Côte 304. The merciless French machine-gun fire on their right flank continues. Pétain's order of the day states: "Courage! We'll get them!"

11 April 1916
Corfu. British and French ships begin transporting Serbian troops to Salonika to augment the Allied force there.

12 April 1916
Mexico. A detachment of Pershing's force enters Parral to buy supplies. As they leave, Carranza's troops fire on them, generating a skirmish that leaves forty Mexicans and two Americans dead. Public outrage forces Carranza to protest to Washington.

13 April 1916
Washington. Carranza's ambassador delivers the First Chief's protest of the Punitive Expedition to the Wilson administration, virtually demanding its withdrawal from Mexico. Wilson rejects the demand.

14 April 1916
Russia. The Second Army makes a final but futile attempt to dislodge the Germans at Lake Narotch. The overall offensive not only has failed to force the Germans to redeploy troops from Verdun, but also has cost the Russians dearly—110,000 casualties, over five times the Germans' 20,000 losses. At Mogilev, Commander in Chief Alexeyev holds a council of war with the three commanders of the armies on the Western and South-Western Fronts (Gen. Alexei Evert, Gen. A.N. Kuropatkin, and Gen. Aleksey A. Brusilov), their chiefs of staff, and General Shuvayev to present his plan for the offensive to recapture Vilna. Although ill-prepared and ill-supplied for undertaking such a venture, the commanders agree, and they set a tentative date in May to begin the offensive.
Turkey. After pausing in response to a resurgence of Turkish resistance and false information about the strength of the bastion, the advance toward Trebizond resumes. General Lyakhov's troops, supported again by shelling from Russian ships, dislodge the Turks from their defensive position at Kara-dere and send them into retreat toward Trebizond.

15 April 1916
Mesopotamia. Gorringe's troops try again, attacking the Turkish defenses at Beit Aisa, but again to no avail. He begins sending aircraft to drop food for the Kut garrison, but the drops cannot meet the daily needs of the troops. Townshend's men face starvation in addition to the malaria, gastroenteritis, dysentery, scurvy, and other ailments that have already claimed hundreds of lives. Townshend's Indian troops, whose religions proscribe the eating of horseflesh, the only available meat, are too weak to perform their duties.

16 April 1916
Luxeuil, France. French officials authorize the *Escadrille Americaine* (which comes to be known as the Lafayette Escadrille) as part of the French Air Force, with an original complement of seven American pilots given the rank of NCO and stationed at this town on the Vosges front.

18 April 1916
Turkey. General Lyakhov's troops capture Trebizond, abandoned by the Turks during the night of 15 April. Trebizond provides the Russians with another coastal base from which to supply their advance into Eastern Anatolia.
German East Africa. Van Deventer's Mounted Brigade, now reduced by disease, hunger, and fatigue to only six hundred men fit for duty, reaches Kondoa Irangi, abandoned by the Germans.

19 April 1916
Chantilly. General de Castelnau, Commander in Chief Joseph Joffre's chief of staff, telephones General Pétain at his headquarters in Souilly to inform him that Joffre has decided to relieve General de Langle de Cary as commander of Army Group Center, placing Pétain in that post. Gen. Robert Nivelle will assume Pétain's current command of the Second Army at Verdun. Although he will remain in overall command, Pétain's new post will take him to Bar-le-Duc, well-removed from the Verdun front, and he fears for what his Second Army soldiers will face under Nivelle, who wholeheartedly supports the murderous struggle.

20 April 1916
Mesopotamia. The effort to relieve Kut collapses as another attack on the Turkish position at Sannaiyat fails. The Tigris Corps' casualties total nearly ten thousand men, one-fourth of Aylmer's entire force. Total losses since January number 23,000, an unqualified disaster, especially considering that Townshend's force at Kut numbers about 12,500—little more than half the men killed or wounded in the relief effort. Turkish casualties are thought to number ten thousand since January.

21 April 1916
Verdun. Twelve days of incessant rain have hindered action at the front. After assessing the results, General Mudra has expressed to Knobelsdorf his growing doubt that the offensive can succeed. In response, Knobelsdorf removes him from command and returns him to the Argonne front.

Rather ironically, on this same day Crown Prince Wilhelm, persuaded by Mudra's arguments, concludes that the offensive has failed and should be ended: "A decisive success at Verdun could only be assured at the price of heavy sacrifices, out of all proportion to the desired gains." Knobelsdorf, of course, strenuously disagrees, and he replaces Mudra with a commander who shares his view, Gen. Ewald von Lochow—the first move in a continuing chess game to counter the Crown Prince's opposition and to keep the Verdun offensive rolling on.

Ireland. Good Friday. Sir Roger Casement comes ashore near Tralee from a German U-boat, having failed in his mission to Germany to obtain weapons for an uprising scheduled for Easter week because a British ship has intercepted the German ship bringing the guns. He is arrested by British authorities when he lands.

24 April 1916

Mesopotamia. In a desperation bid to help Townshend hold out, the paddle steamer *Julnar* sets out after dark with 270 tons of supplies trying to sweep past Turkish guns on the banks of the Tigris. The boat makes it all the way to Magasis, about four miles below Kut, where steel hawsers the Turks have stretched across the river ensnare the boat's rudder. Turkish fire kills or wounds most of the crew, and the survivors are taken prisoner.

Ireland. Over a thousand arms-bearing Irish men and women led by James Connolly, a trained soldier and leader of the Socialist Republican Party, along with Patrick Pearse and other members of the Irish Republican Brotherhood attempt to take control of Dublin. Their aim is to destroy British rule and create an Irish Republic. Against their uprising are aligned the forces of the ten-thousand-man Royal Irish Constabulary (mostly Irishmen), the one-thousand-man Dublin police force (unarmed), and both the Irish Volunteers of the Irish Nationalist Party (supporters of Home Rule) and the Ulster Volunteers (opponents of Home Rule). Both of the latter groups, along with the majority of the Irish, have accepted the postponement of Home

Rule for the duration of the war. The rebels seize fourteen of the city's major buildings, establishing their headquarters in the General Post Office, but fail to take Dublin Castle, the nexus of British rule. Officials at the castle call in reinforcements from outside the city and from England.

25 April 1916

England. In an effort to support the Easter Rising, battle cruisers from the High Seas Fleet bombard Lowestoft and Yarmouth, but the Harwich light force commanded by Commodore Reginald Tyrwhitt drives them off, although losing a submarine in the skirmish. The Germans lose two U-boats, and the battle cruiser *Seydlitz* hits a mine and must undergo repairs. Although Room 40 had apprised Admiral David Beatty that ships from the High Seas Fleet were approaching, the information comes too late for him to reach the scene in time.

26 April 1916

Mesopotamia. Captain Townshend opens negotiations for surrender, sending a letter to Gen. Kahlil Pasha, the Turkish commander at Kut and a nephew of Enver Pasha. Townshend has been authorized to offer £1 million, and he proposes parole for his force and a six-day armistice during which food can be brought into the fort. He also asks that T.E. Lawrence and Aubrey Herbert be allowed to come to Kut to help with the negotiations.

Dublin, Ireland. The British begin in earnest to put down the Easter Rising, as the gunboat *Helga* opens fire, destroying Liberty Hall, headquarters of the Labour Party, and other buildings. Shelling from the *Helga* and British artillery kills many civilians and sets many buildings afire. British troops land at Kingstown and march toward Dublin. Eamon de Valera's fighters ambush them but cannot prevent the British from entering the city.

London. Sir Mark Sykes, principal adviser to the British government on Middle Eastern affairs, and Georges Picot, former French consul-general in Beirut, conclude negotiations on a postwar division of the territories controlled by Turkey. Their agreement contradicts other negotiations Great Britain has conducted via letter with Sherif Hussein of Mecca that promise the Arabs a restoration of lands and autonomy. The secret Sykes-Picot Agreement provides that Russia will acquire several Armenian and Kurdish areas; France will acquire Lebanon, the Syrian littoral, and several areas adjacent to Russia's share; and Great Britain will acquire Mesopotamia, including Baghdad, and the ports of Haifa and Acre; the territories between the British and French shares will become a confederation of Arab states where the two Allies will exercise "spheres of influence"; Alexandretta will be a free port; and Palestine will have an international government.

27 April 1916

Mesopotamia. Hostilities cease at Kut. Townshend and Kahlil meet secretly. The Turkish commander demands unconditional surrender, with Townshend and his men becoming prisoners. When offered the £1 million, Kahlil says that he must confer with Enver Pasha and that Townshend's force must leave the fort, with the Turks providing tents and food from the wrecked *Julnar.*

Dublin, Ireland. Gen. Sir John Maxwell, formerly commander in chief in Egypt, arrives to take command of British troops countering the Easter Rising. Prime Minister Asquith has sent him with orders to subdue the rebellion immediately. The mostly untrained troops sent from England begin shooting Irish men on sight, as the rebels of course do not wear uniforms. Artillery shells set fire to the General Post Office.

28 April 1916

Dublin. Connolly, suffering from two wounds, orders all the women out of the General Post Office in the morning, and in the afternoon he and the remaining rebels abandon the burning building. A force of five thousand British soldiers with armored cars hunts down the rebels—now only two hundred strong—in King's Street, where some of the soldiers bayonet or shoot civilians they find hiding in cellars.

29 April 1916

Mesopotamia. With negotiations failed, Townshend destroys his guns and ammunition and surrenders. Kahlil has the 1,450 sick and wounded British troops exchanged for Turkish prisoners of war and sent to Basra. The remaining twelve thousand British troops he removes to a camp at Shumran as prisoners.

Dublin. Connolly and Pearse surrender. Ruins mar much of Dublin, and citizens jeer the despised rebels but will dramatically change their minds, along with the majority of their countrymen, when the leaders of the Easter Rising are summarily judged and executed.

German East Africa. Van Deventer's infantry, struggling forward in the wake of his Mounted Brigade, arrives in Kondoa Irangi. Most of them, weak from malaria, dysentery, and sores, are unfit for combat, so a force of nearly four thousand Germans and askaris commanded by Maj. Georg Kraut entrenched in the hills south of the town need not fear attack. Kraut also has several guns salvaged from the *Königsberg.*

30 April 1916

Verdun. The French have now recaptured the positions taken by the Germans on Le Morte Homme, restoring the front there to its earlier line. The so-called meat-grinder of Verdun has thus far cost the French 133,000 casualties; the Germans, 120,000—largely resulting from the relentless bombardments of the nearly 4,000 guns both sides maintain at the front.

1 May 1916

Verdun. General Nivelle arrives at the headquarters in Souilly to take command of the Second Army. He declares: "We have the formula!" Joffre has now abandoned the system by which French troops have been rapidly replaced at the front through rotations—there will be no more fresh troops for the "meat-grinder."

The Hague, Holland. A German consul recruits Mata Hari (real name Margaretha MacLeod), a Dutch dancer and courtesan who has lived in Paris since 1905, to obtain information for the Germans. Among her lovers are numerous military officers.

3 May 1916
Verdun. The Germans unleash a ferocious artillery bombardment of Côte 304 with five hundred heavy guns concentrated on a one-mile front.

4 May 1916
Salonika. After two earlier Zeppelin raids, the Allies have augmented their air defenses, so that when *LZ-85* appears for a third bombing raid, artillery fire brings it down in ruins in the Vardan Marshes, where the crew sets it aflame.
Mesopotamia. Kahlil ships the 420 British officers captured at Kut by steamer to Baghdad, the first stage in their journey to Anatolia in Turkey. Most of the regular soldiers will march overland. General Townshend alone is destined for Constantinople and relatively comfortable captivity on an island in the Sea of Marmara.

5 May 1916
Verdun. After two days and one night of their punishing artillery bombardment, the Germans manage to secure a foothold on Côte 304, where the French defenders have

been unable to bring up food supplies or evacuate their wounded because of the bombardment's intensity.
North Sea. The Grand Fleet waits at the entrance to the Skagerrak, hoping to lure out the High Seas Fleet with a seaplane raid on the Zeppelin base at Tondern. But Admiral Scheer does not respond to the provocation.

6 May 1916
Mesopotamia. The British and Indian troops taken prisoner at Kut begin the march toward Baghdad.

8 May 1916
Verdun. After three days of fierce, close-in fighting resulting in ten thousand French dead, the Germans capture Côte 304, depriving the French of a vital defensive position and opening the way to a decisive assault on le Morte Homme. At the same time, however, disaster befalls the Germans occupying Fort Douaumont. A chain reaction of explosions sets afire containers of flamethrower fuel, and the burning liquid flows down the fort's corridors, reaching a

A French mobile infantry mess (by Jean Berne-Bellecour, courtesy of the Anne S.K. Brown Military Collection, Brown University Library)

store of 155 mm shells. The resulting mighty explosion blows up or asphyxiates most of the men inside the fort. The survivors, their faces blackened with smoke, fall victim to machine-gun fire from their own comrades, who take them to be French African invaders, as they race out of the fiery interior. The disaster claims 650 lives.

9 May 1916
German East Africa. Major Kraut's four thousand *Schutztruppe* launch a night attack on van Deventer's force of three thousand men.

10 May 1916
German East Africa. Kraut's offensive continues into the early morning hours. His series of four attacks imperils van Deventer's troops at times, but the South Africans manage to hang on. Ending the assaults, Kraut's men simply disappear into the bush.
Salonika. Lt. Gen. Sir George Milne replaces Gen. Sir Bryan Mahon as commander of the British troops in the Allied force.

11 May 1916
Verdun. Maj. Tricornot de Rose, creator and commander of the French airplane fighter units at Verdun, dies when his Nieuport stalls and crashes.

12 May 1916
Lake Tanganyika. Lt. Comdr. Geoffrey B. Spicer-Simson, inexplicably gone for nearly three months, finally returns to Lukuga and resumes his command just in the nick of time to prevent the increasingly impatient Belgians from launching their own efforts to take control of the lake.

13 May 1916
Vosges. The *Escadrille Americaine,* equipped with Nieuport fighter planes—worthy rivals of the Fokker planes flown by the Germans—makes its first patrol flight over the Western Front.
London. The Asquith government orders the call-up of married men between the ages of thirty-six and forty-one for service.
Verdun. Crown Prince Wilhelm, increasingly disillusioned with the Verdun offensive to the point of despair, receives orders

Italian troops on the move through the Magan Forest on their way to a confrontation with an Austrian offensive in May 1916 (Library of Congress)

from his commander in chief, Gen. Erich von Falkenhayn, to prepare for a new major offensive to begin on 1 June. Falkenhayn code names the new offensive "May Cup."

15 May 1916
Italy. Austrian commander Field Marshal Franz Conrad von Hötzendorf's Trentino offensive, delayed by heavy snows, begins with a four-hour artillery barrage starting at 6:00 A.M. along the front at Folgaria and Lavarone. The shelling destroys much of the Italian artillery and their frontline defensive positions, which the Austrians capture at Costa d'Agra and Monte Coston.
Wilhelmshaven, Germany. Adm. Reinhard Scheer, commander in chief of the High Seas Fleet, wanting to provoke some action, plans to lure Adm. David Beatty into chasing Adm. Franz von Hipper's battle cruisers after they shell Sunderland, with U-boats waiting to torpedo the British ships. Sheer will then engage the British with his own waiting fleet when informed of Beatty's movements by scouting Zeppelins. Scheer's counterpart, Adm. John Jellicoe, has a similar plan to lure the High Seas Fleet into a trap in the Skagerrak, with submarines lying in wait off the Dogger Bank and his own ships at the entrance to the Skagerrak while seaplanes fly reconnaissance. Setting his plan in motion, Scheer sends out the U-boats assembled for the anticipated battle. They have been withdrawn from preying on merchant shipping after protests following the torpedoing of the *Sussex* on 24 March.

16 May 1916
Italy. Pushing forward in their Trentino offensive, the Austrians capture the strongly defended Italian trenches on Soglio d'Aspio.

17 May 1916
Italy. The Austrians capture Monte Maggio and Cima di Campulozzo.

18 May 1916
Italy. The Austrians take Zugna Torta and Linz as their Trentino offensive continues. It is thus far a success.

19 May 1916
Italy. The Trentino offensive stalls momentarily as the Austrians fail in their efforts to take Monte Pasubio and Col Santo, incurring heavy casualties. But the beleaguered Italians evacuate and destroy their forts at Monte Toraro, Monte Campolon, and Monte Melignone, giving the Austrians control of the Della Verena Pass. Archduke Karl Franz Joseph, heir to the Austro-Hungarian throne and commander of the Eleventh Army's XXth Corps, spearhead of the offensive, sends a message to Conrad von Hötzendorf: "Breakthrough completed."

20 May 1916
Verdun. With the advantage of controlling Côte 304, Gen. Max von Gallwitz's troops storm le Morte Homme but fail to take the summit.
Italy. Commander in Chief Count Luigi Cadorna confers at Udine with Gen. Pietro Frugoni, commander of the Second Army, and the Duke of Aosta, commander of the Third Army—both at the Isonzo River front. Deeply concerned that the Austrian XXth Corps may break through into the Venetian Plains, Cadorna and his commanders agree to the possibility of abandoning the Isonzo River front and to otherwise take all necessary steps to shore up the Trentino defense. Cadorna also orders the First Army at the Trentino front to fight to the last man. Rather inexplicably, Archduke Eugen, army group commander in charge of the Austrian offensive, issues orders for regrouping his forces, sending the Third Army into a flanking movement at the Assa Gorge instead of into supporting the XXth Corps' rapid advance and thus providing the Italians with valuable time for reinforcing their frontline troops. The IIIrd Corps of the Third Army, however, succeeds in capturing Cima di Leva and part of the Marcai Ridge.

21 May 1916
Italy. The Austrian Third Army IIIrd Corps captures Monte Cost'alta and the Costesin Ridge to the south of Vezzana.

22 May 1916
Verdun. Following the disastrous explosion in Fort Douaumont, Gen. Charles

Mangin, commander of the Fifth Division of the IIIrd Corps of Nivelle's army, has proposed attacking the fort and quickly received Nivelle's accord. Although the Germans learn of the planned attack on the day Nivelle orders it, 13 May, they could hardly be surprised when it begins anyhow since Mangin has assembled three hundred guns for a five-day artillery bombardment that precedes the attack. Though the fort is badly battered by the bombardment and all the observation turrets are destroyed, the Germans greet the attacking French troops with a devastating artillery shelling as they venture forth from their trenches. Even so the remnants of the 129th Regiment race forward and in less than an hour take three-fourths of Douaumont's superstructure. A few of them enter the fort itself, but the Germans drive them back. Fighting continues through the day in the fort's outer tunnels, and on a rampart the French set up a machine gun that sweeps the entire superstructure. In the evening, premature reports reach both commands that the French have retaken the fort.

23 May 1916
Verdun. The Germans move in reinforcements at Douaumont via a tunnel at the fort's northeast corner. They also set up a mine-thrower that blasts the rampart where the French machine gun is mounted. By nightfall the battle ends, with the French invaders either surrounded and taken prisoner or sneaking back to their lines in the darkness. Their attack force was simply too small to do the job, and their efforts end in debacle, with heavy losses.

24 May 1916
Italy. The Austrians abandon the effort to take Monte Pasubio.

25 May 1916
Italy. The Austrians capture Monte Cimone, opening the possibility of an advance to Arsiero.
German East Africa. Brig. Gen. E. Northey, British commander in Rhodesia, crosses into the German colony from the south with the Nyasaland-Rhodesia Field Force of nearly twenty-six hundred men.

26 May 1916
Italy. The Austrian Third Army's IIIrd Corps captures Monte Kempel, which commands the Assa Gorge and the Assa Valley, and pushes on toward Asiago. Archduke Eugen orders a concentration of the offensive on the Asiago salient in hopes of effecting a breakthrough into the Brenta Valley and then an advance to Bassano.
Northern Rhodesia. Spicer-Simson, after quarreling with the Belgians, has sailed south to assist Brigadier General Northey's advance into German East Africa. He arrives at Kituta, where he meets Lt. Col. Ronald "Kaffir" Murray, commander of Murray's Column, who is about to set out to attack Bismarckburg. Spicer-Simson sails off to blockade the harbor at the German port, but the hilltop fort there discourages him. He turns his ships about and sails back to Kituta.

27 May 1916
Italy. The Austrians reach Arsiero, where trench warfare sets in.
Versailles. Gen. Joseph Galliéni, weak from an operation and depressed by the news of Douaumont, dies.

30 May 1916
North Sea. Apprised by Room 40, which has been intercepting German orders, that Admiral Scheer has a major operation in motion for the following day, both Admiral Jellicoe with the Grand Fleet and Admiral Beatty with the Battle Cruiser Fleet set sail an hour before midnight, Jellicoe from Scapa Flow and Beatty from the Firth of Forth, intending to rendezvous a hundred miles west of the entrance to the Skagerrak.

31 May 1916
North Sea. Heavy winds prevent the use of Zeppelins as spotters, but Scheer has decided to proceed with a revised plan to lure the Grand Fleet into entrapment without using air reconnaissance. With U-boats stationed off the Grand Fleet bases at Scapa Flow, Rosyth, and Cromarty, he sends his two scouting groups commanded by Hipper out at 1:00 A.M., headed for Norway. An hour and a half later, he sails out with

the rest of the High Seas Fleet. Neither the Germans nor the British know the other's fleet is at sea, and they are headed on courses that make their meeting virtually inevitable. In fact, at noon the Admiralty telegraphs Jellicoe that the German fleet is still in harbor in the Jade River estuary. Scheer remains ignorant also because his U-boat trap fails: not a single British ship is torpedoed as they steam out of port, and no message comes from the U-boats advising Scheer that the British have sailed. The weaponry of the mutually approaching fleets contrasts starkly. Six of the Grand Fleet's thirty-seven dreadnoughts mount 15-inch guns; one, a 14-inch gun; fifteen, 13.5-inch guns; and fifteen, 12-inch guns. By contrast, fourteen of the High Seas Fleet's twenty-seven battleships and battle cruisers have 12-inch guns, and the rest have 11-inch guns. So the British have greater fire power. The German ships have a speed advantage, however. At 2:10 P.M., the *Galatea,* in the lead of Beatty's fleet, spots a Danish merchant ship off the Jutland Bank and moves in with the *Phaeton* to investigate. Hipper has also spotted the Danish ship and comes to have a look. The foes sight each other. The *Galatea* signals Beatty: "Enemy in sight. Two cruisers probably hostile in sight bearing ESE course unknown." The *Galatea* and the *Phaeton* open fire at 2:28 P.M. The German light cruiser *Elbing* responds. A shell hits the *Galatea,* but it's a dud. The British cruisers speed off to the northwest, hoping to lure the Germans into confrontation with Beatty's fleet. Aboard the *Lion,* Beatty unsuccessfully tries to signal the Fifth Battle Squadron, sailing northeast since leaving the Moray Firth to rendezvous with Jellicoe, to turn southeast and join the battle. At 3:20 P.M., Hipper's lookouts sight Beatty's fleet approaching. The admiral orders both scouting groups—Rear Adm. Friedrich Bodicker commands the second group—to turn about 180 degrees and steam southward, hoping Beatty will give chase right into the jaws of the waiting High Seas Fleet. Aboard the *Derfflinger,* Chief Gunnery Officer Georg von Hase orders his guns into action against the *Princess Royal,* but the shots go over her. Still,

the weather benefits the Germans: a heavy mist cloaks their ships, rendering Beatty's large guns useless, while the British ships are clearly visible along the western horizon. Having signaled Jellicoe, Beatty opens fire at fifteen thousand yards, but the shots are long. Beatty shifts to a south-southeast course, and Hipper reacts by moving due south—setting the opposed fleets on parallel courses and firing broadside cannonades. The *Queen Mary* misses Beatty's signal that his flagship *Lion* and the *Princess Royal* will focus on Hipper's flagship the *Lutzow* while the *Queen Mary* is to attack the *Derfflinger* and the following ships attack their counterparts down the line. So the *Derfflinger* remains free to fire without reprisal for ten minutes. Shortly after four o'clock, a German shell destroys one of the *Lion*'s turrets, killing most of its crew and setting fire to cordite supplies. At the same time the *Von der Tann,* though suffering direct hits from the *Indefatigable,* slams several shells into her British foe, setting off internal explosions and sending her quickly to the bottom. The Fifth Battle Squadron, commanded by Sir Hugh Evan-Thomas, sails into the battle scene. By now the *Queen Mary*'s guns are hammering the *Derfflinger,* which shifts its sights to this new challenger as the *Seydlitz* does the same. Four 12-inch shells from the *Derfflinger* set off explosions aboard the *Queen Mary* that break the ship in half—over twelve hundred men meet death as she sinks. Thick smoke and water exploding upward from shell bursts obscure the unfolding battle. The big guns of the Fifth Battle Squadron's super dreadnoughts restore the advantage to Beatty, but now the High Seas Fleet looms into sight. Beatty signals the fleet to turn to the northwest and move off, expecting the High Seas Fleet to follow after into the oncoming Grand Fleet. Evan-Thomas, with visibility continually worsening, receives the signal late and remains headed toward the High Seas Fleet, whose lead ships open fire. By 6:00 P.M., a half hour after Jellicoe, aboard the *Iron Duke,* observed that the firing had stopped to his south, the commander in chief has had no message from Beatty for over an hour. Beatty is actually

Naval Warfare

It was a major surprise that, aside from submarines, naval warships played a minor role in the outcome of World War I. It was thought in the decades before the war that the great tradition of decisive naval engagements would have much to do with the course of any major conflict. In fact, launching of the great *Dreadnought* by Britain in 1906 set off a costly naval shipbuilding competition with Germany, and the resulting tensions did much to lead to the final hostilities. However, when the war actually began in 1914, the great fleet built by Germany was still badly out-numbered and outclassed by the British fleet, so German leaders decreed that the High Seas Fleet should remain in port. The investment was too great to risk in combat—a perfectly silly policy conundrum. Aside from the dramatic but essen-tially meaningless escapades of German Admiral Spee in the Pacific during the first months of the war, almost no combat took place on the seas. The British settled into a watchful blockade of the Continent and were content to wait until the Germans "came out." Aside from what were for the most part nuisance raids by small forces, the Germans disobliged the British until May of 1916 when the entire High Seas Fleet disgorged into the seas around Denmark and hoped to draw the British into a fragmented fight. The resulting Battle of Jutland was the only major engagement of the war, and although the mighty dreadnought class ships fought each other for the first time, the battle was inconclusive. The Germans actually did quite well in the face of superior numbers, and the British failed to catch and crush the German Fleet during their only opportunity to do so. The Germans escaped and stayed cooped up for the remainder of the war.

less than six miles away. But where is Hip-per? The *Iron Duke*'s captain records: "Beatty in the *Lion* appeared out of the mist on our starboard bow, leading his splendid battle cruisers, which were engaged to star-board with an enemy invisible to us. I noted smoke pouring from a shell-hole on the port side of the *Lion*'s forecastle and grey, ghost-like columns of water thrown up by heavy enemy shells pitching amongst these great ships." Jellicoe signals Beatty: "Where is enemy's battle fleet?" Beatty is uncertain, but Jellicoe calculates that Scheer is about ten miles distant and de-ploys his fleet for the attack. In the mean-time, Sir Horace Hood with the *Indomi-table* and *Inflexible* and four destroyers comes to Beatty's rescue from the north-east, destroying or damaging three of Hipper's advance cruisers, ending the chase, and preventing Hipper from sight-ing the approaching Grand Fleet, which can now complete its deployment. Hood joins Beatty's vanguard and heads into Hipper's fleet with all guns blazing. The *Invincible*,

after hitting the *Derfflinger* with a few shots, takes a shell amidships, explodes, and breaks in half, with the halves coming to rest on the bottom jutting nearly verti-cally upward—1,026 men die. The Grand Fleet bears down upon the High Seas Fleet, but poor visibility resulting from mist, smoke, and low clouds continues to ham-per operations for both sides—many of the ships simply cannot be seen. Fearing en-trapment, Scheer at 6:35 P.M. orders a ma-neuver that turns all of his fleet 180 de-grees and disappears into the mist. Jellicoe turns to the south. Scheer makes a turn to the east and unintentionally heads straight into the approaching Grand Fleet. Scheer once again turns 180 degrees and once again disappears. At eight-fifteen, Beatty encounters Hipper's battle cruisers and damages the *Seydlitz* and *Lutzow*. Scheer dispatches some of his predreadnoughts to shield his fleet from Beatty, who, lacking the support of the Grand Fleet, calls off the attack as darkness settles. Four more encounters occur before midnight, resulting in collisions, damage by fire, and the sinking of one German ship, the *Frauenlob,* by torpedo.

1 June 1916

North Sea. The final encounters in the Battle of Jutland unfold during the early morning hours. At 1:45 A.M., the British Twelfth Flotilla, led by Capt. Anselan Stirling in the *Faulknor,* sights six German battleships. The *Faulknor* and five other ships in the flotilla unleash seventeen torpedoes. One explodes in the bowels of the *Pommern,* a predreadnought battleship, which suddenly fragments and sinks. Elsewhere, the German dreadnought *Thuringen* spots the British cruiser *Black Prince,* splays searchlights on her, and shells her mercilessly, with the resulting fires exploding her magazines—another total loss. At two-thirty, attracted by the sounds of Captain Stirling's encounter, the cruiser *Champion* and four destroyers from the Twelfth and Thirteenth Flotillas sight Hipper's trailing ships and torpedo a destroyer but make no further effort to attack; they also fail to report the sighting to Jellicoe. Finally at three-thirty, the *Champion* sights four German destroyers moving in an opposite direction, fires desultorily, scoring one torpedo hit, but makes no attempt to turn and give chase. Intermittently, the British make other sightings of the withdrawing Germans but never report them to Jellicoe. The Battle of Jutland ends with a whimper. Hipper's battle cruisers and the High Seas Fleet make good their escape beyond Horns Reef and their own protective minefields.

Verdun. Since February the Germans have maintained a continuing artillery bombardment of the French positions, with their Big Berthas concentrating on hurtling 420 mm shells into Fort Moulainville, although French countershelling has destroyed nine of the original thirteen immobile Big Berthas. German artillery superiority and their capture of le Morte Homme and Côte 304 have rendered the French vulnerable at this salient, but Knobelsdorf's planned "May Cup" offensive shifts the focus to the right bank of the Meuse, the principal targets now being Fort Vaux, the Fleury Ridge, and Fort Souville beyond, and the fortifi-cations at Thiaumont to the west. After a morning barrage, the German troops sally forth from their trenches and, advancing rapidly, capture the Caillette Woods and part of the Fumin Woods, positioning themselves for a determined attack on Fort Vaux while depriving the French of posts from which to fire on their flanks as they move against the fort.

2 June 1916

North Sea. As a result of a communications failure, the German U-boats patrolling the British coast have withdrawn a day early, and the Grand Fleet and the battle cruiser squadrons safely return to their bases. The British losses from the Battle of Jutland number 6,096 men killed and 510 wounded, with 177 taken prisoner; three battle cruisers; three armored cruisers; and eight destroyers. German losses total 2,551 men dead and 507 wounded; one battleship; one battle cruiser; four light cruisers; and five destroyers. In ships' tonnage the British loss is over twice that of the Germans—155,000 tons to 61,000. But the Germans have several badly damaged ships as well, with Hipper's battle cruiser fleet rendered unfit for service. The decisive battle the Admiralty and the Royal Navy longed for has eluded them. Germany claims victory, but Great Britain retains control of the seas, and the blockade of Germany will continue. Admiral Jellicoe reports to the Admiralty that the Grand Fleet is once again ready to put out to sea for action.

Verdun. Vaux, the smallest fortress in the Verdun necklace of fortifications, appears vulnerable to the impending German attack, as its only remaining 75 mm gun turret—the others were removed under Joffre's orders—has been destroyed by direct hit of a Big Bertha shell, so machine guns now constitute its largest weaponry. In addition, water supplies are inadequate and no tunnel has been built to the rear for sending in reinforcements. Commander Maj. Sylvain-Eugene Raynal and his six hundred troops wait expectantly as at dawn the German artillery ceases firing—the barrage had sent over fifteen hundred shells per hour onto the fort. Two battalions of

Communications and Command Control

One of the greatest deficiencies of the Allied armies on the Western Front was the poor state of their communications and command control. The advent of modern war conditions caught the French and British armies without adequate preparation or ideas as to how to communicate between commanders and the front, or how to control battles once set in motion. In truth, these problems were never solved, and the difficulties probably caused many of the millions of needless casualties along the entrenched Western Front. There was no reliable wireless radio technology during World War I, so commanders at the rear were forced to rely on communication methods that had not advanced much over those of a century before. Telephone lines, often laid at great effort before an offensive, usually were destroyed in the early stages of bombardment, leaving runners or carrier pigeons as the principal methods of communication—techniques that had been used by Wellington at Waterloo. The Allied commanders during World War I were notorious as "Chateau Generals" who remained well behind the actual lines and seldom spoke with those who actually did the fighting. The chain of command and communication was rigid and highly centralized, with increasingly specific written orders passing down the hierarchy (and forward in space toward no-man's-land) and gaining unrealistic ideas and illusions as they went. The commands passed successively from the army commander to the corps level to the division to the brigade to the battalion. When the orders arrived at the company level, junior officers were left to sort out whatever might still be relevant and to throw away instructions that were clearly out of touch with reality. However, this entire process could take place only in the absence of fighting. Once a battle started, there were virtually no communications between the rear areas and the front. Local units were left to fend for themselves once a plan was set afoot. In part this helps explain why no genuine breakthroughs were ever achieved. No one knew what was happening after the first few moments of an attack.

An Austrian "galloper" (a mounted messenger) traverses a battlefield in a scene out of previous centuries (courtesy of the Anne S.K. Brown Military Collection, Brown University Library)

the Fiftieth Division attack the fort's north-east and northwest galleries, capturing the former by 5:00 A.M. Fighting rages in the fort throughout the day, ending in the Germans' capture of the northwest gallery as well as entering one of the corridors to the interior.

London. Lord Kitchener meets in a committee room at the House of Commons with his parliamentary critics and defends his policies and tenure at the War Office. His talk is totally successful in winning the MPs to his side. The field marshal has been invited by Czar Nicholas II to visit the Russian fronts so that he can both offer counsel and report back to the Asquith administration on supply and other problems facing the Russian army.

3 June 1916

Verdun. German troops encircle Fort Vaux to the south, cutting it off from contact with the French lines to the rear. With the Germans occupying the top of the fort and advancing along two of the fort's corridors, Raynal's men erect barricades within the corridors, intent on holding the underground interior. German troops inch forward in the totally dark corridors, only three feet wide and five feet high, with grenades exploding about them, shrapnel ricocheting off the walls, and TNT fumes from the explosions choking their lungs. During the night the exhausted Germans withdraw, replaced by fresh troops.

Arras. Two months of tunneling under and blowing up each other's lines—with the advantage going to the British, who have taken over this sector to aid the French effort at Verdun—come to a temporary end with the British setting off four charges under the German trenches. The Germans have managed to advance slightly during fighting over the past two months, but the front is essentially a stalemate.

Greece. Gen. Maurice Sarrail ousts Greek authorities from Salonika, effectively imposing Allied control of the city. Demonstrators protest this usurpation of Greek sovereignty.

Washington. After months of debate on the issue of preparedness, with President Wilson advocating a stronger military to bolster the credibility of his diplomatic efforts among the European nations, Congress has passed the National Defense Act, which now becomes law. The act authorizes an army of nearly 175,000 and provides for the National Guard to be increased to nearly 400,000 men over a five-year period. The act also authorizes the War Department to hold summer training camps for volunteers and to construct and operate a nitrate factory. Perhaps most importantly, the act affirms universal military service.

4 June 1916

Verdun. At dawn, waves of French troops stream toward the western walls of Fort Vaux, but a German bayonet assault drives them off. During the night the Germans have brought in six flamethrowers. Inserting their nozzles into openings in the fort's walls, they blast flames into the interior, trying to smoke out or gas Raynal's men. The effort fails. Near midday Raynal sets free his last carrier pigeon bearing a note that states, "Relief is imperative." The bird reaches Verdun with the message and dies, a victim of the gases released by the German flamethrowers. Raynal realizes that half his troops must be evacuated in order to conserve water and food for those troops essential to maintaining the defense—but how to get them to safety with Germans encircling the fort? Late at night, Raynal sends Officer-Cadet Buffet out to find a way through the German lines, with three hundred escapees following after him in small groups.

London. Lord Kitchener leaves by train for Thurso, Scotland, where he will board ship for his top-secret journey to Archangel, Russia.

Russia. Gen. Aleksey A. Brusilov has planned an offensive along the entire southern half of the Eastern Front from the Pripet Marshes to the north to the Dniester River on the south. His intention is to prevent the Germans from throwing in their reserves—their standard tactic on the front when hit on a narrow sector—while probing for a weak spot on their line and the Austro-Hungarian line where his troops may break through. He also hopes to oblige the Austrians to commit their reserves im-

Austrian troops assault a Russian town (by Fritz Neumann, courtesy of the Anne S.K. Brown Military Collection, Brown University Library)

mediately since Conrad von Hötzendorf has weakened their lines by redeploying troops to the Italian front. Brusilov's two main thrusts involve the Eighth Army advancing along the Rovno-Kovel rail tracks to attack Lutsk and the Ninth Army driving forward across the Dniester into Galicia. At the same time, the Eleventh and Seventh Armies will attack north and south of Tarnopol. The Brusilov Offensive begins with a thunderous artillery bombardment. The attacking Russians achieve only minor gains, but the Austrians will commit their reserves and fulfill Brusilov's hope.

5 June 1916

Verdun. At dawn, the Germans blast an opening in the wall at the southwest corner of Fort Vaux and attack with flamethrowers, but air rushing from the inside hurls the flames back upon them, and the French move in to protect the gap. Observing that the Germans are digging mine shafts, Raynal signals Fort Souville by blinker to pound them with artillery fire—the work ceases. But German shelling subsequently destroys both the blinker and its operator. Inspecting his troops during the

evening, Raynal finds them "crushed with fatigue, silent, and gloomy. If I were to ask one more effort of them, they would have been incapable." He distributes the last of the water supply—a quarter pint per man that stinks of the decaying flesh of the corpses in the fort. Raynal himself has not eaten for two days. Miraculously, Buffet returns from Fort Souville, reporting that most of the escapees have been killed or captured but that a relief attack will be forthcoming—promised by General Nivelle, to whom he reported in person. Buffet heads back out through the German lines, once again safely making his way to Souville.

Russia. As the Austrians have sent the Fourth Army's reserves south to bolster their lines at Sopanov, where the Russians had effected a small breakthrough the previous day, their defenses along the Styr River east of Lutsk are weakened, and the Russian Eighth Army smashes through, capturing both the first and second lines of the Austrians' defensive trenches, taking thousands of prisoners, and routing the remaining Austrian troops.

Arabia. Ali and Feisal, on orders of their father, Sherif Hussein Ibn Ali, Amir of Mecca and Keeper of the Holy Places of

Islam (Mecca and Medina), launch an Arab revolt in Medina against the rule of Turkey. They lead a force of thirty thousand tribesmen and five hundred Arab soldiers trained by the Turkish army. The Arabs can field altogether fifty thousand tribesmen, but they have only ten thousand rifles and no artillery. The Turkish artillery at Medina quickly disperses Feisal's attacking tribesmen.

North Sea. Lord Kitchener, after visiting Admiral Jellicoe aboard HMS *Iron Duke* to discuss the Battle of Jutland, boards the armored cruiser *Hampshire* for the trip to Archangel after 4:00 P.M. About an hour later off the Orkney Islands, the *Hampshire* hits a mine laid by a U-boat before the Battle of Jutland and sinks. Kitchener and his staff drown in the stormy seas.

Field Marshal Earl Horatio Herbert Kitchener (Library of Congress)

6 June 1916
Verdun. The French relief attack at Fort Vaux begins with an unsuccessful artillery barrage in the first hours of the day—the shells sail over the German positions. When the relief forces attack, German machine-gun fire cuts them to pieces or runs them to ground, forcing their surrender.

Russia. Austrian troops flee to Lutsk, where Archduke Joseph Ferdinand expresses determination to hold fast. The city's defense depends upon rattled Hungarian troops who have retreated to the hills at Krupy before the rapidly advancing Russians. If the Russians take Krupy, they can bring their artillery up to bombard Lutsk from the hills.

7 June 1916
Verdun. Major Raynal surrenders Fort Vaux to the Germans. As they are led from the garrison, the severely parched French troops crawl to the first shell hole they see to drink its contaminated water. The Germans, after enduring over twenty-seven hundred casualties in the week-long siege, are astonished to learn that the French defenders have fewer than one hundred.

Russia. Brusilov's troops easily dislodge the Hungarians from Krupy and then turn their artillery loose upon Lutsk. The Austrian Fourth Army falls back beyond the Styr River, abandoning Lutsk to the Russians. The Austrians have lost sixty thousand men, mostly captured by the Russians, and vast quantities of vehicles and supplies.

Arabia. Sherif Hussein at Mecca proclaims the independence of the Hejaz region of Arabia bordering the Red Sea.

8 June 1916
Verdun. At dawn, General Nivelle, presuming that Raynal's garrison endures, sends forth a brigade of Zouaves and Moroccans in a sixth attempt to relieve Fort Vaux. The Germans, having secured the fort, simultaneously launch an attack aimed at Fort Tavannes. Their artillery savages the Zouaves—the survivors turn back—and their machine guns at Fort Vaux slaughter the Moroccans who continue the charge. General Pétain, appalled by the futile carnage in what he terms "the furnace of Verdun," orders Nivelle to terminate the attacks. The French abandon their position at the Thiaumont works and farm to the Germans during the night. At his Stenay headquarters, Crown Prince Wilhelm receives Major Raynal, praises him and his troops, congratulates him on being awarded the Legion of Honor, and as a token of his

admiration, gives the major a captured French officer's sword to replace the one he had surrendered at Fort Vaux.

Trentino. Lieutenant General Cadorna has sent troops forward to positions near Bassano and Valarsa, while moving his headquarters to Treviso. His troops hold fast on Monte Cegnio and stymie the Austrians at Monte Meletta and Monte Lemerle.

Berlin. Conrad von Hötzendorf visits Falkenhayn to seek German help. Concerned that the success of the Brusilov Offensive threatens to destroy chances for victory on the Western Front, Falkenhayn compels Conrad von Hötzendorf to redeploy two of his divisions from Trentino to the Eastern Front and insists that he abandon the Trentino offensive.

Lake Tanganyika. Following a skirmish with Lt. Col. Ronald Murray's column, the Germans escape from Bismarckburg during the night. At the north end of the lake, Col. V.F. Olsen, Danish commander of a five-thousand-man brigade of the Belgian Force Publique, occupies Usumbura. The Force Publique, totaling ten thousand men and commanded by Baron Charles Henri Tombeur, has joined forces with British troops in the western region of British East Africa commanded by Sir Charles P. Crewe, a South African. Their goal is to capture the German colony of Urundi, but as the two commanders despise each other, the joint venture is strained by lack of communication and Belgian fears of suspected British territorial ambitions.

9 June 1916

Verdun. In the early morning, the French recapture their positions lost the night before at the Thiaumont farm.

Lake Tanganyika. Lt. Comdr. Geoffrey Spicer-Simson's flotilla returns to Bismarckburg, now occupied by Murray's Column. He quarrels with Colonel Murray and abruptly invalids himself back to England.

Arabia. Sherif Hussein's tribesmen attack the Turkish garrisons at Mecca and Jeddah.

10 June 1916

Berlin. Although his major offensive on the Western Front has only just begun, Falkenhayn sees no alternative to assisting Conrad von Hötzendorf. He orders Ludendorff and Hindenburg to send five divisions to the southern sector of the Eastern Front and tells Crown Prince Wilhelm to do the same with four of his divisions at Verdun while temporarily halting the offensive there.

11 June 1916

Verdun. Frustrated and constrained by Joffre's and Nivelle's imperviousness—their insensible consignment of men to "the furnace of Verdun"—and concerned over the French troops' morale, yet all too aware of the symbolic importance of Verdun to the French public, Gen. Philippe Pétain writes to Commander in Chief Joffre: "Verdun is menaced and Verdun must not fall. The capture of this city would constitute for the Germans an inestimable success that would greatly raise their morale and correspondingly lower our own." Pétain pleads with Joffre to advance the date for a planned major British offensive at the Somme River in July. But even a significant British victory, he says, "would not compensate in the eyes of public sentiment for the loss of this city, and at this moment sentiment possesses an importance that it would be inexpedient to disregard." Some French commanders have already concluded that the city will fall to the Germans, who appear to be gaining the advantage: including a two-to-one ratio in artillery; the possibility that Oswald Boelke's and Max Immelmann's "Flying Circus" may gain supremacy in the air over Verdun, where they are punishing the American pilots of the Lafayette Escadrille; and, though the Germans may not know it, alarmingly eroding morale among the French troops.

Rome. Mounting criticism of the war forces the resignation of Prime Minister Antonio Salandra, who is succeeded by the aged Paolo Boselli, now given the burden of trying to unite the nation behind a continuing war effort.

12 June 1916

Verdun. Two entire regiments of troops from the Vendee defending the Ravine de la Dame north of Thiaumont have been lost after three days of intense German shelling.

Russia. The Russian Eighth Army's advance has stalled before a surprisingly strong Austrian defense along the Styr River north of Lutsk as German reinforcements begin to arrive, redeployed from the Western Front.

13 June 1916

Arabia. The thousand-man Turkish garrison in Mecca surrenders to the Arabs, but the Turks continue to hold two small forts on the outskirts of the city.

14 June 1916

Trent, Austria. General Baron von Dankl requests relief from command. He is enraged that Conrad von Hötzendorf has falsely accused him of failing to coordinate the tactics of his Eleventh Army in the Trentino offensive. The commander in chief grants the request.

15 June 1916

Trentino. Determined upon one last effort in the Trentino offensive, Conrad von Hötzendorf sends his troops back into battle, hoping to break through at Monte Lemerle.

16 June 1916

Paris. The Chamber of Deputies meets in secret session to discuss Verdun. Several members denounce the conduct of the ongoing battle, revealing that casualty figures have been misrepresented as less than those the Germans suffer—the reverse is actually true.

Arabia. Following bombing raids by seaplanes launched from the *Ben-my-Chree* and shellings by Royal Navy ships, the fifteen-hundred-man Turkish garrison at Jeddah surrenders to the Arabs.

17 June 1916

Trentino. The Austrians' final effort comes to naught. Conrad von Hötzendorf, obliged to redeploy troops to the Eastern Front, calls a halt to the Trentino offensive, which has succeeded in taking only a small section of the Lessini Alps. The offensive has

cost the Austrians five thousand dead, twenty-three thousand wounded, and two thousand taken prisoner. The Italians have suffered twelve thousand casualties and forty thousand taken prisoner.

Verdun. French troops beat back German assaults at le Morte Homme, Thiaumont, and Hill 320.

Argonne. French flying ace Jean Navarre is shot down and permanently grounded with severe wounds.

Russia. German troops assembled for a counteroffensive at the Stokhod River and now commanded by Gen. Georg von der Marwitz attack Gen. Alexei Kaledin's Eighth Army troops south of the Pripet Marshes, gaining a salient of a few miles while inflicting forty thousand casualties on the Russians. At the southern end of the Brusilov Offensive's front, the Russian Ninth Army recaptures Czernovitz as the Austrians continue their retreat.

18 June 1916

Verdun. Two Royal Flying Corps pilots claim to shoot down German air ace Lt. Max Immelmann, who has scored fifteen victories in the skies over the Western Front. The loss prompts Kaiser Wilhelm II to ground Lt. Oswald Boelke lest he too meet death in the air war above Verdun. Boelke says Immelmann's death resulted from a malfunction that caused his machine gun to destroy his Fokker's propeller.

19 June 1916

German East Africa. Brig. Gen. John Alexander Sheppard, commanding one of two forces Gen. Jan Smuts has sent out to conquer the Usumbura highlands, captures Handeni, already abandoned by Maj. Georg Kraut.

20 June 1916

Turkey. After a long journey by riverboat or desert march to Baghdad, 80 miles more from there to Samarra on the Baghdad Railway, and a 380-mile desert march to Ras el Ain, the remnants of General Townshend's Kut force now board open trucks for the remainder of their deadly journey to camps in Anatolia. They must still traverse the Amanus and Taurus Moun-

---

Air Aces

During World War I, the new phenomenon of air combat gave rise to glorification of the fighter pilot, perhaps as a way to invest at least one aspect of the war experience with a traditional haze of heroism, the sort of fuzzy view that had been nearly obliterated by the grinding industrial death machines of the war in the trenches. The epitome of the romantic hero-pilot was the "ace," a flier of single engine pursuit planes who killed his foes in one-on-one combat by virtue of superior physical skills and courage. The French were the first to designate such heroes, awarding the informal accolade of "ace" to any pilot who downed at least five enemy craft (including balloons). Other air forces adopted the same standard, although the British Royal Flying Corps shied away from any official recognition of aces. The German air force eventually raised the number of required kills to ten when it became apparent that five was too few. Following are the leading aces of the war by nationality:

> Great Britain: Maj. Edward Mannock (seventy-three kills)
> France: Capt. Rene Fonck (seventy-five kills)
> Germany: Maj. Manfred von Richthofen (eighty kills)
> Italy: Maj. Francesco Baracca (thirty-four kills)
> United States: Capt. Edward Rickenbacker (twenty-six kills)
> Austro/Hungary: Capt. Godwin Brumowski (forty kills)
> Russia: Maj. A.A. Kazakov (seventeen kills)
> Belgium: Lt. Willy Coppens (thirty-seven kills)

---

tains. Townshend himself, spared the fate of his men, is a prisoner on an island in the Sea of Marmara.

21 June 1916
Mexico. General Pershing, encamped at Dublan, deploys two troops of cavalry to reconnoiter the nearby area in order to ascertain whether a reportedly large Mexican force is indeed assembling. Capt. Lewis S. Morey commands one group. The other group, led by Capt. Charles T. Boyd, encounters 250 Mexican troops commanded by Gen. Felix G. Gomez near Carrizal. In a discussion with Boyd, Gomez informs the American that he cannot allow the cavalry unit to continue on to Ahumada until he receives permission from his superiors. Thinking the Mexicans will give way, Boyd orders an attack. But Gomez's troops surround the Americans, killing twelve, among them Boyd, and capturing twenty-four, including an interpreter. Gomez and twenty-nine of his men also die in the skir-

mish. President Wilson immediately demands release of the American prisoners and prepares a message requesting Congress to authorize him to use American soldiers to drive bandit gangs out of northern Mexico as war with Mexico threatens to erupt in the aftermath of the confrontation.
Athens. A joint statement from the British and French governments to King Constantine demands that Greece demobilize its reserves, hold new elections, and dismiss police officials opposed to the Allies. Prime Minister Skuludis resigns to be replaced by Alexander Zaimis, who accepts the Allies' demands except for holding new elections. As a result the Allies lift a naval blockade they have imposed on Greek ports.

22 June 1916
Verdun. The Germans unleash a new weapon as part of preparation for a major new attack designed to capture the Thiau-

mont works and Fleury and thereafter Fort Souville, giving them the key to the capture of Verdun itself. The weapon is phosgene gas, called Green Cross Gas by the Germans because of the markings on the shells. It penetrates the gas masks of the French artillerymen and kills every breathing creature—men, horses, insects—along the French lines, where the artillery falls silent.

Karlsruhe, Germany. New French bomber *escadrilles* created for attacks on German industrial centers raid Karlsruhe, killing 120 civilians and wounding 150 more.

23 June 1916

Verdun. At 5:00 A.M., as the phosgene gas shelling ceases and regular artillery shelling commences, the thirty thousand men General Schmidt von Knobelsdorf has concentrated along a three-mile front before Fleury go over the top in formations denser even than those that launched the original battle in February. Units of the Alpine Corps, commanded by Lt. Col. Ritter von Epp and 1st Lt. Friedrich Paulus, lead the center of the attack, with Epp's men entering the village of Fleury, which finally falls to the Germans after a full day of fierce combat. Reports reach General Pétain in the afternoon that resistance is crumbling at Thiaumont, where perhaps half of the defending Chasseurs unit has surrendered. He also learns that the Germans are within two and a half miles of Verdun and only twelve hundred yards from Côtes de Belleville, a ridge commanding the city. The French commanders are alarmed, and Joffre sends four divisions of reinforcements—men intended for the Somme offensive. The French have endured thirteen thousand casualties and four thousand taken prisoner, but German losses are also severe. During the night, Knobelsdorf concedes that, without more troops, he cannot take Verdun, and there are no more troops because of the loss of reserves—those units sent off to shore up the Eastern Front. Kaiser Wilhelm II, visiting the front to savor the anticipated great victory, returns in disappointment to his headquarters at Charleville-Mézières. Also during the night French determination mounts. Nivelle issues his Order of the Day, ending with this charge: "They shall not pass."

24 June 1916

Verdun. French troops led by Nivelle's right-hand man, the ferocious and intractable Gen. Charles Mangin, counterattack. Mangin hurls successive waves of troops at the flanks of the German defenders of the salient at Fleury as French artillery rains death on them from overhead. The Germans hold.

Somme River. Premier Aristide Briand, deeply concerned about the fate of the French army at Verdun, visits Gen. Sir Douglas Haig's headquarters to plead with him to move the Somme offensive forward once again. Haig acquiesces and orders the preliminary artillery bombardment to begin today, a week earlier than his revised plan called for. Gen. Sir Henry Rawlinson, commander of the Fourth Army that will stage the attack in conjunction with Marshal Emile Fayolle's Sixth French Army positioned along the southern sector of the front, has assembled over fifteen hundred howitzers and other guns, one hundred of them from the French, and 2 million shells for this bombardment planned to last five days. Following the bombardment, the Allies are to attack along a twenty-five-mile front, with the British responsible for the line from Gommecourt south to Maricourt, over two-thirds of the entire front; the French segment will run from Maricourt to Dompierre.

German East Africa. Brig. Gen. John Alexander Sheppard's troops defeat Maj. Georg Kraut's force in a battle near Makunda on the Lukigura River. The British suffer forty-six casualties, including ten dead. Kraut's dead number thirty-four, including four Europeans. Sheppard takes thirty-two askaris and twenty-one Germans prisoner, but Kraut and most of his force escape into the jungle.

25 June 1916

Petrograd. With nearly 16 million men now drafted into military service, the government perceives a need for reserves to perform labor or serve in the military. Although an 1886 law exempts the Moslems of Russia's Central Asia region from military service, Czar Nicholas II issues a decree authorizing the drafting of 250,000 natives from the region as a labor reserve. Half of them are to come from the Kazakhstan and Kirghiz provinces.

26 June 1916
Washington. A report prepared by Captain Morey proving that the Americans were at fault at Carrizal appears in American newspapers, arousing public sentiment against hostilities with Mexico.

27 June 1916
Russia. While to the south his Austrian allies have fallen back to the Hungarian border in the foothills of the Carpathians, German Gen. Georg von der Marwitz establishes his headquarters at Tartakov to renew his counterattacks against the Russians, but he has suffered heavy casualties and his troops are exhausted.

28 June 1916
Mexico City. Gen. Venustiano Carranza orders release of the Americans taken prisoner at Carrizal, defusing the tension between Mexico and the United States.
Trentino. The Italians have recaptured Asiago, Posina, and Arsiero and now reach Pedescala as the Austrian general retreat continues.
Somme River. Although their infantry attack was planned to begin today, the British decide to postpone it until 1 July while continuing the artillery bombardment of the German lines and the barbed wire strung across the front.

30 June 1916
New York City. Speaking before the New York Press Club, Wilson pleas for peace with Mexico, further easing the tensions evoked by the skirmish at Carrizal.
Verdun. After a week of Mangin's relentless attacks, the Germans still hold fast to their Fleury salient.

1 July 1916
Somme River. After seven days of bombardment—the longest artillery barrage yet known, consuming nearly 1,733,000

shells—British and French troops hurtle forth from their trenches at 7:30 A.M. along a twenty-five-mile front, beginning the long-awaited offensive to relieve the trauma of Verdun. Along this front the German defenses vary—for example, in some sectors the Allied bombardment has had little effect; in others no attack has been anticipated—so the advancing troops encounter different levels of resistance. To the south near Maricourt, the British quickly overrun weak German defenses to take one initial objective, Dublin Trench, while suffering heavy casualties in capturing the linked objective of Dublin Redoubt and the second goal of Montauban beyond. A little farther upriver near the village of Carnoy, they succeed in taking the Pommiers Trench and the Pommiers Redoubt, but at the cost of severe fighting, including hand-to-hand combat, and massive casualties. They also find heavy going still farther north near Mametz and Fricourt, especially the latter, where shattering German fire deprives them of the village's capture. The French "Iron Corps" (the Twenty-second), commanded by Gen. Ferdinand Foch and restored since its services at Verdun, readily succeeds in advancing near Hardecourt, as does the French Sixth Army at the southern tip of the front near Herbecourt. Along the southern sector of the front, then, the Allies experience overall success. But along the entire sector running from La Boiselle to Gommecourt, the northernmost attack point, the offensive encounters chaos and disaster. Here German machine-gun and rifle fire destroys the tightly formed British troops as they advance across no-man's-land. At Gommecourt, for example, Lt. Gen. Sir Thomas Snow, commander of the Third Army's VIIth Corps, relentlessly sends wave after wave of his men to certain death. The British commanders have simply overestimated the effects of their artillery barrage and underestimated the strength of the German line. Thus the modest advances on the southern sector of the front are more than counterbalanced by the carnage and defeat along the eighteen-mile sector to the north. The first day of the Battle of the Somme has cost the British a staggering 57,470 casualties, including 19,240 dead and 2,152 missing—their largest casualty toll of the war. German losses, though not detailed, have apparently also been heavy; French losses, light. Now fully certain that the Somme is the focus of the Allies' summer offensive, Gen. Fritz von Below, commander of the Second Army, withdraws his troops from Fricourt and begins a counterattack on Montauban shortly before midnight. During the night Commander in Chief Erich von Falkenhayn, persuaded of Below's view, orders troops redeployed from the Verdun front to reinforce the defenses along the Somme, thus weakening his position at Verdun—to that extent, at least, 1 July is an Allied success. As the night progresses, the British move up their reserve troops. Gen. Sir Henry Rawlinson, commander of the Fourth Army, who is unaware of the true nature of British losses (estimating them at only sixteen thousand), orders preparations for the attack to resume the following day.

Verdun. French troops recapture the Thiaumont works. General Nivelle, foreseeing a new initiative, orders the reorganization of the front lines under the command of Gen. Charles Mangin.

2 July 1916

Somme River. In the early morning hours, Below's attack on Montauban fails. At 10:30, Gen. Douglas Haig visits Rawlinson's headquarters at Querrieu. Now somewhat better informed and aware of the confusion prevalent in his troops' deployments and problems with his engineering and supply efforts, the Fourth Army commander persuades Haig that a renewed offensive must await his army's reorganization. During the evening, the Germans, having no reserves to bring forward, withdraw from the Flaucourt Plateau after receiving authorization to do so from General von Below's chief of staff.

3 July 1916

Somme River. General von Falkenhayn visits General von Below's headquarters at Saint-Quentin and, insisting that "the first principle . . . must be to yield not one foot of ground," dismisses Below's chief of staff, Major General Grunert, for having authorized withdrawal from the Flaucourt Plateau, replacing him with Gen. Fritz von Lossberg. He informs Below that five divisions of reinforcements, two from Verdun, are en route, and about forty batteries are now being emplaced. Airplane reinforcements have also arrived. The commander in chief has called a halt to Crown Prince Rupprecht's offensive at Verdun to provide for the defense of the Somme. British troops capture parts of La Boiselle and Ovillers after heavy fighting.

4 July 1916

Somme River. British troops pursue the assault in La Boiselle.

Russia. Continuing the Brusilov Offensive, General Lesh's Third Army crosses the Styr River in the Pripet region and drives the Germans back toward the Stokhod River. The Russians also attack at Baronovichi north of the Pripet Marshes.

Mexico City, Mexico. Carranza further defuses the tensions between his country and the United States by suggesting that the two nations enter into direct and friendly negotiations to resolve their misunderstanding.

7 July 1916

Somme River. British troops assault German troops concentrated in the Mametz Wood, which Haig sees as vital to protecting the British right flank during a renewed major offensive. The Germans hold fast.

London. David Lloyd George replaces the deceased Lord Kitchener as mnister of war.

German East Africa. Having come ashore from British ships on 3 July, five hundred Indian infantrymen capture Tanga, the coastal terminus of the Usumbura railway. Control of the port allows for an improved supply system for British troops.

8 July 1916

Somme River. British troops capture the Trones Wood, which Haig also sees as vital to a renewed offensive, but a German counterattack drives them out.

Russia. General Lesh's Third Army drives through the Austrian Fourth Army lines near Lutsk and crosses the Stokhod River, but here on the west bank a combined force of German and Austrian troops commanded by Gen. Alexander von Linsingen holds, stunting Lesh's advance. German troops also halt the advance of the Russian Eighth Army's cavalry twenty-five miles east of their goal, Kovel.

10 July 1916

Somme River. British troops attack German positions in the Mametz Wood.

11 July 1916

Verdun. Persuaded by General von Knobelsdorf, Falkenhayn has authorized a renewed offensive on a restricted front aimed at Fort Souville. It opens with a continuing barrage of phosgene gas loosed on the French artillery positions that appears to silence their guns. But the French have been equipped with new gas masks that effectively neutralize the "Green Cross Gas," and the silent guns are a ruse. As the German troops advance from their trenches, the French guns cut them to pieces. Still the Germans manage to push ahead a few hundred yards.

Mesopotamia. Maj. Gen. F.S. Maude replaces Gen. Sir George Gorringe as commander of the Tigris Corps.

12 July 1916

Verdun. The German offensive resumes but without success. A small remnant of perhaps thirty men of the 140th Regiment, who have been forced forward to escape shelling from the French artillery while their comrades fell back, actually reaches the glacis of Fort Souville and waves a German flag. Although this is observed through field glasses by Gen. Krafft von Dellmensingen, commander of the indomitable Alpine Corps, he has no reserves to send forward, and the French garrison quickly kills or captures the invaders.

13 July 1916

Somme River. British troops capture Mametz Wood and Contalmaison.

14 July 1916

Verdun. Counterattacks by General Mangin's troops drive the Germans back almost to their starting point of three days before, and once again stalemate descends along the front. By now Verdun has cost the French 275,000 casualties, including perhaps 70,000 dead. German casualties number nearly 250,000.

Somme River. Following an unusually short five-minute preliminary artillery bombardment, General Rawlinson's troops attack German positions on Longueval Ridge at daybreak, capturing the ridge by mid-morning. They also succeed in ousting the Germans from Trones Wood and High Wood as attacks and counterattacks at these points continue through the day.

Russia. The fighting at Baronovichi ends, with the Russians suffering eighty thousand casualties.

Russian Central Asia. Reacting to the czar's decree of 22 June that they are to be drafted into a labor reserve, Kazaks riot near Zaisan, close to the border with China.

German East Africa. After sailing from Kisumu in small boats, Sir Charles Preston Crewe's King's African Rifles come ashore and capture Mwanza, the German port on the southern tip of Lake Victoria.

15 July 1916

Somme River. General Rawlinson has received reserves, "Kitchener's Army," draftees from England, along with troops from South Africa, Australia, and New Zealand. He sends the South Africans into a successful assault on the German positions at Delville Wood near the village of Longueval.

Russia. Learning from his intelligence gatherers that the Germans plan to launch a counteroffensive on 18 July, Gen. V.V. Sakharov, commander of the Eleventh Army, sends his troops into a preemptive attack north of Brody during the night. The Russians capture thirteen thousand prisoners and large stockpiles of ammunition, aborting the German plan.

16 July 1916

Russian Central Asia. Kazaks in Zaisan and Karkaralinsk riot, destroying crops in the fields of Russian settlers and killing local Russian officials. Other uprisings center near Verny, resulting in the deaths of two thousand settlers. The Russian army's punitive response to these uprisings becomes brutal, leading to the massacre of tens of thousands of Kazak natives.

17 July 1916
Somme River. British troops capture the Waterlot Farm east of Longueval and the German fortress at Ovillers.

19 July 1916
Flanders. Believing the Germans are close to staging a retreat at the Somme, the British commanders have decided that opening another offensive on a second front will hasten the demoralization of the German armies. The offensive is centered at Loos; its objective is capture of the Aubers Ridge and the village of Fromelles. At 11:00 A.M., the British begin the usual preliminary artillery barrage. By noon, the Germans begin a retaliatory barrage, with telling effects on the British artillery positions and ammunition dumps. The late afternoon infantry attack across marshy land meets heavy German resistance and withering machine-gun fire. The Eighth Australian Brigade manages to make headway and to hold an advance position through the night, but at terrible cost—fifty-five hundred casualties.
Somme River. The Germans counterattack at Delville Wood, Trones Wood, Waterlot Farm, and Longueval.
Sinai. The British have been assembling a force at Romani in anticipation of Turkish moves, but air reconnaissance discovers the Turks have about twenty-five hundred men concentrated at Bir Bayud. The Turks are about to launch an attack against the Suez Canal.

20 July 1916
German East Africa. Maj. Gen. Kurt Wahle's force evacuates Kigoma, the Germans' chief port on Lake Tanganyika.

21 July 1916
Somme River. Meeting at the headquarters of Lt. Gen. Sir Hubert Gough's Fourth Army, British commanders decide to launch a general attack along the entire front stretching from Pozieres to Guillemont on the following day.

22 July 1916
Somme River. The new offensive stumbles at the start, as the French Sixth Army protecting the British right flank south of Guillemont is unprepared. At Pozieres, however, Australian troops manage to advance decisively.
Petrograd. Foreign Minister Sergei Sazonov, trusted by the French and British governments, is forced out of office. Control of the Foreign Ministry falls to Rasputin's henchman, Boris Sturmer, already ensconced as premier.

23 July 1916
Somme River. Australian troops capture the German trenches before Pozieres, rout German machine gunners from their posts in the village, and take control of the right side of the Albert-Bapaume road.

24 July 1916
Somme River. The Australians capture that part of Pozieres not already in their hands. The Germans counterattack at High Wood and Guillemont, but the British hold. Their offensive has managed to push ahead more than three miles along a six-mile front in two days of fighting.

25 July 1916
Somme River. The Australians clear the last of the German defenders from Pozieres, taking full control of the village. Haig, Foch, Rawlinson, and Emile Fayolle, commander of the French Sixth Army, agree to launch a joint attack on 30 July.

27 July 1916
Somme River. British artillery shells German positions at Longueval and Delville Wood. Unrelieved, exhausted, undersupplied, and outgunned, the Germans begin surrendering in larger numbers than usual.
Arabia. The Turkish garrison at Yenbo surrenders to Sherif Hussein's son Abdulla, the amir of Trans-Jordan.

28 July 1916
Austria. The Brusilov Offensive begins again, as Gen. V.V. Sakharov's Eleventh Army captures Brody, and the Seventh and

Ninth Armies attack along the Dniester River.

German East Africa. The Belgian Force Publique unit commanded by Lt. Col. F.V. Olsen occupies Kigoma, the port on Lake Tanganyika evacuated by the Germans a week earlier.

30 July 1916

Somme River. The combined Allied offensive changes little. British troops temporarily capture much of Guillemont, but German counterattacks force them out, inflicting heavy casualties. French troops manage a small gain of territory.

31 July 1916

Somme River. As the first month of the Battle of the Somme ends, the British and the Germans each tally about 160,000 casualties in the fighting here.

2 August 1916

Somme River. Australian troops continue their advance near Pozieres, pushing forward north of the village.

Austria. Erich Ludendorff and Paul von Hindenburg visit Lemberg and Kovel. Falkenhayn has given the latter command of the entire Eastern Front, including the Austro-Hungarian armies, but Field Marshal Count Franz Conrad von Hötzendorf dislikes the idea of German overall command.

German East Africa. Olsen's Belgian Force Publique takes Ujiji on Lake Tanganyika.

3 August 1916

London. Sir Roger Casement is hanged for his role in the Irish rebellion despite appeals by prominent Britons and controversy over the evidence that was presented against him during his trial.

4 August 1916

Isonzo River. The Sixth Battle of the Isonzo begins with two corps of the Italian Third Army undertaking a diversionary artillery and infantry assault near Monfalcone intended to draw Austrian troops into that sector while the Italians mount their major attack at Gorizia, to begin on 6 August.

Egypt. Gen. Sir Archibald Murray, expecting the main Turkish attack to occur near Katib Gannit where deep desert sands will work against the Turks, has concentrated forces near Gilbana Station and El Qantara with the intent of falling upon the Turkish left flank. His main force is near Romani. A skirmish on the third between Turkish and Australian patrols has confirmed his judgment, but as battle commences at Wellington Ridge in the early morning, Murray finds his own right flank in danger from a superior Turkish force. British artillery fire checks the Turks here, but they pursue the flanking attack at Mount Royston to the west while also assaulting the main British force at Romani. New Zealand troops sent from El Qantara as reinforcements save the day at Mount Royston.

5 August 1916

Verdun. French troops recapture the village of Thiaumont.

Isonzo River. The diversionary attack near Monfalcone continues.

Egypt. A dawn attack by Scottish and Australian troops takes control of the Wellington Ridge, as fifteen hundred Turks surrender. Now holding the advantage, the British pursue withdrawing Turkish troops through the afternoon hours. In the late afternoon, the Turks repulse a British attack at the Qatia Oasis. Wearied by the day's struggles, both sides withdraw during the night—the British toward Romani; the Turks, eastward to Oghratina.

German East Africa. Gen. Jan Smuts resumes his advance toward Morogoro from Handeni, while Gen. Louis Jacob van Deventer's force heads for the same objective from Kondoa Irangi, moving down the tracks of the Central Railway toward Kilosa.

6 August 1916

Austria. General Sakharov continues his drive south of Brody, capturing over eighty-five hundred prisoners and advancing to within four miles of Lemberg.

Isonzo River. The Italians launch their major attack near Gorizia, charging the Austrian positions at Monte Sabotino.

Even though the Austrians have not been distracted by the feint at Monfalcone, their front lines crumble in less than an hour, and the Italians take the summit along with eight thousand prisoners. They also attack at Podgora. The Austrians fiercely counterattack at both sites during the night. In a related operation in the Monte San Michele sector on the extensive Carso Plateau, the Italians attack and capture the peaks of Monte San Michele as well as the village of San Martino, but their casualties are heavy.
Egypt. British troops press after the Turks, now dug in at Oghratina.

7 August 1916

Isonzo River. The Austrians counterattack forcefully at both Monte Sabotino and Podgora and also at Monte San Michele, but to no avail.

8 August 1916

Verdun. The Germans once again recapture Thiaumont—this is the sixteenth time one side or the other has taken the village since the Battle of Verdun began.

Isonzo River. The Italians crack the Austrian resistance, capturing their positions on the right bank of the river at Gorizia and entering the city. Under revised orders to pursue and menace the Austrians, the Italian troops, though weary, hasten after their withdrawing enemy.

Egypt. Turkish troops withdraw from Oghratina and set up defensive positions at Bir el Abd. Anzac troops continue the pursuit.

9 August 1916

Isonzo River. The Italians renew their advance at Monte San Michele and reach the Vippacco River.

Egypt. The British attack the Turkish positions at Bir el Abd. The Turks not only hold them at bay but counterattack and attack repeatedly, until in the evening commanding officer Maj. Gen. Sir Henry Chauvel orders his beleaguered and weary men to fall back to Oghratina.

10 August 1916

Somme River. King George V begins a five-day tour of the front.

12 August 1916

Somme River. Haig and Joffre, accompanied by Foch, meet at Beauquesne and agree to a general attack for 18 August extending from the Somme River to High Wood. In the meantime, the British will try to advance at Guillemont and the French at Maurepas. George V and President Raymond Poincaré also meet at Beauquesne.

Isonzo River. On the Carso Plateau, the Italians break through the Austrian line and push on to take Nad Logem and Opacchiasella.

Egypt. The Turks abandon their positions at Bir el Abd, despite their successful defense on the ninth, and withdraw fifty miles eastward to El Arish, where their expedition had begun. Their westward venture has cost 6,000 casualties, with another 4,000 men taken prisoner by the British, whose casualties number only 1,130, mostly Anzacs.

14 August 1916

Isonzo River. The Italians resume their offensive along the entire front.

15 August 1916

Austria. Gen. Platon A. Lechitsky's Ninth Army arrives at Solotwina to the west of Stanislau as the Brusilov Offensive grinds forward. Since the Russian offensive started at the beginning of June its continuing success has resulted in recapturing 15,000 square miles and inflicting a total of 700,000 casualties—including 350,000 taken prisoner—on the German and Austrian forces. But the offensive has also cost the Russians 550,000 casualties.

17 August 1916

Isonzo River. Although the previous three days of fighting have pushed the Italian gains to over three miles along a twelve-mile front, the commander in chief, Gen. Count Luigi Cadorna, calls a halt to the successful offensive. The Italians begin to consolidate their victory, which has exacted a price of 51,232 casualties. Austrian casualties exceed forty-nine thousand.

Bucharest, Romania. After many months of being wooed by both sides, but most intensely by the Allies, Romanian officials sign political and military conventions with the Allies. In return for territorial concessions, including the ceding of Transylvania, provision of munitions, and an Allied offensive launched from Salonika, the Romanians agree to enter the war with an attack on Austria-Hungary to begin no later than 28 August.

Bulgaria. Aware of the Allies' negotiations with Romania and of General Sarrail's plan to launch an offensive from Salonika—scheduled for 1 August but postponed to await the outcome of the Romanian negotiations—the Central Powers have decided on a preemptive strike. To the west, the Bulgarian First Army attacks from Monastir, advancing down the Kenali Valley, pushing back surprised Serbian troops, and seizing Florina's railway station. At the same time to the east, the Bulgarian Second Army marches through the Rupel Pass in the Belasica Mountains and advances into Macedonia. Two divisions of the German Eleventh Army also attack southwest of Lake Doran.

18 August 1916
Somme River. The new Franco-British offensive makes little headway, although the British achieve some gains near Guillemont.
Macedonia. The Bulgarian First Army captures Florina.

19 August 1916
North Sea. Adm. Richard Scheer, with his High Seas Fleet once again seaworthy, sails forth from Wilhelmshaven with eighteen dreadnoughts and two battle cruisers ostensibly to carry out a raid on Sunderland that was precluded by the Battle of Jutland and to taunt the British to be "on watch for attacks by our Fleet." Adm. Sir John Jellicoe's fleet is already at sea in anticipation, forewarned by intelligence from Room 40. The sortie proves an empty gesture, however, as the fleets avoid contact.
Somme River. German troops counterattack as the British advance to Thiepval Ridge and the French capture Angle Wood.

20 August 1916
Macedonia. Suffering heavy casualties, the French fall back before the Bulgarian Second Army, which advances nearly to the Struma River at Orlyak. But here the Bulgars are stopped by the British. On the western sector at Lake Ostrovo, Serbian troops, now reinforced, fight back relentlessly, stymieing the Bulgar advance.

21 August 1916
Somme River. The British advance to the northwest of Pozieres, and at Thiepval Ridge they repulse German counterattacks.

22 August 1916
German East Africa. General van Deventer marches into Kilosa without opposition and sets up headquarters. From here he will move down the Central Railway to meet Smuts at Morogoro for what Smuts hopes will be a decisive battle with Gen. Paul von Lettow-Vorbeck's *Schutztruppe.*

23 August 1916
Somme River. The Germans form their first *Jagdtstaffel,* or *Jasta,* a tactical fighter squadron composed of fourteen planes—a move long advocated by Lt. Oswald Boelcke, who is made commander of *Jasta 2.*
Verdun. Crown Prince Wilhelm, dismayed to learn that his chief of staff, General Schmidt von Knobelsdorf, still hopes to take Verdun, has finally persuaded his father, Kaiser Wilhelm II, himself dismayed by the failure of the Verdun offensive, to relieve Knobelsdorf of his position. The kaiser reassigns Knobelsdorf to command of a corps on the Russian front and appoints Gen. Walther von Luttwitz, who has been serving in Russia, as his successor. Luttwitz fortunately agrees with the Crown Prince's assessment of the futile tragedy being enacted at Verdun.

24 August 1916
Somme River. French troops capture Maurepas. British troops push forward at Thiepval and Delville Wood.
Macedonia. Greek troops, technically not among the belligerents, surrender forts at Kavalla to units of the Bulgarian Second Army.

26 August 1916
German East Africa. General Smuts's Rhodesian and Baluchi troops arrive at Morogoro, but Lettow-Vorbeck has already left, moving southward. As the Germans leave the town, the rear guard torches supplies that could not be carried off. The Germans have also dynamited the railroad tracks and some of the cars. Smuts now controls the Central Railway, which links Dar es Salaam, the main German port on the Indian Ocean, with Kigoma, the main port on Lake Tanganyika and now in British hands. But his elusive quarry, Lettow-Vorbeck, who fights and runs to fight another day, evades him.
Macedonia. The Bulgar offensive comes to a halt.

27 August 1916
Romania. After sending a declaration of war to Vienna, the Romanian army, marching through passes in the Alps, invades Transylvania. Falkenhayn, having felt certain that no such move would occur until late September following the harvest season, is astonished—another mistake to be held against him, in the opinion of the kaiser, who declares: "The war is lost." The kaiser has staunchly supported Falkenhayn, but Chancellor Theobald von Bethmann Hollweg has been urging his dismissal. The chancellor, convinced that Germany cannot win the war, wants Falkenhayn replaced by commanders who have the needed credibility and stature with the public to win acceptance of a peace settlement negotiated on the basis of the status quo now prevailing on the Eastern and Western Fronts—namely, Hindenburg and Ludendorff.

28 August 1916
Somme River. British troops capture most of the German positions at the Delville Wood.
Pless. Kaiser Wilhelm II accepts the resignation of Gen. Erich von Falkenhayn as chief of the General Staff and names Gen. Paul von Hindenburg, hastily recalled from the Eastern Front with Ludendorff for consultation, as his replacement. The kaiser reassigns Falkenhayn, who wishes to continue in military service to his country, as commander of the German and Austrian forces opposing Romania.
Mesopotamia. Gen. F.S. Maude becomes commander in chief of British forces, replacing Gen. Sir Percy Lake. The new commander begins work immediately on restoring morale and strengthening his forces with reinforcements, equipment, and hospital facilities.

29 August 1916
Pless. General Hindenburg is officially installed as chief of the General Staff of the Army in the Field. His longtime Eastern Front partner, Gen. Erich Ludendorff, becomes first quartermaster-general and, at Hindenburg's insistence, shares equal authority and responsibility with the chief. The German public welcomes the change in military leadership.
Transylvania. Invading Romanian troops occupy Kronstadt, Petroseni, and Kezdiasarhely—all already evacuated.
Macedonia. Military partisans of Eleutherios Venizelos in Salonika stage a coup, forcing officers loyal to King Constantine to leave the city and setting up the "National Defense" movement under the protection of General Sarrail.

1 September 1916
Salonika. Gen. Maurice Sarrail, wishing to gain total control over the city, has instigated demonstrations by military partisans of Venizelos, who favors the Allies. The leaders renounce King Constantine and declare Greece an ally of the Allied powers. At the same time, an Allied fleet anchors at Salamis to put pressure on Constantine by suggesting support for a coup. Both King George V and Czar Nicholas II object to such blatant interference in Greece's internal affairs.

2 September 1916
London. During the night, the Germans send their largest fleet of Zeppelins—twelve naval airships and four army airships—to bomb the British capital. Unknown to the Germans, the machine guns of British airplanes now have incendiary ammunition that can torch the hydrogen

This striking double portrait in 1913 before the war demonstrates the uncanny likeness of royal cousins Czar Nicholas of Russia (on the left) and King George of Great Britain (Library of Congress)

that fills the Zeppelins. One of the army Zeppelins falls victim to this ammunition, crashing in flames and killing its sixteen crew members. The massive raid fails.

3 September 1916
Somme River. A fourth general Allied offensive, intended to begin on 30 August but postponed because of poor weather, opens with an attack by the British Fourth Army and the French Sixth Army. The British make some headway at Guillemont, but Australian troops fail in their assault on Mouquet Farm. The French succeed in capturing Foret and much of Clery.
Pless. Despite Hindenburg's and Ludendorff's advocacy for resuming unrestricted submarine warfare, a council that also includes Bethmann Hollweg and Grand Adm. Henning von Holtzenzendorf meets with the kaiser and decides to postpone resumption until a peace initiative is concluded.
Bulgaria. Gen. August von Mackensen, now commanding a mixed force of Bulgar, German, and Turkish troops, begins to attack in the Dobrudja region of Romania.
German East Africa. Dar es Salaam falls to Smuts's troops. Lettow-Vorbeck's deceptive tactics have convinced the British that the Germans are defending the port, but the German commander and his *Schutztruppe* are gone, and Comdr. Max Loof and his crewmen have remained behind only to destroy the harbor, the ships at anchor there, the railway, and other useful facilities. The British prize is 450 civilians, 80 of them hospitalized.

4 September 1916
Somme River. British attention now focuses on Guillemont. Covered by a creeping barrage, whereby the artillery arches its shelling to remain just ahead of the advancing troops (now a standard tactic on all fronts), British troops overrun the Germans to capture this longtime objective and are poised to attack the German lines at Ginchy.
Verdun. The Tavannes Tunnel, a railway tunnel stretching fourteen hundred yards underneath the Meuse Hills, has been used by the French as a storage facility, a hospi-

tal, a route for troops moving to and from the front, a barracks, and a communications center. It sometimes shelters as many as four thousand men. During the night a fire starts among some rockets and spreads to a grenade depot, which explodes and sets afire gas stores, exploding still other grenades. The chain reaction gorges the tunnel with flames and smoke, as men flee for their lives.

5 September 1916
Cambrai, France. Hindenburg and Ludendorff tour the Western Front. Seeing the Verdun battlefield with their own eyes, they are appalled. Both compare Verdun to hell. Ludendorff declares it "a nightmare for both the staffs and the troops. . . . Our losses were too heavy for us." After meeting with commanders and their chiefs of staff from all sectors at Crown Prince Rupprecht's headquarters at Cambrai, the commanding duo sense that losses on the Western Front have greatly attenuated the German army's strength—bleeding the Germans white while trying to inflict that same fate on the French. They will alter policy accordingly, ordering a halt to Falkenhayn's hold-at-any-cost defense and terminating the attacks at Verdun, where German casualties now total 281,333 men. They will also allow commanders at the front greater leeway in making decisions. (French losses at Verdun number 315,000.)

6 September 1916
Transylvania. Romanian troops capture Hermannstadt (Sibiu), the capital city of Transylvania.

7 September 1916
Verdun. After three days, the Tavannes Tunnel inferno subsides. Five hundred bodies charred into dust are found near the air shafts; another five hundred men have been totally consumed. Somehow the French manage to keep the disaster a secret from the Germans.

9 September 1916
Somme River. British troops capture the village of Ginchy.
Romania. General Mackensen's force cap-

tures Silistria, a city on the south bank of the Danube River that Romania took from Bulgaria in 1913 when Bulgaria was hamstrung by a struggle with Greece and Serbia.

12 September 1916
Somme River. The French Sixth Army resumes its offensive, halted during the previous six days by unfavorable weather.
Macedonia. An offensive planned by Gen. Maurice Sarrail to dislodge the Bulgars from their conquests opens at 6:00 A.M. The main thrust of the offensive centers on Mount Kajmakcalan, a peak from which Bulgar artillery positions dominate Monastir and the plains to the north of Lake Ostrovo. The Serbian First Army spearheads this part of the Allied attack, succeeding in taking the foothills of the mountain. French troops assault the Bulgarian positions at Monastir but to no avail.

13 September 1916
Macedonia. The British objective is Machukovo in the Vardar River sector of the front, but the village is protected by defensive bastions built on the river by the Germans and also by German troops supporting the Bulgars. Of the four attacking British battalions, three lose half their strength in the futile effort to breach these defenses.

14 September 1916
Isonzo River. At dawn, Italian artillery opens fire preliminary to renewed attacks by the Second and Third Armies, as the Seventh Battle of the Isonzo begins. Initial success gives the Italians control of San Grado di Merna and other objectives.
Somme River. During the night, British troops move into positions preparatory to launching on the following morning a major new offensive planned by General Rawlinson and approved by General Haig.

15 September 1916
Somme River. The British attack begins at 6:20 A.M. on a wide front stretching from Bouleaux Wood to Mouquet Farm. The troops advance behind a creeping barrage. They are meant to be supported by forty-nine tanks—their first appearance in battle—but only eighteen of these actually participate, as fifteen have failed to find their assembly sites and others bog down in the great shell craters of no-man's-land. In a few cases, the tanks fire on their own infantry because of the confusion of battle and difficulties in maneuvering. German shells destroy some of the strange new weapons. But where the tanks succeed in their role, astounded German troops give way or surrender in large groups. Improved communications and aerial reconnaissance also help the British effort. They capture Courcelette, push near the Mouquet Farm, secure Martinpuich, and take High Wood and Flers; they are stopped, however, at Bouleaux Wood and the nearby Quadrilateral.

16 September 1916
Somme River. As rains descend on the battlefield, German artillery bombards British positions. Though severely strained by troop commitments on the Eastern and Southern Fronts, the Germans move in five divisions of relief troops and launch unsuccessful counterattacks near Courcelette and against the French lines. The British offensive stagnates as Rawlinson's forces concentrate on consolidating their gains of the previous day.
Transylvania. The Romanian Second Army captures Baraoltu. General Falkenhayn arrives to assume command of the Ninth Army.
Isonzo River. The Italian Second Army captures Monte Rombon but is forced to withdraw. Appraising the new Isonzo offensive as unpromising, Gen. Count Luigi Cadorna calls it off and plans to try again later.
Cambrai. General Hindenburg orders construction of a defensive system of fortifications about twenty-five miles to the rear of the front. Known to the Germans as the "Siegfried Line" and termed the "Hindenburg Line" by the Allies, the system will be built by prisoners and civilians.
Romania. Mackensen's force attacks the Russian Dobrudja Army along a line between Rasova and Tuzla on the Black Sea.
Macedonia. French troops, after five days

of struggle, finally break through to capture Boresnica, sending the Bulgars into retreat toward Florina, seven miles distant and the major objective of the French drive.

17 September 1916
Macedonia. French and Russian troops capture Florina.

19 September 1916
Transylvania. Falkenhayn has amassed a superior force, including Gen. Krafft von Dellmensingen's topflight Alpine Corps, that outnumbers the Romanians by thirty-five battalions to twenty-five and boasts more than a three-to-one advantage in artillery. He attacks the Romanian First Army to the east of Hermannstadt, crossing the Carpathian Mountains and driving toward Petroseni.

Macedonia. After several days of slow advance, Serbian First Army troops capture the eastern peak of Mount Kajmak-calan, but the Bulgars still hold the crest of the ridge there and the western peak of the mountain.

German East Africa. Belgian troops commanded by Baron Charles Henri Tombeur, after several weeks of marching eastward along the Central Railway, capture Tabora, where Gov. Heinrich Schnee had moved his government and Maj. Gen. Kurt Wahle had concentrated his five-thousand-man force. Both the government and Wahle's troops, divided into three separate columns, have already evacuated the town and withdrawn to the southeast, with Schnee and his staff accompanying Wahle's column. Schnee's wife remains in Tabora in the governor's house. Numerous children and about 140 other women also remain behind. The Belgians liberate two thousand prisoners of war—Britons, Belgians, Italians, French, and Russians. Tombeur, content with his victories, does not pursue Wahle's troops.

22 September 1916
Arabia. Ghalib Pasha, Turkish governor general of the Hejaz region, surrenders the garrison of At Taif, with two thousand troops, to Abdulla ibn-Hussein, whose offensive has been effectively supported by

Egyptian artillery rushed from the Sudan by Gen. Sir Francis Reginald Wingate.

23 September 1916
London. Twelve naval Zeppelins stage a night raid on the capital, their bombs creating major fires in east London, but British fire destroys *L-32* and *L-33,* two of the Germans' new "super Zeppelins."

25 September 1916
Athens. Eleutherios Venizelos, having remained publicly silent about the mounting tension between his partisans and those of King Constantine, sails for his native Crete with a French escort.

Somme River. After a nine-day delay enforced by ongoing heavy rains, the British resume their offensive. The objectives are positions at Morval and Gueudecourt at the south of the front and Thiepval Ridge to the north. The British succeed in capturing Morval and Lesboeufs, but the German defense stops them at Gueudecourt.

26 September 1916
Somme River. Canadian troops of the Fifth Army join the offensive, attacking at Thiepval and driving the Germans out of the village, which artillery shelling has reduced to rubble. The French Sixth Army joins the offensive near Morval but to little effect.

Macedonia. Bulgarian troops counterattack and drive the Serbian First Army from the positions they had captured on Mount Kajmakcalan.

Transylvania. Falkenhayn's Ninth Army attacks the Romanian positions at Hermannstadt. The Alpine Corps breaks through the Rotenturm Pass.

Romania. Mackensen's troops capture Turturkai, a fortress on the Danube River, taking twenty-five thousand prisoners.

28 September 1916
Somme River. Canadian troops push ahead to the north of Courcelette and also north of the village of Thiepval. The Germans have abandoned their positions at Combles and Gueudecourt, allowing Allied troops to take control of these villages, as the British turn over part of their southern sector

of the line to the French Sixth Army and the first phase of the Battle of the Ancre draws to its conclusion.

29 September 1916
Transylvania. Falkenhayn's Ninth Army sends the Romanian First Army into hasty retreat. The fleeing Romanians hurl artillery guns and trucks into the Oly River to clear the road out of Hermannstadt so that their troops can escape. The Germans retake Hermannstadt and capture three thousand Romanian soldiers and thirteen guns. Now Falkenhayn is free to move eastward and attack the Romanian divisions concentrated near Brasov.
Somme River. Haig wants to keep pressure on the Germans, who he believes have lost 370,000 men so far in the Battle of the Somme and are severely strained. He orders a second general attack along the Ancre River front to commence on 12 October.
London. During a press interview, David Lloyd George, secretary of state for war, discourages peace initiatives by nonbelligerent nations: "The fight must be to a finish. . . . The whole world—including neutrals of the highest purposes and humanitarians with the best of motives—must know there can be no outside interference at this stage." His primary audience is Woodrow Wilson, who since February has been searching for ways to end the war. But the Allies are not interested in peace now; they wish to pursue their war aims. For the French, these include expelling German troops from French soil, retaking Alsace and Lorraine, extracting reparations from Germany, and winning guarantees that preclude future invasions by Germany. British aims include total victory and probably, though not officially stated, acquiring German colonies and somehow reducing Germany's naval and commercial status. The Germans, occupying French land, have no interest in accepting a return to the prewar European territorial, economic, and political realities as a condition for peace.

30 September 1916
Macedonia. The Serbian First Army has steadfastly stopped and then pushed back the Bulgars, recapturing ground on Mount Kajmakcalan. It now takes control of both its eastern and western peaks. The Allies have secured a line of advance extending from the mountain westward to the Mala Prespa Lake, but the advance now stagnates.

1 October 1916
Somme River. The second phase of the Battle of the Ancre begins as General Rawlinson sends his troops into the battle of the Transloy Ridges in an effort to advance and consolidate his line near the village of Le Sars prior to the start of the major offensive that General Haig plans.
Transylvania. German troops storm through the Vulcan Pass in the Petroseni region.
London. Despite their earlier losses, the Germans send another raid by eleven Zeppelins against London. British fighter planes set fire to *L-31,* a "super Zeppelin" commanded by the renowned Heinrich Mathy, who jumps to his death as his ship plummets to earth.

2 October 1916
Somme River. Rains deluge the entire front as Rawlinson's men continue to push forward.
Macedonia. Sarrail's combined French and Russian force drives the Bulgars from their redoubts on San Marco.

3 October 1916
Romania. Continuing his drive from Bulgaria, Mackensen forces the Romanians back across the Danube River. Falkenhayn's Ninth Army battles the Romanians at Kronstadt, while in the Petroseni region the Germans push the Romanians back to the Transylvania-Romania border.

5 October 1916
Somme River. Rawlinson's troops succeed in taking their initial objectives, the last one—a mill to the northwest of Eaucourt-l'Abbe—falling to them during the night. But the deluge continues, turning the entire Somme front into a quagmire that compounds the difficulties of moving troops and supplies.

6 October 1916
Macedonia. Under General Sarrail's orders, French artillery opens fire in the afternoon on the Bulgarian trenches at the Florina sector of the front, as French and Russian troops rush into a head-on attack against the Bulgarian line. They are stopped cold. To their right, Serbian troops make some headway along the Crna River between Brod and Scacevir.

Cadore region, Italy. Since the beginning of October, Italian troops have scaled several mountains to now gain control of the crest above the Avision River.

7 October 1916
Macedonia. Serbian troops manage to establish a bridgehead on the Crna River between Brod and Scacevir, but the Germans begin transferring troops from the Vardar sector to bolster the Bulgar defense here. At the direction of Hindenburg and Ludendorff, Gen. Otto von Below arrives at Skopje to assume command of the German Eleventh Army and the Bulgarian First Army, comprising the Macedonian Army Group.

8 October 1916
Newport, Rhode Island. With orders issued to the High Seas Fleet on 6 October to resume U-boat attacks on merchant ships, although not without prior warning, *U-53* sinks five ships (three British, one Dutch, and one Norwegian) in the first U-boat action of the war off the coast of the United States.

9 October 1916
Macedonia. Eleutherios Venizelos, having proclaimed in Crete a revolution designed to bring Greece into the war on the side of the Allies, arrives in Salonika to establish a provisional government with control of the "National Defense" movement and to create an army that will join the fight against the Bulgarian and German armies.

Isonzo River. The Eighth Battle of the Isonzo begins with an Italian artillery shelling of the Austro-Hungarian lines on the Carso Plateau. The Italian plan is to attack on the plateau east of Gorizia and the Vertojbica River, with major attacks at Nad Logem and Monte San Marco. The Italian Second and Third Armies, reinforced for the renewed offensive, comprise 225 battalions, with 1,305 guns. The Austrian Fifth Army, also reinforced, confronts them with 107 battalions and 538 guns stretched from Gorizia to the Gulf of Trieste on the Adriatic Sea.

10 October 1916
Mogilev, Russia. Swayed by the Czarina Alexandra (who is in the thrall of Rasputin), Czar Nicholas II officially orders cessation of the offensive. Brusilov has succeeded in forcing the Germans to redeploy forty-four divisions from other fronts, presumably relieving pressure on the French at Verdun, and has also forced the Austrians to forego pursuing the advantage accruing from their victory at Caporetto on the Trentino front. But whatever success the Brusilov Offensive may have achieved has been bought at enormous cost: 1,412,000 casualties. Before the offensive began, the Russians had already suffered a total of 5,366,000 casualties. The repercussions of such staggering losses and of rapidly growing social and economic turmoil on the home front promise tragedy for the regime.

Athens. Constantine's government receives an ultimatum from the Allies demanding surrender of the Greek fleet.

Isonzo River. Shortly before 3:00 P.M. the Italian attack begins, immediately encountering tenacious Austrian resistance.

11 October 1916
Athens. Constantine's government accedes to the ultimatum received from the Allies the day before. The Allies unload ammunition from some of the ships and tow away over twenty-four vessels, confiscated by the French navy.

12 October 1916
Isonzo River. The Eighth Battle of Isonzo concludes with the Italians overcoming a stubborn Austrian defense to capture a major salient between the Vippacco River and Hudilog and other objectives, while taking eighty-two hundred Austrian soldiers prisoner. Severe weather interrupts continuance of the offensive.

Trentino. After three days of assaulting Austrian positions, the Italians capture the Cosmagon Alps and Monte Roite.

13 October 1916
Romania. The Austrian First Army enters the fray, attacking in the area of the Trotus River valley, but a resolute Romanian defense holds fast.

14 October 1916
Somme River. After three days of fighting, British troops have managed to drive the Germans out of their trenches on the southern end of the so-called Schwaben Redoubt, but the Germans continue to hold the remainder of the redoubt.

15 October 1916
Macedonia. The impatient General Sarrail has ordered a renewed assault, so the combined force of French and Russian troops advances against the Bulgars in the early afternoon, meeting initial success but falling victim to enfilades of machine-gun fire. Their casualties near twenty-one hundred.

16 October 1916
Arabia. The renowned Arab expert Sir Ronald Storrs arrives at Jiddah on a mission from Cairo to gather information. With him is Capt. T.E. Lawrence. Abdulla ibn-Hussein meets them and apprises them of the state of the Arab revolt, which has simply attenuated even though sixteen thousand men remain in the field at Rabigh Mecca, and Yanbu' al Bahr.

18 October 1916
Somme River. The Transloy Ridges phase of the Battle of the Ancre comes to an end as Rawlinson's troops, attempting to advance, founder amid the mire, flooded trenches, and water-filled craters of the front. One of two tanks breaks across the front line, but the troops are too exhausted to follow; the tank turns back.
Arabia. Doubtful of Abdulla's capabilities as a leader, Lawrence leaves Jiddah to meet with Abdulla's brother Ali ibn-Hussein at Rabigh and subsequently with the third brother, Feisal ibn-Hussein, in command at Yanbu' al Bahr.

19 October 1916
Verdun. The relative status quo the front has experienced over recent weeks sunders as a French offensive planned by the triumvirate of Generals Pétain, Nivelle, and Mangin erupts with a cannonade of the German positions at Douaumont. The offensive's objective is the recapture of Fort Douaumont, and the French have effected certain advantages promising success. Three divisions will initiate the infantry attack, followed by three more divisions, both groups backed up by two divisions held in reserve. Pétain has amassed a superiority in guns—650 against at most 500 for the Germans—and among them are two new weapons, the 400 mm "super-heavies" made by Schneider-Creusot, the most massive guns France has yet devised, more powerful even than the Krupp "Big Berthas." And the advancing troops will be covered by a continuous creeping barrage instead of the usual suddenly silent artillery as the troops go over the top.
Romania. In the Dobrudja sector, Mackensen's army pursues the offensive with the objective of taking the major port, Constanta. Russian troops on the front fall back rapidly, giving their Romanian allies minuscule support.

20 October 1916
Romania. Mackensen's army captures Tuzla on the Black Sea.
Macedonia. Learning that the Serbians have captured the town of Brod, General von Below sends a message to OHL at Pless. The supreme command decides to deploy reinforcements to bolster the German forces in Macedonia.

21 October 1916
Somme River. British troops resume the attack on the German positions at the Schwaben Redoubt, taking five thousand yards of their enemy's trenches.
Macedonia. Rains have transformed major sectors of the front into a slough, precluding significant operations by Sarrail's army.
Vienna. Friedrich Adler, son of the leader of the Social Democrats, Viktor Adler, walks into a hotel restaurant where Prime

Minister Count Karl von Sturgkh has just finished eating lunch, draws a pistol, and shoots the prime minister. The dead count seems a victim of the growing economic and political turbulence in Austria-Hungary, which is divided by many ethnic groups and movements.

22 October 1916

Verdun. In the afternoon, the French cannonade ceases, cheers arise from the French trenches, and the German artillery, heretofore quiet, opens up on the line of the expected French attack. But there is no attack. Nivelle has tricked the Germans into revealing the placements of their artillery, and the French barrage begins again, now focused on destroying the German guns.

Romania. Bulgarian cavalry in Mackensen's army gallop up the coast into Constanta in full view of the Russian Black Sea Fleet, which steams off into open water. Romanian and Russian forces retreat to a line to the north of the railway connecting Constanta with Cernavoda, where German troops capture the main bridge spanning the Danube River.

23 October 1916

Verdun. For four days, Fort Douaumont has withstood the pounding of the French artillery, the worst damage being the loss of an artillery observation turret on 21 October. But near midday the French unleash the "super-heavies," firing at ten- to fifteen-minute intervals with impressive accuracy and wreaking catastrophe on the fort's interior and the garrisoning troops. The sixth direct hit penetrates a major depot filled with rockets and small arms ammunition, setting off a great explosion. Threatened by a repeat of the 8 May disaster and believing that to remain in the fort is suicidal, the commanding officers order its evacuation. As night falls and the "super-heavies" cease their shelling while fires continue to rage within the fort, the Germans move out.

Wilhelmshaven. Twenty-four destroyers under the general command of Capt. A. Michelsen steam out of port headed for Zeebrugge. The Admiralty alerts Admiral Jellicoe in case Michelsen's movements presage putting to sea of the High Seas Fleet.

24 October 1916

Verdun. The French attack sweeps forward in a morning mist. German field guns, reduced to perhaps only a hundred by the barrage of 22 October, remain silent until twelve minutes into the sally, too late to prevent the French troops from advancing into their lines. Exhausted and demoralized, German troops surrender in droves. Lifting fog reveals Fort Douaumont, and French troops rush in, capturing twenty-nine Germans—two unwittingly left behind when the fort was evacuated and the others who had entered after the evacuation. The day's victory restores to the French much of the ground lost in May and June. They also capture six thousand German prisoners.

Arabia. T.E. Lawrence visits Sherif Hussein's third son, Feisal, in the hills of Al Hamra overlooking Yanbu' al Bahr, from which a small force of Turkish troops has driven him. Lawrence immediately discerns in Feisal the leader the Arab revolt needs to succeed.

25 October 1916

Romania. Units of Falkenhayn's Ninth Army have traversed the mountains and pushed forward, trying to reach the plains of Wallachia, but they stall now before Romanian defenses near Targu Jiu and farther to the north above Curtea de Arges, where the onslaught of winter impedes further advance by the Alpine Corps.

Isonzo River. Interrupted by inclement weather, the Italian offensive along a line from Monte San Marco to the Adriatic begins again with an artillery bombardment of the Austrian positions.

German East Africa. German troops commanded by Maj. Gen. Kurt Wahle attack South African troops at Iringa but are repulsed. The South Africans trap one of Wahle's columns, forcing its surrender, as Wahle withdraws toward Mahenge.

26 October 1916

Verdun. The Germans counterattack four times without success.

English Channel. Michelsen's destroyers set out from Zeebrugge and raid British net barrage drifters and other ships in the straits between Dover and Calais. The Germans sink two destroyers and seven drifters. The British destroyer *Zulu* is damaged by a mine and her sister ship, the *Nubian,* by a torpedo. (The latter's undamaged bow section will later be welded to the former's undamaged stern section to create the *Zubian.*) Michelsen's flotilla escapes to Zeebrugge.

27 October 1916
Verdun. A final German counterattack fails, as the French push forward four hundred yards beyond Fort Douaumont.

28 October 1916
Verdun. The French pursue their offensive, commencing an artillery bombardment of Fort Vaux.
Somme River. Capt. Oswald Boelcke, commander of the *Jasta 2* squadron, mastermind of the tactics of aerial combat, and Germany's leading airman with forty victories in the skies over the Western Front, dies in a midair collision with his fellow airman Lt. Erwin Boehme while dogfighting with Royal Flying Corps planes above the village of Pozieres.
Isonzo River. The Italians pause briefly after three days of bombardment preliminary to a renewed attack.

1 November 1916
Isonzo River. Italian artillery resumes its bombardment as the Ninth Battle of the Isonzo opens, with the infantry attacking shortly after 11:00 A.M. and breaking through the Austrian lines.
Arabia. T.E. Lawrence sails from Jiddah to Port Sudan en route to Khartoum to report his findings to Gen. Sir Francis Wingate.

2 November 1916
Verdun. After five days of bombardment by French artillery, the German garrison at Fort Vaux abandons the fort during the night.
Mesopotamia. Lt. Gen. Sir S.F. Maude, content to allow the experts to handle affairs at Basra, leaves for the front to organize and supply his forces preparatory to launching an offensive.

3 November 1916
Verdun. The French offensive concludes when, during the morning, French troops reclaim possession of Fort Vaux.
North Sea. Two German U-boats become stranded in fog off the west coast of Jutland, and Admiral Scheer dispatches to their rescue a flotilla that includes four dreadnoughts. They save one of the U-boats, but a British submarine torpedoes the dreadnoughts SMS *Kronprinz Wilhelm* and SMS *Grosser Kurfurst.* The two ships return safely to harbor but must be drydocked for repairs. The near loss of the dreadnoughts upsets Kaiser Wilhelm II and leads Scheer to conclude that the naval war is now best left to the U-boats.

4 November 1916
Isonzo River. The ninth battle ends with the Italians having pushed the Austrians back at various sites on the Carso Plateau, gaining three miles beyond Vallone but failing to reach their major objective, Salone. Severe weather and heavy casualties (twenty-eight thousand men) induce Cadorna to terminate the offensive.
Arabia. In Mecca, Sherif Hussein is crowned "King of the Arabs."

5 November 1916
Berlin. The Two Emperors' Manifesto issued by Kaiser Wilhelm II and Franz Joseph declares Poland a semi-independent kingdom, comprised mostly of the former Russian part of the nation, under the protectorate of Germany and Austria-Hungary.

7 November 1916
Washington. Into the late night, election reports indicate that Woodrow Wilson has failed to win re-election as president of the United States. But returns from the western states reverse the outcome, as Wilson defeats Republican candidate Charles Evans Hughes and secures four more years in the White House.

11 November 1916
Macedonia. Serbian troops capture a thou-

sand prisoners in the Crna sector of the front, as General Sarrail, having reorganized his forces, anticipates capturing Monastir.

Romania. The Germans have reorganized and reenforced under Falkenhayn, who places General Kühne in charge of the front and provides him massive superiority over the Romanian forces—thirty-three battalions to fourteen—at the Vulcan and Surduc Passes. The Germans begin a new drive toward the plains of Wallachia, and Kühne smashes through the Surduc Pass.

13 November 1916
Somme River. With Haig's approval, Lt. Gen. Hubert Gough commits the IInd and Vth Corps of his Fifth Army to the Battle of the Ancre in an effort to advance the British front line along the Ancre River from the Quadrilateral to Beaumont Hamel. In less than three hours, the IInd Corps succeeds in achieving its objectives, taking the rest of the German trenches at Schwaben Ridge and the south bank of the Ancre and two major bridges at Beaucourt. The Vth Corps, following the use of gas at Beaumont Hamel, fights its way into the village, but has less success at Redan Ridge and fails at Serre.

Romania. John Norton-Griffiths arrives in Bucharest. A munitions expert who devised the mining of the Messines Ridge, he has been sent by the British government to make certain the extremely valuable Romanian oil fields and grain stores do not fall into German hands as the Romanian army retreats. He has authority to promise the Romanian government compensation for any losses resulting from his assignment. Unable to obtain government approval, although he understands that he has the monarchy's support, Norton-Griffiths sets out on his mission in defiance of the officials.

14 November 1916
Romania. Kühne's troops advance to Bumbesti Jiu on the plains of "Little Wallachia." Farther north, Krafft's Alpine Corps takes Caineni.

15 November 1916
Romania. Kühne's cavalry division, com-

manded by Gen. Count von Schmettow, which has been protecting Kühne's right flank, rides into Targu Jiu, as the Romanians fall back before the German advance.

Chantilly. Allied commanders confer on plans for 1917 while the political leaders meet in Paris. Joffre advocates continuing the strategy of 1916—that is, pursuing large-scale attacks on the German lines on the Western Front. The commanders agree that the Western Front should be primary; that they should keep pressure on the Germans as much as possible whenever the weather allows through the winter; that if one of them is attacked, the others will create diversionary offensives elsewhere on the fronts; and that they will be prepared to begin major new offensives as early as February.

18 November 1916
Somme River. Having consolidated gains during the intervening days, Gough's Fifth Army pushes toward Grandcourt and advances a thousand yards beyond Beaucourt and Beaumont Hamel, bringing to a successful conclusion the Battle of the Ancre.

Verdun. Unsatisfied with the gains achieved in October, Gen. Robert Nivelle secures Joffre's approval of another offensive along a six-mile front extending from Vacherauville on the Meuse River to Damloup.

19 November 1916
Somme River. With the British success along the Ancre River consolidated, the Battle of the Somme concludes. Through the duration of the battle—over four and a half months—the casualties for both sides well surpass a million men: the Germans have lost 660,000; the British and French, 630,000.

Macedonia. Though slowed by winter weather, Sarrail's troops have pushed ahead toward Monastir. The Germans, intent on avoiding entrapment, have abandoned Monastir during the night, and French and Serbian cavalry enter the town and assume control.

Athens. The Allies present an ultimatum to Constantine's government demanding that official representatives of the Central

French mounted trooper, 1916 (by Jean Berne-Bellecour, courtesy of the Anne S.K. Brown Military Collection, Brown University Library)

Powers be sent home and that all war matériel be surrendered to Allied forces.

20 November 1916
Romania. Schmettow's cavalry reaches Slatina on the Olt River.

21 November 1916
Vienna. Shortly before 10:00 P.M., the eighty-six-year-old Emperor Franz Joseph dies. He had been monarch of the Habsburg kingdom of Austria since 1848 and of the combined Austria-Hungary kingdom since 1867. His grand nephew, Archduke Karl, succeeds him as Karl I. The new emperor will force Prime Minister Count Istvan Tisza, a Hungarian, out of office and will assume supreme command of the Austro-Hungarian army.
Berlin. Arthur Zimmerman becomes foreign minister, replacing Gottlieb von Jagow.

22 November 1916
German East Africa. Murray's Column, the force of British South African Police commanded by Lt. Col. Ronald Ernest Murray, captures a German force operating south of Tabora that includes seven German officers and forty-seven men of other European nationalities.

23 November 1916
Somme River. Manfred von Richthofen shoots down Maj. Lanoe Hawker, Great Britain's premier flying ace, over Bapaume. It is Richthofen's ninth victory.
Romania. As Kühne's infantry arrives at Slatina on the Olt, Gen. August von Mackensen, having paused in his Dobruja offensive, begins a new offensive on the Danube River across from Zimricea, where he has assembled a combined force of German, Austro-Hungarian, Bulgarian, and Turkish troops. During an obscuring fog, his troops quietly cross the river in barges and capture Zimricea, in preparation for an advance against the Romanian capital, Bucharest.
London. Gen. Sir Douglas Haig, following the Chantilly Conference of 15 November, has been in London holding discussions with Gen. Sir William Robertson, chief of the Imperial General Staff, and Admiralty officials, advocating his purpose to concentrate in 1917 on driving the Germans out of Flanders. Prime Minister Asquith gives Haig his approval of this resolve and the other strategies agreed to at Chantilly.
Salonika. Venizelos's Provisional Government declares war on Germany and Bulgaria.

24 November 1916
Petrograd. Prime Minister Boris Sturmer resigns, succeeded by Alexander Trepov.

29 November 1916
Scapa Flow. Adm. David Beatty succeeds Adm. Sir John Jellicoe as commander in chief of the Grand Fleet.

30 November 1916
Athens. Constantine's government rejects the Allies' ultimatum of 19 November. Allied ships disembark troops at Peiraeus.

1 December 1916
Romania. Although overextended, the

Germans have successfully withstood Romanian attacks meant to save Bucharest, in part because a Romanian staff car carrying officers with the attack plans mistakenly drove straight into a German position. As the German noose tightens around Bucharest, the government abandons the capital, withdrawing to Jassy.

Athens. The Allies re-embark the troops landed at Peiraeus after a three-and-a-half-hour skirmish between their sailors and marines and Constantine's troops.

3 December 1916

Romania. A final Romanian effort collapses in defeat as Falkenhayn's Ninth Army sweeps down on them from the rear. Those not taken prisoner fall back to Bucharest.

4 December 1916

London. First Lord of the Admiralty Balfour, hoping to defuse press and public criticism of and demands for change at the Admiralty resulting from the Germans' raids in the English Channel in October and November as well as merchant shipping losses to the U-boats, secured Admiral Jellicoe's acceptance of the post of First Sea Lord on 22 November. Jellicoe now assumes the post, replacing Adm. Sir Henry Jackson, who has no regrets about leaving the Admiralty.

5 December 1916

Warsaw. In order to put into effect the Two Emperors' Manifesto, the German governor-general of Warsaw and his Austrian counterpart in Lublin establish a Provisional Council of State for Poland in Warsaw. Among its twenty-five members chosen by the two emperors is Josef Pilsudski, an opponent of Russian interests in Poland who largely favors ties to Austria and who organized the Polish Legion for service in Galicia. He heads the council's Military Commission.

Romania. General Mackensen sends a note to the Romanians in Bucharest inquiring whether the city will undergo siege. The note is brought back unopened—the Romanian troops have already abandoned the capital. Their only alternative was to accept being surrounded.

6 December 1916

German East Africa. Lt. Col. Paul von Lettow-Vorbeck and his *Schutztruppe* fail in their efforts to capture Kibata and the British supplies of food and ammunition there that his troops need. He moves off northward across the Rufiji River.

7 December 1916

Romania. General Mackensen occupies Bucharest. Falkenhayn's Ninth Army turns to the north in hopes of capturing the oil fields and refineries at Ploesti, but Falkenhayn is too late: John Norton-Griffiths has done his work. The oil fields at Ploesti, Targoviste, and elsewhere are aflame and their refining facilities in ruins—a severe loss to the German war effort, as it will be months before production can be restored. (Norton-Griffiths will also succeed in destroying many of the grain stores and making his way safely out of Romania, returning to England by way of Russia and Scandinavia.) The Romanians retreat toward the Siret River and Russia, with the Germans following after. The Romanians have endured three hundred thousand casualties, half of them prisoners. German casualties number two hundred thousand.

London. After months of in-fighting, Lloyd George's machinations and parliamentary disgruntlement with the conduct of the war have won, the final twist being formation of a new, small War Council with Lloyd George as chairman and Asquith excluded. Both Lloyd George and Asquith have resigned their positions, and now David Lloyd George becomes prime minister and forms a new cabinet. Among the fallen is Arthur Balfour, replaced as first lord of the admiralty by Sir Edward Carson.

8 December 1916

Athens. Allied ships begin a blockade of Greece declared on 2 December.

11 December 1916

Macedonia. Gen. Maurice Sarrail receives orders from General Joffre to terminate his offensive, already bogged down by heavy snows. German artillery is still within range of Monastir.

A German gun crew, 1915 (by J.A. Sailor, courtesy of the Anne S.K. Brown Military Collection, Brown University Library)

12 December 1916
Berlin. Chancellor Theobald von Bethmann Hollweg tries to initiate a peace-making process, presenting a speech in the *Reichstag* and also having Ambassador Count Johann von Bernstorff deliver a request to the White House, inviting Wilson's intervention. Other neutrals are also invited to participate. Bethmann Hollweg is concerned that the kaiser will accede to pressures from Hindenburg and Ludendorff to resume unrestricted U-boat warfare, and believes that will bring the United States into the war on the Allies' side. He is also convinced that Germany cannot win the war and that his own position is in jeopardy. Nevertheless, he makes no concrete offers of terms for peace and even speaks boastfully of Germany's war successes and determination.

13 December 1916
Mesopotamia. Maj. Gen. F.S. Maude's troops, well rested and reinforced to a total of 150,000 (of whom about 72,000 will concentrate on the central front on the Tigris River), open their long-awaited offensive with an artillery bombardment of Turkish positions at Sannaiyat. Maude has no intention of attacking the strong garrison at Sannaiyat, however, but merely wishes to provide a feint so that during the night his troops can secretly pass by on the Tigris's right bank toward their actual objective, the recapture of Kut. The ruse works.

14 December 1916
Mesopotamia. Maude's troops cross the Shatt-al-Hai River and arrive at Kala Haji Fahan. From here a cavalry brigade moves on toward the bridge over the Tigris River at Shumran, above Kut, while the rest of the troops prepare for an advance to Kut the following morning. Although the cavalry is repulsed at Shumran, during the night RFC planes bomb the bridge, rendering it unserviceable.

15 December 1916
Verdun. Fulfilling his promise to keep the pressure on the Germans, Nivelle sends the French Second Army into a limited offensive on a bitter winter day, retaking Louvemont and Bezonvaux and extending the front line two miles beyond Fort Douaumont. During the night, Nivelle

leaves his headquarters at Souilly ostensibly to assume command of "the Armies of the North and the Northwest."

Mesopotamia. As a British flotilla bombards the garrison at Sannaiyat, Maude's troops advance to positions across the river from Kut, confronting a strong Turkish garrison at Hai salient.

18 December 1916
Washington. Through the State Department, President Wilson releases a message he has worked on for weeks that calls on all the belligerent nations to reveal their terms for peace, asserts that all nations of whatever size want guarantees of security against aggression, and advocates consideration of forming "a league of nations to insure peace and justice throughout the world." Wilson does not offer himself as mediator but says he would be available if wanted. His primary purpose at the moment is to keep alive the initiative offered by Bethmann Hollweg.

20 December 1916
Mesopotamia. After five days of consolidating his position, Maude sends troops to attempt a crossing of the Tigris, but without success. As winter rains set in, Maude pauses and digs in.

21 December 1916
Egypt. Gen. Sir Archibald Murray, after months of preparation, has his Sinai force ready to advance to El Arish and beyond. The preparations have included building a railway for movement of supplies, completing a water pipeline to Romani, and assembling a Camel Transport Corps of thirty-five thousand camels with Egyptian drivers. Leader of the advance is Lt. Gen. Sir Philip Chetwode. Chetwode occupies El Arish without firing a shot.

22 December 1916
Verdun. Gen. Charles Mangin, Nivelle's ruthless right hand, leaves Souilly to take command of the Sixth Army. With the departure of Nivelle and Mangin, the ten-month Battle of Verdun—the longest battle in history—comes to an end. Over the course of the battle, France has suffered 377,231 casualties; Germany, 337,000—a total exceeding 700,000, including perhaps 420,000 dead. The dreadful toll evokes the final futility of Verdun.

23 December 1916
Egypt. Again apprised by air reconnaissance of a Turkish force at Magdhaba, Chetwode sends mounted horse and camel brigades to the attack. Although not easily persuaded by a day-long fight, the Turks finally abandon and surrender the town at 6:30 P.M.

26 December 1916
Paris. Prime Minister Aristede Briand, reacting to parliamentary opposition to Gen. Joseph Joffre that has increased throughout the year, has been whittling away at Joffre's powers. He now takes the final step, forcing Joffre's resignation as commander in chief of the French armies. Joffre is named Marshal of France, the first general to be so honored since 1870, and he enters the oblivion of retirement. His successor as commander in chief is Gen. Robert Nivelle.

30 December 1916
Petrograd. During the early morning hours, Rasputin visits the home of Prince Felix Yusupov at the prince's invitation. The prince gives him cakes laced with cyanide and then fires several shots into his back, but the monk lives. The count and his co-conspirators, including the czar's cousin Grand Duke Dmitri, beat and kick the wounded Rasputin as he drags himself across the floor, and they shoot him repeatedly. Then they bind him and take him to the Neva River, where they shove him down into the river's freezing waters through a hole in the ice. Rasputin drowns.
Allied capitals. After separately denouncing Bethmann Hollweg's call for a peace conference as insincere, the Allied governments issue an official joint response rejecting the proposal as a public relations gimmick, accusing Germany of criminal actions, and asserting their continuing agreement never to make peace individually. For the present, neither Bethmann-Hollweg's nor Wilson's proposal has any chance of success.

In January, the German high command, now in control of nearly the entire German state, decides to gamble on unrestricted submarine warfare: if the U-boats can strangle the Allied war effort and starve Great Britain without drawing the Americans into the conflict too soon, then Germany will win the war. They announce the policy and begin to sink commercial ships on February 1. The ploy comes within a whisker of triumph—Britain is close to the limit of endurance before the adoption of the convoy system alleviates the problem—but the gamble fails when the United States declares war in April, although it will be many months before the weight of American arms is felt on the Western Front.

In Russia, the Romanov empire disintegrates. Bread riots in March in Saint Petersburg grow into a full-fledged revolution, and the czar abdicates, soon to be arrested with his entire family. A provisional government attempts to govern the country and even tries to continue the war effort, but to no avail. Thousands desert from the army, and those who stay refuse to obey orders, often shooting their officers. Workers' and soldiers' councils (called "soviets") are established and begin to wield power. A mild offensive by the remnants of the army in June collapses, and Russia is effectively removed as a belligerent. A German advance rushes to take Riga in September. Two months later, revolutionaries storm the Winter Palace in Saint Petersburg, and a Marxist faction, called Bolsheviks, seizes control of the Russian state. By December, the Bolsheviks are negotiating a peace with the Germans.

On the Western Front, the Germans withdraw in many sectors to a fortified line (known as the Hindenburg Line) and wait for the Allies to attack. Ludendorff is in nearly complete control of civilian affairs as well as military operations. After March, troops can be withdrawn from the East and fed into the Western Front. The French and British decide on another grand offensive and launch attacks in April. As the meat grinder devours men, mutinies break out among the French regiments and by spring have become general, but the Germans fail to perceive that nearly the entire French army has taken itself temporarily out of action. In May, Pétain is made commander in chief, and he quells the mutinies and restores order. Meanwhile, British offensives near Arras take another big toll. A large new offensive begins in July in the Ypres region and lasts until November, with heavy losses and almost no gain. Near Cambrai in November, the British use coordinated tank and infantry attacks to break the German defenses, but they cannot follow up swiftly enough. Within days the Germans take back all that was lost.

To the south, the Italians try an offensive in the Trentino in June but achieve little. The combined Germans and Austrians, however, make one of the most successful assaults of the war in the fall and push the Italians armies backward pell-mell all the way to the Piave River.

In the Balkans, the Allied army of Salonika fails in a campaign against the Bulgarians. In Mesopotamia and Palestine, however, the British and the Arabs (led by T.E. Lawrence) begin a gradual series of advances that grind away at the Turks.

1 January 1917

Egypt. While reconnoitering at Sheikh Zowaiid, British cavalrymen have discovered that the village has a substantial water supply. Here, ten miles southeast of Rafah, Chetwode's troops concentrate for the advance to Rafah. The Turks' retreat into Palestine has left the Sinai effectively free of Turkish troops.

London. Prime Minister David Lloyd George leaves for a conference of the Allies in Rome with a British delegation that includes Gen. Sir William Robertson, chief of the Imperial General Staff. The focus of the Rome conference is the possibility of shifting the major war effort to the fronts in Italy and the Balkans, as Lloyd George advocates.

Submarines

When World War I began, the submarine was a very old weapon, invented during the American Revolution almost a century and a half before. However, the submarine had not been used extensively or effectively until the German navy brought its U-boat fleet to bear against commercial shipping during 1917. The modern submarine used during World War I was small, cramped, and incredibly uncomfortable for its crew, but it was a deadly weapon at sea, especially when it struck without warning by launching underwater torpedo attacks. Both sides had reasonably large numbers of submarines when the war began, but neither the Central Powers nor the Allies ever used submarines to any major advantage against opposing navies. The British had minor success in the Gallipoli campaign, and the Germans attempted to use their U-boats against the British blockade in the North Atlantic, yet these were essentially sideshows. The main usefulness of the submarine was as a commerce destroyer. Subs could roam the shipping lanes virtually undetected, and once freed from the self-imposed restriction of surfacing to warn victims before an attack, the underwater warships proved able to devastate shipping. Subs were vulnerable to cannon fire when on the surface, but there were practically no good offensive weapons to detect or damage a submarine that remained submerged. When Germany began unrestricted submarine warfare in early 1917, the result was very nearly to starve Great Britain into submission. Only the belated adoption of the convoy system managed to avert defeat.

---

3 January 1917

Arabia. Capt. T.E. Lawrence has been trying to prepare defenses for Yanbu' al Bahr, to which Feisal ibn-Hussein has been forced to retreat after being defeated by the Turks in early December 1916. Lawrence is deeply impressed by the patience and steadfastness Feisal evidences in dealing with his restless Bedouin tribesmen. The British captain now leaves Yanbu' al Bahr with Feisal and the remnants of his force, heading for Al Wajh, which Feisal had earlier proposed to attack.

6 January 1917

Mesopotamia. Certain that he must secure the right bank of the Tigris River before assaulting Kut, Lt. Gen. Sir F.S. Maude issues orders to begin operations against the Turkish position at Khudhaira Bend in the river above Kut.

9 January 1917

Egypt. Chetwode's troops attack the major Turkish defenses at Rafah at a site known as "The Reduit." Although the British outflank "The Reduit," taking Rafah and effectively surrounding the Turks, their attack stalls in the late afternoon as Turkish reinforcements approach. But a final assault leads to a Turkish surrender, with over sixteen hundred taken prisoner. Not wanting to expose his force to counterattack from Palestine, Chetwode withdraws, but his advance to Rafah has secured Egypt and the entire Sinai for the British.

Pless. During a meeting of the War Council, Chancellor Bethmann Hollweg accepts the inevitability of capitulating on the issue of unrestricted submarine warfare to Gen. Erich Ludendorff, whose influence with the kaiser exceeds his own. Ludendorff and his collaborator, Field Marshal Paul von Hindenburg, are now effectively in control of policymaking. Although recognizing the possibility, even likelihood, that unrestricted submarine warfare will cause the United States to join the Allies, Ludendorff believes that American entrance into the war will be too little too late. He has the total support of the German navy and the assurances of navy officials that unleashing the U-boats to curtail shipments of grains and other supplies to Great Britain will so cripple that nation that the British will be rendered incapable of continuing the war beyond August 1917.

9 January 1917
Mesopotamia. To distract the Turks' attention from his objective at Khudhaira Bend, Maude has staged actions all along his line but at some cost, with serious casualties at Sannaiyat. A one-hour artillery bombardment of the Turkish lines at Khudhaira Bend begins at 7:30 A.M. The troops attack at 9:00 A.M. and capture the Turks' first line, but a fierce Turkish counterattack recaptures part of it. As night approaches, a British counterattack accompanied by an artillery shelling regains the lost ground, giving the British an advance of a thousand yards for the day at a cost of seven hundred casualties.

10 January 1917
Washington. The Allied governments respond to Pres. Woodrow Wilson's statement of 18 December. They place blame for the war on Germany and Austria-Hungary and outline some general terms, including restoration of Belgium, Serbia, and Montenegro, with reparations; restoration of areas in France, Russia, and Romania occupied by the Central Powers; European security guarantees; deprivation of any Turkish European presence; and restoration of lands and sovereignty to Slavic, Italian, Romanian, and Czech peoples under foreign dominance. No mention is made of the German colonies.
Mesopotamia. In the morning, the British discover that the Turks have abandoned the remainder of the front line they had still clung to at the end of fighting the previous day. The British occupy the trenches.

11 January 1917
Mesopotamia. At two in the afternoon, the British attack under cover of artillery, but the Turks have reinforced their troops during the night. In less than an hour, their counterattack drives the British back upon their own lines, where machine-gun fire halts the Turks.

15 January 1917
Washington. A Joint High Commission of American and Mexican officials established to discuss the tensions between the two countries and to suggest remedies disbands because Gen. Venustiano Carranza has rejected (27 December) a protocol the group had agreed to (the Mexicans reluctantly) that mandated the withdrawal of the Punitive Expedition led by Gen. John J. Pershing only when conditions in the northern Mexican states permit. Carranza insists on immediate withdrawal of the expedition without any preconditions.
London. At Lloyd George's invitation, Gen. Robert Nivelle visits London to advocate his plan for the spring 1917 Western Front campaign. Nivelle's plan is to use the tactics he applied at Verdun in three limited attacks along a front from Arras to Rheims. He has declared to the Second Army that "victory is certain." The victory will be assured by heavy use of artillery, which so far in the war has accounted for well over half of all casualties, in a creeping barrage that will allow the infantry to rapidly overrun the German batteries and hasten on to take their trenches in a "decisive battle." One sticking point is that Nivelle wants the British to extend their part of the front twenty or twenty-five miles south of the Somme River. British Commander in Chief Sir Douglas Haig, while appearing to be accommodating, agrees to an extension of only eight miles, thus annoying Nivelle and setting the stage for controversy between the two commanders and their governments. Lloyd George, however, welcomes Nivelle in hopes that his plan for brief and limited actions will obviate major offensives by the BEF and also will set the stage for dismissing Haig, whom he distrusts for callously undertaking battles that generate enormous casualties.

16 January 1917
Berlin. Foreign Minister Arthur Zimmermann believes from messages sent by Heinrich von Eckhardt, the German minister in Mexico City, that Gen. Venustiano Carranza is definitely pro-German. Zimmermann thinks Carranza would be will-

ing to permit U-boat bases in Mexico and would agree to stop providing oil to the Royal Navy at Tampico. Wanting to encourage hostilities between Mexico and the United States as a means of preventing American involvement in the war, Zimmermann wires a message to Mexico City via Stockholm, Buenos Aires, and Washington, D.C.—forwarded from there by Count Bernstorff. The message tells Eckhardt that, if Germany's unrestricted submarine warfare draws the United States into the war, then Eckhardt should offer Mexico an alliance promising "Joint conduct of the war. Joint conclusion of peace. Ample financial support and an agreement on our part that Mexico shall gain back by conquest the territory lost by her at a prior period in Texas, New Mexico, and Arizona." Eckhardt should also ask Carranza to invite Japan to join the alliance.

18 January 1917
Washington. Facing the possibility that the United States will become involved in the European fighting and not wanting open hostilities with Mexico, Wilson decides to withdraw the Punitive Expedition from northern Mexico.

19 January 1917
Mesopotamia. Shifting their tactics after 11 January, Maude's troops have executed small advances supported by artillery for a week. During the night of 18-19 January, the Turks finally succumb, retreating from their trenches to cross the river. The first phase of Maude's offensive ends, with the stage set for an attack on the Hai salient.

20 January 1917
German East Africa. Gen. Jan Smuts confers his command on Maj. Gen. A. Reginald Hoskins and leaves for England to attend the Imperial War Conference. He believes that Lettow-Vorbeck will be defeated within a few months, ending the war in East Africa.

22 January 1917
Washington. President Wilson addresses the Senate. He reviews responses to his peace initiatives and declares: "The question upon which the whole future peace and policy of the world depends is this: Is the present war a struggle for a just and secure peace, or only for a new balance of power? . . . [There] must be, not a balance of power, but a community of power: not organized rivalries but an organized common peace. . . . First of all . . . it must be a peace without victory." He advocates equality of nations and of rights, freedom of the seas, reduction of armaments, and other policies. He concludes: "These are American principles, American policies. We could stand for no others. And they are also the principles and policies of forward-looking men and women everywhere, of every modern nation, of every enlightened community. They are the principles of mankind and must prevail."

23 January 1917
Russia. The German Eighth Army, commanded by Gen. Friedrich von Scholtz, launches an offensive on the northern sector of the front aimed toward Riga. The Germans encounter fierce resistance.
English Channel. Learning that a flotilla of German destroyers is en route to Zeebrugge, Vice Adm. Sir Reginald Bacon, commander of the Dover Patrol, sends a fleet of two dozen destroyers and cruisers commanded by Rear Adm. Sir Reginald Tyrwhitt out of Harwich to intercept the Germans. Tyrwhitt's HMS *Centaur* spots the German flotilla, but the Germans lay down a smoke screen and scatter. In the resulting confusion, Tyrwhitt's force damages two of the German destroyers, but the German flotilla escapes destruction, with most of the ships returning safely to Zeebrugge.

25 January 1917
Mesopotamia. The British assault on the Hai salient begins successfully, capturing eighteen hundred yards of the Turks' front lines on both banks of the river. But four Turkish counterattacks supported by a large German mortar and carried out by troops using only hand grenades retake the lost positions while inflicting eleven hundred casualties on the British.

Arabia. Lawrence and Feisal enter Al Wajh, taking the city from the Turks, who quickly surrender after a bombardment from British ships off the coast—an easy, nearly bloodless victory for Feisal that suddenly gives the Arabs the upper hand, as the Turks go on the defensive.

26 January 1917
Mesopotamia. In twelve hours of fierce fighting, Punjabi troops retake the line gained and then lost the day before.

27 January 1917
Mexico. Units of the Punitive Expedition begin withdrawal to bases in Texas.

31 January 1916
Washington. Shortly after 4:00 P.M., Count Bernstorff delivers to Secretary of State Robert Lansing at the State Department a note informing him that Germany will resume unrestricted submarine warfare on the following day. The note justifies this move on the grounds that the Allies "desire to fight to the bitter end" and are determined to carve up Germany, Austria-Hungary, Bulgaria, and Turkey—thus Germany is forced to continue fighting, and with any weapon available. The count expresses deep regret, and tears well in his eyes as he says goodbye to Lansing. Two memoranda accompanying the note state that, beginning 1 February, German U-boats will sink without prior warning all ships in waters around Great Britain, France, and Italy and in the eastern Mediterranean; that there will be a certain grace period for merchantmen and passenger liners; and that the United States will be allowed to send one ship per week out of Falmouth, England, if it is guaranteed not to contain contraband and is marked with red-and-white stripes. On this same afternoon, in response to Wilson's speech of 22 January, an aide to Bernstorff travels to New York to provide Col. Edward M. House with the terms Germany desires in accepting peace. The terms include restitution of that part of Alsace the French have occupied; provision of a frontier to protect Poland and Germany from Russia; restitution of those parts of France occupied by

German troops, with financial compensation but also with adjustments to the frontier; restoration of Belgium with guarantees for German security; restoration of German colonies; "freedom of the seas"; and an end to restrictive commercial treaties. But of course the resumption of unrestricted submarine warfare ends any hope of continuing the effort to pursue a process toward peace. When Wilson learns of Bernstorff's note, he says: "The break that we have tried so hard to prevent now seems inevitable." The president is ready to sever diplomatic relations with Germany, though not to go to war.

1 February 1917
Berlin. Germany defines zones surrounding the British Isles, off the French coast, and in the Mediterranean Sea as waters wherein U-boats will sink any ship without warning. The U-boat fleet assigned this task consists of 105 submarines.
Washington. Reacting to Germany's announcement of the resumption of unrestricted submarine warfare, which President Wilson tells his cabinet came as an "astounding surprise," the government of the United States terminates diplomatic relations with Germany and orders Count Bernstorff to leave the country.
Mesopotamia. With his troops having doggedly pushed forward a thousand yards at the Hai salient, General Maude tries to finish the job of driving the Turks from the site, but the day's attack founders, with two brigades of Sikh troops suffering a thousand casualties in rigorous battle.

3 February 1917
Russia. General Scholtz's drive toward Riga concludes after achieving fractional gains and sustaining heavy casualties. Because of the losses, Hindenburg and Ludendorff reject Scholtz's request for reinforcements, and fighting on the Eastern Front comes to an end for the rest of the winter.
Mesopotamia. After regrouping his troops, Maude tries again, this time succeeding in clearing the Turkish trenches.

5 February 1917
Mesopotamia. The Turks have withdrawn

from the Hai salient and repositioned their defensive line from the "Licorice Factory" at the confluence of the Tigris and Hai Rivers across from Kut northeastward to Yusifiya on the Tigris.

9 February 1917
Mesopotamia. Maude's troops attack at the "Licorice Factory," breaking through the Turks' front line.

10 February 1917
Mesopotamia. The British capture the "Licorice Factory" and begin to push the Turks back to the Tigris.

13 February 1917
Neuchâtel, Switzerland. Emperor Karl of Austria-Hungary wishes to make peace, as he fears continuation of the war will result in the disintegration of the empire. His messenger and friend, Count Thomas Erdody, tells the emperor's brother-in-law, Prince Sixtus of Bourbon-Parma, and his brother Prince Xavier, both French sympathizers and veterans of the Belgian army, that Karl wants to negotiate a peace settlement. Sixtus inquires whether Karl wants to negotiate publicly or in private, and the count returns to Vienna to get Karl's answer.
Paris. French intelligence officers arrest and imprison Mata Hari, suspecting her of spying for a German official at The Hague.

17 February 1917
Somme River. The British have harassed the Germans with small raids as the winter proceeds. Now during the night they attack on a large scale north of the Ancre River, but German artillery stops them after a gain of several hundred yards that costs twenty-seven hundred casualties.
Mesopotamia. Persistent pressure leading to widespread surrender by Turkish troops has given Maude control of the right bank of the Tigris River between Kut and Yusifiya. But as long as the Turks hold Sannaiyat, his supply ships cannot move up the river, so Maude temporarily halts the action on the right bank, menaced by heavy rains, and at noon sends his troops against the Turkish front lines at Sannaiyat.

Initially successful, they fall back before a Turkish counterattack.

21 February 1917
Neuchâtel, Switzerland. Count Erdody returns with documents from Emperor Karl and Austrian Foreign Minister Count Ottokar Czernin to present to Prince Sixtus. Count Czernin's statement is uncompromising on the terms already outlined by the Allies, and Karl's comments also seem unpromising.

22 February 1917
Mesopotamia. At Sannaiyat the British forge ahead, capturing a major portion of the Turkish second-line trenches but at a cost of 1,332 casualties.

23 February 1917
Mesopotamia. Having decided to cross the Tigris River at the Shumran Bend, Maude sends his troops over in ferries in the early morning, taking the Turks unawares. Although the Turks throw together a tough resistance, by the end of the day the British have secured a bridgehead on the left bank, losing only 350 men in the process. At the same time, the assault at Sannaiyat resumes but beginning only after noon, giving the beleaguered Turks the opportunity to withdraw. By midnight, Sannaiyat falls to the British.

24 February 1917
Mesopotamia. While the British troops who have taken Sannaiyat pursue the retreating Turks and occupy Kut, those at Shumran Bend push forward to the barracks at Dahra Bend.

25 February 1917
Washington. President Wilson learns of the contents of the Zimmermann telegram. British agents had intercepted the message, which was actually transmitted by the United States' Department of State via London and Washington under a communications arrangement set up by Colonel House and Count Bernstorff as a means of promoting peace efforts. The British, not wanting to reveal that they have been tapping American and German telegraph

transmissions, have waited until it could appear that they garnered the message from sources in Mexico City. They have forwarded the contents of the Zimmermann telegram to Wilson through Walter Hines Page, American ambassador to Great Britain.

English Channel. Sailing out of Zeebrugge, two German flotillas of destroyers head for Dover. The Dover Patrol drives off one flotilla, while the second briefly succeeds in shelling Margate, Westgate, and the North Foreland wireless stations before hastily returning to Zeebrugge.

26 February 1917

Washington. Although angry and disaffected with the Germans because of the Zimmermann telegram, Wilson has accepted the urgings of Frank L. Polk, acting secretary of state in Robert Lansing's absence, to wait until Lansing's return to Washington to make public the telegram's content. But he has already decided to ask Congress for the authority to enact "armed neutrality" to protect American shipping, significantly cut back under the German U-boat menace. While he addresses the Congress on this question in the afternoon, a messenger brings to the House chamber news that a U-boat has sunk the Cunard liner *Laconia,* with the loss of two American lives. The president asks Congress to pass legislation authorizing the government to provide arms to American ships, if necessary, and to use any other means needed to protect American ships and citizens. He assures his listeners that whether such a move leads to war rests entirely with Germany's response.

Calais. Lloyd George, Gen. William Robertson, French Premier Aristede Briand, French Minister of War Gen. Louis Lyautey, Haig, and Nivelle confer. Nivelle points out Haig's refusal to extend the British lines as he has requested; Haig, in turn, explains that such extension would have placed BEF units at the northern end of the Hindenburg Line when they were not prepared to penetrate such an imposing defense. Lloyd George invites Nivelle to draw up a resolution to the disagreement. The proposal Nivelle presents at the end of the

day has actually been agreed to beforehand by him and the British prime minister—they had been consulting through an intermediary for ten days before the Calais meeting. The proposal gives Nivelle command of all BEF operational, supply, and administrative functions, with direct communication between himself and Robertson. These functions are to be carried out by the BEF chief of staff and the British quartermaster general, who will be stationed at French headquarters. Haig retains control of discipline. Haig and Robertson are outraged.

Petrograd. Serious trouble has been brewing on the Russian home front, with public opposition to the war increasing through the fall and winter months along with severe shortages of food and fuel. The first overt sign occurs when a crowd of several hundred people marches through the streets of the capital breaking store windows, shouting revolutionary slogans, and singing the *Marseillaise.*

Mesopotamia. Delays and lack of coordination prevent the British from outflanking and defeating the Turkish forces retreating toward Baghdad. The British reach Nahr-al-Kalek on the Tigris, with three of Maude's gunboats joining them there.

27 February 1917

Calais. The controversy is ironed out. Nivelle receives command of the BEF only for the duration of the offensive, and the proposal about the British chief of staff and quartermaster-general is deleted. The agreement will become effective on 1 March. The conference ends with the participants nursing acrimony.

28 February 1917

Washington. Lansing had returned the day before, and he and Wilson have awaited confirmation of the contents of the Zimmermann telegram. Now satisfied that the telegram is authentic, Wilson authorizes Lansing to release it for newspaper publication after 10:00 P.M.

Mesopotamia. British cavalry move forward to investigate Al Aziziyah, finding it already abandoned by the Turks, but then return to Nahr-al-Kalek, where Maude pauses to regroup and to reestablish his overextended lines of supply and communication before advancing on Baghdad.

1 March 1917
Washington. American newspapers headline the Zimmermann telegram story, evoking public rage against Germany. In the House of Representatives, the rage takes the form of overwhelming approval, by a vote of 403 to 13, of the bill introduced to give the president authority to effect "armed neutrality."

2 March 1917
Persia. In conjunction with the British expedition in Mesopotamia, the Russians have launched an offensive from the Caucasus moving down through Kermanshah to pressure the Turks and to advance on Baghdad from the northeast. Their advance reaches Hamadan and Kangavar in western Persia.

4 March 1917
Washington. With the Congress legally obliged to adjourn at noon, Robert La Follette, Frank Norris, and other senators committed to keeping the United States out of the war filibuster the Senate "armed neutrality" bill to death—much to the consternation of their colleagues and the president.
Berlin. Zimmermann acknowledges that the content of the telegram he sent to Mexico is authentic.

5 March 1917
Paris. As French officials readily discern the benefits of any possibility of driving a wedge between Austria-Hungary and Germany, Pres. Raymond Poincaré meets for two hours with Prince Sixtus.
Washington. Wilson is inaugurated for a second term as president. In his address, following summary statements about his administration's achievements, the president declares: "The tragical events of the thirty months of vital turmoil through which we have just passed have made us citizens of the world. There can be no turning back. Our own fortunes as a nation are involved, whether we would have it so or not."

Mesopotamia. General Maude resumes the advance toward Baghdad, where the Turks are furiously digging in on the west bank of the Tigris to prevent encirclement and to protect their railway link to Samarra—needed for movement of supplies and troops, especially in the event retreat becomes necessary. Their commander, Kahlil Pasha, had assumed Baghdad was safe from the British and that he could concentrate on stopping the Russians, so his defenses are thin—only ten thousand troops and fifty guns. One of Maude's cavalry brigades reaches Zor, where it encounters a Turkish force. The resulting skirmish costs the British twenty-eight dead and fifty-six wounded.

6 March 1917
Mesopotamia. British cavalry discover the Turks have abandoned Ctesiphon, where Kahlil Pasha had extensively entrenched for a decisive battle.

8 March 1917
Paris. Following discussion with Premier Aristede Briand, who also serves in the role of foreign minister, Poincaré meets for a second time with Prince Sixtus, explaining that the irreducible terms for peace are that Alsace and Lorraine be returned to France, Constantinople be ceded to Russia, Belgium be restored, and Serbia be granted autonomy. He adds that peace must be made at the same time not only with Great Britain, France, and Russia, but also with Italy, which has not been mentioned in the documents from Karl and Czernin.

9 March 1917
Washington. Assured by Congressional authorities on the Constitution and by the attorney general that, as commander in chief, he has authority to arm merchant ships without Congressional approval, Wilson announces the decision to do so and calls Congress into special session to begin on 16 April.
Mesopotamia. Maude's troops reach Diyala and succeed in crossing the Diyala River despite strenuous Turkish counterattacks. To the south of the Tigris, British troops moving to encircle Baghdad en-

counter a strong Turkish defensive line extending from Tel Aswad to Qarara. The British suffer 768 casualties in an attack the Turks easily repulse.

10 March 1917
Petrograd. The demonstrations have grown in size and frequency, augmented by more than two hundred thousand striking workers from the local war matériel manufacturing plants, and the government has lost control of the city. Czar Nicholas II issues orders to the commandant of the city's military garrison to use force in quelling the demonstrations.
Mesopotamia. Since Gen. Kahlil Pasha and Gen. Kiazim Karabekir Bey, commander of the troops that have fallen back before Maude's advance, have decided to concentrate their defenses on a line from Lake Aqarquf (the Umm at Tubal sandhills) to the Tigris, the British find the Tel Aswad defenses evacuated. The British advance in a sandstorm that obliterates vision and communications as the Turkish artillery pounds away. In the afternoon Kahlil Pasha gives the order to retreat to the north.

11 March 1917
Mexico. Gen. Venustiano Carranza is elected president of Mexico along with a new Congress.
Mesopotamia. British troops occupy Baghdad, ending three hundred years of Turkish control of the city. They also occupy Kadhimain on the Tigris River to the north of Baghdad.

12 March 1916
Petrograd. A reserve battalion of one of the military garrison's regiments mutinies, killing their commanding officer and joining the street demonstrators. The president of the Duma had telegraphed the czar at Mogilev (army headquarters) the day before describing the situation in the city as anarchy and advocating formation of a new government. The czar responded by proroguing the Duma, but the majority of the members decide to continue meeting in the Tauride Palace in defiance of the czar. They elect the Temporary Committee to help restore order to the capital. Also meeting

in the palace, labor delegates from the War Industries Committee, left-wing Duma members, representatives of the rebellious troops, and others form the Soviet of Workers' and Soldiers' Deputies.

13 March 1917
Washington. The United States government recognizes the Carranza government, designating Henry P. Fletcher as ambassador to Mexico.
Mesopotamia. British troops advance to Kasirin on the Tigris.

14 March 1917
Petrograd. The Petrograd Soviet, hoping to obtain the allegiance of the capital's military garrison, issues "Order Number 1," which upends the customary system of military discipline by providing that the troops are to elect committees to determine the issuance of arms and resolve grievances, that the troops obey only those orders from the Provisional Government that do not conflict with orders from the Soviet, and that the troops can forego or modify signs of respect traditionally granted their officers. With this directive officers lose virtually all their authority, and the directive is adopted nationwide, not just in Petrograd.
Mesopotamia. British troops attack a rear guard of the retreating Turks, inflicting 1,000 casualties while enduring 518, and succeed in capturing the Khan al Mashahidah station on the rail line connecting Baghdad to Samarra.

15 March 1917
Petrograd. Fresh troops sent into the city by the czar join the demonstrators. The entire Petrograd military garrison of 170,000 men has now gone over to the rebels. The conflict in the streets has so far caused thirteen hundred dead and wounded.

16 March 1917
Petrograd. Attempting to fill the void left by the collapse of authority, the Temporary Committee, with the consent of the Petrograd Soviet, announces establishment of the Provisional Government composed

Mutinies

The armies of France, Italy, Germany, and Russia all experienced large-scale mutinies during the war; although considering the horrible conditions under which the common soldiers fought, it is surprising that there were not more uprisings. The French and Italian mutinies were not the result of organized resistance to commanders or governments, nor were they the products of conspiracies or ideological dissent. Rather, the mutinies grew from the complete physical and psychological exhaustion of frontline troops who could endure no more and simply gave up fighting the enemy. The most serious and widespread mutiny was among the French army in the spring of 1917. The horrendous casualties and sickening conditions around Verdun after the German offensive and subsequent failed French counteroffensive produced intolerable conditions among the French frontline troops, and in May they began to refuse orders. Before it was over, the mutiny spread to sixteen army corps, and eventually only a handful of trustworthy people were left along the entire Western Front. For the most part, the mutineers had no political or military program of their own. They just refused to take orders that would have sent them forward in yet another of the senseless slaughters that passed for offensives. Indeed, the mutineers often held their posts in the trenches. No officers were killed and there was scarcely any violence despite the huge numbers of men involved. The French government named Pétain to quell the mutinies, which he did successfully by a display of good sense and common humanity. Only a handful of mutineers were executed after the restoration of order, even though more than twenty-three thousand men were convicted. Fortunately for the Allies, the Germans did not learn of the mutinies until it was too late to take advantage of the weakened state of the French defenses. The British army (which avoided all but minor problems) was called upon to take the brunt of offensive action during the remainder of 1917, but the French army was restored to nearly full effectiveness by the following spring. In the fall of 1917, the Italian Second Army completely collapsed in the face of the German-Austrian assault at Caporetto. More than half a million men refused to fight when the offensive from the east smacked into the Italian defenses. A couple hundred thousand soldiers surrendered to the rapidly advancing enemy, but nearly four hundred thousand more simply threw down their arms and turned away from battle. The entire army withdrew from the front in defiance of orders and began a leisurely stroll toward home, the men apparently believing that the war would end if they refused to resist the Germans and Austrians. When it became obvious that the enemy was not going to stop just because an Italian army had melted away, the mutineers allowed themselves to be reorganized. Some were shot as deserters, but most were simply reformed into the semblance of fighting units and the conflict resumed on a new line. Mutinies among the Germans and Russians were more political in nature and reflected fundamental national distress rather than local military conditions. The German army began to break apart during the final weeks of the war when the situation on the Western Front deteriorated rapidly and it became evident that the nation was doomed to defeat. Political agitators found sympathetic ears among troops who were starving and battered by Allied advances. When coupled with a widespread mutiny in the German navy, the disaffection and outright rebellion among much of the retreating army in the fall of 1918 was the catalyst for a social and political revolution. The same pattern had been seen earlier in Russia, where the large-scale mutiny of the long-suffering army was the key element in bringing down the Romanov imperium.

of Progressive Bloc members of the Duma. Prince George Lvov is designated premier. Since the Mensheviks in the Soviet believe this welcome "bourgeois revolution" should not include Socialists (overriding the weak Bolsheviks in this decision), only one Socialist is appointed to the government for the purpose of creating a liaison between the government and the Soviet. This lone Socialist is Alexander Kerensky, vice chairman of the Soviet, named minister of justice in the Provisional Government. At Pskov, where Nicholas II has been taken by revolutionary soldiers, members of the Temporary Committee, supported by counsel of army generals, have convinced the czar that he must abdicate. He signs an act of abdication that confers the throne on his brother, Grand Duke Michael. The czar also accepts the appointment of Prince Lvov as premier.

Somme River. With the Hindenburg Line completed, the Germans begin to withdraw from areas captured in the Somme region. A formidable defensive complex of tunnels, galleries, concrete dugouts, and trenches ranging in places to a depth of eight thousand yards, the Hindenburg Line extends ninety miles from the Aisne River just east of Soissons northward through Saint-Quentin and on to Arras. It took five months to build, the work being done mostly by Russian prisoners of war, assisted by Belgian and German workers. In preparing to withdraw, the Germans destroy railroads, bridges, towns, dwellings, waterways, fruit trees—anything of potential use to the Allies—and remove the civilian population. Crown Prince Rupprecht objects to the harshness of this scorched earth policy but is obliged to go along.

17 March 1917

Petrograd. Swayed by hostility to the monarchy in the capital, Grand Duke Michael renounces the crown. The Provisional Government announces both his renunciation and the czar's abdication. The Romanov dynasty, begun by Michael Romanov in 1613, comes to an end.

Paris. Under insurmountable pressure from a Chamber of Deputies enraged by the recalcitrance of War Minister Lyautey,

who was forced to resign on 14 March, Premier Briand now also resigns. He is replaced by the seventy-five-year-old Alexandre Ribot. Paul Painlevé, who does not think highly of Nivelle, becomes minister of war.

United States. Newspapers report that since 16 March three American ships— *City of Memphis, Illinois,* and *Vigilancia*— have been sunk by U-boats.

English Channel. Once again during the night, two flotillas of German destroyers leave Zeebrugge and cross the channel barrage, one to disrupt shipping and the other to attack the English coast. Outnumbering the Dover Patrol ships in the channel, the first flotilla sinks HMS *Paragon* with shells and a torpedo, and the other shells Ramsgate and Broadstairs. They return safely to Zeebrugge before destroyers dispatched from Deal have time to reach the scene.

18 March 1917

Mesopotamia. Maude's troops sweep to the west of Baghdad to capture Nukhta and to the northeast to capture Buhriz and Ba'qubah on the Diyala River.

19 March 1917

Geneva. Prince Sixtus has written a letter to Emperor Karl advising him that the opportunity for negotiating a peace with Russia is heightened by the revolution and the new government, that if Germany negotiates the peace it will come at Austria's expense, and that he should preclude an offensive against Italy. He presents the letter to Count Erdody, who tells him that Karl must see him and Xavier in Vienna and promises safe conduct. The brothers agree to make the journey.

Hindenburg Line. The Germans successfully complete their withdrawal to the Hindenburg Line, conceding the initiative on the Western Front to the Allies and embracing a policy of "strategic defense."

20 March 1917

Petrograd. Responding to pressure from the Petrograd Soviet, the Provisional Government places the czar and his family under house arrest at Tsarskoye Selo, intending to allow them to leave some time later for asylum in England.

New York City. Former president Theodore Roosevelt issues a statement calling for war with Germany.

Washington. At a meeting of all the members of his cabinet, the president requests advice on whether to call a special meeting of Congress before 16 April and what to ask of the convened Congress. The cabinet members unanimously support calling an earlier special session and asking Congress to declare war. During the night the president decides his cabinet is right.

21 March 1917
Washington. Pres. Woodrow Wilson issues a proclamation calling Congress into special session on 2 April.

22 March 1917
Washington. President Wilson officially recognizes the revolutionary government of Russia, whose assumption of power is well received in the United States and appears to bolster the view that the war against imperial Germany and Austria-Hungary now more clearly involves the advancement of liberty and democracy.

New York City. A rally of twelve thousand people at Madison Square Garden cheers Roosevelt, supporting his call for war.

23 March 1917
Vienna. Prince Sixtus and Prince Xavier meet with Erdody and Emperor Karl at the emperor's castle. Karl tells them: "It is absolutely necessary to make peace; I want it at any price." A stumbling block for him is Italy. He will consider a settlement with Italy only after the other three Allies have agreed to make peace.

Mesopotamia. After a pause to consolidate his victories, Maude sends troops out of Ba'qubah to take Shahraban, but just beyond they meet heavy resistance, supported by an artillery bombardment, and suffer twelve hundred casualties.

Persia. The Russian force advancing from the Caucasus comes to a dead halt at Banen, completely snowed in.

24 March 1917
Vienna. Czernin stresses to Prince Sixtus and Prince Xavier that any negotiations must be held in strictest secrecy to prevent Germany from discovering that Austria is pursuing a separate peace. Karl gives Sixtus a letter detailing peace terms.

Washington. Secretary of the Navy Josephus Daniels meets with shipbuilders and places orders for twenty-four destroyers. The navy currently has 300 ships, 130 shore stations, and 60,000 men in uniform.

25 March 1917
Petrograd. To ensure a supply of grains, the provisional government declares the grain trade a monopoly controlled by the government and mandates that grains be sold only to representatives of the government at prices fixed by the government, thus exacerbating discontent among the peasants, who already were disgruntled by their inability to appropriate the lands of their landlords.

26 March 1917
Palestine. Commander in Chief Gen. Sir Archibald Murray, now headquartered at El Arish, has assigned Lt. Gen. Sir Charles Dobell, commander of the Eastern Force, the task of taking Gaza after first securing the Wadi Ghazze, a ravine and water source six miles southeast of the coastal city. Camel and cavalry units grouped in a force known as Desert Column, commanded by Gen. Sir Philip Chetwode, spearhead the attack along with units of two infantry divisions. Although the natural obstacles, including huge cactus hedges, are formidable, by the end of the day the attack succeeds in forcing the Turks back into the city, which should readily fall to the British troops the following day. But at their headquarters in In Seirat, Dobell and Chetwode misapprehend the real situation and order the mounted troops to withdraw to Wadi Ghazze. The withdrawal allows the desperate Turks a chance to reinforce the Gaza garrison.

Arabia. After meeting earlier with Abdullah ibn-Hussein and failing to persuade him to pursue more aggressive tactics, T.E. Lawrence himself leads an attack at Aba el Na'am on the railway that traverses the Hejaz region. He and his men take thirty prisoners.

27 March 1917
Petrograd. Pressured by the Allies, the Provisional Government has continued Russia's participation in the war. Now the Petrograd Soviet threatens that policy by issuing a public statement urging the peoples of the world "to take into their own hands the decision of the question of war and peace." Singling out the workers of Germany and Austria, the statement incites them to "throw off the yoke of your semi-autocratic rule" and to refuse service in the war perpetuated by "kings, landowners, and bankers." The statement also renounces secret negotiations and territorial claims.
Palestine. Because of the previous day's misunderstandings, the British assault on Gaz fails. At 6:30 P.M., under orders from General Dobell, the men withdraw across the Wadi Ghazze.

28 March 1917
Arabia. Lawrence attacks the Hejaz railway again, striking this time at Mudahrij.

29 March 1917
Mesopotamia. The Turks have concentrated a force of five thousand at the Hahrwan Canal near Sindiya. Maude's troops, blinded and disoriented by mirages created on the canal waters and victimized by intense heat, fail to outflank the Turks and suffer 514 casualties in a frontal assault. During the night, the Turks withdraw northward to the Shatt al Adhaim.

31 March 1917
Mesopotamia. Despite heavy resistance, British troops pushing doggedly forward from Shahraban complete their mission as the Turks withdraw across the Diyala River at Khanaqin.

1 April 1917
Paris. Prince Sixtus meets again with President Poincaré, presenting Karl's letter in which the emperor agrees to the terms proposed by Sixtus except for the issue of Constantinople—he is concerned that the current Russian government will not endure. Although the demurrer on Constantinople raises questions, Poincaré makes clear his desire to pursue a separate peace

with Austria-Hungary in order to disadvantage Germany.

2 April 1917
Washington. Shortly after 9:00 A.M., President Wilson addresses the Congress and members of his cabinet and the Supreme Court in the House Chamber of the Capitol and requests that Congress declare a state of belligerency between the United States and Germany. He concludes his speech with these words: "The world must be made safe for democracy. Its peace must be planted upon the tested foundations of political liberty. We have no selfish ends to serve. We desire no conquest, no dominion. We seek no indemnities for ourselves, no material compensation for the sacrifices we shall freely make. We are but one of the champions of the rights of mankind. . . . It is a fearful thing to lead this great peaceful people into war, into the most terrible and disastrous of all wars, civilization itself seeming to be in the balance. But the right is more precious than peace, and we shall fight . . . for democracy, for the rights of those who submit to authority to have a voice in their own Governments, for the rights and liberties of small nations, for a universal dominion of right by such a concert of free peoples as shall bring peace and safety to all nations and make the world itself at last free."
Compiègne. A council of war called by Ribot meets to discuss the spring offensive planned to begin on 16 April. Despite objections to his plans stated by Painlevé and Generals Philippe Pétain and Joseph Micheler that generate his own offer to resign, Nivelle remains in command with authority to begin his offensive.

7 April 1917
Washington. Passed by both houses of Congress over modest opposition (the vote was 82 to 6 in the Senate, 373 to 50 in the House), the declaration of war with Germany is brought to the White House, where at 1:18 P.M. the president signs it. It is understood that American involvement in the war will be slow to build, as the United States army currently has only 5,791 officers and 121,797 enlisted men in its ranks, with an

Pres. Woodrow Wilson delivers his war message to a joint session of the U.S. Congress in April 1917 (Library of Congress)

additional 80,446 officers and men serving in the National Guard, most of the latter still deployed along the Mexican border.

9 April 1917

Arras. Gen. Douglas Haig's part of Nivelle's offensive opens, supported by 2,817 guns and mortars that have been shelling the positions of Gen. Baron Ludwig von Falkenhausen's Sixth Army for four days with telling effect, destroying trenches, disrupting communications, and preventing food deliveries to the front line. The Royal Flying Corps has fought for four days to achieve supremacy in the air over the front, losing 75 planes and 105 crewmen. The British infantry has the advantage of a connected series of caves and mine shafts, expanded by tunneling, that accommodate thirty thousand troops who can move well out into no-man's-land before emerging into the open. The Third Army (350,000 men), commanded by Gen. Sir Edmund Allenby, moves out from Ar-

ras at the center of the attack, while the First Army, commanded by Gen. Sir Henry Horne, pushes toward Vimy Ridge. The southern, or right, flank is entrusted to Lt. Gen. Sir Hubert Gough's Fifth Army. Canadian troops of the First Army on the far left advance and capture part of Vimy Ridge overlooking Bailleul, while Allenby's troops sweep ahead, taking Fampoux on the north bank of the Scarpe River as night falls. With the help of a single tank christened "Lusitania," which knocks out German machine-gun posts one by one, Allenby's men also advance toward Feuchy, taking that objective in the afternoon, while to their right other units push through Neuville Vitasse toward Wancourt. But here and on the far right, the Hindenburg Line holds. Allenby's successful troops have captured fifty-six hundred prisoners and thirty-six guns. Cold, hail, and snow set in during the night, impeding movement of the horse-drawn artillery to the forward positions.

An Allied soldier grotesquely frozen in death on the Western Front (by Reni-Mel, courtesy of the Anne S.K. Brown Military Collection, Brown University Library)

10 April 1917
Arras. The British have failed to take advantage of the salient at Fampoux that opened a gap of ten thousand yards in the German line, and now their advance creeps forward, deterred by German machine-gun fire. Long-range British guns devastate Monchy-le-Preux, but in the afternoon German reserve infantry and artillery move to the front to bolster the defense. Ludendorff, dismayed that Falkenhausen failed to implement the new German defensive strategy—for example, not bringing up reserves in time to thwart the British attack—dismisses the baron from command.
Mesopotamia. Deferring a plan to attack at the Shatt al Adhaim, the British turn to meet the threat of a seven-thousand-man Turkish force from the northeast. The British halt the advance at Chaliya.

11 April 1917
Arras. Three tanks assist the British attack on Monchy, but German fire knocks out two of them and a British artillery shelling of the town inadvertently destroys the third. Two units of cavalry gallop to the attack from the east, as Scottish troops move in from the west, but German machine-gun fire destroys the cavalry and a German counterattack drives the British infantrymen back. Overhead, Manfred von Richthofen achieves his fortieth kill, equaling Boelcke's record.
Folkestone, England. French Premier Alexandre Ribot meets with British Prime Minister David Lloyd George and shows him the letter from Emperor Karl transmitted by Prince Sixtus. They disagree about informing Italy, Ribot insisting on secrecy because of the extreme hostility between Italy and Austria-Hungary.

12 April 1917
Arras. With Canadian troops now in full control of Vimy Ridge, the Germans withdraw.
Petrograd. As order and authority have virtually disappeared in the countryside following the collapse of the monarchy and its local police officials, Prince Lvov declares authorization by the Provisional Government for officials in the provinces to use troops to impose order. The first All-Russian Conference of Soviets calls on the Provisional Government to begin negotiations with the Allies for an agreement that disclaims attaining territories or indemnities as part of a peace settlement—a rejection of Allied goals.

A Scots infantryman (by Jean Berne-Bellecour, courtesy of the Anne S.K. Brown Military Collection, Brown University Library)

14 April 1917

Arras. Needing to keep the Germans occupied as the time for Nivelle's major offensive approaches, Haig sends two battalions against the German line to the east of Monchy, driving them back, but the German counterattack regains the lost ground and forces the British back on Monchy.

Washington. Wilson appoints journalist George Creel as chairman of the Committee on Public Information approved by Congress to oversee the truthfulness of news stories while providing speakers, news stories, pamphlets, movies, posters, and other means of affecting public support for the war effort.

Arabia. Having failed to move Abdullah, Capt. T.E. Lawrence returns to Al Wajh. Here Feisal has been joined by Auda abu Tayi, a sheikh of the Howeitat tribe who becomes an adherent of Lawrence's plan to attack Aqaba. Capturing Aqaba from the land entails crossing six hundred miles of desert—a strenuous endeavor in which the Howeitat could be most helpful.

15 April 1917

Mesopotamia. Unable to advance at Chaliya, the Turks withdraw into the foothills of the Jabal Mountains. The British turn eastward to move against the Turkish position on the Shatt al Adhaim.

16 April 1917

Aisne River. Nivelle's long-planned and oft-postponed offensive begins. But the Germans are well prepared, having captured the plan of attack and then learned of the date when British and French military attachés at The Hague mentioned it at a state dinner. The Germans have also been warned of an impending attack involving two weeks of French artillery bombardment. German airplanes control the air over the twenty-five-mile front, precluding French air reconnaissance. At 6:00 A.M., Gen. Charles Mangin's Sixth Army attacks along the Chemin des Dames while General Mazel's Fifth Army, which includes two Russian brigades sent to France in April 1916, attacks along a line from the Sixth Army's right flank near Hurtebise Farm to the sector north of Rheims. Al-

though both armies manage to push forward modestly along most of the front, the hoped-for quick breakthrough and destruction of the German line fails. Strong resistance and counterattacks by Gen. Otto von Below's First Army and Gen. Hans von Böhn's Seventh Army prove too formidable, even though the French take more than ten thousand prisoners. Both sides suffer extensive casualties.

Petrograd. Provided safe passage through Germany by German officials who believe that his role as an agitator may weaken Russia's continuing commitment to the war, Vladimir Lenin arrives in the capital.

17 April 1917

Aisne River. While Mangin consolidates his position and Mazel pauses because of unfavorable weather, Nivelle sends the Fourth Army, commanded by Gen. Francois Anthoine, into battle in the Champagne sector, attacking toward Moronvilliers. Anthoine achieves a small advance. On Mangin's left flank, the Germans withdraw during the night toward the Chemin des Dames, leaving Vailly, Aizy, Sancy, and Jouy burning in their wake.

18 April 1917

Aisne River. Below's troops counterattack fiercely at Juvincourt, where the French had achieved a three-mile salient, but the French line holds.

Mesopotamia. At the Shatt al Adhaim, the British distract the Turks with a feint attack on their left flank. Surprising the Turkish front by crossing the river on pontoons, they capture twelve hundred and rout the remainder.

19 April 1917

Palestine. Based on misleading reports from General Murray portraying the Gaza expedition as "most successful," Lloyd George believes all is well and sets Jerusalem as Murray's next objective, necessitating another attack on Gaza. But this time the Turks are fully prepared. Although Murray sends against them three divisions supported by tanks and 150 guns, this second attack on Gaza fails dismally—the Turks not only hold but counterattack. The

British lose sixty-five hundred men and two thousand animals; Turkish losses are only two thousand.

20 April 1917
Saint-Jean-de-Maurienne, France. Ribot and Lloyd George at a meeting of Allied political leaders maintain the secrecy of Prince Sixtus's intermediary efforts, but raise the question of pursuing peace negotiations with Austria-Hungary to test the Italian response. Italy's minister of foreign affairs, Baron Sidney Sonnino, adamantly rejects the idea, insisting on the pursuit of total victory so that Italy will be guaranteed accession of Trentino, Trieste, Dalmatia, and the Adriatic Islands. His response torpedoes Sixtus's effort.
English Channel. For a third time, the Germans send two groups of destroyers out from Zeebrugge for a raid on Dover. Although the Dover Patrol is unaware of the German ships' approach, two of the patrol's destroyers, HMS *Swift* and HMS *Broke,* scouting southwest of the Goodwin Sands, come upon one of the flotillas. The *Broke* rams one of the German destroyers, and after the British sailors repulse a German attempt to board her, the British ship breaks free. The German destroyer sinks. The *Swift* does in another of the destroyers as British reinforcements begin to appear on the scene, sending the other German ships into flight. The results of the skirmish discourage any subsequent German raids on the Dover coast.

21 April 1917
Aisne River. After learning that Nivelle plans to continue his offensive, even throwing the Tenth Army into an effort to break through the German defenses between Barry-au-Bac and Hurtebise Farm, Gen. Joseph Micheler, commander of the Reserve Army Group, expresses concern over the supply of artillery shells and recommends a much-reduced offensive.
Mesopotamia. British troops moving up the rail line toward Samarra launch an attack on a Turkish defensive line near Istabula defended by eleven thousand troops. During the night, the Turks fall back to consolidate their position.

22 April 1917
Petrograd. Pressured by the other Allies to continue the war effort until Germany is defeated and by Russian socialists to advocate a negotiated peace with no claim to territorial accessions, the Provisional Government issues a declaration to the people of Russia stating that Russia has no desire or intention "to dominate other peoples"—an effort to placate the Petrograd Soviet.
Mesopotamia. The British attack again at Istabula, meeting fierce resistance.

23 April 1917
Aisne River. Nivelle receives a note from Pres. Raymond Poincaré expressing doubts about the possibilities of any further success for his offensive. Government officials are appalled by the heavy losses at the Aisne front—thirty thousand dead, one hundred thousand wounded, and four thousand taken prisoner.
Arras. To assist the French effort on the Aisne front, Haig resumes his offensive. The British attack at 4:45 A.M. along a nine-mile line extending from Gavrelle through Roeux and Guémappe to Fontaine les Croiselles—only a minimal advance is expected. Although they manage to capture Gavrelle and Guémappe and push to the east of Monchy le Preux, along most of the line tough German resistance and counterattacks lasting into the morning of 24 April hold the advance to one or two miles. In the skies, such German aces as Manfred von Richthofen, his brother Lothar, and Hermann Göring duel with British aces Albert Ball, William Bishop, and others.
Mesopotamia. The British advance at Istabula and, meeting no resistance, push on to the Samarra Railway Station, capturing 16 engines and 250 trucks laden with supplies. Their successful three-day operation costs 2,228 casualties; the Turks have 3,700 casualties, with 700 taken prisoner.

24 April 1917
Mesopotamia. As one of Maude's units occupies Samarra, another at the Shatt al Adhaim attempts to outflank the Turks at Danuba.

Salonika. With the blessing of the leaders of France, Great Britain, and Italy (who met in Rome in January for the only time during the war), Gen. Maurice Sarrail, commander in chief of the Allied forces in Macedonia, and Lt. Gen. Sir George Milne, commander of the British Salonika Army, have planned a combined offensive against the German and Bulgarian forces on the Salonika front. Joint French, Italian, Serbian, and Russian forces will attack in the Crna River sector, and the British will focus on the Lake Dojran sector. As heavy snow deters operations in Sarrail's sector to the west, Milne's offensive opens first. British troops begin the assault in the darkness of night shortly before 10:00 P.M. But the Bulgars have long anticipated the attack and are well entrenched, with concrete dugouts commanding the ridges of the mountainous region. The British attack ends in overall failure.

Boston, Massachusetts. After conferring with British and French naval representatives in Washington, Secretary of the Navy Josephus Daniels has concurred in focusing American naval efforts on patrolling the American Atlantic coast, the Caribbean, the Gulf of Mexico, and the coasts of Canada and South America, while also sending a token force for service in European waters. Six American destroyers now sail out of Boston Harbor for Queenstown, Ireland. These and any American ships subsequently sent to Europe will be under the overall command of Rear Adm. William S. Sims, who arrived in London on 10 April.

Dunkirk, France. German destroyers from Zeebrugge raid Dunkirk, sinking a French destroyer.

25 April 1917

Salonika. Concluding that the Bulgarian defenses at Dojran are impregnable, the British withdraw.

Washington. Marshal Joseph Joffre and a French delegation begin a visit to discuss war tactics with American officials.

26 April 1917

Paris. At the minister's request, General Haig visits Defense Minister Painlevé, who assures him the French offensive will continue but indicates that he wishes to replace Nivelle with Gen. Philippe Pétain.

27 April 1917

Aisne River. Nivelle receives orders from the government to forego his planned offensive at Brimont Ridge in May.

28 April 1917

Arras. Having decided to continue the offensive, Haig and his commanders determine first to take Roeux and its chemical works, Oppy, and Arleux, and to move forward near Monchy le Preux. But the assault fails overall, with only the Canadians succeeding with the capture of Arleux.

Corfu. British, French, and Italian officials meet to discuss tactics for combating the U-boat threat in the Mediterranean Sea, but they remain unprepared to launch any operations against the Austrian fleet harbored at Pola. The Austrians meanwhile are planning a major operation against the Otranto Barrage, a system of nets, 120 net drifters, and 30 motor launches strung across the Straits of Otranto to try to prevent U-boat passage between the Adriatic and Mediterranean Seas.

Washington. President Wilson issues an executive order providing for government censorship of telegrams and of telephone and telegraph lines and authorizing the navy's operation of all wireless stations for the duration of the war.

29 April 1917

Aisne River. Nivelle asks Micheler whether Mangin should be relieved of command. Surmising Nivelle's intent to save himself by sacrificing Mangin, Micheler asserts: "General, your intentions are infamous, cowardly, dastardly." At Mourmelon-le-Grand, two hundred men of the Twentieth Regiment, survivors of the first day's battle in which German machine guns mowed down four hundred of their comrades, refuse to obey the order to return to the battle. Arrested by military police, they are sent to the front, except for fifteen who are held for trial and possible execution.

Arras. Manfred von Richthofen shoots down his fifty-second victim.

Mesopotamia. The Turkish troops withdrawing northward on the Shatt al Adhaim have dug in at Band-i-Adhaim, where the British bear down on them.

30 April 1917
Mesopotamia. The British attack in a sandstorm at Band-i-Adhaim, and the Turks retreat into the Jabal Mountains. Maude's conquest of Baghdad and Turkish Mesopotamia is secure, as he assumes responsibility for governance, public health, finance, hospitals, and other services in the former Turkish nation.
London. Alarmed by monthly increases in shipping losses to German U-boats, Prime Minister David Lloyd George visits the Admiralty to advocate a policy of using convoys. Also alarmed—April losses of neutral ships have risen to 834,549 tons from 291,459 tons in January, and the British have lost 155 ships in April, up from only 35 in January—Admiralty officials have already decided to try the convoy system. Admiral Jellicoe has finally dropped his opposition to the idea.

1 May 1917
Petrograd. Rejecting the plea from the All-Russian Conference of Soviets, Minister of Foreign Affairs Pavel N. Milyukov sends a note to the Allied governments supporting the ideas of achieving a "decisive victory," Russia's commitment to the Allies'

war effort, and postwar guarantees and penalties to prevent the recurrence of war. The note generates a crisis between the Provisional Government and the Petrograd Soviet.
Mesopotamia. Royal Flying Corps airplanes bomb Turkish troops retreating into the Jabal Mountains beyond Band-I-Adhaim, killing fifty.

2 May 1917
Aisne River. General Mangin is relieved of command.
Washington. Marshal Joffre visits Wilson at the White House and requests that an American division be sent to France within a month. The president agrees.

3 May 1917
Arras. Convinced that Nivelle's offensive is ending, Gen. Douglas Haig has decided that the British offensive's objectives should be limited to keeping pressure on the Germans and securing a favorable position along the Scarpe River as a preliminary to a larger operation planned for Flanders in the summer. The renewed attack begins at 3:45 A.M., an hour and a half before dawn, along a sixteen-mile line running from Arleux to Bullecourt. Once again, Canadian troops achieve the day's major success in capturing Fresnoy at the western tip of the front. At the opposite end of the front, Australian troops manage

An Allied convoy at sea in the Atlantic. The convoy system narrowly saved Britain from starvation in 1917 and 1918 (Library of Congress)

to gain a small salient at Bullecourt, where the Germans counterattack them repeatedly. But elsewhere along the front, the offensive goes nowhere.

4 May 1917
Paris. Allied political and military leaders confer on war strategy. Lloyd George and other British representatives make known their concern over shipping losses and their desire to drive the Germans out of Belgium, where German U-boats launch their attacks with impunity out of the harbors at Zeebrugge and Ostend.
Queenstown, Ireland. The six American destroyers that set sail from Boston on 24 April arrive to begin coastal patrol missions.

5 May 1917
Petrograd. For two days, demonstrators assembling in the streets have shouted demands for Milyukov's resignation.

7 May 1917
Arras. British troops, hoping to link up with the Australians, secure a foothold in the southeast section of Bullecourt. Albert Ball, Britain's most famous ace, apparently falls victim to vertigo and flies his plane into the ground.
Doullens. General Haig meets with his commanders and informs them that the combined British-French offensive is ending and that future attacks will try to effect the attrition of the German forces, with a subsequent major British effort at Ypres followed by a general advance in Flanders. Thus Haig commits the BEF to a third battle at Ypres, to be preceded by capture and consolidation of the Messines-Wytschaete Ridge.
Petrograd. Testifying before a joint meeting of the Provisional Government and the Petrograd Soviet about the status of the Russian military, Gen. Mikhail Alexeyev declares, "The army is on the very brink of ruin." Morale and discipline have so thoroughly collapsed that the commanders have lost authority over their troops.

8 May 1917
Arras. The Germans, counterattacking with fierce determination, recapture Fresnoy.

Salonika. Informed that in June one of his divisions and two of his cavalry brigades will be sent to Palestine, General Milne has decided to try another night attack at Dojran. His troops reach and hold the lower slopes of the Petit Couronné.

9 May 1917
Salonika. After the coming of daylight, the British position on the slopes of the Petit Couronné proves untenable, and the troops are unable to advance. As the day proceeds, all the men return to their starting point. Heavy losses and no gains make this second effort as costly and futile as the first. At the same time, Sarrail launches his offensive on the Crna River, where Russian troops sweep forward. But as the other Allied forces founder and cannot come to the Russians' support, Bulgarian and German troops isolate them and kill or capture the entire force. Serbian troops attack Bulgar positions on the Dobropolje Ridge.
Arabia. Leaving Al Wajh, T.E. Lawrence sets out with Auda abu Tayi and forty tribesmen for the Howeitat encampments to the northeast.

10 May 1917
Salonika. Sarrail has ordered the cancellation of a planned Italian attack on the Crna, but the message does not get through. The 8:00 A.M. attack generates severe Italian casualties.

12 May 1917
Zeebrugge. Admiral Bacon sails a large force—twelve destroyers from Harwich and forty-one ships of his own squadron—to try to destroy the locks at Zeebrugge and to sever the canal line between this port and Bruges used by the U-boats. With a smoke screen hiding the flotilla from the Knocke battery on land, the British ships open fire at 5:00 A.M., expending 250 rounds of shells. Thinking the job done, Bacon orders a withdrawal, but the locks remain intact.

14 May 1917
Arras. British troops finally succeed in capturing Roeux.
Salonika. After persistent assaults, the

Dead Italian infantrymen, all killed by a single blast of shrapnel in May 1917 (Library of Congress)

Serbians have managed to capture and secure the lower slopes of the Dobropolje Ridge.

Straits of Otranto. During the evening, the Austrian offensive against the Otranto Barrage opens with two destroyers attacking an Italian convoy of three merchant ships accompanied by a destroyer, sinking the destroyer, blowing up one of the merchants, and damaging or setting afire the other two. Then three Austrian cruisers begin destroying the barrage itself, dividing the line in segments and sinking the net drifters one at a time. The Austrians sink fourteen drifters and disable three others out of a fleet of forty-seven deployed for the night. Hearing from Valona that the attack is in progress, Admiral Acton boards the cruiser *Dartmouth* and sets out from Brindisi with a fleet of British, French, and Italian destroyers and cruisers to attack the Austrian ships. Although both sides draw blood, the Austrians manage to escape to the north, while the *Dartmouth* is badly damaged by a torpedo, and one of the

French destroyers sinks after hitting a mine. The night's losses convince Italian Commander in Chief Luigi Cadorna that the net drifters cannot be protected during hours of darkness, so the Straits of Otranto each night will now be open to U-boat passage.

Washington. Secretary of the Treasury William Gibbs McAdoo announces a bond issue amounting to $2 billion for sale to the public and termed the "Liberty Loan of 1917."

15 May 1917

Aisne River. Gen. Philippe Pétain becomes commander in chief of the French Armies of the North and North-East, replacing the discredited Nivelle who had so confidently predicted the success of his now-failed offensive.

Salonika. British troops attacking along the lower Struma River capture several Bulgarian outposts.

17 May 1917

Arras. After two weeks of relentless fighting, British troops finally take Bullecourt, as the Germans withdraw. Nothing remains of the village but rubble. The Battle of Arras ends, except for continuing British efforts to consolidate their advance. Given the objective of engaging German reserves, the six-week battle has been a success, but it has cost the British 150,000 casualties, over 87,000 of them endured by Allenby's Third Army.

Salonika. A combined Italian-French attack to the north of Monastir fails, as the Germans and Bulgarians have reinforced their front lines.

18 May 1917

Amiens. Haig and Pétain meet. The French commander in chief promises that French troops in Belgium will support the British offensive at Ypres.

Washington. Pres. Woodrow Wilson signs the Selective Service Act passed by Congress, allowing for the creation of a vastly enlarged American army. The act designates the draft system as "selective service"

rather than using the unpopular term "conscription." Wilson and Secretary of War Newton D. Baker choose Maj. Gen. John J. Pershing to be commander of the American Expeditionary Force. To placate the French, Baker announces that a division of the AEF commanded by Pershing will leave for France as soon as possible.

19 May 1917

Petrograd. Trying to resolve the governmental crisis, leaders of the Provisional Government and the Petrograd Soviet, over the objections of the Bolsheviks, agree to a combined government that includes five socialists in addition to Kerensky, who becomes minister of the army and navy. Lvov continues as premier. Milyukov resigns.

Washington. Concerned over rapidly rising food prices, President Wilson has chosen Herbert Clark Hoover as administrator of a committee of the Council of National Defense. He announces that he wants Hoover to have authority to fix prices, in-

Gen. John "Black Jack" Pershing (on the right), commander of the American Expeditionary Force, confers with other Allied officers in France (Library of congress)

vestigate food stocks and the methods of pricing and distribution, take measures to prevent hoarding and waste, and oversee licensing and requisitioning. Such authority will require Congressional approval.

22 May 1917
Petrograd. Kerensky forces General Alexeyev to resign as commander in chief, appointing Gen. Aleksey A. Brusilov in his place. The new commander plans an offensive similar to the one of 1916, although focused on the southern sector of the front with an advance toward Lemberg. But there is little possibility of mounting any effective new Russian offensive on the Eastern Front, quiet since October, as over 2 million men have deserted, with few replacements available. Brusilov must depend greatly on shock battalions set up by Alexeyev with volunteers taken from units throughout the army.
Salonika. Sarrail's and Milne's offensive peters out, having succeeded only in capturing and holding a few Bulgarian outposts at a cost of fourteen thousand men killed, wounded, or captured. The Italians blame the offensive's failure on Sarrail.

23 May 1917
German East Africa. Belgian troops capture Capt. Max Wintgens, who in February, without orders, had marched off on his own with seven hundred askaris from Maj. Georg Kraut's force—much to the surprise of both the British and Col. Paul von Lettow-Vorbeck—raiding and destroying in areas the Allies had regarded as already safe and apparently heading for Tabora. Suffering from typhus, Wintgens has no choice but to surrender in order to obtain treatment. Lt. Heinrich Naumann assumes command of his vagabond force, which is pursued by the Belgians; a special British force called EDFORCE after its commander, Brig. Gen. W.F.S. Edwards, sent to quash Wintgens and headquartered in Tabora; and another special force, the Tenth South African Horse, dispatched to East Africa for the purpose by Gen. Louis Jacob van Deventer, who has just replaced Brig. Gen. A.R. Hoskins (ordered to Mesopotamia) as commander of the KAR forces previously led by Smuts. Naumann now has a force of fifty Europeans and five hundred askaris; the British and Belgian forces involved in his pursuit number four thousand.

25 May 1917
Ghent, Belgium. With the Zeppelin now obsolete for use as a bomber, the Germans have developed the Gotha airplane specifically for the strategic bombing of London in the daytime. Twenty-three Gothas leave their airfields at Ghent for their first bombing raid. Failing to reach London because of massive clouds, the Gothas bomb Folkestone on their return journey. Their toll is 95 dead and 195 wounded.

28 May 1917
Aisne River. Troops of the Thirty-sixth Infantry Division sent to the rear for rest refuse to return to the fighting at Craonne in the Chemin des Dames; sixty even take the train into Paris. But by mid-morning all are en route back to the front, although fourteen face courts-martial. Several such minor episodes of mutiny or "indiscipline" (the commanders' term) have occurred among the French troops during April and May.
New York City. With a large coterie of officers, General Pershing sails aboard the White Star liner *Baltic* for London and Paris to make preparations for the later arrival of units of the AEF.
Arabia. T.E. Lawrence arrives at the first of the Howeitat encampments.

30 May 1917
Aisne River. Troops of the Fifth Infantry Division hold protest meetings, expressing support for their officers while objecting to participating in futile offensives.
Messines. British artillery begins a week-long bombardment of German positions on the Messines Ridge in preparation for a long-planned attack.

2 June 1917
Doullens. With a promise from General Haig of strictest secrecy, General Pétain's chief of staff reveals to Haig that the French army has been afflicted with mutiny, precluding the possibility of offensive actions,

A British field howitzer fires a round during the Battle of Messines Ridge in June 1917 (Library of Congress)

in particular a planned attack at Malmaison. The revelation presents Haig with a quandary concerning whether to pursue the Flanders campaign. He decides that at this late date it is best to proceed with the assault on Messines Ridge planned for 7 June.

3 June 1917
Aisne River. After two days of protests and marches at Ville en Tardenois by dissident soldiers, two thousand in all, singing the *Internationale* and waving red flags, trucks transport the rebellious troops to other sites. Similar protests with troops refusing to return to the front—some 250 incidents in all—continue at various cantonments. Of the French army's total strength of 3.5 million, about thirty-five thousand are estimated to be involved in these protests—enough to alarm the high command.

Leeds, England. The Independent Labour Party, to which Ramsay MacDonald has defected after resigning from the Labour Party, has aligned with the Socialist Party to lead a conference at Leeds to advocate a peace settlement. Over eleven hundred delegates attend, including MacDonald,

Bertrand Russell, and Philip Snowden. The conference increases anxiety in the government over a growing peace movement.

4 June 1917
Ostend, Belgium. Hoping to destroy the German submarine base at Ostend, Admiral Bacon has sent a flotilla of cruisers and destroyers to shell the dockyards. They open fire at 3:00 A.M. The attack proves fruitless, however, despite several direct hits on the dockyard. The ineffective British attacks on Zeebrugge and Ostend leave the job of closing the ports to Gen. Douglas Haig and his Flanders offensive, intended to be supported by twenty-four thousand soldiers disembarked by the navy at Westende as the advance of Haig's troops warrants. In the English Channel, some other means must be found to stop the U-boats.

5 June 1917
Aisne River. Three hundred soldiers of the Fifth Infantry Division pass the motion: "We shall not move back to the trenches."

Washington. When signing the Selective

Services Act, President Wilson had designated 5 June as registration day. Now over nine and a half million men between the ages of twenty-one and thirty register for the draft.

7 June 1917

Messines. Haig has assigned to Gen. Sir Herbert Plumer's Second Army the job of clearing the Germans from the Messines Ridge. Since the previous summer, Plumer's men have been tunneling under the ridge and have placed twenty caches of explosives at intervals beneath the German positions. Although the Germans have suspected that the British are mining the ridge, their own tunneling has been too shallow to detect the British shafts, some of which are eighty feet below the surface. In addition, even though officers of Gen. Sixt von Armin's Fourth Army have recommended evacuation of the ridge positions after questioning British prisoners, the general has decided to stay put because withdrawal means ceding six miles of terrain to the enemy. Plumer's plan is simple: blow up the German positions and send in troops to occupy the ruins. For the infantry attack, he has the artillery support of 2,233 guns against the Germans' 630 and total superiority in the air, where British planes outnumber the Germans' 300 to 50 and have forced Richthofen's renowned "Flying Circus" to abandon the front. At 3:10 A.M., nineteen of the mines set by the British tunnelers explode simultaneously. Watching British soldiers compare the explosion's effects to an earthquake, with blasts of flames and dust surging skyward. "The earth seemed to tear apart," says one. "The whole ground came up and went back down again. It was like a huge mushroom." The advancing British and Anzac troops, protected by a creeping barrage, encounter light resistance, as the force of the explosion has killed ten thousand German troops. By midday, Plumer's men capture most of their objectives, ejecting the Germans from the heights of the Messines-Wytschaete Ridge and pushing their lines back three or four miles along an eight-mile front. Hastily mounted German counterattacks fail to dislodge them.

8 June 1917

Paris. The government confers upon General Pétain the right to execute rebellious soldiers immediately. Widely liked and admired by the soldiers, Pétain assumes the task of resolving the causes of the mutinies and placating the rebellious troops throughout the French army. Although arrests and courts-martial continue in order to enforce discipline, Pétain halts all offensive operations and makes a sincere effort to improve the troops' living conditions, including provision of better food and quarters, consistent leave policies, and uninterrupted periods of rest and relaxation. The two Russian brigades that fought at the Aisne, where they suffered six thousand casualties, have also become rebellious—one brigade maintains loyalty to the Russian Provisional Government; the other brigade adopts Bolshevik precepts—and are sent into quarantine at a camp at La Courtine in mid-France.

Liverpool, England. General Pershing and his staff arrive and, following welcoming ceremonies, board the train for London, where the American commander and his staff will meet with Prime Minister Lloyd George, Jan Christian Smuts, Gen. Sir William Robertson, Adm. Sir John Jellicoe, Adm. William S. Sims, Winston Churchill, and other officials.

10 June 1917

Trentino. The Trentino Offensive, planned in December by Gen. Count Luigi Cadorna for the spring but delayed by the Tenth Battle of the Isonzo, finally opens at 5:15 A.M. with an artillery bombardment. Cadorna has assembled ten divisions, a new army called the Sixth Army, and fifteen hundred guns for his offensive intended to drive the Austrians—units of the Army Group Tirol commanded by Field Marshal Count Franz Conrad von Hötzendorf—from the Asiago Plateau and force their withdrawal from the Assa River valley. Although the Austrian lines are obscured by heavy mists, the Italian shelling wreaks extensive destruction upon their defensive positions. After nearly five hours of shelling, Italian troops begin to advance as the mists slowly dissipate. Their attack on the

Austrian positions in the Monte Ortigara sector ends in hand-to-hand combat. Although in some sectors of the front the Italians manage to advance by the end of the day, overall the Austrians hold fast while inflicting heavy casualties that prompt the commander of the Sixth Army to recommend to Cadorna that the offensive be terminated. But the commander in chief determines to pursue the offensive, allowing a two-day respite—a fateful pause.

11 June 1917
Athens. Carrying out a policy of firmness decided upon by Prime Ministers Lloyd George and Ribot that is intended to bring Venizelos to power, the French envoy in Athens delivers an ultimatum demanding that King Constantine abdicate the Greek throne. British and French troops invade Thessaly; French troops take the Isthmus of Corinth.

13 June 1917
London. Before noon, fourteen Gothas flying in formation make their first attack on London with the intent of bombing the heart of the city—six others that began the flight have had to turn back. Liverpool Street Station and its environs are the center of the attack that results in 162 dead and 432 wounded—a great shock for the British, whose fighter planes so far prove ineffectual against the Gothas.
Trentino. The Italians' pause has allowed the Austrians to reinforce their lines and even to plan a counterattack, although the Austrian Supreme Command has refused to shift troops from the Isonzo front for the effort.
Boulogne, France. General Pershing and his accompanying officers arrive to welcoming ceremonies and board the train for Paris.

14 June 1917
Athens. Having abdicated the throne on 12 June in favor of Alexander, his second son, Constantine leaves the capital to begin exile in Switzerland.
Messines. Plumer's Second Army consolidates a successful battle, with the Germans withdrawing from the last of the positions

they have held on the Messines-Wytschaete Ridges. But the Battle of Messines Ridge costs Plumer seventeen thousand casualties, largely caused by German artillery and machine-gun fire directed at his troops as they dig in. German casualties total twenty-five thousand, including those blown up in the giant explosion of 7 June.

15 June 1917
Trentino. At 2:30 A.M., the Austrians counterattack, taking the Italians by surprise. They break through the Italian line but then fall back, thwarted in hand-to-hand fighting. At dawn, the Italians launch a series of counterattacks, all successfully repulsed even though Italian artillery fire batters the Austrian lines.
Washington. President Wilson signs into law the Espionage Act, defining the nature of war crimes and granting the president power to regulate exports through creation of the Exports Council.

16 June 1917
Compiègne. General Pershing and his staff meet with French Commander in Chief Gen. Philippe Pétain. After hearing Pershing's depiction of the American support that is to come, the pessimistic Pétain responds simply: "I hope it is not too late." Pershing returns to Paris to begin plans for dealing with the eventual arrival of the AEF.

18 June 1917
Russia. The Russian Seventh and Eleventh Armies begin Gen. Aleksey A. Brusilov's planned offensive aimed at Lemberg.
Trentino. Italian artillery opens twenty hours of firing at 8:00 A.M. preparatory to an assault along the entire front from Porta Lepozze to the Assa Gorge, with major thrusts against Austrian positions at Monte Forno and Monte Ortigara.

19 June 1917
Trentino. At 6:00 A.M., the Italian assault begins, spearheaded by elite Alpine troops who capture Austrian positions in the Ortigara sector, taking possession of the mountain's main summit. But elsewhere, including some positions on the Ortigara, the Austrians hold fast, preventing a sig-

nificant Italian advance. During the night, the Austrians reinforce their positions at Porta Lepozze and Monte Campigoletti.

London. Gen. Douglas Haig has traveled to the city to try to persuade the War Cabinet that he is right about pursuing what he sees as the advantage opened by the Battle of Messines Ridge and unleashing the large-scale Flanders offensive he has planned. But the members of the War Cabinet—Lloyd George, Andrew Bonar Law, Lord Curzon, Smuts, Viscount Alfred Milner, and Gen. Sir William Robertson—respond pessimistically. Prime Minister Lloyd George remains especially disaffected over the prospects on the Western Front.

20 June 1917

Russia. The offensive of the Seventh and Eleventh Armies ends as the troops refuse to continue fighting.

Trentino. Italian airplanes bomb Austrian positions, but even though Cadorna has 145 airplanes against the Austrians' 26, his offensive shows signs of faltering.

London. Haig receives unexpected support before the War Cabinet from Admiral Jellicoe, who asserts that shipping losses are so great that, unless the British can seize the ports at Zeebrugge and Ostend from the Germans, the war cannot continue. "There is no good discussing plans for next spring—we cannot go on," declares the first sea lord.

23 June 1917

Russia. General Kornilov's Eighth Army attacks with some success, capturing seven thousand Austro-Hungarian prisoners.

24 June 1917

Trans-Jordan. At Minifir, T.E. Lawrence leads a raid on the railway that links Amman with Der'a. His purpose is to convince the Turks that his ultimate target is Damascus, whereas, of course, he intends to attack Aqaba.

25 June 1917

Trentino. Reinforced once again, the Austrians launch an early morning artillery barrage and infantry attack against the Ital-

ian positions on Monte Ortigara, recapturing the main summit.

26 June 1917

Trentino. At the Porta Lepozze sector, the Italians cease fire and withdraw to new positions at the Porta Maora.

Compiègne. General Pershing makes a second visit to General Pétain's headquarters and requests that the AEF, when it arrives, be given the Lorraine sector of the Western Front between the Argonne Forest and the Vosges Mountains, so that the American army can make use of the ports at Saint-Nazaire, La Pallice, and Bassens and the railroads connecting them to the front.

27 June 1917

Athens. Eleutherios Venizelos arrives in the capital, assumes the premiership, and declares his Provisional Government the official government of Greece. The new government declares war on the Central Powers.

London. Though doubtful of the accuracy of Jellicoe's assessment, after mulling over his and Haig's arguments, the War Cabinet is sufficiently persuaded to authorize Haig to continue preparations for his offensive while Lloyd George tries to determine how much support can be expected from the French. Content with the final outcome of the War Cabinet's deliberations, the commander in chief returns to Flanders to pursue his plans. The delay in pressing whatever advantage resulted from the Battle of Messines Ridge, however, affords the Germans time to construct concrete bunkers and other strong defensive installations along the Flanders front, where Crown Prince Rupprecht of Bavaria, commander of the German northern army group, and his chief of staff, Gen. Hermann von Kuhl, are certain the British offensive will concentrate—a view supported by General von Armin's new chief of staff, Col. Fritz von Lossberg, recently appointed to this post by Gen. Erich Ludendorff.

28 June 1917

London. Prime Minister David Lloyd George appoints Gen. Sir Edmund Allenby commander of the Egyptian Expeditionary Force. The prime minister's assignment to Allenby comes in a simple statement: "I'd like you to take Jerusalem as a Christmas present for the nation."

30 June 1917
Trentino. Austrian troops surprise the Italians and force them back to the northeastern slopes of the Porta Maora, recapturing the last of the positions lost to the Italian offensive. Cadorna's failed offensive, accompanied by disproportionate losses, demoralizes the Italian troops. The offensive has cost Cadorna's Sixth Army 23,736 soldiers and officers killed, wounded, or taken prisoner. The Austrian losses are only 8,828.

2 July 1917
Russia. The offensive on the South-Western Front intended to take Lemberg ends as General Kornilov's troops also refuse to continue. The offensive's casualties total 38,700.

6 July 1917
Russia. German and Austrian troops begin a counterattack against the Russian Eleventh Army, pushing the Russians back toward the Seret River.
German East Africa. At Mhindi soldiers of General van Deventer's Third King's African Rifles attack a detachment of Lettow-Vorbeck's *Schutztruppe* commanded by Capt. Eberhard von Lieberman, who withdraws to Narungombe, forty miles to the west of Kilwa, where the Germans build strong defenses.
Trans-Jordan. Capt. T.E. Lawrence, Auda abu Tayi, and their force of Howeitat tribesmen capture Aqaba after a nearly two-month trek across the desert and a successful attack on Turkish troops at Aba el Lissan, an escarpment outside Aqaba, where they kill 300 Turkish soldiers and take 160 prisoners. The coastal city gives the Arabs a base within a hundred miles of Allenby's operations in Palestine from which to advance toward Damascus. Lawrence will report to Gen. Sir Edmund Allenby in Cairo and obtain his support for continued operations.

7 July 1917
London. The Gotha bombers return— twenty-two this time—dropping their bombs on the city and the East End. The raid's toll is 54 dead and 190 wounded. The British still have no effective means of combatting the Gothas. The public responds with anger and demands for more aircraft to protect London.

8 July 1917
Russia. The Russian offensive on the northern sector of the Eastern Front begins, but only two of the six divisions assigned to the offensive actually participate, and officers must use guns to force soldiers of one division to muster for the line of attack.

10 July 1917
Russia. The offensive on the northern sector ends, as Russian troops return to their own initial positions.

11 July 1917
London. Responding to the crisis created by the Gotha bombings, Parliament establishes a committee chaired by Jan Smuts, now a member of the War Cabinet, to study defense tactics.
Berlin. Responding to Social Democratic Party advocacy of a peace settlement "without annexations or indemnities" and of political reforms, Kaiser Wilhelm II grants, in principle, equal suffrage to the peoples of Prussia.
Ypres. Attempting to achieve air superiority before the Flanders offensive begins, five hundred British and two hundred French airplanes take to the air.

13 July 1917
Berlin. Victimized by Ludendorff's plotting against him and blamed for everything from food shortages to demoralization of the sailors in the High Seas Fleet, Chancellor Theobald von Bethmann Hollweg is forced out of office. Undersecretary of State Georg Michaelis replaces him, but all the real power now lies in the hands of Ludendorff and Hindenburg.
Russia. With the overall offensive a shambles, although there has been modest suc-

cess on the Romanian front, Kerensky has removed Brusilov from command and placed Gen. L.G. Kornilov in charge. Kornilov orders a halt to the entire offensive.

16 July 1917
Ypres. Allied artillery opens fire on the German lines in order to prepare for the beginning of the Flanders offensive.

19 July 1917
German East Africa. The Third King's African Rifles attacks Captain von Lieberman's positions at Narungombe, defended by eight companies of *Schutztruppe* with two field guns and forty-eight Maxim machine guns. Initially the attack goes badly, as the KAR's right flank founders in a swamp and falls victim to the German machine guns. By noon so many of the KAR officers have been killed that African NCOs command most of the platoons and companies. The Germans attack with bayonets, but the KAR troops stand their ground and counterattack. As the sun sets, the Germans attack again, and again the KAR troops hold and counterattack, capturing a machine gun. During the night Lieberman's men disappear into the bush.
Berlin. The *Reichstag* passes the Peace Resolution—supported by the Social Democratic Party, the Center Party, and the Progressive Peoples Party—by a vote of 212 to 120. The resolution calls for "a peace of understanding and reconciliation" that bars "compulsory" annexation of territory and any forms of political, economic, or financial "oppression."

20 July 1917
London. Wanting to remove Adm. Sir John Jellicoe as first sea lord, Lloyd George first moves to neutralize Jellicoe's primary supporter, first lord of the admiralty Sir Edward Carson, by moving him into the War Cabinet and replacing him at the Admiralty with Sir Eric Campbell Geddes. The prime minister also finally gives approval to Haig's planned offensive in Flanders.
Washington. In the Senate Office Building, the draft begins as a blindfolded Newton D. Baker reaches into a jar and selects the first number in the lottery—each man in each local board region with the number becomes draftable. The drawing continues throughout the day until 10,500 numbers have been selected.

21 July 1917
Western Front. General Pétain's tactics in resolving the mutinies and his appeals to patriotism have largely succeeded in meeting his goal of restoring the army's "feeling that it was a single organism co-operating for a common purpose." As the weeks pass, discipline revives among the troops. Over twenty-eight hundred have received sentences, and of these, fifty have been condemned to death. Miraculously, the Germans have not learned of the mutinies until it is too late to reap any advantage.

25 July 1917
Paris. At the end of a two-day trial, a military court sentences Mata Hari for espionage. She is to be executed by firing squad.

26 July 1917
Ypres. The combined British and French air squadrons achieve control of the air space above the Flanders front, as the outnumbered German airmen withdraw.

27 July 1917
Ypres. As the projected date for the opening of Haig's Flanders offensive approaches, soldiers of the Guards Division of Gen. Hubert Gough's Fifth Army discover that the Germans have evacuated three thousand yards of their front line after British artillery shelling and occupy the abandoned trenches. Gough has an advantage in artillery of nearly two to one, with 2,174 howitzers, field guns, and heavy guns. Haig has designated the Fifth Army's nine divisions as the spearhead of the Flanders offensive.

30 July 1917
Ypres. During the night and early morning hours of 29-30 July, General Gough's assault forces assemble at the front lines for the initial attack of the Flanders offensive. Joining them are 136 tanks deploying in an arc to the east of Ypres.

31 July 1917
Ypres. At ten minutes before 4:00 A.M., British, Anzac, French, and Belgian troops go over the top to begin the Third Battle of Ypres, called by the British soldiers simply Passchendaele. Gough's Fifth Army carries the center of the attack to the east of Ypres along the Ypres-Roulers railway and to the northeast of Ypres, advancing against Gen. Sixt von Armin's Fourth Army and units of Gen. Otto von Below's Sixth Army. To the south Gen. Sir Herbert Plumer's Second Army and to the north the French First Army supplement the Fifth Army's assault. Along the entire front, the Allies succeed by midday in capturing their initial objectives, German outposts and first-line defenses, but in pressing beyond the second line of the German defenses, they confront counterattacks that force them back to their first objectives. The tanks supporting the Allied attack prove ineffectual, deterred by the cratered terrain and prey to German shelling; the Germans knock out nineteen of the fifty-two tanks with Gough's Thirtieth Division. Twenty-two other tanks break down with mechanical failures. The farthest advance achieved by the Fifth Army as night approaches is about thirty-five hundred yards. During the afternoon, heavy rains begin.

1 August 1917
Ypres. Allied troops hold fast against German counterattacks and consolidate their gains.

Slogging through a rain on the Western Front, 1917 (by A. Barrere, courtesy of the Anne S.K. Brown Military Collection, Brown University Library)

2 August 1917
Ypres. As the rains continue for the third day, the battlefield becomes a quagmire interspersed with water-filled shell craters. As the infantry assault pauses, the British artillery begins bombarding the Gheluvelt Plateau, but German batteries to the rear of the plateau escape the effects. Haig postpones resuming the general offensive. Driving the Germans from their first and second lines of defense has already cost the Allies twenty-three thousand casualties; they have taken six thousand prisoners.

3 August 1917
Ypres. The rains and the artillery shelling continue. The mud muffles the explosive effects of the shells.
German East Africa. Units of the King's African Rifles stage an attack from three directions against Lettow-Vorbeck's main positions in the southeast corner of the colony, but the German defenses are so strong that the attack fails totally, with the Germans successfully assaulting the KAR supply column.
Washington. Edward N. Hurley, head of both the Shipping Board and the Emergency Fleet Corporation by appointment of President Wilson, commandeers all large-hulled ships under construction in the United States for military transports or convoys. At the end of June, the government had confiscated all interned enemy ships and returned them to service flying the American flag.

5 August 1917
London. Smuts's committee has recommended creating three fighter squadrons and a system of antiaircraft guns to protect London from the Gothas, with a single commander to be in control of the London Air Defence Area. Brig. Gen. E.B. Ashmore returns from France to assume the command.

7 August 1917
London. In his maneuverings to bring about the removal of Sir John Jellicoe as first sea lord, Prime Minister David Lloyd George engineers the dismissal of the admiral's close friend, Sir Cecil Burney,

Trenches became miserable, wet ditches during a rainstorm (by A. Barrere, courtesy of the Anne S.K. Brown Military Collection, Brown University Library)

as second sea lord. His successor is Vice Adm. Sir Rosslyn Wemyss, given the added title of deputy first sea lord.

10 August 1917
Ypres. After allowing time for the ground to dry while continuing the artillery bombardment, the British launch an attack against the German positions on the Gheluvelt Plateau, but German counterattacks drive them back. They achieve only a small gain at Westhoeck.
Washington. Pres. Woodrow Wilson signs the Lever Act, passed by Congress authorizing the president to control foods, fuels, fertilizers, and machinery used for food production, so that he is freed to create the Food Administration with Herbert Clark Hoover in charge, which he had advocated in a May public announcement.

12 August 1917
Chatham, England. As 10 Gothas appear

to bomb the naval base at Chatham, 132 Sopwith Pups take to the air to drive them off. Heading for the Channel, the Gothas drop their bombs on Southend, killing 32 and wounding 46.

14 August 1917
Peking. The Chinese government, which had severed diplomatic relations with Austria and Germany on 14 March, declares war on the two nations. It is a meaningless gesture, but it allows China to seize those German holdings not already in Japanese hands and provides China a seat at the peace conference. China is in a state of political and social turmoil, with the warlords still maneuvering for power and an opposition government established in Canton.

15 August 1917
Rome. Pope Benedict XV publicly issues a call for peace dated 1 August in which he advocates evacuation of occupied Belgium and France, restoration of the German colonies, and a peace settlement providing for disarmament and international arbitration of disputes. Through his nuncio at Munich, Cardinal Pacelli, the pope announces that the government of Austria-Hungary is seeking a peace settlement and that demands for a settlement without annexations or indemnities are increasing among left-wing political parties in Germany.

16 August 1917
Ypres. Delayed for two days by heavy rains, a major attack by the French and British planned for 14 August begins with an advance into the Gheluvelt Plateau. Although one of Gough's divisions manages to capture Langemarck, the attack as a whole fails.

21 August 1917
Russia. German troops capture Riga, a major Russian port on the Baltic Sea.

22 August 1917
Margate. Fifteen Gothas remain serviceable, but four turn back with engine trouble as the bombers try one more daytime raid

on England. Antiaircraft guns destroy one over Margate. A Royal Naval Air Service plane sends another crashing into the sea. The others quickly unload their bombs over Ramsgate and Dover and flee, leaving behind eight dead and twelve wounded Britons. Assessing the new effectiveness of the English defenses, Capt. Rudolf Kleine, commanding officer of the Gotha squadron, cancels future daytime raids and begins training his crews for night flying.

Ypres. As a result of the stagnated Flanders offensive, General Haig and Adm. Reginald Bacon decide to postpone the amphibious operation to land troops on the Belgian coast.

25 August 1917

Ypres. Haig and Plumer confer. Haig overcomes Plumer's deep reluctance, gaining his agreement that Plumer's Second Army will assume the major burden of the Flanders offensive, as Gough's assaults have attained only meager results. The Fifth Army's limited attacks will continue, however, as Plumer requires time to make plans and preparations for the resumption of the general offensive. Thus far the offensive has cost the British sixty-eight thousand casualties, including fifteen thousand dead. The farthest advance the British have achieved is only four thousand yards.

26 August 1917

Verdun. Despite the army's problems resulting from the mutinies, Gen. Philippe Pétain launches a successful offensive along an eleven-mile front, capturing le Morte Homme, so hard won by the Germans in February 1916.

27 August 1917

Ypres. Gough's troops vainly try to slog forward in the muddy soup of the battlefield, gaining no ground.

Washington. Responding to Pope Benedict XV's peace appeal, Wilson declares that there can be no return to the prewar status nor a peace settlement as long as the current German government remains in power.

29 August 1917

Ypres. General Plumer submits his plans for continuing the offensive to General Haig. He recommends shifting the main focus to the south to take advantage of control of the Messines Ridge; advancing in a series of short thrusts at six-day intervals, each having the objective of taking about fifteen hundred yards, to maintain artillery coverage and discourage counterattacks; and emplacing artillery in the greatest concentration to date for the war—one gun every 5.2 yards. The barrage system for the artillery defines five zones of fire totaling a depth of a thousand yards as a hell of high explosives, shrapnel, and machine-gun bullets. The infantry density is also the highest yet, with each attacking corps responsible for only a thousand yards of front.

1 September 1917

Riga, Russia. Opening an offensive against the Russian bridgehead at Riga, Gen. Oskar von Hutier's Eighth Army artillery launches a two-hour barrage of gas shells at the Russian positions on the east bank of the Dvina River at Borkowitz beginning at 4:00 A.M. and followed by a bombardment of explosive shells. The German infantrymen cross the river, capturing the islands of Berkowitz and Elster, and discovering that the Russian troops of the Twelfth Army have fled. They push forward, taking prisoners and establishing a bridgehead of over seven miles.

Chaumont, France. General Pershing moves his headquarters and staff to this small town (population fifteen thousand) in Lorraine to be near the front he has chosen as the center for the American Expeditionary Force's operations. The American First Division, commanded by Maj. Gen. William L. Sibert, has recently arrived and is training near Valdahon. Maj. George C. Marshall is chief of operations.

2 September 1917

Riga. The Twelfth Army has abandoned the Riga bridgehead, but General von Hutier's troops encounter strong opposition from the Russian troops and difficult terrain as they try to push ahead in the Tirul

Marshes toward the Gross Jegel River.

Berlin. Adm. Alfred von Tirpitz and other conservatives found the German Fatherland Party to oppose the proponents of peace and the *Reichstag*'s Peace Resolution by supporting the policies of the High Command—i.e., Hindenburg and Ludendorff.

3 September 1917

Chatham, England. Undertaking their first night raid, four Gothas led by Captain Kleine bomb the naval station at Chatham, killing 131 sailors and wounding 90.

Riga. The Germans cross the Gross Jegel and pressure the Russians, retreating along the railway that links Riga with Pskov.

4 September 1917

London. General Haig meets with the War Cabinet after sending a dispatch admitting the Flanders offensive has fallen behind schedule but blaming this failure on weather and a shortage of heavy shells. He hears Lloyd George's view of the current status of the war: Russia cannot continue, so Germany can transfer troops from there to the Western Front, where, given the problems of the French army and the stalemate at Ypres, there is little cause for optimism, and offensive measures should at least temporarily be halted—probably until the Americans can arrive in force in 1918. Lloyd George wishes to divert support to the Italians. Perturbed by Haig's tactics and his offensive's failure, the prime minister mutters: "Blood and mud, blood and mud. They can think of nothing better." Nevertheless, Haig leaves the meeting with the War Cabinet's tacit approval to continue.

Riga. Hutier's troops reach the southern bank of the Aa River.

5 September 1917

Riga. The Russian Twelfth Army succeeds in escaping annihilation, retreating to Wenden. Riga falls to General von Hutier's Eighth Army, which has suffered only forty-two hundred casualties in the offensive. Russian losses are twenty-five thousand.

6 September 1917

Egypt. British agents blow up a munitions

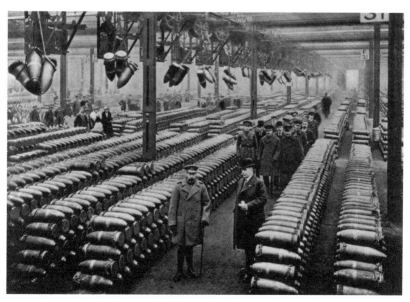

British King George V visiting an English munitions factory. Despite the impressive rows of shells seen here, the British suffered throughout the war from shortages of artillery ammunition (Library of Congress)

depot at Haidar Pasha intended for use by the Yilderim, or Lightning, force set up by the Germans for an attack on Baghdad. The action supports Gen. Sir Edmund Allenby's plans for marching against Gaza. Allenby has assembled three corps, including three divisions of mounted troops, for his campaign for which the ultimate objective is the capture of Jerusalem.

10 September 1917

German East Africa. Gen. Louis van Deventer moves his headquarters to Kilwa, planning to launch a decisive campaign against Lettow-Vorbeck with forces from here and Lindi.

11 September 1917

Italy. Meeting in Udine with Lord Derby, Britain's minister of war, Gen. Count Luigi Cadorna promises to continue offensive operations against Austria-Hungary and elicits a commitment from Lord Derby that Great Britain will send him needed heavy artillery.

12 September 1917

Petrograd. Troops led by commander in chief of the army, Gen. Lavr Kornilov, who hopes to take control of the Provisional Government, have been forced to stop forty miles from the city because the railroad tracks have been torn up, and his coup attempt fails. Kerensky has Kornilov and other generals arrested and assumes the additional post of commander in chief.

16 September 1917

La Courtine, France. At the behest of the French, three thousand troops of the Russian brigade that remain loyal to the Provisional Government have encircled the Bolshevik troops at the camp. They subdue all but five hundred of them with artillery fire, and even these diehards finally surrender. The ringleaders are shot. Thus ends the potential menace these troops represented to the French government.

19 September 1917

German East Africa. The King's African Rifle forces set off to the southwest from Lindi and to the south from Kilwa to be-

gin van Deventer's major campaign against Lt. Col. Paul von Lettow-Vorbeck.

20 September 1917

Ypres. The renewed offensive Plumer has planned begins at 5:40 A.M., as his Second Army troops move out in the wake of a devastating creeping barrage that renders most of the frontline German troops dead, wounded, or stunned. By early afternoon, the British and Anzac troops capture all their major objectives except an area of the Gheluvelt Plateau called "Tower Hamlets Spur." The artillery barrage pauses until British troops spot Germans moving up to counterattack at about 4:00 P.M. A renewed barrage stops the counterattack, and the British consolidate the day's gains.

Montreuil, France. The French high command receives a message from General Cadorna that Italy will have to abandon plans for further offensive operations in favor of defense because of an expected Austrian counteroffensive. Annoyed, the British and French halt a shipment of two hundred pieces of artillery already en route to the Italians. Cadorna has been taken in by an Austrian ruse.

23 September 1917

Arras. At 6:00 P.M., six British airplanes discover German ace Werner Voss, credited with forty-eight kills, flying alone and give chase. Maneuvering adeptly, Voss evades their fire while scoring hits on two of his attackers. But A.P.F. Rhys-Davies finally gets Voss's triplane in his Lewis gun's sights—the German ace is apparently wounded or has fainted—and rakes the triplane's entire fuselage with fire. Voss plummets to his death.

Ypres. Continued attempts to capture "Tower Hamlets Spur" and secondary objectives set for Gough's Fifth Army on the northern sector of the front result in over twenty thousand casualties by the end of the third day of the British offensive. But Plumer's tactics succeed in taking the fifteen hundred yards set as the offensive's initial objective.

24 September 1917

London. The Gothas return to raid London at night, although only three reach the city, so the casualties are light—thirteen dead and twenty-six wounded.

26 September 1917

Ypres. The second stage of Plumer's plan opens at 5:50 A.M. with his troops once more advancing behind a horrendous artillery barrage that again leaves the German survivors dazed and ready to surrender. The continuing barrages thwart German counterattacks launched within easy range of the British guns, as Plumer's plan envisioned. So again Plumer's troops succeed in capturing their objective, a more limited advance of a thousand yards and occupation of all of Polygon Wood. Once more, however, the cost is heavy—fifteen thousand casualties.

28 September 1917

Kent, England. Two Riesen (Giant) airplanes for the first time join with twenty-five Gothas to raid England. The Riesen are massive, with biplane wings measuring over 138 feet. But the raid is a failure. Fifteen of the Gothas have to turn back, six crash-land when reaching their airfields in Belgium, and British antiaircraft fire destroys three.

Ypres. Meeting with Plumer and Gen. Hubert Gough, Commander in Chief Douglas Haig declares himself sufficiently satisfied with the progress of the renewed offensive that, following the third step of Plumer's plan, he intends to try to break through the German lines.

Mesopotamia. With Baghdad secure, Gen. F.S. Maude, commander of the Mesopotamian Force, has sent troops forward on both the Tigris and Euphrates Rivers. On the Euphrates they force the surrender of the Turkish garrison of over thirty-five hundred at Ar Ramadi.

30 September 1917

London. Eleven Gothas stage another night raid on London, but they inflict little damage. Shell fragments generated by "blind barrage firing," a new British defense tactic, prove nearly as destructive as the German bombs.

German East Africa. Near the border of

British East Africa at Mount Kilimanjaro, the Fourth King's African Rifles and units of the South African Horse and the Cape Corps surround Lt. Heinrich Naumann's nomadic force, by now reduced to 14 Europeans and 165 askaris. This force, led first by Capt. Max Wintgens and now by Naumann, has traversed two thousand miles of territory in eight months, keeping the British and the Belgians on edge with their daring and freedom of movement.

2 October 1917

German East Africa. Entrapped near Mount Kilimanjaro, Lieutenant Naumann formally surrenders. The British charge him with murder, but lack of evidence eventually precludes a trial.

4 October 1917

Ypres. Plumer begins the third step of his plan with an attack launched at 6:00 A.M. This time the creeping barrage and the infantry attack begin simultaneously without any preliminary artillery shelling. Trying to devise a countermeasure to the new British tactics, Col. Fritz von Lossberg has moved his counterattack reserves to the front lines instead of holding them in the rear, so the German troops are densely massed at the front. The result is catastrophe. The British barrage exacts thirty thousand German casualties. British casualties, however, are not light, and their advance is a modest seven hundred yards. The rains return.

6 October 1917

Italy. Italian air reconnaissance reveals that there will be no general Austrian counteroffensive. The Germans and Austrians have forty-three divisions deployed along the entire Italian front, and nearly thirty of them are in the Isonzo River sector, an indication that any offensive will be centered here. In fact, the primary thrust of the offensive is to be at Caporetto and Tolmein (Tolmino). The German Fourteenth Army, comprised of two Austrian and two German divisions commanded by Gen. Otto von Below, will spearhead the offensive. General von Below has 1,845 guns, thus providing enormous superiority over the artillery available to Gen. Luigi Capello, commander of the Italian Second Army that opposes Below.

7 October 1917
Ypres. Generals Plumer and Gough at Haig's request visit the commander in chief at GHQ at Montreuil. Both generals urge termination of the offensive. But Haig insists on continuing, arguing the need to keep pressure on the Germans as long as the French army remains incapacitated and to reach higher ground for ceasing operations for the winter. He wants another attack launched on 9 October. The primary objective is to be Passchendaele Ridge.

13 October 1917
Ypres. Haig summons Gen. Sir Arthur Currie, commander of the Canadian Corps of General Plumer's Second Army, to GHQ at Montreuil and assigns his corps the task of spearheading the capture of Passchendaele Ridge. Currie believes the task can be done but estimates a cost of sixteen thousand casualties. Heavy rains beginning on 9 October have again turned the battleground into a mire. Currie insists on time to prepare his troops and to ensure adequate artillery support.

15 October 1917
Vincennes. In the early morning, Mata Hari stoically dies before a firing squad. During her final day on earth, she has reportedly declared: "Death is nothing, nor life, either, for that matter. To die, to sleep, to pass into nothingness, what does it matter? Everything is an illusion."

17 October 1917
North Sea. Two German light cruisers attack a convoy en route from Great Britain to Scandinavia, sinking nine of the twelve merchant ships in the convoy and both of the British destroyers escorting them.
German East Africa. Sensing that van Deventer has sent a major force against him, Lettow-Vorbeck has seized the initiative and marched with five *Schutztruppe* companies to engage the King's African Rifle units commanded by Brig. Gen. Gordon Beves, a South African. The clash oc-

curs at Mahiwa on the Lukuledi River, where Lettow-Vorbeck has deployed and entrenched his troops on a ridge. The British attack at daybreak. Attacks and counterattacks, including bayonet charges, consume the day.

18 October 1917
German East Africa. After a quiet night, the fighting at Mahiwa resumes as day dawns. Lettow-Vorbeck has correctly assumed that Beves would send his men into a frontal assault, and his troops inflict a dreadful toll on the KAR throughout the day, with both sides forced to fall back in exhaustion during the night. British losses total 2,700 men, more than half the 4,900 sent against Lettow-Vorbeck. Among Lettow-Vorbeck's total force of 1,500, there are 95 dead and 422 wounded. "With the exception of Tanga," says Lettow-Vorbeck, "it was the most serious defeat . . . [the British] had suffered." But Lettow-Vorbeck's own losses are irreplaceable, and he cannot afford another such "victory."

20 October 1917
Mesopotamia. Moving up the Tigris River, General Maude's troops capture Jabal Hamrin on the Diyala River after three days of pressing after the rapidly retreating Turks.

21 October 1917
Nancy. The first American troops to move into position at the front occupy the line in the Sommerville sector.

24 October 1917
Isonzo River. At 2:00 A.M., Austro-German forces open their counteroffensive with a massive artillery bombardment of thirty-five hundred guns along the whole Isonzo front, lobbing gas shells into the Italian positions at the Tolmein sector with devastating effect. At 7:00 A.M., Below's troops attack, with four companies commanded by Capt. Erwin Rommel in the lead. They sweep forward against minimal opposition, crossing the Isonzo River and by 4:00 P.M. occupy the town of Caporetto. They achieve a fifteen-mile breach of the Italian lines between Flitsch and Tolmein.

Assessing the catastrophe during the night, Cadorna orders the immediate dispatch of four divisions from Trentino and elsewhere to reinforce the front. He also sends orders to hold the Monte Maggiore at all costs and secretly instructs the Duke of Aosta and Lieutenant General Capello to prepare defenses along the Tagliamento River.

Trans-Jordan. Allenby has asked T.E. Lawrence to raid the railway in the Yarmuk Valley and render it useless as an aid to his offensive against Gaza. Lawrence leaves Aqaba with a force of Bedouins and Indian machine gunners to make the raid. The raid fails.

25 October 1917

Petrograd. The Bolsheviks, supported by the majority of the Petrograd military garrison, seize control of the government.

Isonzo River. Lieutenant General Capello, who had been ill and thus uninvolved during the few days leading up to and including the battle, informs General Cadorna at his headquarters at Udine that the entire Italian line east of the Isonzo River has fallen to the Austro-German forces. By midday, Monte Stol falls, and Below's troops menace Luico. Capello, still ill, appears at headquarters and urges a general withdrawal to as far as the Tagliamento River. Cadorna agrees. Capello returns to Cividale but is so incapacitated that he must turn over command to General Montouri, who at about 9:00 P.M. advises a now-wavering Cadorna that the present Italian positions can be held. At this very moment, two corps of Italian troops are hastily retreating from the mountains.

26 October 1917

Ypres. The Canadian Corps, supported by a heavy artillery barrage, begins the advance toward Passchendale in the rain at 5:30 A.M. Though encountering heavy resistance, they attain their first objective by four-thirty in the afternoon, occupying the south slopes of Bellevue Spur to the northeast of Laamkeek.

Isonzo River. Below's troops take Monte Maggiore, which Cadorna considers crucial to the Italian defense. Austro-German troops enter the Friuli-Venetian Plain.

London. Reacting to a plea for help from Cadorna and to confused reports out of Italy, Lloyd George orders that two divisions be sent from the Western Front to support Cadorna as soon as possible.

27 October 1917

Isonzo River. General von Below's troops take Cividale and reach the Torre River, routing the Italian troops, now in rapid flight. Left with no other choice, Cadorna orders a general retreat of the Second Army, the Fourth Army (positioned to the northwest of the front), and the Duke of Aosta's Third Army (stationed at the Carso sector of the Isonzo River front) to the Tagliamento River. The Second Army retreats chaotically, hounded by Below's troops.

29 October 1917

Italy. Cadorna has ordered the Second Army to hold the Torre River long enough to allow the Third Army to cross with as much of its equipment as possible; but German units, driving toward Cadorna's headquarters at Udine, breach the Second Army's line, dividing its forces in half. In the evening, General von Below, now pressured by Ludendorff to return five divisions to the Western Front, orders his troops to capture the bridges over the Tagliamento River before the Italians can destroy them.

30 October 1917

Ypres. The Canadians renew the attack, taking Bellevue Spur against rigorous German opposition.

Italy. Gen. Ferdinand Foch, sent by the French government, arrives in Italy and visits General Cadorna at his current headquarters at Treviso. He had already offered aid to Cadorna, informing him that the French were prepared to send four divisions to Italy.

31 October 1917

Italy. Impeded by confusion and Italian resistance, Below's troops fail to reach the Tagliamento River in time to seize the bridges. The Italians cross over and pause along the entire length of the river's west bank. They have, however, lost 250,000 prisoners to the Austro-German forces, and Cadorna realizes that he now must fall back all the way to the Piave River. Chief of the Imperial General Staff Sir William Robertson, dispatched by Lloyd George, arrives in Italy and meets with Foch and Cadorna at Treviso.

Palestine. Leaving his encampments intact and periodically shelling Turkish positions at Gaza to convince the Turks that his efforts are aimed at Gaza, Allenby has slowly moved his troops to the southeast preparatory to attacking Beersheba. During the night, Allenby has concentrated 40,000 British troops with 116 guns for the attack. The Turkish garrison consists of four thousand infantry, one thousand cavalry, and four batteries of artillery circled by only one line of redoubts and trenches. Since mid-September Gen. Erich von Falkenhayn has been moving troops of the Seventh Army from Aleppo, intending to concentrate them at Beersheba for an attack on Allenby's right flank, but they have yet to reach their destination. The first objective of the British attack is Hill 1070. They begin an artillery barrage of the hill at 5:55 A.M. The troops advance at eight-thirty and capture the hill, allowing the artillery to move closer. Following an hour-and-a-half barrage, the troops attack. Though meeting some stiff resistance, especially at Tel es Saba, they overrun the Turkish defenses. At 4:40 P.M., the cavalrymen of the Desert Mounted Corps gallop off toward Beersheba, four miles distant, charge past Turkish trenches, and sweep into the town, taking fourteen hundred prisoners and fourteen guns while mopping up. Beersheba, with its vital wells, is in British hands.

London. Foreign Secretary Arthur J. Balfour has issued a declaration on the settlement of Jews in Palestine that the War Cabinet approves. The Balfour Declaration reads: "His Majesty's Government view with favour the establishment in Palestine of a national home for the Jewish people, and will use their best endeavours to facilitate the achievement of this object, it being clearly understood that nothing shall be done which may prejudice the civil and religious rights of existing non-Jewish communities in Palestine, or the rights and

political status enjoyed in any other country." The wording is mostly the work of Lord Milner, who is sympathetic toward Zionism, as is Assistant Foreign Secretary Lord Robert Cecil. In addition, Zionist leader Chaim Weizmann has influence with Lloyd George. British government officials think support of Zionist ambitions is desirable in light of the dissolution of the czarist government in Russia and the anticipated fall of the Ottoman Empire, but the declaration creates anxiety and doubt about British intentions among Arab leaders, especially Sherif Hussein.

1 November 1917

Italy. The Italian Third and Fourth Armies and the sparse remnants of the Second Army emplaced on the west bank of the Tagliamento manage to fend off German efforts to cross over. General von Below decides to try to turn the Italian left flank on the upper Piave River, employing the Austrian Tenth Army in this task.

Palestine. With Beersheba in his control, Allenby assaults the Turkish positions outside Gaza, which British artillery and ships have shelled continually since 27 October. The assault moves in a sweep from Umbrella Hill, southwest of the town, on a line to the sea. It begins at 11:00 P.M. Within half an hour, the British capture Umbrella Hill, commanding the Turks' left flank. Traveling from Aleppo, Gen. Erich von Falkenhayn arrives in Jerusalem.

2 November 1917

Italy. Below's troops force their way across the Tagliamento River on a damaged railway bridge at Cornino and by a foot bridge near Pinzano. With this breakthrough, Below can abandon his plan to use the Austrian Tenth Army and can harry the Italian Third and Fourth Armies straight on.

Palestine. At 3:00 A.M., the British begin a ten-minute artillery barrage and then unleash their main attack on the Turkish defensive positions at Gaza. By 6:30 A.M., they have carried all their main objectives, including Sheikh Hasan on the coast. This initial victory costs twenty-seven hundred casualties.

Washington. Secretary of State Robert

Lansing and Ambassador Viscount Kikujiro Ishii of Japan exchange official notes in which Lansing recognizes that Japan has special interests in China and, in return, the ambassador commits Japan to adhere to the Open Door policy by which all nations have equal access to involvement in Chinese commerce and industry. The governments of Japan, China, and other nations interpret the ambiguous wording of the Lansing-Ishii Agreement as giving the United States' tacit approval to Japanese political and economic policies in China, despite Lansing's denials. The Chinese feel betrayed by the United States.

3 November 1917

Berlin. After weeks of preparation, the Zeppelin *L-59* leaves Staaken near the capital, bound for German East Africa on an extraordinary journey to deliver supplies to Lettow-Vorbeck. The *L-57* had originally been designated for the journey but had been destroyed by fire nearly a month earlier. The *L-59,* a huge airship 743 feet long and over 78 feet in diameter, carries a cargo of fifteen tons—small arms and ammunition making up nearly three-fourths of it. Lt. Comdr. Ludwig Bockholt's first destination is Jamboli, Bulgaria. With him is an all-volunteer crew of twenty-one men.

Italy. Cadorna informs the Italian government of his plan to withdraw to the Piave and establish a defensive position on the river's west bank.

4 November 1917

Bulgaria. The *L-59* arrives in Jamboli after a twenty-eight-hour flight.

Italy. Prime Minister David Lloyd George and French Premier Paul Painlevé meet with Italian officials to discuss how many troops the British and French should provide. The two prime ministers also agree to seek Cadorna's dismissal.

5 November 1917

Mesopotamia. Maude's troops moving up the Tigris attack strongly held trench lines at Tikrit, to which the Turks have fallen back after being forced to abandon Ad Dawr on 2 November. Surmounting the Turks' counterattacks, the British conquer their trenches and finally force them into retreat. The British attack costs 1,800 casualties, including 161 dead; the Turks lose 1,500 men, including 300 dead. The British advance pauses.

6 November 1917

Ypres. At 6:00 A.M., General Currie's Canadian troops attack the Germans a third time and sweep toward their objectives, capturing Passchendaele village in a little over an hour and securing their other objectives by 9:00 A.M.

Palestine. Dry winds and low water supplies have deterred Allenby's attack on Gaza, and the Turks have sent in a division of reserve troops to reinforce the garrison. Allenby renews the attack, with his troops advancing steadily. During the night hours, the British capture the Ali Muntar Knoll, while the Turks set fire to their supplies depot at Tel es Sheria and abandon the redoubt at Hareira.

7 November 1917

Italy. Meeting at Rapallo, Lloyd George, Painlevé, and Italian Prime Minister Vitorio E. Orlando (who succeeded to the premiership when the government fell in October because of the military crisis) create the Supreme War Council, a prelude to a unified Allied command. The council has two functions: organizing monthly meetings of the chiefs of state at Versailles, and providing a permanent professional military staff.

Palestine. At dawn, the British attack and capture Tel es Sheria. The Turks withdraw from Gaza, leaving Allenby in control of both Gaza and Beersheba and the territory between them.

Petrograd. Red Guards organized by Leon Trotsky and aided by sailors from the Kronstadt base seize control of the city's bridges, railway stations, and other facilities as Vladimir Lenin, leader of the Bolshevik Party, initiates a coup to take over control of the government. In Moscow the Bolsheviks seize the Kremlin and other strategic locations, but their opponents muster a stiff resistance.

8 November 1917

Rome. Meeting with King Victor Emmanuel of Italy, Lloyd George and Painlevé secure his agreement to dismiss Cadorna. **Petrograd.** Troops and sailors loyal to the Bolsheviks capture the Winter Palace, seat of the Provisional Government. Alexander F. Kerensky has already left in a car (provided by the U.S. embassy) for the headquarters of the northern armies, where he hopes to find loyal troops to put down the Bolshevik uprising. But Lenin is now in effective control of the capital and of the national government through the Congress of Soviets. Civil war looms.

9 November 1917
Italy. Cadorna receives notice of his dismissal. Gen. Armando Diaz replaces him in command and completes establishing the defensive position on the Piave.

10 November 1917
Ypres. The Canadians push on, crossing the Passendaele-Westroosebeke road and securing Passchendaele Ridge after only an hour's battle. In two weeks of fighting, the successful Canadians have endured 15,654 casualties. The Third Battle of Ypres, or Passchendale, ends. But Haig's Flanders offensive falls significantly short of his original goals of advancing inland beyond Ghent and freeing the Belgian coast. His small victory, in fact, has come at tremendous cost. Since the offensive began at the end of July, the British forces have suffered 80,000 killed or missing, 230,000 wounded, and 14,000 taken prisoner. German losses are 50,000 killed or missing, 113,000 wounded, and 37,000 captured.

Russia. Kerensky has made good his escape to the army headquarters at Pskov. From there seven hundred loyal Cossacks led by Gen. Peter Krasnov march toward Petrograd, capturing Tsarskoye Selo.

11 November 1917
Moscow. Bolsheviks take control of the city.

Mons, Belgium. At a conference held to determine German strategy for 1918, Gen. Erich Ludendorff concludes that conditions in Russia and Italy will make it possible to focus on the Western Front and move troops to effect a decisive blow there, even though the Germans and the Allies will confront each other with nearly equal

French infantrymen draw field rations in the trenches of the Western Front (courtesy of the Anne S.K. Brown Military Collection, Brown University Library)

forces. The blow must be struck early, perhaps as early as the end of February, before the United States can provide sizable forces to the front. "We must beat the British," Ludendorff asserts. Beating the British first would permit subsequent concentration on France as a lone enemy. Ludendorff plans to spend the next three months training German troops in new tactics emphasizing infiltration—sending teams of infantrymen to thrust quickly to the enemy's rear—with artillery groups following close behind to stifle counterattacks and with planes supporting the advance from the air.

13 November 1917
Italy. Gen. Sir Herbert Plumer arrives in Mantua to take command of the British troops being assembled to help the Italians.
Palestine. At 7:00 A.M., Allenby's army attacks a force of twenty thousand Turks dug in at four villages to the east of Junction Station trying to guard the branch railway to Jerusalem. Although meeting some stiff resistance, the British troops by early evening drive the Turks from the villages— they withdraw northward to Ramallah (Ramle), ceding Junction Station to Allenby. Allenby's casualties number 616; the Turks have 400 dead and 1,000 taken prisoner.

15 November 1917
German East Africa. Lettow-Vorbeck evacuates Chiwata, where he has taken his sick and those wounded at the Battle of Mahiwa. His destination is the Rovuma River, the border of Portuguese East Africa (Mozambique). Lacking sources of supplies needed to continue his mission but determined never to surrender, he has decided that his only recourse is to cross into Portuguese territory, seize new supplies there, and fight on.
Petrograd. General Krasnov's effort to overthrow the Bolsheviks disintegrates, as Kerensky has failed to win support for Krasnov from generals at the front. The general's Cossacks abandon the fight— they are greatly outnumbered. The Petrograd Bolsheviks arrest Krasnov. Kerensky, who is with the general, escapes arrest and flees the country disguised as a sailor.

16 November 1917
Italy. As French and British troops move into positions supporting the Italians, General von Below launches an attack on the Italian positions along the Piave River that makes meager progress.
Paris. Defeated in a vote of confidence by the Chamber of Deputies, Painlevé resigns as premier. President Raymond Poincaré calls in Georges Clemenceau, a man he intensely dislikes, to form a new government. The president says to Clemenceau: "You have made it impossible for anyone else to form a cabinet; now see what you can do."
Palestine. After more than a week of pressing after the withdrawing Turks, an Anzac unit of Allenby's army captures Jaffa. Another unit takes Ramallah. With the Turks in apparent disarray, Allenby decides to march on Jerusalem instead of pausing to rebuild his communications and supply systems.
Moscow. Bolshevik forces finally triumph as their outnumbered opponents surrender, giving control of the city to the revolutionaries.

18 November 1917
Palestine. Allenby begins the advance to Jerusalem.
Mesopotamia. Commander of the Mesopotamian Force Lt. Gen. Sir F.S. Maude dies suddenly, apparently stricken with cholera. Lt. Gen. Sir W.R. Marshall replaces him as commander.

20 November 1917
Cambrai. Hoping for a success to counterbalance the dismal results of the Third Battle of Ypres, Gen. Sir Douglas Haig has approved a surprise attack by Gen. Sir Julian Byng's Third Army in the Somme sector, which Byng thinks can effect a major breakthrough leading to the capture of Cambrai. Byng has assembled 1,000 guns for the assault and a special force— 378 tanks from Brig. Gen. Hugh Elles's Tank Corps, 324 of which will spearhead the attack with the other 54 in reserve— the first large-scale use of tank warfare. The troops and tank crews have undergone intensive drill during the days leading up to

the attack. General Elles leads them into battle in his tank, "Hilda." At 6:20 A.M., the British guns roar and the tanks plunge into no-man's-land along a six-mile front. Advancing behind a creeping barrage, the tanks quickly overrun the German outposts and their first line of trenches, dropping fascines (ten-foot-long rolls of wooden poles bound together) in the trenches and passing over them. The tanks open gaps in the Germans' rows of barbed wire, allowing the infantrymen following in their tracks to stream rapidly forward. Rumbling forward in such great numbers, the tanks terrify the German troops, many of whom flee to the rear. Near Ribecourt, "Hilda" ditches, and a disappointed Elles returns to his headquarters. The German defenders at Flesquieres check the rapid advance, with their well-trained gunners knocking out thirty-nine of the British tanks. Elsewhere the British achieve their major objectives, capturing Gramcourt, Marcoing, Havrincourt, and Ribecourt while advancing up to four thousand yards and rending a breach in the Hindenburg Line along the entire six-mile front. The British capture forty-two hundred prisoners and a hundred guns but suffer four thousand casualties during the day's fighting. During the night the Germans begin to move in reinforcements.

London. Lloyd George's government survives a crisis as the opposition in Parliament finally approves formation of the Supreme War Council that the Allied leaders had agreed to at Rapallo. Colonel House meets with the prime minister to discuss war goals. President Wilson has appointed House as the American representative on the Supreme War Council.

21 November 1917
Jamboli, Bulgaria. The *L-59,* forced to turn back on 13 November and again on 16 November by menacing weather conditions, lifts off in clear weather to resume the journey to East Africa. Flying at two thousand feet, the Zeppelin passes over Adrianople, the Sea of Marmara, and eastern Turkey and then out over the Mediterranean Sea without being spotted by Allied aircraft. Off the western tip of Crete,

however, *L-59* encounters a thunderstorm and lightning that threaten its destruction. To save his ship, Bockholt descends to one thousand feet. Electrified and glowing from surges of lightning, the imperiled ship survives and continues its journey.

Cambrai. British troops, weary from the previous day, push ahead only marginally, but during the night General Haig decides the offensive should continue. He hopes to capture the Bourlon Ridge because it would give the British artillery a commanding view of the Germans' rear lines.

Palestine. Advancing toward Jerusalem, Allenby's Seventy-fifth Division captures the village of Nabi Samwweil.

Petrograd. People's Commissar of Foreign Affairs Leon Trotsky publicly renounces Russian claims to the Bosporus and urges the United States and the other Allies to effect an armistice and begin peace negotiations quickly.

22 November 1917
Italy. General von Below sends his troops against the center of the Italian line; the Italians hold, although ceding Monte Tomba to the Austro-German troops.

Cambrai. A German counterattack recaptures Fontaine, taken by the British the day before.

Petrograd. The government sends to the Allied governments a Peace Decree, proposed by Lenin and approved by the Congress of Soviets on 8 November, proposing that the belligerents agree to an immediate armistice and begin negotiations for a peace settlement without territorial annexations or payments of indemnities. The decree arouses hostile reactions in the Allied capitals. People's Commissar for Foreign Affairs Leon Trotsky begins publishing the contents of secret agreements the Allies have made, including the Treaty of London, that reveal goals of territorial aggrandizement and other dubious purposes. Trotsky had discovered copies of the agreements at the Foreign Ministry.

23 November 1917
Egypt. After surviving seemingly impossible flying conditions and extremes of temperature that heat and cool its gas and

force the crew to shift its ballast, the *L-59* remains on course, flying northwest of Khartoum. But the German Admiralty has received reports that Lettow-Vorbeck has been forced out of the Makondi Highlands, where *L-59* is to rendezvous with him, and appears to face defeat. The *L-59* receives orders to return home. Frustrated and disheartened after traveling twenty-eight hundred miles and nearing his objective, Lieutenant Commander Bockholt turns *L-59* west from Khartoum and then heads north.

Italy. Below launches a final attack on the Italian's Piave line. General Foch, believing the defense of the Piave will hold, departs for France.

Cambrai. General Byng sends his Fortieth Division, supported by one hundred tanks, against the German defenses at Bourlon Ridge, but the Germans hold fast, inflicting four thousand casualties. Baron Manfred von Richthofen's "Flying Circus" arrives and begins to attain supremacy in the air over the battlefield.

24 November 1917
Cambrai. Again the British fail to take Bourlon.

25 November 1917
German East Africa. Lettow-Vorbeck enters Portuguese East Africa, crossing the Rovuma River near its confluence with the Ludjenda River. His *Schutztruppe* force now numbers two hundred Europeans and two thousand askaris. They immediately confront a force of a thousand Portuguese sent to prevent their crossing the river and severely defeat them, capturing all of the supplies the Portuguese have brought.

Bulgaria. Surviving sometimes harrowing difficulties on the return trip, *L-59* arrives and lands safely at Jamboli. After four days in the air, the Zeppelin still has enough fuel left for three more days of flying. Although her mission was aborted, the *L-59* has achieved the first intercontinental flight and also the longest sustained flight on record—being airborne for 95 hours and flying a total of 4,220 miles without interruption.

Petrograd. Gen. N.V. Krylenko becomes commander in chief. His first act is to send

a peace delegation to the German forces in position near Dvinsk.

26 November 1917
German East Africa. A force of Germans commanded by Capt. Theodor Tafel marching to join Lettow-Vorbeck in Portuguese East Africa encounters a detachment of Indian troops. In the ensuing battle the Indians lose 40 percent of their men.

Trans-Jordan. After being taken prisoner and being savagely treated in Der'a while reconnoitering there disguised as an Arab—his true identity was not discovered—T.E. Lawrence managed to escape his captors. He now arrives back in Aqaba in poor physical condition.

27 November 1917
German East Africa. Members of Tafel's force—30 Europeans, 180 askaris, 640 carriers, and 220 African women—surrender to the Indians they had defeated the previous day.

Italy. The Italians have successfully held off General von Below's troops along the entire Piave front, and now British and French troops are in position to bolster their defenses. Three German divisions are recalled to the Western Front. The Caporetto offensive ends. It has cost the Italian army 10,000 dead, 30,000 wounded, 293,000 captured, and 400,000 deserters, but at least now the military and political situations stabilize.

Cambrai. After five days of trying and failing to take Bourlon, General Haig admits defeat and cancels the Cambrai offensive. Once again, stalemate reigns on the Western Front.

Petrograd. A note sent by Gen. Max von Hoffmann, commander of the German forces on the Eastern Front, informs Krylenko that the Germans are ready to negotiate an armistice with Russia and that the negotiations can begin on 1 December at Brest-Litovsk.

28 November 1917
German East Africa. Apparently assuming that he has been abandoned by Lettow-Vorbeck, who is only a day's march distant, Tafel destroys his weapons and sur-

renders the remainder of his force. A few diehards with Tafel refuse to surrender, however, and continue the trek to find Lettow-Vorbeck.

30 November 1917
Cambrai. After two days of relative quiet, the Germans begin a massive bombardment of British positions at 8:30 A.M. in preparation for a major counterattack. As airplanes strafe and bomb along the eight-mile front in conjunction with the attack, German troops rush forward in small groups, bypassing British strongpoints. As the infantrymen advance, the artillery follows immediately. At first the surprised British fall back, but then they rally and hold.

1 December 1917
Cambrai. German troops capture Masnieres and Les Rue Vertes at the center of the front, but the counterattack begins to falter from exhaustion.
Versailles. The Supreme War Council meets for the first time, with Clemenceau as president. Colonel House evidences disappointment that the council, in his view, shows insufficient interest in coordinating military strategy and in developing a coherent diplomatic stance.

3 December 1917
Cambrai. After a one-day respite, the Germans renew their push, taking La Vacquerie in the southern sector of the front, while at the center the British withdraw to concentrate their strength around Marcoing. Haig decides to withdraw the troops from the Bourlon salient to positions that can be consolidated and held through the winter months.
London. The War Cabinet decides to support "in principle" Gen. Alexei Kaledin's anti-Bolshevik movement among the Cossacks known as the Volunteer Army and any other group opposed to the Bolsheviks. At Rostov, Kaledin, the ataman or hetman (governor) of the Don Cossacks since 8 June, has declared his region independent.

4 December 1917
Cambrai. During the night and into the following morning, the British evacuate,

falling back in the northern sector virtually to their original positions before the battle. At the center they continue to hold Havrincourt, Flesquieres, and Ribecourt; to the south they have already been driven back beyond their starting line. Thus the British abandon to the Germans most of what they had won during the first days of the Battle of Cambrai.

6 December 1917
Jassy, Romania. With Russia sidelined, Romanian government and military commanders agree to negotiate an armistice with Gen. August von Mackensen, removing Romania from the war.

7 December 1917
Cambrai. The British complete their withdrawal. Byng's Third Army has endured the loss of 44,207 men and 158 guns. The German Second Army's losses total 41,000 men and 145 guns. The Germans have learned the value of new infiltration tactics, and the British have learned the value of the tank. Otherwise, the Battle of Cambrai changes nothing on the Western Front.

8 December 1917
Palestine. After pausing several days to consolidate the areas already captured and to move up reinforcements, Allenby's army, with Gen. Sir Philip Chetwode's XXth Corps in the lead, begins an assault on Turkish forces manning the defensive positions on the hills surrounding Jerusalem and captures some of the strongest redoubts.

9 December 1917
Palestine. During the previous night and the early morning hours, the Turks evacuate Jerusalem, bringing to an end four hundred years of Turkish rule over the Holy City.

11 December 1917
Palestine. General Allenby enters Jerusalem on foot through the Jaffa Gate. In a proclamation read from the steps of the Citadel, the general informs the inhabitants that they are free to go about their

business without fear and that all the sacred places and practices "will be maintained and protected according to the existing customs and beliefs of those to whose faiths they are sacred." The successful expedition has cost the British 1,667 casualties.

12 December 1917
North Sea. Four German destroyers spot a convoy in the waters between Great Britain and Scandinavia. They attack, sinking one of the British destroyer escorts, incapacitating the other, and sending every merchant ship in the convoy to the bottom. The German ships return home unharmed.

13 December 1917
Petrograd. Lenin orders the Red Army to destroy Kaledin and his supporters in the Cossack region. The army plans to divide the Don Cossacks from the Ukraine.

14 December 1917
Chaumont, France. General Pershing removes Sibert from command of the First Division and appoints Brig. Gen. Robert L. Bullard commander. Sibert returns to the United States.

15 December 1917
Brest-Litovsk. German and Russian negotiators sign an armistice.

17 December 1917
Washington. Returning from London, Colonel House presents a disquieting report to the president on his failure to persuade the Allied leaders to publicly announce liberal goals for the war and the peace to follow. Wilson realizes that he must prepare a statement of American aims to force the issue.

20 December 1917
Brest-Litovsk, Russia. Representatives of the Central Powers and the Russian government meet at the headquarters of Prince Leopold of Bavaria to negotiate a peace settlement.

24 December 1917
London. Controller of the Navy Sir Eric Geddes, appointed by Lloyd George in May to curtail the power of First Sea Lord Sir John Jellicoe, achieves the prime minister's long-term goal: he abruptly and without any warning sends Jellicoe a brief note informing him of his dismissal as first sea lord. The startled admiral responds that he will begin leave immediately.
Mannheim, Germany. The Royal Flying Corps sends ten de Havilland airplanes from the airbase at Ochey, France, on the first long-distance raid. From thirteen thousand feet, the planes bomb Mannheim and Ludwigshafen.

26 December 1917
Washington. Pres. Woodrow Wilson issues a proclamation giving the federal government control of the nation's railroads.

27 December 1917
London. Vice Adm. Sir Rosslyn Wemyss succeeds Jellicoe as first sea lord.

28 December 1917
London. The Channel Barrage Committee, established by Sir Eric Geddes, removes Vice Adm. Sir Reginald Bacon (an ally of Jellicoe) from command of the Dover Patrol and appoints Adm. Roger Keyes in his place.

Songs of War

The hell of warfare may seem an unlikely muse, yet its context invariably evokes an outpouring of songs. Every lengthy war that Americans have been involved in, for example, from the American Revolution to World War II at least, has generated numerous noteworthy songs—no war more so than World War I. The American experience of the war gave us many songs that form an ongoing part of our popular music. Among the enduring examples, George M. Cohan's *Over There* may stand out–it was even sung as American troops launched into battle. But there are many others. To this day most Americans probably are familiar with *There's a Long, Long Trail,* created by Stoddard King and Zo Elliott a few years before the outbreak of war but altered to become the great love song of the troops in the American Expeditionary Force. Still sung is *Pack Up Your Troubles* by George Asaf and Felix Powell. The troops' favorite marching song, the still-memorable *Mademoiselle from Armentieres,* had probably hundreds of verses. Many of the enduring songs were sentimental, such as *Till We Meet Again* by Raymond Egan and Richard Whiting, *Keep the Home Fires Burning,* and *Just a Baby's Prayer at Twilight.* And some were amusing: *K-K-K-Katy* and *Oh! How I Hate to Get Up in the Morning.* The British troops also had many songs, but without a doubt most notably *It's a Long, Long Way to Tipperary.* They were partial to the American Civil War song *John Brown's Body* as a marching tune.

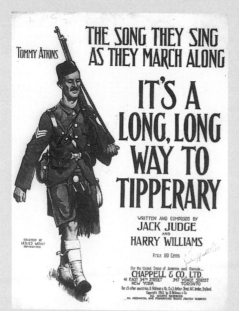

Among their hauntingly sad melodies was *Après la Guerre,* and the French had Louis Bousquet's *Madelon.* Not surpisingly, given its lengthy duration, World War I in fact produced hundreds of songs–a sizable number of them well laced with censurable obscenities. These songs served a variety of purposes, including helping to sustain public support for the war effort, boosting the troops' morale and camaraderie, and serving as a tool for the enlistment of new troops. Whatever their uses during the war, these songs provide a continuing evocation of the most significant watershed of the twentieth century.

The sheet-music cover for one of the war's most popular homefront songs (courtesy of the Anne S.K. Brown Military Collection, Brown University Library)

The final year of the war opens with the main issues on the Western Front still hanging in the balance. The U-boat attacks on shipping may still bring Britain down, and the Americans have not yet begun to make their weight felt on the battlefront. Ludendorff decides on a series of huge offensives in a bid to win the war before the end of summer. He orders the German army to begin to build up matériel and to train in special new tactics that promise to assist in breaking even the strongest Allied defenses. Three and a half million men are assembled on a relatively narrow front, many of them storm troopers with the assignment to rapidly overrun trenches and strong points. The first attacks are launched along the Somme in March, and the Germans advance rapidly, often penetrating deeply past the old trench lines. The British and the French try to rally and counter, but for weeks the Germans hold the upper hand.

At virtually the same time that Ludendorff begins his ultimate offensive, the first American troops enter the trenches. They are poorly trained and have to be equipped to a large extent by the other Allies, but they are strong in numbers, enthusiastic, and add new life to the war-weary defenses.

In response to the new German successes, the Allies finally agree on a unified high command and appoint French marshal Ferdinand Foch as supreme Allied commander. He slowly assumes control of all the Allied armies and begins to direct the resistance to the sustained German offensive.

In August, the tide begins to turn. The Germans start to retreat, and the Allies begin their own series of offensives that, within weeks, push back the German salients and even breach the Hindenburg Line. In addition, the German economy and civilian government begin to collapse. By September, it seems clear that there is no longer a will to fight. Even the frontline troops signal the need for peace. Ludendorff is ousted by late October, and an armistice is signed on November 11.

5 January 1918

London. While Woodrow Wilson dithers over his statement of war aims, continually revising it after discussions with Colonel House and other advisers, Prime Minister David Lloyd George preempts the president, outlining his aims in a speech to the Trades Union Congress that he hopes will induce the Labour Party to remain part of his coalition while placating the Liberal Party and antiwar groups. Lloyd George declares that Great Britain intends no aggression against the German people. He insists that territorial settlements following the war must be based on "the consent of the governed," but that Germany must make reparations to Belgium and return Alsace and Lorraine to France. Germany's colonies will not be returned. The prime minister advocates allowing independence for Poland, granting Italy legitimate territorial concessions, and giving the minority peoples in the Habsburg Empire self-government. He also calls for an international organization to resolve future disputes. Never consulted beforehand or apprised that the prime minister intended to make such a public statement, Wilson takes offense, feeling that Lloyd George's proposals are so near his own as to preclude delivery of his speech. Colonel House persuades him otherwise, convincing Wilson that Lloyd George's statement actually improves the climate for his own.

8 January 1918

Washington. Wilson presents his statement of war aims, the Fourteen Points, to a hastily convened joint session of Congress. Wilson advocates "open covenants, openly arrived at"; freedom of the seas; "removal, so far as possible, of all economic barriers and the establishment of an equality of trade conditions among all nations"; disarmament "to the lowest point possible consistent with domestic safety"; "free, open-minded, and absolutely impartial adjustment of all colonial claims"; "evacuation of all Russian territory"; evacuation and restoration of Belgium; evacuation and restoration of invaded parts of France, while the "wrong done to France by Prussia in 1871 in the matter of Alsace-Lorraine . . . should be righted"; readjustment of the borders of Italy; autonomous development for the peoples of Austria-Hungary; evacuation of Romania, Serbia, and Montenegro; sovereignty for the Turkish parts of the Ottoman Empire and autonomy for other areas under Turkish rule; an independent Poland; and formation of "a general association of nations . . . under specific covenants for the purpose of affording mutual guarantees of political independence and territorial integrity to great and small states alike."

Western Front. After a tour of the Western Front, Ludendorff decides on the scope of his spring offensive, code named "Saint Michael." Ludendorff is assembling on the Western Front over 3.5 million men in nearly 195 divisions, with two-thirds of the total concentrated on a 60-mile front defended by 33 British divisions, several of them 15 or 25 miles to the rear. The front Ludendorff has chosen centers on the Somme River and extends from Lens to just south of La Fère on the Oise River. His troops are being trained in infiltration tactics, with the youngest and ablest soldiers formed into special groups called *Sturmabteilungen* (storm troops). Equipped with light machine guns, flamethrowers, and trench mortars, they will sweep around strongly defended sites to rush to the rear of the British lines and attack their artillery. The storm troops will be followed by units of infantrymen, machine gunners, artillery, and engineers. Ludendorff is optimistic. Once the British are pushed back in the Somme sector, he intends to shift suddenly to attack in Flanders and drive them back to the sea. (Gen. Douglas Haig has a total of 1,097,906 troops in France and Belgium.) As a backup, Ludendorff has developed plans for attacking the French in the Aisne sector, if that possibility offers itself.

16 January 1918
Trans-Jordan. Sherif Nasir leads his Bedouin tribesmen in the capture of Tafila, taking 150 Turks prisoner.

18 January 1918
Mesopotamia. Maj. Gen. L.C. Dunsterville arrives in Baghdad. His assignment is command of a force whose daredevil mission is to cross overland to Rasht on the Caspian Sea and from there to make their way to Baku—the purpose being somehow to prevent the Germans from seizing the oil fields at Baku and the port as an opening to Afghanistan. Dunsterville's force is intended eventually to total 150 officers and 300 NCOs supported by 5 squadrons of armored cars, with 8 cars to a squadron.

19 January 1918
Petrograd. The Bolsheviks dissolve the Constituent Assembly, convened only the day before but with the Bolsheviks and the Social Revolutionaries making up a minority of delegates. Red Guards order the assembly to disband, and the delegates have no choice. The Bolsheviks announce that they will hereafter rule by decree.

20 January 1918
Trans-Jordan. Zeid, youngest brother of Feisal, arrives in Tafila with Maj. T.E. Lawrence and Jafar Pasha, commander of the Arab regular army, to discover Sherif Nasir's tribesmen quarreling as a result of old feuds.

23 January 1918
Trans-Jordan. Turkish troops arrive from Karak, attack the Bedouin outposts at Tafila, and drive the Arabs off. Lawrence organizes a defensive position on the plain to the northeast of Tafila.

25 January 1918
Trans-Jordan. At Tafila the Arabs, instructed by Lawrence, train their machine guns to splay an enfilade on the advancing Turks, while Lawrence swings his cavalry in a wide circle and attacks the Turks' left wing, routing them and taking two hundred prisoners and twenty-seven machine

guns. It is a small but brilliant tactical victory for Lawrence, but the Arabs, suffering from the winter cold, refuse to follow through by moving northward.

26 January 1918
London. Foreign Secretary Lord Balfour sends a note to each of the Allied governments requesting that they grant Japan the mandate to represent Allied interests in the Far East, including authorizing Japan to intervene in Siberia to protect the Trans-Siberian Railroad and the war supplies depoted in Vladivostok. The American government, regarding direct intervention in Russia as premature, rejects the idea.

27 January 1918
Mesopotamia. General Dunsterville sets out from Baghdad with eleven officers and four NCOs and their batmen in cars and vans bound for Baku.

28 January 1918
Berlin. Stimulated by the slowness of the peace process at Brest-Litovsk, food shortages and rationing, and strike calls by the Independent Social Democratic Party (USPD—a movement that broke away from the SPD in April 1917), joined by Spartacus (formed by Rosa Luxemburg and Karl Liebknecht in January 1916), the Berlin Union of Metalworkers launches a strike. Five hundred thousand workers in the capital and about one million nationwide are involved. The strikers' slogans call for peace without claims to territory and for democracy in Germany.

3 February 1918
Berlin. Under threats of violent enforcement of a return to work, strike leaders call off the strike. German workers do not yet embrace revolution, but the strike impels the government to secure a peace settlement at Brest-Litovsk soon.
Rome. Alarmed by losses of their merchantmen—fifty-four in January alone—to Austrian U-boats operating in the Mediterranean, Allied naval officials confer and decide to bolster both their antisubmarine patrols and the Otranto Barrage, which was destroyed during 1917 by violent weather,

in an effort to keep the U-boats bottled up in the Adriatic Sea.

10 February 1918
Brest-Litovsk. Trotsky, who had assumed leadership of the Russian delegation to the peace conference a month earlier, has been stalling, arguing for terms that cede no Russian lands to Germany. Although Foreign Minister Baron Richard von Kuhlmann, who heads the German delegation, favors conciliation—a peace without annexation of territory—Ludendorff remains adamant in demanding territorial concessions. So Trotsky plays his last card: "No war—no peace," with Russia neither signing a peace agreement nor continuing the war. Kuhlmann is willing to accept this simple resolution that leaves Germany in control of Russian areas now occupied, but Ludendorff is not. The real German power at the peace conference is Ludendorff's representative, Gen. Max von Hoffmann, who ensures that Ludendorff's wishes are fulfilled.
Warneton, France. At 9:00 P.M., 195 Australian troops led by nine officers head into no-man's-land for an attack on the frontline German trenches at Warneton. As the noise of their artillery's barrage covers their efforts, they blow holes in the Germans' barbed wire. Men hidden in holes raise plywood figures that simulate crouching soldiers and draw the Germans' fire. The daredevil raiders pierce the German lines and storm through their trenches, killing or capturing defenders as they go. By 11:00 P.M., the Australians and their prisoners begin to withdraw across no-man's-land, menaced by German shells. The raid costs the Australian Third Division eight dead and thirty-eight wounded or missing, but their prisoners provide valuable information about the buildup for Ludendorff's planned offensive.

11 February 1918
Persia. General Dunsterville's convoy reaches Hamadan, where he confers with General Baratov, former Russian commander in Persia, who has lost control over his troops.
Russia. At Rostov, Gen. Alexei Kaledin

A German officer in 1918, still looking confident (by Reni-Mel, courtesy of the Anne S.K. Brown Military Collection, Brown University Library)

speaks impassionedly to the Cossack Assembly. Kaledin's anti-Bolshevik stance proves hopeless since Red Army troops menace Rostov and his support by the Cossacks has withered. Following his speech, Kaledin walks alone to a private room, where he shoots himself.

13 February 1918
Bad Homburg. The Crown Council (comprised of the kaiser, Hindenburg, Ludendorff, Kuhlmann, and Chancellor Count Georg von Hertling, who had replaced Michaelis the previous November) approves the plan to begin an advance on 19

February along the entire Russian front from Finland to the Ukraine as a means of forcing the Russian government to accept a peace treaty. The majority of members of the *Reichstag* oppose the move.

16 February 1918
Persia. Dunsterville reaches Rasht, where the British and Russian consuls advise him that Bandar-e-Pahlavi (Enzeli), his next destination, is under Bolshevik control.

17 February 1918
Persia. At Bandar-e-Pahlavi, General Dunsterville learns from the head of the Bolshevik Committee that orders from Baku are to stop him from proceeding.

20 February 1918
Persia. Through the auspices of the head of the Bolshevik Committee, Dunsterville has obtained gasoline for his return trip. He reaches Manjil as Red Guard troops from Baku arrive too late in Bandar-e-Pahlavi to place him and his men under arrest.

24 February 1918
Trans-Jordan. Ill and frustrated after a violent quarrel with Zeid over the Arabs' refusal to advance to the north, Lawrence leaves Tafila and travels to Beersheba to offer Allenby his resignation as a leader of the Arab Revolt. The resignation is refused.

26 February 1918
Petrograd. German troops, set in motion on 18 February, have advanced north and east over two hundred miles, capturing Helsinki and threatening Petrograd. The Russian government capitulates and accepts the peace terms tabled at Brest-Litovsk. Lenin has argued that there is no alternative if the revolution is to be saved.

3 March 1918
Brest-Litovsk. German and Russian delegates sign the Treaty of Brest-Litovsk. By the treaty's terms, Russia cedes about a third of her populace, farmlands, and factories, and three-fourths of her coal and iron mines to the Germans. To Germany goes control of Poland, the Baltic states,

and the Ukraine, all now supposedly independent states—areas actually conquered by Russia over the previous two hundred years and inhabited by non-Russians. Turkey receives Kars, Ardahan, and Batum. "This is a peace that Russia, grinding her teeth, is forced to accept," Trotsky grumbles. It is an ignominious end to Russia's role in the war, most especially since that role has exacted a toll of 2 million dead, 4 million wounded, and about 2.5 million taken prisoner.

4 March 1918
Washington. Wilson announces that Bernard Baruch will head the War Industries Board, with full power to appoint and control all committees except the committee empowered to fix prices, which reports directly to the president. Gen. Peyton C. March is appointed Army Chief of Staff.

5 March 1918
Romania. German and Romanian delegates sign a preliminary peace agreement. The Treaty of Buftea cedes to Germany and her allies all of Dobrudja and to Hungary territories along the Carpathian boundary. Romania agrees to a massive troop reduction, evacuation of all occupied areas, and the passage of Austrian and German troops destined for the Ukraine. The Allies regard this separate peace as a violation of their 1916 alliance with Romania and thus consider it an end to Romania's claims to Transylvania, Bukovina, and Banat.

9 March 1918
Western Front. Col. Douglas MacArthur, chief of staff of the Forty-second "Rainbow Division," takes part in two practice raids on German lines in the Lunéville sector. MacArthur had suggested the designation "Rainbow" because members of this National Guard unit represent twenty-six states and the District of Columbia.
Mesopotamia. With the winter rains over, Gen. W.R. Marshall, commander of the Mesopotamian Force, resumes the offensive on the Euphrates River. Arriving at Hit, the British find the town unoccupied. The Turks have withdrawn to Khan al Baghdadi and dug in there.

11 March 1918
Washington. Wilson sends a message to the Congress of Soviets meeting in Moscow, now the seat of government and capital of Russia, urging that body to reject the Treaty of Brest-Litovsk. The congress responds derisively. By some accounts, the first cases of influenza—107 stricken recruits—occur at an army base in Kansas. This is the beginning of a flu epidemic that will infest all the army bases at home, not to mention the civilian populace, and troops and civilians throughout Europe, Africa, India, and most of the rest of the world.

12 March 1918
Mesopotamia. General Marshall receives orders to support military efforts to prevent the Turks from moving through northwest Persia, and Dunsterville is named commander under his own authority.

14 March 1918
Somme River. British commanders, relying on information gleaned from reconnaissance and interrogation of prisoners, are convinced that 21 March is the date for the German offensive.
Russia. German troops take control of Odessa and the part of the Russian fleet harbored there, giving Germany effective control of the Black Sea.

18 March 1917
Somme River. The British send aloft five bombers escorted by twenty-five fighters on a reconnaissance flight over areas where the command thinks Ludendorff may be concentrating troops. Suddenly German fighters appear en masse—Manfred von Richthofen's *Jagdgeschwader I* alone comprises thirty Fokker triplanes and Albatros and Pfalz fighters. The British are badly outnumbered. In the ensuing Battle of Le Cateau, the German fighters down three of the British bombers and seven fighters while losing only one Albatros. Air power forms a major adjunct to Ludendorff's planned offensive; he has assembled 730 planes at the front. The British had 579 before this skirmish.

21 March 1917

Somme River. Poised for Ludendorff's offensive are Gen. Otto von Below's Seventeenth Army on the northern sector, Gen. Georg von der Marwitz's Second Army at the center, and Gen. Oskar von Hutier's Eighteenth Army to the south. Opposite them from north to south are Gen. Sir Henry Horne's First Army, Gen. Sir Julian Byng's Third Army, and Gen. Sir Hubert Gough's Fifth Army. Gen. Douglas Haig has agreed with Gough that his troops are likely to face the brunt of the attack but has responded to Gough's warnings and pleas by offering minimal reinforcements. The British have created "battle zones" extending from one to two miles behind their foremost lines as their main defensive positions. At 5:00 A.M., the Germans begin the largest and most concentrated artillery bombardment to this time, as six thousand guns rain death and destruction on Gough's and Byng's front lines and battle zones simultaneously—a front forty miles long. Intended to create gaps in the British defenses, the bombardment also delivers gas throughout their positions. For hours, the German guns alternate the heaviest shelling between the front lines and the battle zones. Then at 9:30 A.M., with a morning fog settled on the battlefield, the storm troops race forward from their trenches and quickly bypass the strongest British outposts, leaving the second and third waves of troops to mop them up. Aided by the fog, the new tactics prove brilliantly successful against the Fifth Army's center, as Hutier's advancing troops virtually eliminate the eight battalions of the defending Eighteenth Corps. Only fifty survivors reach the battle zone, only to be overrun later as the Germans drive through and well beyond these defenses. To the north, however, the Germans meet heavier resistance from the Third Army because General Byng has ignored Haig's orders and moved more of his men into the frontline trenches. Elsewhere British resistance improves as the fog lifts. At midday, both German and British aircraft take to the skies to duel for supremacy over the battlefield, with the Germans losing eight planes and the British seven. Despite the British troops' strong resistance in some sectors of the ground battle, the Germans succeed in effecting an advance along the entire forty-mile front. As daylight fades, a quiet descends on the battlefield. The Germans move their reserves forward, but the British have no reserves close enough to provide reinforcements. During the night, troops on the edges of the salient at the center of the Fifth Army pull back. Other British troops bypassed by the German advance try to find their way to the rear, many losing their lives en route.

Russia. Unable to provide transport to bring the Czechoslovak Army Corps from Russia to France, General Foch has sent orders that the corps should move to Vladivostok. The corps now becomes known as the Czechoslovak Legion. Organized in August 1914 as a unit of the Russian army, the corps originally comprised fewer than a thousand men recruited from the Czechoslovak community in Russia, but by mid-1917, as part of the Eleventh Army, its numbers had swollen to seven thousand. During the Kerensky Offensive, the Eleventh Army had entered Austria-Hungary, where two Austrian regiments, mostly Bohemian, joined its ranks. The Provisional Government in March 1917 had granted the corps the right to recruit Czechoslovak prisoners of war, and it soon had expanded to thirty thousand. Following the Treaty of Brest-Litovsk, with the support of Thomas Masaryk, leader of the Czechoslovak independence movement who intends in time to use the corps to help achieve his goal of an autonomous state, and of Gen. Ferdinand Foch, the corps had asked to join the Allies on the Western Front. Promised a million rubles by the French for the use of the corps, the Bolsheviks released the corps to the tutelage of the French army.

22 March 1918

Somme River. With their positions and resolve hardened, Byng's Third Army troops stunt the advance of Below's Seventeenth Army along the northern sector of the front. But in late afternoon, massive waves of Below's soldiers dislodge the Third Army from the ruins of Vracourt, forcing Byng to withdraw his flanks during the night. At the center of the front, Hutier's troops relentlessly drive back Gough's Fifth Army. Gough's troops on the southern tip of the front also fall back, surrendering Tergnier and positions on the Oise Canal. By the end of the day, the Germans hold all of the Fifth Army's battle zone. In the continuing large-scale air battle, the Germans lose eleven planes; the Royal Flying Corps, nineteen.

23 March 1918

Somme River. General von Hutier's troops resume their hard push forward, and the British Fifth Army crumbles and reels to the rear. Ludendorff's offensive has now opened an enormous salient at the center of the British line and yet has failed to destroy the BEF. Ludendorff sees no choice but to continue. He moves more troops in, redeploying them from Flanders, and orders Hutier to attack to the west and south, possibly menacing Paris. Apprised of the desperate British position, General Pétain has sent twelve French divisions into the Noyon sector to begin reinforcing the British, but they are unable to move fast enough to come up behind Gough's forces, who are retreating in disarray.

Laon, France. In anticipation of the spring offensive, Ludendorff had approved creation of a giant cannon by the Krupp Works. Named *Wilhelm Geschutz* in honor of the kaiser, the cannon extends 112 feet in length, weighs 138 tons, and hurls shells 75 miles. Transported by train to the forest of Crépy-en-Laonnois and there hidden among the trees and camouflaged to prevent detection from the air, the great gun is emplaced to bombard Paris in an effort to destroy civilian morale. The Germans fire the first shell at 7:26 A.M. At regular intervals of about fifteen minutes thereafter, other shells follow. Parisians and the War Ministry assume the city is being bombed from the air. The shelling ceases for a while and then begins again, with the last of twenty-two shells hitting the city at 2:45 P.M. By now, authorities know that Paris is the target of a long-range cannon whose first-day toll is sixteen dead and twenty-nine injured.

24 March 1918

Somme River. The Third Army's Vth Corps, bordering the northernmost position of the Fifth Army, has held fast but in the early morning realizes that withdrawal is inevitable and abandons the Flesquieres salient. A full-scale British retreat begins. By evening, General von Hutier's troops have completed a total advance of seventeen miles from their starting line. General von Below's troops are fifteen miles from where they began. Deeply concerned, General Pétain goes in search of Haig and finds him at Dury at 11:00 P.M. Pétain expresses pessimism over the possibility of rescuing Gough's Fifth Army and concern about the prospect of his own forces being attacked in the Champagne sector, convincing Haig that he can expect no help from the French commander. The two commanders agree upon the Somme River as the new dividing line between their armies. Haig hastens back to GHQ at Doullens and wires a message to London requesting that Minister of War Lord Milner and Chief of the General Staff Sir Henry Wilson, who in February through Lloyd George's insistence replaced Robertson in this post, be sent to the front to confer with him. Prime Minister David Lloyd George's concern had already prompted him to dispatch Lord Milner, who, having missed Haig at GHQ, motors on to Versailles to confer with Sir Henry Rawlinson, Great Britain's representative to the Supreme War Council.

Laon. At 6:45 A.M., the great gun resumes shelling Paris, whose residents have assumed that the gun was destroyed the previous day. The bombardment continues at shorter intervals than the day before, with twenty-two shells falling on the city and its suburbs.

25 March 1918

Somme River. Sir Henry Wilson arrives at GHQ in Doullens. He listens indulgently to Haig, although he has little use for the commander or his ideas on the conduct of war.

Laon. Nicknamed "Big Bertha" by the Parisians, the Germans' huge gun continues the siege, lobbing six shells into the city.

26 March 1918
Somme River. Allied leaders meet at Doullens, already menaced by the Germans—Hutier's Eighteenth Army has advanced another five miles; Below's Seventeenth Army, another six miles. Milner, French President Raymond Poincaré, French Premier Georges Clemenceau, and Generals Wilson, Haig, Pétain, Foch, and a few others attend the meeting. As British troops retreat through the streets of the town, the conferees confirm Haig's and Pétain's previous decision on the Somme River as the boundary between their forces, decide that Pétain can free twenty-four divisions to bolster Haig, and agree that a unified command is needed. The Allied leaders grant Gen. Ferdinand Foch, Wilson's and Milner's candidate for the job, authority to coordinate the actions of the two Allies' armies, working closely with generals in chief who are to supply him with "all necessary information." Clemenceau snorts at Foch: "Well, you've got what you wanted." The general's riposte: "A fine present . . . you give me a lost battle and tell me to win it."

Mesopotamia. The British have sent cavalry and three armored cars traveling secretly by night well around the Turkish positions at Khan al Baghdadi to a site on the Aleppo Road six miles beyond the town. Marching up the river from Hit and Shahiliyah in the early morning darkness, the British main column attacks just after sunrise. Throughout the day, they relentlessly drive the Turks from their defensive positions, taking a thousand prisoners. As retreating Turks move up the Aleppo Road at about midnight, they encounter the British cavalry, and another thousand surrender as the rest flee.

Moscow. The government grants the Czechoslovak Legion permission to travel across Siberia to Vladivostok, to which Masaryk is already en route. The legion will board the Trans-Siberian Railway for the journey.

French leader Georges Clemenceau (on the left) visiting the Somme theater (Library of Congress)

27 March 1918
Mesopotamia. On the Aleppo Road at Wadi Hawran, the British armored cars force the surrender of two thousand more Turks withdrawing from Khan al Baghdadi. The cavalry moves upriver, taking Alus and Al Hadithah and five hundred more prisoners.

28 March 1918
Arras. General von Below's Seventeenth Army stages an attack (code named Mars) on Byng's Third Army positions at Arras that fails totally. The German advance farther south in the Somme sector continues, however, reaping so far a total of seventy thousand prisoners and eleven hundred guns.
Mesopotamia. British armored cars push on to 'Anah and beyond, capturing the Turkish commandant and the head of the German Euphrates Mission bearing official documents before turning back to 'Anah. In their March sweep along the Euphrates River, Marshall's troops have garnered 6,000 Turkish prisoners and a large supply of ammunition while enduring only 159 casualties, including 36 dead.

29 March 1918
Laon. After a three-day silence, "Big Bertha" opens up again. Although only four shells land on the city, one does the greatest damage yet, hitting the crowded Church of Saint-Gervais and killing seventy-five while wounding ninety others.

1 April 1918
London. Confirming its commitment to air warfare, the British government creates the Royal Air Force as a separate branch of the military and establishes the Air Ministry. Over 58 percent of Great Britain's frontline aircraft are fighter planes; by contrast, over half of the German and French planes are devoted to reconnaissance.

3 April 1918
Western Front. The first American troops to serve in France have now been in the Ansauville sector (near the Saint-Mihiel salient) and the Sommerville sector (stretching north from Switzerland) for

A French aviator, 1918 (by Reni-Mel, courtesy of the Anne S.K. Brown Military Collection, Brown University Library)

nearly three months while training with the French army. Although involved only in repelling German raids, including gas shellings, they have suffered over 640 casualties, 549 in the Ansauville sector.
Beauvais, France. Clemenceau, Lloyd George, and other Allied leaders, including Pershing and Gen. Tasker H. Bliss, meet. Recognizing that greater military coordination still remains to be achieved, they unanimously agree to give Marshal Foch "the strategic direction of military operations." Foch is now commander in chief of the Allied forces, although control of tactics and the right to appeal decisions to their respective governments remains with the commanders of each nation's troops.

4 April 1918
Russia. German troops reach Sevastopol, taking control of Crimea. They now have full access to the Caucasus and Georgia and the rail lines across the Caucasus to Baku.

9 April 1918
Lys River. General Haig has expressed his concern to Marshal Foch that a German

attack may be likely against the British lines north of Arras, but Foch, preferring to cluster a major force near Amiens, has refused to redeploy French troops to relieve the British line south of the Somme so that they can reinforce the Flanders positions. In the meantime, General Ludendorff, fearing that the left flank of the German salient has become vulnerable to attack by the French, has halted the Somme offensive in favor of pursuing the second part of his original plan. At 4:14 A.M., Gen. Ferdinand von Qaust's Sixth Army unleashes a barrage of artillery shells and gas presaging the anticipated assault. Its primary focus is the Portuguese Corps of Gen. Sir Henry Horne's First Army defending the Lys River front near Neuve-Chapelle, which the German commanders regard as most susceptible to attack. (Sharing this same view, Haig had planned to remove the Portuguese troops from the front line during the night of this very date.) At 8:45 A.M., Quast's troops go over the top. They find the Portuguese line essentially abandoned and race ahead three miles without encountering resistance, reaching the British defensive line along the Lys and Lawe Rivers. The British put up a stiff resistance; the struggle is especially desperate along the Lawe River. In the late afternoon, one of Quast's divisions finds a bridge still standing across the Lys at Bac Saint Maur and crosses over. The Germans capture six thousand men of the Portuguese Corps. The British find the remaining thirteen thousand dispersed in rear areas.

London. Lloyd George, assessing the demoralizing British failure at the Battle of the Lys, tells the House of Commons: "We have entered the most critical phase of this most terrible war. There is a lull in the storm, but the hurricane is not over."

10 April 1918

Lys River. Gen. Sixt von Armin's Fourth Army now joins in the offensive, attacking Gen. Sir Herbert Plumer's Second Army to the north of Armentières. At midday, the British evacuate Armentières, rendered undefensible by Quast's advance the previous day. The Sixth Army takes the city while pursuing the attack across the Lys River above Bac Saint Maur, pushing toward Bailleul.

11 April 1918

Lys River. Both German armies continue to advance, with the Sixth Army driving toward Hazebrouck. Alarmed, General Haig issues this order at the end of the day: "Every position must be held to the last man. . . . With our backs to the wall and believing in the justice of our cause each one must fight on to the end. The safety of our homes and the freedom of mankind alike depend upon the conduct of each one of us at this critical moment."

12 April 1918

Lys River. Though florid and rather trite, General Haig's order rouses the troops. Although the Germans force Horne's men back still farther, resistance along the line stiffens.

Portuguese East Africa. Near Medo, a column of the King's African Rifles clashes with German troops led by Capt. Franz Koehl in jungle terrain choked with bamboo and elephant grass. After a day of bloody combat, the Germans withdraw, leaving the battleground and its wounded and dead to the British.

13 April 1918

Russia. The generals previously arrested by Kerensky had escaped in December and made their way to Cossack territory, where they organized a Volunteer Army, now numbering about nine thousand men led by Gen. L.G. Kornilov. They have crossed the Kuban River and are poised to attack Yekaterinodar (Krasnodar). A shell fired by Red troops from the city hits the farmhouse where Kornilov is staying and kills the general. His disheartened officers and troops, now commanded by Gen. A.I. Denikin, abandon the attack and withdraw.

14 April 1918

Somme River. Conceding him still more power needed to impose unity on the Allied military effort, British and French leaders name Marshal Ferdinand Foch as Allied commander in chief.

Lys River. For two days, strong British

resistance holds the Germans. The crisis seems to be over.

17 April 1918
Lys River. After a few days' pause, the Germans resume the offensive along the entire front from Bethune to Dixmude but achieve only modest gains near Bailleul and Mount Kemmel and toward Ypres.

18 April 1918
Lys River. With the British line holding fast, three French divisions—Foch has relented somewhat—relieve Plumer's troops on the sector between Meteren and Mount Kemmel.
Washington. President Wilson creates the National War Labor Board, giving its members authority "to promote and carry on mediation and adjustment in the field of production necessary for the effective conduct of the war" in all cases where existing agreements or laws do not provide for means of effecting settlements.

21 April 1918
Somme River. The great German air ace Baron Manfred von Richthofen meets his end, apparently the victim of ground fire, although Capt. A.R. Brown, a Canadian pilot flying a Sopwith Camel, claims the victory. Richthofen's skill in aerial combat had exacted eighty kills (seventy-nine British airplanes and one Belgian plane) and earned him Germany's highest military award, the *pour le Merite,* or Blue Max.

22 April 1918
Dover. Vice Adm. Roger Keyes aboard HMS *Warwick* commands a squadron of ships that sets out at 5:00 P.M. for a long-planned assault on the ports at Zeebrugge and Ostend intended to end their role as U-boat bases. The plan is to sink three old cruisers loaded with cement in the entrance to the Bruges canal at Zeebrugge to block the canal. As a diversion, the cruiser HMS *Vindictive,* converted to an assault ship, will come alongside the mile-long mole at Zeebrugge under cover of a smoke screen and disembark marines to attack the German gun positions before the cement-laden cruisers move in.

23 April 1918
Zeebrugge. One minute after midnight, the *Vindictive* reaches the mole, although not at the spot originally intended since the ship's smoke cover was dispersed by winds, leaving her exposed to German fire. Tucked against the jetty by two ferry boats, the cruiser unloads the landing parties, but her guns are useless in their support because of her position. Splayed by German firing, the block ships cannot reach their intended sites for scuttling. The crews release the charges to sink the ships and escape to a waiting launch. Only one of two submarines involved in the operation arrives on time and purposely smashes headlong into the mole's cross braces. The crew escapes to a skiff and blows up the submarine, rending a hundred-foot gap in the jetty. The *Vindictive,* under tow by one of the steamers, withdraws into open water. The raid at Ostend fails as the two ships sent to block the port lose their way because the Germans have removed one marker buoy and moved another. One ship runs aground, and the second plows into it. The daring British operation, resulting in five hundred casualties, fails in its objective—the Germans are able to quickly dig a new channel at Zeebrugge—but boosts British morale.
Compiégne. Foch and Haig agree on a system of *roulement* proposed by Foch by which weary British divisions will replace French divisions at quiet sectors of the Western Front, freeing the French troops for service in a general reserve. Four British divisions, accompanied and commanded by their officers, will begin the *roulement,* three being transferred by mid-May to the Aisne River sector to serve with the French Sixth Army commanded by Gen. Denis Duchêne and the fourth to the sector southeast of Chalons controlled by Gen. Henri Gouraud's Fourth Army.

24 April 1918
Lys River. With a six-day lull in the fighting, Plumer is able to relieve more of his troops on the front lines, and Foch sends two more divisions into the Flanders sector.
Somme River. German troops attack at

Villers-Bretonneux in the company of thirteen tanks and breach the British line, opening a salient and capturing the village and the Abbe and Hangard Woods. This is the German's first use of a large number of tanks to support an attack. In response, the British converge twenty tanks upon the salient for a counterattack. Ludendorff's goal is the capture of Amiens, but the Australians' counterattack, during which a few tanks from both sides battle each other for the first time in the war, recaptures Villers-Bretonneux and secures Amiens from menace.

25 April 1918
North Sea. Admiral Scheer has brought the High Seas Fleet out of the Jade Basin to attack British ships convoying a Scandinavian merchant fleet, but he has been misinformed about their whereabouts and has turned back. The *Moltke* develops serious problems, losing a propeller and a gear wheel, and must be towed. The *Moltke*'s call for help alerts the British. Admiral Beatty dispatches the Grand Fleet, now harbored at Rosyth, to give chase—its only show of force since 19 August 1916. Out of Rosyth steam thirty-one battleships, four battle cruisers, two heavy cruisers, twenty-four light cruisers, and eighty-five destroyers. But they are too late, as Scheer's fleet reaches safety, with only the *Moltke,* now on its own steam, limping behind. The British submarine *E-42,* well ahead of the fleet, slams a torpedo into the *Moltke,* but the wounded German ship makes it to harbor. Once more Beatty is disappointed.

26 April 1918
Russia. On orders from Moscow, guards detaining Nicholas II and the royal family at Tobolsk in Siberia move them to Yekaterinburg in the Ural Mountains.

27 April 1918
Mesopotamia. With the Euphrates under control, General Marshall's new assignment is to drive the Turks out of Kurdistan. Heading northward from the Tigris River, his troops take Qarah Tappah without opposition and press on toward Kulawand,

where Lewis guns and a cavalry charge quickly subdue the withdrawing Turks. Six hundred become prisoners.

Jerusalem. Dr. Chaim Weizmann, head of the recently created Zionist Commission, and other members of the commission meet with Arab notables to assure them that the perception that they are to be ousted from their "present holdings" results either from a misconception of Zionist aims or from "the malicious activities of our enemies." The Arabs seem mollified.

28 April 1918
Russia. The first contingent of the Czechoslovak Legion, numbering two thousand men, arrives in Vladivostok.

29 April 1918
Lys River. Following a German surprise attack that achieves a modest gain at Mount Scherpenberg, the Battle of the Lys culminates, the Fourth and Sixth Armies' impetus spent.

Meuse River. In the Toul sector near Saint-Mihiel, where American pilots are training, Lt. Edward V. Rickenbacker shoots down a German plane, scoring his first air victory.

Mesopotamia. Marshall's troops capture Tuz Khurmatu and Daquq. The first action costs 194 casualties but secures 1,300 prisoners and 12 guns.

1 May 1918
Aisne River. Since mid-April, Gen. Erich Ludendorff has planned to shift the focus of his offensive once more, this time to an attack on the Chemin des Dames at the center of the Aisne River sector, his purpose being to force the French to redeploy troops from Flanders and set the stage for a German breakthrough there. Seeing the Chemin des Dames as a "weak spot in the French front," Ludendorff issues orders to Crown Prince Rupprecht for his army group to begin preparations for the offensive, code named Blücher. The Seventh Army commanded by Gen. Hans von Böhn will carry the right and center of the attack; the First Army commanded by Gen. Fritz von Below, the left. The plan of the attack is exceptionally thorough and well-

First Lt. Eddie Rickenbacker poses with his "Hat in the Ring" squadron fighter plane. Rickenbacker, a champion race car driver before the war, became America's greatest ace and one of the enduring heroes of the conflict. (Library of Congress)

guarded. The Germans increase activity in Flanders to deceive the Allies into thinking the attack will occur there.

Russia. The Austrians and Germans have a treaty of alliance with the separatist government of the Ukraine allowing German forces to enter the country. Already occupying Kiev, the Germans have pushed eastward and now take Taganrog on the Sea of Azov.

Laon. After firing on Paris for the entire month of April, "Big Bertha" falls silent.

Abbeville. The Allied Supreme War Council meets, with the foremost question on the minds of the French and British leaders being whether Pershing will allow American troops to be amalgamated into their own forces and commands. But Pershing adamantly insists on maintaining the AEF's independence. He also rejects a plan that Newton D. Baker had agreed to providing for shipment to France of 120,000 American soldiers per month for four months.

2 May 1918

Abbeville. Under intense pressure from the other Allies, Pershing gives a little. He ac-

cepts transporting 120,000 American troops through June and agrees to discus-

American doughboys (by Lucien Jones, courtesy of the Anne S.K. Brown Military Collection, Brown University Library)

An American field kitchen (by F. Journey, courtesy of the Anne S.K. Brown Military Collection, Brown University Library)

sion of a possible extension of this plan. In return, he obtains Allied agreement that the AEF will remain independent and that the British must provide shipping for forty thousand more American soldiers than already provided for during May and June.

7 May 1918

Romania. After two months of negotiations, Germany and Romania sign a final peace treaty. The Peace of Bucharest incorporates the earlier peace conditions. In addition, Romania cedes her two major ports to the Germans and Austrians, leaving the little nation landlocked. Romania also grants Germany a ninety-nine-year lease on Romanian oil wells and the right to keep an army of occupation in Romania. The defeated nation also agrees to provide food to Germany and her allies at fixed prices. The harshness of this treaty and the Treaty of Brest-Litovsk hardens the resolve of the Allies to pursue the defeat of imperial Germany.

Mesopotamia. Marshall's troops, having taken Taza on 3 May, enter Kirkuk, discovering six hundred ill or wounded Turks.

8 May 1918

Russia. German troops at Taganrog have been joined by General Denikin's Volunteer Army and another small anti-Bolshevik army. This combined force captures Rostov, which the Red Army had earlier wrenched from the Volunteer Army's control.

9 May 1918

Dover. Admiral Keyes sends a second raid against Ostend, with the *Vindictive* and the *Sappho* as designated block ships. But the *Sappho* is forced to turn back with engine trouble, and the *Vindictive* loses her way in dense fog in the Ostend canal entrance and runs aground.

Washington. Prof. Thomas Masaryk arrives in the capital to advocate the cause of his countrymen now in Siberia.

20 May 1918

Washington. President Wilson signs the Overman Act, which authorizes the president to reorganize the functions of the executive branch's varied agencies in any way he deems fit, including abolishing bureaus and offices or creating new ones, consolidating existing agencies, and redefining duties—an extraordinary grant of authority to the chief executive by the Congress.

Moscow. The government orders the Czechoslovak Legion, now dispersed at various points along the Trans-Siberian Railway between the Volga River and Vladivostok, to surrender their arms. When the Czechs refuse, Trotsky orders the Red Army to forcibly disarm and detain them.

22 May 1918

Portuguese East Africa. Near Korewa, a British column nearly manages to surround Koehl's column of *Schutztruppe,* still recovering from the battle near Medo. Eleven Germans and forty-nine askaris die in the fighting. Most of the *Schutztruppe* escape, but they lose their transports and a large quantity of ammunition.

24 May 1918

Mesopotamia. Too far removed from their supply sources, Marshall's troops leave Kirkuk and reestablish bases at Tuz and Kifri from which to watch over the Persian border.

26 May 1918

Aisne River. The German buildup for the attack on the Chemin des Dames is complete—3,719 guns are in place to support the infantry. Ludendorff's goal is a salient of exactly twelve miles and no more, which he believes will be a sufficient penetration toward Paris to force the French to redeploy troops from Flanders while the Germans hastily transport reserves to the attack there. General Duchêne has ignored warnings from American intelligence and from his own men about the German buildup along the Aisne front and also warnings from British officers there as part of the *roulement* that his defenses, his forward trenches in particular, are inadequate. He has also disregarded his orders by concentrating his defense in the forward trenches.

Russia. Refusing to capitulate to the Red Army, members of the Czechoslovak Legion capture Chelyabinsk.

27 May 1918

Aisne River. At 1:00 A.M., the German artillery barrage begins along a twenty-four-mile front from Berry-au-Bac to Chavignon facing the entire Chemin des Dames. For over two and a half hours, the shelling pounds roads and bridges and French front lines, artillery, command posts, and rear lines as far back as the Vesle River. A creeping barrage falls on the infantry positions at the Chemin des Dames itself. In the early morning, "Big Bertha," silent for nearly a month, joins in the destruction, hurling fifteen shells into Paris and its suburbs that cause four deaths. At 3:40 A.M., German infantry plunge forward, meeting minimal resistance from the shattered French and British troops. In less than two hours, they break through Duchêne's center and capture the eastern end of the Chemin des Dames Ridge. By 9:00 A.M., storm troops reach the Aisne, and the infantry sweeps down the south slope of the ridge after them. The French blow up most of the bridges, but frequently without sufficient thoroughness to prevent access and crossing. Duchêne sends forward his few reserves, but the Germans cross the Aisne and smash ahead, opening a gap between the French right and the British left. By day's end, the German salient extends twelve miles into Duchêne's center, south of the Vesle River, and they control the entire Chemin des Dames. Throughout the day, German aircraft have dropped gre-

nades and strafed roads used by the retreating Allied troops, while also preventing the French from evacuating or blowing up their airfield at Magneux. The German attack has destroyed four Allied divisions and badly mauled four others. Duchêne confronts catastrophe.

Russia. German and Austro-Hungarian troops extend their control nearly to the mouth of the Don River, capturing the Donbass coalfields north of Rostov.

28 May 1918

Aisne River. The German advance continues as Duchêne squanders his reserves, committing them to the fighting without careful forethought on where they might best serve. The Germans capture Fisme and the airfield nearby at Magneux, abandoned by the French with planes, hangars, and fuel tanks left intact. German troops cross those sections of the Vesle along the front not reached the day before. Gen. Philippe Pétain orders holding of the flanks northwest of Soissons and south of Rheims. He appeals to Foch to send reserves to the front, but the commander in chief quite presciently judges the offensive may "only be a feint" and decides to wait and see how it develops. His counterpart Ludendorff, however, becomes enthralled by the amazing success of the offensive's first two days and, violating his own dictum to adhere rigidly to the Blücher plan, commits reinforcements to the attack and brings up reserve troops. He now envisions capturing Paris.

Somme River. American troops of the First Division's Twenty-eighth Regiment, supported by the French, attack German positions in the ruined town of Cantigny near Montdidier, killing or capturing all the Germans in the town. The Germans respond with a series of counterattacks, but the Americans hold fast. The small battle costs the First Division 1,067 casualties; German casualties number over 1,600, including 225 taken prisoner.

29 May 1918

Aisne River. The Blücher offensive resumes, with the Germans driving ahead along the entire front, capturing Fere-en-

A member of the American First Division in France (by Lucien Jones, courtesy of the Anne S.K. Brown Military Collection, Brown University Library)

Tardenois and crossing the Ourcq River at the center of the salient. Clemenceau visits the front in the afternoon and receives gloomy reports from Duchêne and the other commanders. Pétain orders preparations for a counterattack and moves forward every reserve unit he can find, some now finally released by Foch.

Russia. Czechoslovak Legion units capture Penza after defeating Red Army troops.

30 May 1918

Aisne River. Pétain's plan to counterattack fades as the Germans drive ahead for the fourth day, pushing the center of their sa-

lient nearly to Château-Thierry and to the Marne River, actually forming a bridgehead on its south bank near Jaulgonne. French resistance on both German flanks, however, begins to stiffen. At Pétain's request, Gen. John Pershing extends American aid to the French. Marines with the AEF's Second Infantry Division assemble for the journey to the front to support the Sixth Army's XXIst Corps at the very center of the German salient—the American troops' destination is Belleau Wood. Pershing commits the Third Division to positions on the Marne. Panic imbues Paris: over a million residents have fled, members of the Chamber of Deputies assail Foch and Pétain and call for Duchêne's discharge, and the government prepares plans to move to Bordeaux.

Aisne River. French resistance holds the Germans to a modest gain, extending down the Ourcq toward Meaux. The German advance now totals forty miles, and they have captured fifty thousand prisoners and eight hundred guns.

Russia. Czechoslovak Legion troops capture Tomsk.

1 June 1918

Aisne River. Exhaustion, declining discipline, distance from supply lines, and increasing opposition begin to take their toll on the Blücher offensive. The French limit the Germans to a slight advance.

Marne River. Throughout the course of the day, the American reinforcements from the Second Division sent by Pershing—26,600 men of the Ninth Infantry, Twenty-third Infantry, and two marine regiments—arrive west of Château-Thierry near Belleau Wood. With them is Brig. Gen. James G. Harbord, Pershing's trusted chief of staff, who left the staff in early May to assume command of the Marine Brigade.

Versailles. The Allied Supreme War Council meets, with Pershing among the attending generals.

Portuguese East Africa. Col. Paul Emil von Lettow-Vorbeck and his column of *Schutztruppe* cross the Lurio River near the village of Vatiua and move south into hilly bush country. They are pursued by six columns of British troops and one of Portuguese troops.

2 June 1918
Aisne River. For the second day, the French contain the German advance.
Versailles. On the Supreme War Council's second and last day of discussing a response to the Aisne offensive, General Pershing, while maintaining a coolheaded appraisal of the situation, asserts that he will insist on transport of 250,000 American soldiers per month from the United States in June and July to bolster the Western Front and commits American troops currently being trained behind the British lines to redeployment with the French.

3 June 1918
Marne River. French troops dislodge the Germans from their bridgehead on the south bank of the Marne River at Jaulgonne. The AEF's Third Division moves into defensive positions on the Marne near Château-Thierry.

5 June 1918
Aisne River. Crown Prince Rupprecht orders the Seventh Army and the First Army to consolidate their frontline positions. The Blücher offensive ends in exhaustion. With the artillery and support infantry units of the AEF Second Division now in place to the west of Château-Thierry, Gen. Jean Degoutte, commander of the French XXIst Corps, has given them control of a sector of over five and a half miles between the Marne and Ourcq rivers with the understanding that they will repulse any German assault.

6 June 1918
Marne River. At 5:00 A.M., the Marine Brigade of the AEF's Second Division commanded by General Harbord attacks German positions west of Belleau Wood, which German troops occupy. At 5:00 P.M., the marines launch a second attack, this one directed against the German defenses in Belleau Wood and in the nearby village of Bouresches. The marines attack in successive waves across open fields of wheat stud-

An American soldier (by Lucien Jones, courtesy of the Anne S.K. Brown Military Collection, Brown University Library)

ded with red poppies, as the British troops had done in 1916, recklessly exposing themselves to German machine-gun and rifle fire. They succeed in driving the Germans out of the village and in taking Hill 142 west of the woods. But the price is dear: 1,087 casualties.

7 June 1918
Russia. Omsk falls to the Czechoslovakian Legion.

8 June 1918
Matz River. To protect the right flank of the Aisne salient, Ludendorff has ordered an offensive by General von Hutier's Eighteenth Army beginning on 7 June intended

The end of innocence: an American doughboy at the front in France, 1918 (Library of Congress)

to push forward to a line six miles beyond the Matz River (which joins the Oise above the Aisne), extending between Montdidier and Compiègne. Difficulties with assembling troops and artillery have forced Hutier to postpone the offensive until today. The Eighteenth Army's primary opponent is Gen. Georges Humbert's Third Army, but confronting Hutier's left flank is the Tenth Army commanded by the fearsome Gen. Charles Mangin. German deserters have informed the French that the German offensive will begin at midnight with an artillery barrage, so Humbert unleashes his artillery at ten minutes before midnight.

Russia. The Czechoslovakian Legion captures Samara.

9 June 1918

Aisne River. Clemenceau removes Duchêne as commander of the Sixth Army, replacing him with General Degoutte.

Matz River. Despite the preemptive bombardment by the French, Hutier's artillery barrage proves deadly, hitting the Third Army first with gas, followed by high explosives that destroy the frontline trenches and batteries, command posts, roads, and telephone lines to the rear. Beginning at 3:00 A.M., the German infantry attacks, advancing rapidly. By the end of the day, Hutier's men advance six miles, devastating three of Humbert's divisions and taking eight thousand prisoners.

Adriatic Sea. Hoping to sunder the Otranto Barrage, the Austrians send four light cruisers and eight torpedo boats to attack the barrage's nets and the patrols protecting the area. With the attacking ships already en route, a support group of four dreadnoughts and three predreadnoughts, with an escort of seven torpedo boats, steams out of the harbor at Pola and heads south to be in place to protect the attack ships from a possible Allied counterattack.

10 June 1918

Matz River. Though hammered by a fierce

A dramatic but improbable scene drawn for the cover of *Collier*'s magazine, showing a Briton, an American, and a Frenchman capturing a German machine-gun position (by F.C. Yohn, Library of Congress)

barrage from Humbert's artillery, Hutier's troops push ahead another two miles. Humbert's right center crumbles, placing his right flank in grave danger. To avert disaster, he pulls back the entire right flank six miles. Pétain and Gen. Emile Fayolle, commander of the army group, send reinforcements to be placed under command of Mangin. Fayolle orders Mangin to relieve Humbert's right flank by attacking toward Ressons sur Matz from the southwest. Foch arrives and urges Mangin to attack like a "thunderbolt." In the presence of Foch, Fayolle, and Humbert, Mangin orders his commanders to prepare for an attack at 11:00 A.M., with no preliminary artillery bombardment. Mangin asserts: "The attack will be ruthless, pressed to the limit. This will be the end of the defensive battles we have fought for the past two months. From now on we attack; we must succeed. Go back to your men and tell them just that." Foch approves.

Adriatic Sea. Two Italian motor boats patrolling the waters off the island of Premuda spot the Austrian support group of dreadnoughts heading for the Otranto Barrage at 3:15 A.M. Commander Luigi Rizzo races to attack the unsuspecting Austrians; at two hundred yards' distance, he launches two torpedoes—both hit the dreadnought *Szent Istvan*—and speeds away. The dreadnought's engines remain intact, and the captain decides to continue. But soon the ship begins filling with water, lists, and sinks. With the Otranto attack no longer secret, the Austrians terminate the operation and return to harbor.

11 June 1918

Marne River. Because the marines attacking Belleau Wood have been so close to the enemy line that no artillery support is possible and they remain pinned down after four days of combat, their commanders pull back the frontline troops and, to the surprise of the Germans, let loose an artillery barrage on the enemy positions that sunders the trees of Belleau Wood. Renewing the attack on the dazed Germans, the marines take three hundred prisoners and most of Belleau Wood.

Matz River. Mangin's troops assemble in a morning mist that conceals them from the Germans. As the mist disperses at eleven-thirty, they surge forward, covered by a rolling barrage and fire from fighter planes. Tanks follow. The French rapidly retake Mery, Belloy, and Fretoy, capturing a thousand prisoners and nineteen guns. But German artillery in the woods above Belloy brings the advance to a halt. As hoped, Humbert holds the Germans.

Russia. Warned that the Germans intend to capture Murmansk to use as a U-boat base, Wilson in April had approved sending a warship to the port; 150 American marines now also arrive.

12 June 1918

Matz River. Both sides attack. Gen. Hans von Böhn's Seventh Army now joins in the battle, striking from the east and driving toward Compiègne. But Pétain and Fayolle have greatly reinforced Humbert's artillery, and the guns' shelling, combined with the French infantrymen's renewed momentum, force the Germans back to their starting line of 9 June. Ludendorff terminates the offensive. French losses in the four-day battle total 35,000 men and 70 tanks (144 tanks saw action). The French learn some lessons from the battle about the value of Pétain's defensive tactics and of Mangin's swift counterattack. General Pershing's armor expert and observer at the scene, Maj. George S. Patton Jr., learns some lessons about the potential of tank warfare, including the desirability of eliminating mechanical failures. The French victory quiets the political furor in Paris and secures Clemenceau's hold on the premiership.

13 June 1918

Marne River. The battle in Belleau Wood, again a foot-by-foot struggle for ground, explodes as the Germans counterattack ferociously but fall before the Americans' fire.

14 June 1918

Persia. Advancing into northwest Persia, Turkish troops capture Tabriz.

15 June 1918

Piave River. With Russia out of the fighting, Austrian leaders, including Emperor Karl, see the possibility of redeploying troops to mount a decisive offensive against the Italians. They had planned for the offensive to begin on 20 May, but lack of horses and motor vehicles for hauling artillery and men to the front, disrepair of train engines, inadequate and insufficient food and clothing for the soldiers, and lack of spirit have caused the offensive to be slow materializing. Field Marshal Count Franz Conrad von Hötzendorf has persuaded the young emperor that the primary thrust of the offensive should be in the Sette Comuni sector of the Piave front and should be the task of the expanded Eleventh Army. Army Group Boroevic will support the Eleventh Army by attacking from the Lessini Alps against the Italians' flank. On the very day of the offensive, the Austrian armies remain short of artillery, gas shells, ammunition, food, and horses; and a diversionary attack on 13 June at the Tonale Pass has already come to naught. Deserters have apprised the Italians of the offensive, and the Italians preempt the Austrian attack by starting an artillery bombardment four hours before the Austrians had planned to begin. The Austrian artillery sticks to the plan and commences firing at 3:00 P.M. The Italian artillery wins the duel.

16 June 1918

London. The government issues a pledge (known as the Declaration to the Seven Syrians) that future governments of the area occupied by Allied forces in Arabia will come into being on the principle of "consent of the governed" and that areas still under Turkish control "should obtain their freedom and independence." Arab leaders assume that this pledge includes a reassurance about the future of Palestine.

Piave River. At 7:00 A.M., the Austrian infantry moves out on the Sette Comuni front, advancing through rugged terrain and struggling across the river. In the afternoon they confront stiff opposition that drives them back to their starting line. At the Montello sector, however, Army Group Boroevic's troops manage to establish five bridgeheads across the Piave, advancing two miles and holding their ground. Nevertheless, by evening the Battle of the Piave is already over, although the Austrian command is not prepared to admit it.

18 June 1918
Persia. A force of about ten thousand Cossacks led by a Colonel Bicherakov, to whom they are intensely loyal, has gained control of the area between Qazvin and Manjil and now reaches Rasht.
Piave River. As his troops have successfully thwarted the Austrian assault, except at the Montello, Gen. Armando Diaz begins a counterattack against Gen. Svetozar Boroevic's troops. The beleaguered Boroevic asks Emperor Karl for permission to withdraw. The emperor stalls.

22 June 1918
Persia. Colonel Bicherakov returns from a visit to Baku with the intent of transporting his troops, with four of the British armored cars and some of Dunsterville's officers, across the water to Alyaty, and from there marching 150 miles to the west to capture the bridge over the Kura River and prevent the advance of 12,000 Turkish troops moving through Azerbaijan.
Russia. Gen. A.I. Denikin and his Volunteer Army of "White Russians" open an offensive against the Red Army in the northern Caucasus.

23 June 1918
Piave River. Finally receiving permission to withdraw on 20 June, Boroevic has removed first his wounded and then his viable troops surreptitiously over two nights. Now realizing that Boroevic is evacuating the Montello, the Italians inflict heavy casualties on the last of the Austrians to cross the Piave. The Battle of the Piave costs the Italians an estimated eighty-five thousand losses. The Austrians have lost seventy thousand, but in addition they suffer demoralization and desertion.

26 June 1918
Marne River. After twenty continuous "days of hell" fighting at Belleau Wood, often hand to hand, American troops finally

dislodge the Germans. During the prolonged struggle, the Marine Brigade suffers fifty-two hundred casualties, a loss of half its strength. Losses of the Third Brigade Infantry, which relieved the weary marines for part of the battle, total thirty-two hundred men. To honor the courageous marines, General Degoutte orders that Belleau Wood be renamed Bois de la Brigade de Marine.

27 June 1918
Persia. Dunsterville's force, nicknamed "Dunsterforce," takes control of Bandar-e-Pahlavi (Enzeli).

3 July 1918
Persia. Colonel Bicherakov's force sets sail for Alyaty.
Portuguese East Africa. Lettow-Vorbeck and his *Schutztruppe,* always searching for supplies, capture Nhamacurra, just inland from the Indian Ocean, and find aboard a river steamer a British doctor who provides needed medical supplies. At the railroad station they defeat a force of British and Portuguese troops, taking 540 prisoner. Of the defenders, 209 lose their lives, many of them drowned or devoured by crocodiles while taking flight in the waters of the Nhamacurra River. Lettow-Vorbeck's valuable plunder includes 350 rifles, 10 machine guns, clothing for his entire outfit, over 660,000 pounds of food, and huge quantities of wine and schnapps. Guessing correctly that the British and Portuguese are racing south to prevent him from reaching the port of Quelimane, Lettow-Vorbeck decides to avoid them by turning northward.
Versailles. The Supreme War Council considers a plan proposed by Gen. Franchet d'Esperey for an attack by the "Armies of the Orient" headquartered in Salonika against the Bulgarians. General d'Esperey was appointed to the Allied command at Salonika in June to succeed Gen. Louis Guillaumat, recalled by Clemenceau to aid in the defense of Paris. (Guillaumat had succeeded Sarrail in December 1917.) The new commander has quickly won the confidence of the Allied officer corps at Salonika, including the British commander,

Lt. Gen. Sir George Milne. (Finding his name difficult, the British refer to d'Esperey as "Desperate Frankie.") Unsympathetic to d'Esperey's plan—Western Front commanders want to keep the focus and troops there, and Lloyd George wants to redeploy some of Milne's troops to help Allenby in Palestine—the council refers the plan to a subcommittee.

6 July 1918
Washington. Under pressure from Allied leaders and his own advisers to commit American troops to intervention in Siberia, Wilson expresses disapproval of interfering in Russia's civil strife but agrees to send "policing expeditions" to support the British troops in Murmansk and the Japanese troops in Vladivostok and to ensure that supplies sent to the White Russian forces do not fall into the hands of the Bolsheviks.

7 July 1918
Marne River. Intelligence reports gained through patrols, prisoners, and air reconnaissance coming to Commander in Chief Philippe Pétain have indicated that Ludendorff plans a major offensive on the Marne front. Air reconnaissance alone substantiates the German buildup. (There are now over thirty-three hundred planes in the northeast sector of the Western Front, including the dead Richthofen's squadron, commanded by Hermann Göring.) Pétain now understands that the objectives of this offensive are Rheims, Epernay, and Chalons, which means that the Fifth Army of Gen. Henri Berthelot will take the brunt of it. To Berthelot's left, General Degoutte's Sixth Army's right, containing AEF units, will also come under fire, as will the leftward units of Gen. Henri Gouraud's Fourth Army. Pétain also knows that the date of the attack is 15 July. With Foch's approval, Pétain plans his own offensive to be commanded by Mangin and to begin on 18 July against the German salient in the Aisne River sector. Its chances of success will be greater if the Germans are preoccupied on the Marne. Ludendorff confronts a growing opposition: he has 207 divisions on the Western Front, but the Allies have 203, and

17 of these are American, twice the size of the European divisions (the AEF now comprises over one million troops). For the first time, the Germans are outnumbered. Ludendorff views the impending battle as a *Friedensturm,* a decisive battle to attain peace, because he believes its success will finally permit destruction of the BEF in Flanders.

Constantinople. Five RAF de Havilland 9 bombers based on islands in the Aegean Sea attack the city, setting fire to an ammunition factory.

9 July 1918
Berlin. The German high command forces the resignation of Baron Richard von Kuhlmann as foreign minister. The army commanders have opposed him for months, as Kuhlmann has advocated conciliatory peace terms and sees the Brest-Litovsk Treaty as merely temporary—to be sub-

A member of the American Expeditionary Force in France, 1918 (by F. Journey, courtesy of the Anne S.K. Brown Military Collection, Brown University Library)

stantively revised when a general peace is negotiated. Adm. Paul von Hintze replaces him.

15 July 1918

Aisne River. With the success of the Aisne offensive, the Germans have been able to move "Big Bertha" closer to Paris, situating the giant cannon in the Chatel Woods six miles north of Château-Thierry and only fifty-eight miles from Paris. After a respite of five weeks, the capital city once again rumbles with explosions of the gun's shells, fifteen altogether.

16 July 1918

Persia. A brigade of Gen. Sir William Marshall's Mesopotamian Expeditionary Force sent from Ruz to assist Baku arrives at Hamadan after traveling overland 350 miles in six days over formidable terrain.

Marne River. Knowing that the German artillery softening up is to begin at ten minutes after midnight, the French have opened their own barrage forty minutes earlier. Gas shells—American troops' first experience with gas—comprise a major part of the German bombardment. When the German attack comes, General Gouraud, employing Pétain's defensive tactics, holds the Germans to a modest advance and thereby protects the French right flank. The left flank, protected by Degoutte's Sixth Army, also mostly holds, with the American troops proving steadfast. But at the center, Berthelot, who had only recently assumed command and has been unable to impose Pétain's tactics, holds a line defended by both French and Italian units. They give way along a five-mile front, allowing the Germans to cross the Marne. French artillery and aircraft zero in on this sector, attacking the temporary bridges the Germans have installed, and the Italian troops hold their second-line defensive positions. Pétain rounds up some reinforcements, including two British divisions that Foch manages to persuade Haig to release.

Russia. The Soviet of Yekaterinburg in the Urals (where the royal family is detained), concerned that White Russians may set free the czar, have decided that the family should be executed. Red Guards shoot Nicholas II, the czarina, their children, and their retainers in a basement room of the house they occupy.

Aisne River. "Big Bertha" ceases firing after launching only four shells into Paris. French artillery makes the gun's new site untenable, and the Germans move it out of the area.

17 July 1918

Marne River. The Germans renew the attack, again making headway against the French center but nowhere else. As the day closes, the German offensive slows. Ludendorff, realizing that his objectives are beyond reach, cancels the offensive and departs for Crown Prince Rupprecht's headquarters at Tournai to plan another offensive. Although they have fallen well short of his goals, the five Ludendorff offensives of 1918 have nevertheless gained the Germans ten times as much ground as the Allies captured in 1917, while garnering 225,000 prisoners and 2,500 guns and inflicting close to 448,000 casualties on the British and 490,000 on the French. But the cost to Ludendorff—963,300 casualties—is also staggering, and unlike the British and French, he has no pool of recruits left. He also is in peril of losing his ally Austria-Hungary, and he has no new ally to counterbalance the ever-growing presence of the Americans.

Aisne River. American troops of the First and Second Divisions begin to move toward the frontlines southwest of Soissons for an attack in conjunction with Gen. Charles Mangin's Tenth Army, which is scheduled for 18 July.

18 July 1918

Aisne River. As planned by Pétain, a counteroffensive against the Germans' Aisne salient by the Sixth and Tenth Armies, commanded by General Mangin and supported by the AEF First and Second Divisions, begins at 4:35 A.M. Taken by surprise, the Germans quickly fall back. Alarmed by news of the retreat, Crown Prince Wilhelm orders the withdrawal of Böhn's Seventh Army troops still occupying the Marne salient. Ludendorff hastens back from Flanders.

19 July 1918
Marne River. The French Fifth and Ninth Armies, along with two British divisions released by Haig, join the counteroffensive, which lashes at both German flanks.

Aisne River. Badly battered in two days of fighting, the American Second Division receives permission to retire from the front near Soissons, where its objective has been to establish a line beyond the road connecting Soissons to Château-Thierry. French troops replace them. The American First Division troops also fail to attain their objective but do eke out an advance at a cost of three thousand casualties, including Maj. Theodore Roosevelt Jr.

20 July 1918
Marne River. The British and Americans each commit two more divisions to the Allied counteroffensive. Crown Prince Wilhelm designates a series of defensive positions for his armies to fall back to in succession.

Aisne River. American First Division troops advance toward Bersy-le-Sec near the Soissons-Château-Thierry road, but French troops on their flanks fail to keep up.

21 July 1918
Aisne River. The First Division captures Bersy-le-Sec, moving to within three miles of Soissons. The exhausted troops await the arrival of French relief troops. Stiff German resistance in the Soissons battle has cost the two American infantry divisions half of their soldiers and over half of their officers.

24 July 1918
Melun, France. Pétain, Haig, and Pershing meet with Foch at his headquarters at the chateau of Bombon. All clearly feel that the Allied forces now control the initiative on the Western Front. Foch asserts that their objective should be to eliminate all of the German salients and in particular to free the railway lines serving the areas north and northeast of Paris. He accepts Pershing's plan of attack against the Germans' Saint-Mihiel salient.

26 July 1918
Russia. A *coup d'etat* gives control of Baku to the Central Caspian Dictatorship, which plans the arrest of the local commissars. The commissars join about twelve hundred Red Guards in taking thirteen ships and sailing for Astrakhan, but the Caspian fleet, allied with the dictatorship, brings the escapees back for imprisonment.

28 July 1918
Amiens. Following up on his directive of 24 July calling for freeing the railway network surrounding Paris in order to ensure communication and transport between the northern and eastern sectors of the Western Front, Foch has instructed that all attacks to achieve this objective must occur at brief intervals and be unanticipated by the Germans. He awards command of a combined British-French attack near Amiens meant to further this plan to Gen. Douglas Haig. The attack itself falls to two armies: Gen. Sir Henry Rawlinson's Fourth Army positioned east of Amiens and Gen. Marie Debeney's First Army to the south of Rawlinson facing Montdidier. Haig and both field commanders will maintain strictest secrecy.

Aisne River. The Rainbow Division, trying to dislodge the Germans from positions on the Ourcq River, attacks the village of Sergy, which changes hands seven times during the day but finally falls to the Americans.

Palestine. Maj. T.E. Lawrence returns to Aqaba after visits to Jiddah, Cairo, and Allenby's headquarters to discuss plans for the fall offensive.

29 July 1918
Amiens. Haig makes known his goal: to push General von der Marwitz's Second Army back to a line between Morcourt and Hangest—a modest advance to be followed by pressing the Germans toward Chaulnes.

31 July 1918
Russia. Turkish troops reportedly occupy the heights above Baku, so the colonel has sailed on to Derbent with most of his men, planning to move in behind the Turks from the north.

Persia. Part of the brigade sent by General Marshall to defend Baku reaches Qazvin.

3 August 1918
Persia. Alarmed by reports of Turkish troops at Baku, General Dunsterville begins sending troops from his force by steamer from Bandar-e-Pahlavi to assist in the city's defense.
Russia. The Japanese land a division of troops at Vladivostok. They had previously landed troops on 5 April but only for a temporary stay. Now they plan to build a force in Siberia that will eventually total over seventy thousand troops.

5 August 1918
Russia. The first contingent of the troops sent by Marshall arrives in Baku.
Somme River. "Big Bertha" re-emerges. Sited in the Corbie Woods near Beaumont-en-Beine, the cannon begins a fourth period of shelling Paris, firing seventeen times on the city.

6 August 1918
Persia. Dunsterville sends a second contingent of troops to Baku, providing a total of 324 British soldiers to the city's defense.

7 August 1918
Marne River. After more than two weeks of attacks and counterattacks, the Allies have forced the Germans back to the front line of 27 March, and the Second Battle of the Marne reaches its end.

8 August 1918
Amiens. The Allied offensive begins as units of Rawlinson's Fourth Army, spearheaded by Australian and Canadian troops, go over the top at 4:20 A.M. behind a rolling barrage, taking the Germans completely by surprise. By 10:00 A.M., the Canadians push beyond Mézières and overrun German positions between Beaucourt and Cayeux, destroying entire regiments and artillery emplacements. By the end of the day, the Canadian and Australian troops have attained all of their objectives except for those on their right flank, where Debeney's troops move forward more slowly to the south of Mézières. The French fall short of reaching the Morcourt-Hangest line, but they advance six miles and take thirty-five hundred prisoners. British troops take over twelve thousand prisoners. Disarray afflicts Marwitz's army. Ludendorff refers to 8 August as "the black day of the German army." The war is at a turning point.

9 August 1918
Somme River. After five days of shelling, "Big Bertha" fires a final round into Paris that explodes in Aubervilliers. Falling back before the advancing Allies, the Germans dismantle the gun and haul it away to be carved up by acetylene torches.
Amiens. German troops reform, establishing a new line of defense. German air squadrons, among them Göring's, arrive from other sectors, overcoming British superiority in the air. German fire knocks out a third of the 145 British tanks still in combat—the British had fielded 414 tanks on the first day of battle. And so the British offensive begins to wind down, achieving a small advance. Debeney's First Army, however, encircles Montdidier from the south, forcing Hutier's Eighteenth Army troops to withdraw.

10 August 1918
Amiens. Debeney's troops capture Montdidier—or rather, the ruins of Montdidier—and push the Germans back toward Roye. Foch orders that the offensive continue, and Haig acquiesces, against Rawlinson's judgment. Haig orders Rawlinson to drive the Germans back to the Somme River and to establish bridgeheads on the river's north bank southward from Péronne.
La Ferte-sous-Jouarre. The United States First Army (soon to total 1.2 million men) officially comes into existence, with Pershing as commander. Col. George C. Marshall becomes chief of operations. Pershing issues orders to transfer the army's headquarters to Neufchâteau, where preparations will begin for an offensive against the Germans' salient at Saint-Mihiel, an operation Foch has awarded to the Americans.

Russia. American troops land at Vladivostok.

11 August 1918
Amiens. The offensive inches forward, thwarted by German counterattacks.
Avesnes, France. Meeting with Kaiser Wilhelm II at the kaiser's headquarters, the stress-plagued Ludendorff states his belief that the Allies now hold the balance of power and that "the war must be ended." He offers his resignation, but the kaiser rejects it.

12 August 1918
Amiens. The offensive pauses as both the British and the French take time to consolidate their positions and regroup their troops, preparatory to a resumption of their attacks. The French First and Third Armies have suffered 24,232 casualties; the British Fourth Army's casualties number 22,000. But Rawlinson's and Debeney's troops have inflicted over 75,000 casualties on Marwitz's and Hutier's armies, including close to 30,000 taken prisoner.
Spa, Belgium. The General Staff advises Kaiser Wilhelm II that no hope remains of effecting a decisive victory on the Western Front and that the Austrians are threatening to sue for peace. The kaiser concludes: "We have reached the limits of our physical endurance. The war must be ended."

14 August 1918
Spa. Despite the views voiced on 12 August, at a meeting of the Crown Council Ludendorff insists that Belgium and northern France can be held and used to impose Germany's will upon the Allies—a negotiated peace on his terms. Meanwhile, stepped-up propaganda at home will sustain the German people's support of the war. Ludendorff's view denies both the military reality on the Western Front and the economic reality within Germany.

15 August 1918
Sarcus, France. After receiving orders from Foch to have Rawlinson's Fourth Army begin an attack on 16 August against Hutier's positions on the Roye-Chaulnes line, Haig visits Foch's headquarters to reject the order, arguing that the attack would gain little ground while costing too many lives—apparently he has been persuaded by Rawlinson. Haig's counterplan is to have the British Third Army and subsequently the First Army attack along a line between Albert and Arras where he believes the terrain better lends itself to using tanks. Foch accepts this plan but shows his annoyance by taking command of the French First Army away from Haig.

16 August 1918
Russia. A final contingent of Marshall's troops arrives in Baku, bringing the Mesopotamian Force's representation in the city to 524 troops and 20 officers.

17 August 1918
Russia. British and Russian troops advance from their positions outside Baku with the intention of taking Novkhani across the peninsula to the north from Baku, but because of a communications failure, they have no artillery backup, and Turkish troops quickly outflank them and force their retreat. Seven Russians die and eight Russian and British troops are wounded.

19 August 1918
Russia. One hundred more British troops accompanied by three officers arrive at Baku.
Constantinople. A single RAF de Havilland bomber drops bombs and leaflets on the city.

21 August 1918
Aisne River. Mangin's Tenth Army troops push forward toward Chauny and Noyon.
Amiens. Gen. Sir Julian Byng's Third Army attacks north of Albert, capturing most of the first day's objectives.

22 August 1918
Amiens. Rawlinson's Fourth Army troops on the Ancre River join the offensive begun the day before by the Third Army and retake Albert, where they discover that the "Leaning Virgin" atop the local church's tower has toppled. The British Army harbors the superstition that the war will end soon after the statue falls.

Trans-Jordan. T.E. Lawrence arrives in El Azrac, where Feisal and his main army have assembled.

23 August 1918
Amiens-Aisne River. French and British armies attack along the entire front from Soissons to Arras. Although the French gain little, troops of Rawlinson's Australian Corps commanded by Lt. Gen. Sir John Monash smash ahead near Chuignes, where the retreating Germans leave behind a fifteen-inch caliber cannon they had used to shell Amiens—the largest weapon captured by the Allies in the war. Byng's troops also advance, approaching Bapaume.

24 August 1918
Portuguese East Africa. At Namarroe a column of *Schutztruppe* led by Capt. Erich Muller, to whom Lettow-Vorbeck delegates command with total trust, encounters a King's African Rifle column and drives it off, capturing two machine guns, forty thousand rounds of ammunition, and extensive supplies.

25 August 1918
Ludwigshafen, Germany. In one of the most daring air raids of the war, the Royal Air Force sends two Handley-Page bombers at night to bomb the Badische Anlin factory at Ludwigshafen. One of the planes descends to two hundred feet above the target to assure accuracy. Since winter weather began to lift in early March, the RAF has sent frequent and repeated bombing raids against German industrial cities. **Constantinople.** RAF de Havilland 9 bombers again return, bombing near the War Office and the railway station.

26 August 1918
Amiens. As ordered by Haig, Gen. Sir Henry Horne sends the Canadian Corps of his First Army into the offensive, striking to the southeast from Arras to menace the rear of the German troops fighting Byng's Third Army. They sweep ahead four miles. During the night Ludendorff issues orders for a general but timed withdrawal to a line extending from Péronne through Ham to Noyon.

Russia. The pilots of two planes sent from Qazvin have been flying reconnaissance over Baku and report that the Turks have assembled 12,500 troops for an assault on the Russian and British defensive positions. The assault begins a little after 10:00 A.M. at Volchi Vorota, a volcano northeast of the city where the defenders have dug in. Deterred only by machine-gun and rifle fire, the Turks manage to take the hill by one o'clock, but British troops later drive them off of Binagadi Hill, previously abandoned by Armenian troops. The British reinforce their positions at the Balajari railroad station, the initial goal of the Turkish assault that falls short because of heavy losses. Although outnumbered ten to one, the British suffer only fifty-two dead and forty-three wounded.
Black Sea. General Denikin's Volunteer Army captures the port city of Novorossisk, giving it access to the Black Sea and its supply lanes.

27 August 1918
Constantinople. RAF Camels and de Havilland 9s strafe and bomb Constantinople, Galata, and Nagara, attacking the airfields at the latter two sites.

30 August 1918
Somme River. The Australian Corps of Rawlinson's Fourth Army, following Marwitz's withdrawing troops, crosses the Somme River and establishes a base at Clery.

31 August 1918
Somme River. When Australian general Sir John Monash tells General Rawlinson that he plans to storm the German position on Mont Saint-Quentin—a hill just north of Péronne that commands approaches to the city held by five divisions and thought to be impregnable to frontal attack—the commander replies: "So you think that you are going to take Mont Saint-Quentin with three battalions. What presumption! However, I don't think I ought to stop you." At 5:00 A.M., one brigade of the Australian Corps, with only 1,320 men and officers, heads into the assault. By the end of the day, the highly capable and fearless Australians secure a foothold on the mountain.

At the same time, their comrades drive the Germans from the Bouchavesnes spur, also to the north of Péronne.

Sarcus. General Foch has proposed to Pershing that the troops of the AEF be divided and placed under the French Second and Fourth Armies for an offensive against the German positions at Mézières. Determined to maintain the independence of the AEF, Pershing has a letter delivered to Foch in which he concedes Foch's capacity to decide strategy as Allied commander in chief but insists: "Finally, however, there is one thing which must not be done and that is to disperse the American Forces amongst the Allied Armies; the danger of destroying by such dispersion the fine morale of the American soldier is too great, to say nothing of the results to be obtained by using the American Army as a whole." Foch finally capitulates and accepts Pershing's plan to send the American First Army against the Germans at Saint-Mihiel.

Russia. Following two days of shelling, the Turks attack British and Armenian positions at Stafford Hill, Warwick Castle, and Diga, outer defensive positions to the north of Baku, and capture all three.

Portuguese East Africa. Lettow-Vorbeck narrowly avoids disaster near Lioma when attacked by three King's African Rifle battalions. He loses twenty-nine of his European troops, seventeen of them dead, and two hundred askaris, plus forty-eight thousand rounds of ammunition and abundant supplies. But his men inflict such heavy losses on the British force that for a while Lettow-Vorbeck will be free to move without being hounded. He continues marching northward toward German East Africa.

1 September 1918
Somme River. Monash's Australian troops capture Péronne.
Russia. At Baku the Turks advance again, forcing the British to retreat to the railway and the Russians to fall back. Now poised to attack Baku itself, the Turks pause to await reinforcements to replace heavy losses. General Dunsterville, who had witnessed the fighting on Stafford Hill, warns the Baku dictators that he will withdraw his men unless their Russian and Arme-

nian troops muster an extraordinary effort to defend the city—although about six thousand strong, they have thus far faltered from poor organization and lack of will.

2 September 1918
Somme River. In the early morning, the Canadian Corps, the Royal Naval Division, and the Lowland Territorials of Horne's First Army break through the complex of concrete and barbed wire fortifications and the troops east of Arras comprising the Drocourt-Queant "switch line," the forwardmost link in the Hindenburg Line. This breakthrough suggests that this formidable barrier, constructed over many months and known to the Germans as the Siegfried Line, is not impregnable. In the early afternoon, Ludendorff accepts reality and issues orders for another general withdrawal, all the way to the Hindenburg Line in the southern sector of the Somme front. The gains achieved in March and April, including the salient won at the Battle of the Lys, will be abandoned. The British have advanced 14 miles, inflicting an estimated 115,600 casualties on the

A French infantryman battles at close range in the midst of barbed wire (by Georges Scott, courtesy of the Anne S.K. Brown Military Collection, Brown University Library)

Germans, including 46,241 taken prisoner. The victory has cost Haig 89,000 troops killed or wounded.

3 September 1918
Somme River. After 9:00 A.M., realizing that the Germans are withdrawing, the First and Third Armies move forward in their wake nearly to the Canal du Nord. Haig orders a pause for rest and reformation before undertaking an assault on the main Hindenburg Line.

4 September 1918
London. After meeting with General Guillaumat, who has come to London to persuade Lloyd George of the virtues of d'Esperey's plan for an attack against the Bulgarians in Macedonia, the prime minister gives his consent. (The Supreme War Council's subcommittee, to which the plan was referred on 3 July, recommended its approval on 3 August.)

8 September 1918
Meuse River. Ludendorff issues orders to withdraw from the Saint-Mihiel salient.

9 September 1918
Palestine. Gen. Sir Edmund Allenby, who was obliged to do little more than make raids during the spring and summer months because a contingent of his troops equal to five divisions was redeployed to the Western Front during Ludendorff's offensives, is ready to march again. His Egyptian Expeditionary Force (EEF) has been reformed and reinforced with Indian cavalry from France and 32 battalions from India; he now has 57,000 rifles, 12,000 sabres, 540 guns, and 350 machine guns. Opposing him are Turkish forces with 26,000 rifles, 3,000 sabres, 402 guns, and 600 machine guns, with 6,000 more troops in garrisons on the Hejaz railway. The numbers at the front are clearly in Allenby's favor, although reserve troops swell the Turks' total force in the Palestine-Syria region to a hundred thousand. Allenby issues orders for an offensive in the Jordan Valley whose initial objective is to drive the Turks out of Nablus, Samaria, Tulkarm, and Caesarea and to capture the railway lines connect-

ing Haifa, Jenin, and Afula. A major part of the offensive falls to the Desert Mounted Corps. To Feisal ibn-Hussein and his Arab army of eight thousand men, encamped about fifty miles east of Amman, Allenby assigns the task of destroying Turkish communications links to the north and west of Der'a as a means of forestalling Turkish reinforcements arriving from the north. Every effort is to be made to preserve secrecy everywhere because Allenby wants the advantage of total surprise.

10 September 1918
Salonika. General d'Esperey receives final approval from the Allied governments to pursue his plan for attacking the Bulgarians. Already at work on the preparations, he quickens the pace. Believing correctly that the Bulgarians will be expecting an offensive to proceed up the valley of the Vardar River, he instead has chosen to launch a surprise attack by Allied troops operating from bases in the rugged terrain of the seven-thousand-foot-high Moglenitsa Mountains, the border between Serbia and Greece.
Spa, Belgium. As the Western Front and German morale crumbles, Gen. Paul von Hindenburg tells the kaiser that Germany's need to negotiate an armistice is "immediate."

11 September 1918
Meuse River. Pershing has assembled American troops from throughout France to form his First Army for the Saint-Mihiel offensive. He has 216,000 men and an additional 48,000 French troops who will assist the attack by his left flank. The French have also provided 3,000 guns for the artillery barrage and 206 tanks, some with American crews. The Allies also have fifteen hundred aircraft for the offensive. Commanded by Col. William Mitchell, this air armada includes 609 planes piloted by Americans; the rest have French, British, Italian, and Portuguese pilots. Opposing this vast assemblage are only seventy-five thousand German troops.

12 September 1918
Somme River. New Zealand troops of Byng's Third Army attack Hindenburg

American artillerymen fire their French-made field gun in fighting in the Saint-Mihiel salient in September 1918. Most American units were equipped with French artillery (Library of Congress)

Line positions at Havrincourt, southeast of Cambrai, and attain control of the outer fortifications. Haig wishes to take such German outposts to provide observation points from which to overlook and study the Hindenburg Line preparatory to a large-scale assault on its main fortification.

Meuse River. At 1:00 A.M., the Allied artillery opens fire, blasting the Germans' frontline trenches as well as the rearward defenses and artillery emplacements while rain drenches the battlefield. After four hours, the artillery shifts to a creeping barrage, and the American and French troops and tanks swarm forward into no-man's-land, the Americans thrusting forward from the southeast and the French from the west. They advance rapidly, finding the Germans' front trenches abandoned—the withdrawal ordered by Ludendorff had already begun. From the southeast, the Americans race ahead, reaching their first and, in some areas, their second goals by the end of the day, forming a bulging line running from Nonsard to Xammes and eastward beyond Thiaucourt. Attacking from the northwest,

the Yankee Division encounters stiff resistance, however, as the Germans had not begun to withdraw from that part of the salient. Their progress is slow, although they manage to open a narrow salient toward Vigneulles.

13 September 1918

Meuse River. Realizing that the Germans have an escape route between the American pincers moving toward each other from the southeast and northwest, Pershing has ordered the advancing troops to make haste. Units of the Yankee Division capture Vigneulles in the early morning. By 6:00 A.M., troops of the IVth Corps from the southeast link up with them, closing the escape route while simultaneously eliminating the German Saint-Mihiel salient. In the air, Capt. Eddie Rickenbacker tangles with Richthofen's Flying Circus, downing one Fokker (his sixth kill) and escaping attack by three others. Pershing's First Army now controls the Saint-Mihiel sector at a line from Haudiomont to Vandieres that confronts and overlooks the

Germans' Michel Line, a defensive position in front of the Hindenburg Line that the Germans feverishly labor to complete before the expected resumption of the American advance. But the Americans have reached Foch's goal and are obliged to stop. Their victory costs 7,000 casualties but reaps 15,000 German prisoners and 450 guns.

14 September 1918
Russia. The nearly two-week pause has allowed Dunsterville and the Baku dictators to strengthen the city's defenses, and their garrison is augmented by the arrival of six hundred of Bicherakov's men following their victory at Petrovsk. Reconnaissance flights indicate that the Turkish force menacing the city has swollen to fourteen thousand infantry and five hundred cavalry with forty guns. At 9:00 A.M., the Turks advance, with their main thrust directed against British and Armenian positions at Wolf's Gap to the west of the city. A second thrust drives against the defenses at Balajari. Although counterattacks initially hold the Turks, their numbers prove too great. At 4:00 P.M., Dunsterville, with the agreement of the dictators, orders his men to slowly withdraw to three ships waiting in the harbor and evacuate Baku. The Turks move artillery into place and shell the city. The dictators change their minds and order Dunsterville, already aboard ship with his men, either to remain or have his ships attacked. Dunsterville ignores the order. Although attacked by a guard ship, the troop carriers escape and arrive safely at Bandar-e-Pahlavi.
Macedonia. General d'Esperey's offensive begins with an artillery bombardment by five hundred guns along a line from Monastir to the Vardar River, convincing German commander Gen. Friedrich von Scholtz that the attack will occur at Monastir, so he sends reinforcements there.
Meuse-Argonne. The first units of Pershing's First Army, which are being redeployed to the Argonne sector, arrive there to begin preparations for continuing the Allied offensive. Altogether five hundred thousand men of the First Army will assemble for the Argonne attack.

15 September 1918
Macedonia. At 5:30 A.M., the Allied offensive begins, with Serbian and French troops at the center of the front heading toward the Crna River and capturing a strong Bulgarian redoubt on a peak called Sokol. The Bulgarians resist fiercely, sending repeated counterattacks against the Allies.

16 September 1918
Persia. At Bandar-e-Pahlavi, General Dunsterville receives orders from General Marshall to return to Baghdad.
Serbia. Serbian troops capture the summit of Kozyak Mountain.
Palestine. RAF planes bomb Der'a, and Arab raiders led by Maj. T.E. Lawrence destroy a section of the railway linking Der'a with Amman.
Washington. President Wilson receives a note from the Austro-Hungarian government passed on by Swedish emissaries suggesting that a "confidential non-binding conversation" be held in a neutral nation to discuss peace terms. Unimpressed, the president responds at once: "The United States will entertain no proposal for a conference upon a matter concerning which it has made its position and purpose so plain."

17 September 1918
Serbia. After receiving reports that his troops have forged a six-mile-deep salient on a twenty-mile front in two days of fighting, d'Esperey orders Milne to send his British and Greek troops into the battle on the salient's right flank in the sector just to the east of Lake Dojran to compound the pressure on the Bulgarians. Alarmed by the Allies' incursion, General von Scholtz asks Field Marshal Paul von Hindenburg to send a German division to shore up the Bulgarian defense, but Hindenburg's focus is on the Western Front. Scholtz orders a withdrawal and tries to muster a defense that will prevent the Franco-Serbian troops from capturing Gradsko and its supply depot, which would bisect the German and Bulgarian forces.
Palestine. Lawrence and his men blow up a section of the railway between Der'a and Damascus, and Feisal's troops take

Muzeirib. Gen. Otto Liman von Sanders, German commander of the Turkish forces, dispatches reserve troops from Haifa to relieve Der'a.

18 September 1918
Somme River. The British Third and Fourth Armies attack along a seven-mile front centering on Epehy. Monash's Australian Corps drives ahead three miles, capturing five thousand German prisoners and seventy-six guns.

Serbia. British and Greek troops attack, but while the Greeks take the village of Dojran, the British fail totally in their efforts to dislodge the Bulgarians from the hills above Lake Dojran.

Palestine. During the night, two of Allenby's brigades secure a foothold in the watershed of the Judean Hills opposite the Wadi es Sarnieh—the first step in Allenby's offensive.

19 September 1918
Somme River. On the basis of the previous week's successes in puncturing the Hindenburg Line, Field Marshal Haig advises Marshal Foch that his armies will be prepared for a general offensive against the Hindenburg Line on 26 September. This offensive will extend along virtually the entire Western Front, the two hundred miles between the Meuse River and Flanders. Since beginning their counteroffensive on 8 August, the combined British armies have advanced an average of about twenty-five miles along a forty-mile front, and they have taken fifty thousand prisoners. British casualties number 180,000—grievous but far less than the horrendous losses suffered on the Somme front in 1916.

Serbia. The British renew the attack on the hills at Lake Dojran and fail again, suffering a second day of heavy casualties. Pleased with their success in this sector, the Bulgarians propose a counteroffensive that will drive all the way to Salonika, but the Germans object on the grounds that such an attack would take the Bulgarians dangerously beyond their defensive positions. Gen. Kuno von Steuben suggests a gradual retreat along the Crna River that would lure the French and Serbian troops

farther into the mountains, where the Bulgarians can attack and destroy their flanks. The Bulgarian commanders accept this idea.

Palestine. Beginning at 4:30 A.M., Allenby's artillery shells the Turkish positions on a front from the Judean Hills to Qalqiliya. RAF planes bomb Nablus, Tulkarm, and the telephone exchange at Afula, destroying communications between Tulkarm and Nazareth. Allenby's troops charge the surprised Turks, taking their front lines and sweeping ahead to capture Jiljiliya and Qalqiliya and to swing past and above Tulkarm to close off the retreating Turks' escape route, already the target of RAF bombing and strafing. By 5:00 P.M., Allenby's troops have captured Tulkarm station, seven thousand Turkish prisoners, and a hundred guns.

20 September 1918
Serbia. German and Bulgarian troops between the Crna River and Lake Dojran begin to fall back, but the Bulgarian troops in the hills at Dojran express dismay at being ordered to leave their strong defensive positions, occupied later in the day by British and Greek troops. RAF bombers spot the retreating Bulgarians in the ravines alonside the Strumica Road and wreak havoc on both men and transports. Abandoning arms and supplies, the Bulgarian troops flee into the mountains.

Palestine. At 5:30 A.M., the Thirteenth Cavalry Brigade of Allenby's EEF enters Nazareth, site of Liman von Sanders's headquarters, which the brigade attacks. While the Germans on Liman von Sanders's staff engage the British troops in street fighting, the general escapes. The cavalry takes fifteen hundred prisoners and leaves the city. British troops capture Afula at 8:00 A.M. Later in the day, Australian cavalry take Jenin and El Lajjun. Beyt Shean also falls to the British, who by day's end hold the entire coastal plain south of Nazareth.

21 September 1918
Palestine. RAF planes bomb and strafe Turkish troops retreating from Nablus along the Wadi Far'a, sending them into flight. The Thirteenth Cavalry Brigade re-

turns to occupy Nazareth; other cavalry brigades capture Nablus.

22 September 1918
Serbia. Advancing Serbian troops reach the Vardar River. French troops, supported by Greek and Italian troops, push ahead to the northeast of Monastir. General d'Esperey orders "unceasing and resolute pursuit" of the retreating German and Bulgarian troops, with cavalry units to take the lead in the advance.
Palestine. British troops capture the Jisr ed Darniya and four thousand retreating Turks who enter Beyt Shean.

23 September 1918
Serbia. A French colonial cavalry unit composed of Moroccan horsemen leaves from Novak with orders from d'Esperey to take Prilep and thereafter to advance all the way to Skopje on the upper Vardar River and capture it.
Palestine. Allenby's cavalry captures Haifa and Acre. By now the Turkish Seventh and Eighth Armies (the former commanded by Mustapha Kemal), which formed the central opposition to Allenby's advance, in effect no longer exist.

25 September 1918
Meuse River. Prowling alone in his Spad over the Toul sector and Verdun, Lieutenant Rickenbacker spots two German photographic planes escorted by five Fokkers. He shoots down two of the Fokkers and returns safely to base. It is his first day as a squadron commander.
Serbia. A Serbian cavalry unit captures Gradsko. British troops cross the border into Bulgaria.
Palestine. During the night, Australian cavalry capture Samakh near the Sea of Galilee. They find 100 dead Germans and take 364 prisoners, but lose 78 men in hand-to-hand fighting. On the far east sector of the initial front, the British capture Amman.

26 September 1918
Palestine. The British VIIIth Corps, having taken Amman the day before, pushes on twelve miles to the northeast and captures Zarqa Station. At Jenin, Allenby con-

fers with his corps commanders and orders continuation of the advance. The next objectives are Damascus and Beirut.
Argonne. The French Fourth Army, commanded by Gen. Henri Gouraud, and the American First Army, commanded by General Pershing, begin the planned resumption of the Allied offensive, attacking General von Gallwitz's Fifth Army on a front between the Aisne River and Haumont that falls nearly in its entirety to the Americans. The American attack, launched with three hundred thousand troops, centers on the Argonne Forest. It opens with a three-hour artillery barrage beginning at 5:30 A.M. Although impeded by many felled trees in the forest, Pershing's troops surge forward in a misty rain well beyond the Michel Line while bypassing Montfaucon, sited on a hill and highly fortified by the Germans. Lt. Col. George S. Patton's tank brigade accompanies them.
Cambrai. Haig has his troops in readiness on a front from Saint-Quentin to Bullecourt—forty British and two American divisions. Opposing them, however, are fifty-seven German divisions on the Hindenburg Line. During the night, the British begin their preliminary shelling of the German positions. Near Saint-Quentin it will continue for fifty-four hours.

27 September 1918
Palestine. The Tenth Cavalry Brigade takes Irbid after the Turkish Fourth Army, still numbering five thousand, withdraws during the night following skirmishing. The Australian Mounted Division that captured Samakh now takes Er Ramtha, southwest of Der'a. Feisal's troops head off the retreating Turkish Fourth Army at Sheikh Saad, capturing a sizable number.
Meuse-Argonne. While forging ahead and extending their two-day advance to seven miles, Pershing's troops also occupy Montfaucon. But German counterattacks slow the Americans' progress.
Cambrai. Following eight hours of artillery shelling, including mustard gas, at the Cambrai sector, Horne's First Army and Byng's Third Army attack the dazed troops of Quast's Sixth Army and Marwitz's Second. They surge across the Canal du Nord

and smash through the Hindenburg Line, advancing to within three miles of Cambrai. **New York City.** Trying to prevent a traditional peace settlement that entails alliances, territorial aggrandizement, and arms competition, Woodrow Wilson addresses an audience of five thousand war bond sellers in the Metropolitan Opera House and assures them that, while the Allies cannot compromise with the discredited governments of the Central Powers, nevertheless the peace must afford "impartial justice in every item of the settlement, no matter whose interest is crossed; and not only impartial justice, but also satisfaction of the several peoples whose fortunes are dealt with." Desiring to prevent a return to nationalisms, trade wars, and other traditional barriers to a long-standing peace, Wilson declares: "No special or separate interest of any single nation or any group of nations can be made the basis of any part of the settlement which is not consistent with the common interest of all." The vital tool to ensure such a peace, Wilson asserts, is the League of Nations; and the league's constitution and statement of objectives "is in a sense the most essential part, of the peace settlement itself." The league would embrace no political or economic "special covenants and understandings"—the ma-jor source, in his view, of modern wars. Wilson invites responses to his statement from other Allied leaders.

28 September 1918
Meuse-Argonne. Thirteen artillery batteries brought forward by the Germans pound American units in the Argonne Forest. Rains render supply roads nearly impassable, and the American assault falters.
Flanders. A third front of the Allies' general offensive erupts as the entire Belgian army, commanded by King Albert and supported by British and French forces, surges forward to capture Houthulst Forest and Passchendaele.
Spa. In the presence of his astonished staff, Ludendorff, thoroughly exasperated and distraught, vents his frustration in a diatribe of self-defense and accusation—heaping invective on the kaiser for weakness, on the German people for cowardice, and on the Imperial Navy for an inadequate U-boat campaign. During the night, still overwrought, he visits Hindenburg and tells him that the war is lost and that Germany has no choice but to relinquish the conquered areas of France and Belgium and pursue a peace based on Wilson's Fourteen Points, which, in fact, he has not read. Hindenburg agrees.

Soldiers of the small Belgian army on duty in the tiny sliver of the Western Front they occupied during the war (by Jean Berne-Bellecour, courtesy of the Anne S.K. Brown Military Collection, Brown University Library)

Portuguese East Africa. With many of his men suffering from influenza, some falling behind to face death or capture, Lettow-Vorbeck has determinedly pushed on. He crosses the Rovuma River, reentering the home territory of German East Africa near Nagwamira. His men kill eight hippopotamuses for the evening's dinner.

Palestine. The Tenth Cavalry takes Der'a. Their orders are to link up with Feisal's troops and march to Damascus.

29 September 1918
Saint-Quentin. After hammering the German positions for two days with shells and gas, Rawlinson's Fourth Army and units of Debeney's First Army, joined by two American divisions, launch the fourth assault of the Allies' offensive. They breach the Hindenburg Line, advance three and a half miles, and capture forty-two hundred prisoners and seventy guns.

Serbia. The French Moroccan cavalry brigade advances on Skopje, now the headquarters of Scholtz and his staff. Bulgarian soldiers in the town quickly surrender while the Germans resist, but by 9:00 A.M. the cavalry controls the town. In the evening, news of Skopje's surrender reaches Salonika, where d'Esperey is already discussing terms of an armistice with Bulgarian officials. The news jolts the Bulgarians and hardens d'Esperey's position. He demands use of Bulgarian railways to transport his troops as part of the armistice concluded during the night.

Spa. Secretary of State for Foreign Affairs Adm. Paul von Hintze, supported by Ludendorff's and Hindenburg's own subordinates, submits proposals for Germany to seek an armistice. Finally accepting reality, Ludendorff and Hindenburg agree to his proposals, as the kaiser does also later in the day. Wilhelm II says simply: "The war is finished, though differently than we had thought."

30 September 1918
Saint-Quentin. American troops extend their advance beyond Nauroy but suffer huge casualties near Bony, where they are attacked from the rear by German troops emerging from tunnels they had failed to

mop up in their headlong charge. The 107th Regiment loses over half its men.

Flanders. Momentum remains with the successful Allied advance commanded by Haig, with 39,000 German troops and 380 guns captured.

Salonika. The armistice signed by the Bulgarians and by d'Esperey for the Allies takes effect at noon, freeing the "Armies of the Orient" to take control of Bulgaria and Serbia, to advance from Serbia into Austria-Hungary, or to attack Turkey, the main target of the largest contingent in the British Salonika Army.

Palestine. British cavalry engage Turkish troops at Kau Kab and Kiswe, only ten miles south of Damascus.

Spa, Belgium. Georg von Hertling submits his resignation as chancellor to Kaiser Wilhelm II. Pressed by his advisers, who are concerned by deteriorating political and economic conditions at home, the kaiser grants a form of parliamentary government to the German people in an effort to save his throne.

1 October 1918
Syria. The Third Australian Light Cavalry of General Allenby's army enters Damascus at dawn. Soon afterwards T.E. Lawrence and his Arab troops arrive in the city. The Battle of Megiddo—a stunning British success—concludes with twenty thousand Turkish prisoners held in Damascus and the three Turkish armies defending Palestine reduced to an unarmed mob.

Flanders. Mud generated by continuing rains slows the Allies' attack at the northern sector of the front to a halt short of the Roulers-Menin line. To date the Belgian, British, and French troops have captured 11,000 prisoners and 350 guns.

2 October 1918
Meuse-Argonne. The men of the "Lost Battalion" of the Seventy-seventh Division, who have been cut off for three days, strike out toward the valley of Charlevaux seeking contact with other American units. They discover themselves completely surrounded by German troops and machine-gun sites.

Berlin. An emissary sent by Ludendorff presents an appraisal of Germany's mili-

The battlefields and trench lines in Flanders were turned into muddy morasses by rain. A British field artillery company attempts to drag its gun free by the most elemental methods. (Library of Congress)

tary posture to the *Reichstag*, informing the members that there is no hope of forcing the Allies to sue for peace. He insists, however, that the army can endure for months and achieve local victories. He concludes with the admonition that the nation must stand firm "to give evidence that a firm will to carry on the war exists, if the enemy will grant us no peace, or a peace only under humiliating conditions." Members of the *Reichstag* listen, thunderstruck. Friedrich Ebert, leader of the SPD, sits afterwards in stunned silence.

3 October 1918

Syria. With order returned to Damascus through Lawrence's efforts, General Allenby arrives in the city to confer with Feisal, who arrives shortly after the general. Allenby informs Feisal that the French will exercise civil jurisdiction over Syria and that a French liaison officer will be assigned to his army, to which Feisal strenuously objects. Allenby reminds Feisal that he is still a subordinate in Allenby's command and must carry out orders—the political discussion will have to await the end of the war. He instructs Feisal to prepare his army to continue their advance, and Feisal leaves. Lawrence informs Allenby that he cannot work with a French liaison officer and requests a leave, which Allenby grants. The Arab Revolt is over.

Berlin. The liberal Prince Maximilian of Baden, who has for several months been writing letters to Crown Prince Rupprecht arguing that Kaiser Wilhelm II must abdicate to save Germany from disaster, becomes chancellor. His first act, actually instigated by Ludendorff, is to send a note to Pres. Woodrow Wilson accepting the Fourteen Points and the principles discussed in Wilson's address in New York on 27 September as "a basis for the peace negotiations."

4 October 1918

Syria. Advancing up the Mediterranean coast from Haifa, the Meerut Division of Allenby's army occupies Tyre.

6 October 1918

Meuse-Argonne. The "Lost Battalion's" commander, Maj. Charles W. Whittlesey, has sent out runners—all killed by the Germans. He has four carrier pigeons, sending them homeward one at a time with details of his position, now under friendly fire by American artillery. The fourth pigeon, though struck and wounded three times by German bullets, gets through. A runner sent with a map of the "Lost Battalion's" position also gets through, and relief troops move to the rescue.

Syria. The Meerut Division enters Sidon.

Washington. Wilson receives Prince Max's note and seeks Colonel House's counsel on how to respond. The colonel opposes making a direct reply.

Zagreb. Serbo-Croatian and Slovenian leaders proclaim Yugoslavia united.

7 October 1918

Washington. Wilson receives a note from the Austrian government proposing an armistice and negotiation of a peace settlement based on the president's publicly stated principles.

8 October 1918

Argonne. German machine-gun units pin down a platoon of sixteen American troops attacking near Chatel-Chehery, killing six, wounding three, and leaving Cpl. Alvin York in command. Leaving his men to guard their prisoners, York heads out alone. York kills over two dozen soldiers of the German battalion pinning down his men, first using his rifle and then his service revolver. He returns with the entire German battalion—132 men, with 35 machine guns—as prisoners.

Washington. Learning of Prince Max's note, Theodore Roosevelt, some senators, and some newspapers call for "unconditional surrender." Advised by House and Lansing that his reply to Prince Max must placate the American public's war sentiments and feelings of hardness toward Germany, Wilson responds with a note of inquiry that probes the Germans' intentions and sincerity.

Syria. The Meerut Division captures Beirut.

9 October 1918

Versailles. Allied leaders confer on the

American soldiers relax at a Red Cross frontline canteen in the fall of 1918 (Library of Congress)

content of Wilson's response to Prince Max and draft a note to the president warning of German duplicity and requesting him to send a representative to Paris to explain American policy. Both Lloyd George and Clemenceau are piqued that the Germans' initial peace overture has gone to Wilson.

10 October 1918
Meuse-Argonne. Though their progress has been painstakingly slow, the Americans now have control of the Argonne Forest.

12 October 1918
Souilly, France. General Pershing, who has decided that the First Army has become unwieldy in size and ordered creation of a Second Army, turns over field command of the First Army to Gen. Hunter Liggett.
New York City. Wilson, while in New York to participate in a Columbus Day parade, receives word of Prince Max's response to his note of inquiry. The prince assures the president that he speaks not just for the government but for "the German people" and that Germany is ready to evacuate occupied Belgium and France. He suggests a "mixed commission" to prepare for the evacuation.

13 October 1918
Syria. Allenby's troops occupy Tripoli.

14 October 1918
Washington. Wilson publicly releases his response to Prince Max's second note. With an eye on American opinion, he takes a hard stand: all submarine warfare must cease, Germany must define the nature of its government, the Allies' military superiority must be preserved, Allied military advisers will decide the process of evacuating France and Belgium.
Argonne. In a daring raid, a battalion of the American 126th Infantry captures ten German machine-gun emplacements, opening the way to conquest of the Côte Dame Marie just south of Romagne. During the night, the Americans discover that the Germans have evacuated the position.

16 October 1918
Meuse-Argonne. American troops finally

achieve the objective Pershing had set for the first day of the offensive (26 September). They reach a line from Grandpre to just north of Cunel and Brieulles, having crossed the Germans' Kriemhilde Line. Liggett now assumes command of the First Army.

18 October 1918
Mesopotamia. Ordered on 1 October to attack the Turks at Mosul, General Marshall sends a corps of the Mesopotamian Expeditionary Force with two cavalry brigades and armored cars to make the assault.
New York City. Colonel House sails for Paris.
Washington. Masaryk publishes a Czechoslovak Declaration of Independence designed to appeal to American public opinion.

19 October 1918
Flanders. General Plumer's Second Army, serving with King Albert, crosses the Lys River and prepares to advance toward the Scheldt River.
Washington. In response to an Austrian note received on 7 October, Wilson sends a note to Vienna pointing out that among the Fourteen Points is a guarantee of autonomy to the peoples of the Habsburg Empire.

20 October 1918
Washington. Wilson receives a response from Prince Max protesting charges of Germany's being inhumane, but accepting the idea that military advisers determine the evacuation process and giving assurances that the German government truly represents the German people.
Mitilini, Lesbos, Greece. Maj. Gen. Sir Charles Townshend, commander of the defeated army at Kut and since then a prisoner of war, has been released by the Turks to serve as their emissary to ask for surrender terms. The triumvirate that had ruled Turkey—Enver Pasha, Talaat Pasha, and Djevad Pasha—has escaped across the Black Sea in a German ship, and Izzet Pasha has put together an interim cabinet whose only objective is peace. They have sent out Townshend, who now boards HMS *Agamemnon,* the flagship of the Brit-

"Over the Top": the defining moment of World War I on the Western Front when infantrymen (in this case Americans) launch an assault from their trench line across no-man's-land (Library of Congress)

ish commander in the Mediterranean, Adm. Sir Somerset Gough-Calthorpe.

23 October 1918
Turkey. A unit of Allenby's Desert Mounted Corps, having traversed 550 miles in 38 days, arrives at Aleppo and demands surrender of the Turkish garrison. Mustapha Kemal, commander of the garrison and what remains of his Seventh Army, refuses.
Washington. Wilson responds to Prince Max's note of 20 October by demanding an end to military control of Germany and acceptance of his terms for peace. He expresses distrust of those who have been deciding German policies and asserts that the United States would prefer to deal with a "constitutional" government in Germany.

24 October 1918
Piave River. Under political pressure to ensure that Italy ends the war in a favorable position, General Diaz has reluctantly

ordered a final offensive centered on the Piave and Mount Grappa. His goal is to split the Austrian forces in the Trentino from those on the Piave by creating a salient extending toward Vittorio Veneto and beyond. The Italians' artillery barrage begins at 5:00 A.M. Flooding on the Piave has forced Diaz to make the Grappa his main focus, rather than the Piave as intended. The attack goes poorly.

25 October 1918
Turkey. Arab troops who have joined Allenby's troops outside Aleppo enter the city during the night and engage the Turks in street fighting. The Turks withdraw.

26 October 1918
Turkey. The Desert Mounted Corps unit enters Aleppo. At Haritan, Indian troops skirmish with Mustapha Kemal's rear guard but retire. The Turks withdraw, and the British advance halts. During the advance, the Desert Mounted Corps has taken

47,000 prisoners, while experiencing only 533 battle casualties, including 125 dead. The Egyptian Expeditionary Force's campaign as a whole has captured 75,000 prisoners, including 200 German and Austrian officers and 3,500 troops; they also have seized 360 guns and destroyed 400 more. Allenby's tactics, especially the use of cavalry, achieve an exceptional victory.

Mesopotamia. After three days of fighting, the British defeat the Turks at Al Fathah and continue their advance toward Mosul.

Paris. Colonel House arrives in the French capital to discover that Clemenceau and Lloyd George, although both annoyed that Wilson has assumed the role of peace broker without consulting them, still anticipate the president's fulfilling the responsibilities of that role. Clemenceau provides House with Foch's recommended terms for an armistice.

Mitilini, Lesbos. Representatives of the Turkish cabinet arrive to negotiate a peace settlement with Admiral Gough-Calthorpe, empowered by the British cabinet to conduct discussions.

Spa. Outraged that Ludendorff has issued an order describing Wilson's armistice proposals as "unacceptable," Kaiser Wilhelm II summons the commander and accepts his resignation. Gen. Wilhelm Groner replaces Ludendorff in the position of first quartermaster general. Hindenburg remains to ensure needed continuity—politics forbids sacking both commanders, as public dismay might become unmanageable.

27 October 1918

Washington. Wilson receives another note from Germany informing him that the current government is in control, including control of the military, accepts his terms, and awaits "proposals for an armistice."

Wilhelmshaven. Units of the High Seas Fleet leave harbor destined for a rendezvous near the island of Wangerooge at the entrance to the Jade Basin, where Admiral Scheer has ordered the entire fleet to assemble for a final battle with the Grand Fleet—"a glorious end, even though it be a fight to the death," in the words of Adm. Adolf von Trotha. But with the war clearly

lost, the sailors view the plan not as glorious, but suicidal. Passive resistance spreads among the crews as the fleet converges on Wangerooge.

Piave River. After three days of attacks by the Italians at the Grappa, the Austrians counterattack, and this sector of the front settles into stalemate.

Meuse-Argonne. After nearly two weeks of fierce fighting, sometimes hand-to-hand, American troops finally gain control of Grandpre.

28 October 1918

Piave River. Diaz's focus now centers on the Piave, where his Eighth Army comes into full play.

Vienna. After informing Kaiser Wilhelm II of his intentions, Emperor Karl sends an appeal to Pres. Woodrow Wilson to intervene immediately to secure an armistice for Austria-Hungary without waiting for Germany to begin negotiations.

Spa. Kaiser Wilhelm II signs amendments transforming the Reich from a constitutional monarchy to a parliamentary monarchy.

29 October 1918

Washington. Wilson presents to the cabinet a note from the Austrian government accepting all of his conditions for a peace settlement and urging him to arrange immediate preparations for an armistice.

Jade Basin. Crews take control of their battleships, and the units of the High Seas Fleet already assembled near Wangerooge stay put. Red flags fly over two of them.

Piave River. The Austrians surrender. The Battle of Vittorio Veneto, a final futile struggle, has cost the Austrians 30,000 dead and 427,000 taken prisoner. Diaz's forces have paid a toll as well—40,000 casualties.

30 October 1918

Mesopotamia. Marshall's troops defeat the Turks at Ash Sharqat and Qayyarah on their march to Mosul. The Turkish Sixth Army disintegrates, and its commander surrenders. Since the offensive against Mosul began, the British have taken 11,500 prisoners and 51 guns.

Paris. Lloyd George and Clemenceau request from Colonel House a detailed explanation of the Fourteen Points. As the war winds down, they begin to object to some of Wilson's principles, Lloyd George being especially opposed to Point Two, freedom of the seas.

Mitilini, Lesbos. Aboard HMS *Agamemnon,* Admiral Gough-Calthorpe and Turkish envoys sign an armistice to take effect at noon the following day. Terms of the armistice provide for occupation of the Dardanelles and Bosporus forts by the Allies, clearing away of all mines to give access to the Black Sea, surrender of all Turkish war ships, demobilization of the Turkish army, freeing of all prisoners, and evacuation of all Germans and Austrians. Outside the boundaries of Turkey itself, the Ottoman Empire, most of its external lands already occupied by Allied armies, ceases to exist. Defeated Turkey's overall losses in the war total 2,920,000 men, including 325,000 dead.

31 October 1918
Mesopotamia. The armistice with Turkey takes effect at noon.

Budapest. Radicals led by Count Mihaly Karolyi seize control of the government and declare Hungary an independent republic.

Jade Basin. Marines arrest over a thousand crewmen of the High Seas Fleet after they have defied the order to leave port five times. But with reduced crews, the fleet cannot sail, and the commanders order the squadrons to return to disparate harbors. During the night the Third Squadron, manned by over twenty-five thousand sailors, arrives in the harbor at Kiel.

Vienna. In the name of Emperor Karl, Archduke Josef appoints Mihaly Karolyi, leader of the Independent Party, as premier. Count Istvan Tisza, former premier of Hungary, is assassinated.

1 November 1918
Meuse-Argonne. Marshal Foch has ordered a full-scale renewal of the Allied offensive on the entire Western Front. Pershing has set Sedan, twenty-five miles to the north, as the center of the First Army's advance. The American artillery begins the new offensive with a barrage that

starts at 3:30 A.M. Two hours later, the infantry moves out over an eighteen-mile front, the center and right entering open countryside and the left attacking into the Loges Wood. On part of the front, the Americans advance five miles by day's end. During the night, the Germans, who had already planned to fall back to the Meuse River, evacuate Loges Wood and Champigneulle.

Austria-Hungary. French units of General d'Esperey's army capture Belgrade, and d'Esperey now plans to advance to Budapest, Vienna, and eventually Berlin.

Padua. Delegates from Austria-Hungary and the Allied nations sign an armistice.

Meuse-Argonne. The American drive continues, taking another seven miles of land from the Germans.

3 November 1918
Meuse-Argonne. During the night, American troops march to the north of Belval Wood behind German positions, capturing withdrawing German troops as they go.

Kiel, Germany. After the Third Squadron's officers refuse to meet with representatives of the sailors, who demand release of the arrested men, and deny all the sailors the right to convene, three thousand Kiel men and women demonstrate in support of the sailors. When the demonstrators begin to march toward the center of the city, a military patrol stops them and orders their dispersal. They refuse the order, and the patrol fires. Eight demonstrators fall dead and twenty eight are wounded.

4 November 1918
Argonne. Although encountering stiffer resistance and taking increased losses from the Germans as their retreat approaches the Meuse River, the Americans continue the push, capturing Beaufort.

Cambrai. The renewed offensive in the British sector of the front begins, with Byng's Third Army and Rawlinson's Fourth Army crossing the Sambre Canal and reaching the Mormal Forest.

Kiel. During the night, sailors form councils, disarm officers, and take control of their ships, raising red flags and liberating the sailors arrested in Kiel. They disseminate demands, including abdication of the Hohenzollerns, release of arrested sailors and political prisoners, and universal suffrage for both men and women.

5 November 1918

Meuse-Argonne. Recognizing the emotional value that the French attach to Sedan, where they surrendered to the Germans in 1870, the American First Army has shifted slightly to the east to let the French Fourth Army enter the city first. Even so, the Americans' more rapid advance brings them near the city ahead of the French, and Pershing, wanting to prove the quality of his army, gives orders for the First Army to take Sedan.

Kiel. The sailors' mutiny wins support as workers organized by the Social Democratic Party call a general strike.

Washington. The Republican Party captures both houses of Congress in the elections. In the Senate, they have a margin of two; in the House, a margin of forty-four—a setback for President Wilson as peacemaker.

6 November 1918

Meuse-Argonne. American troops reach the Meuse River and are within five miles of Sedan.

Germany. By evening, mutinous sailors control Lubeck, Hamburg, Cuxhaven, Bremen, Bremerhaven, Wilhelmshaven, and the garrisoned towns in Schleswig-Holstein. As the rebellion spreads, SPD and USPD representatives try to organize the sailors.

Northern Rhodesia. Encountering major opposition near Songea and realizing that it will only increase, Lettow-Vorbeck has headed west out of German East Africa in mid-October. He left behind his sick and wounded, including the courageous but ill Gen. Kurt Wahle, and passed to the north of Lake Nyasa and entered Northern Rhodesia. He has fallen back from Fife, which he had hoped to capture but found too strongly defended by police and volunteers, and now reaches Kajambi on the Chambeshi River.

7 November 1918

Meuse-Argonne. Trying to beat other units to Sedan, the First Infantry Division night-marches toward the city, crossing the positions of two Ist corps units, one of them MacArthur's Forty-second Division, and thus generating turmoil and confusion. The French protest, leading to a reprimand.

Germany. Rebellious sailors reach Cologne; the insurrection spreads in the Rhineland. In Berlin, sailors arrest seventeen hundred troops arriving to preserve order; Socialist leaders and *Reichstag* members call for Kaiser Wilhelm II's abdication and Crown Prince Wilhelm's renunciation of the throne. In Munich, Kurt Eisner, a pacifist leader of the Socialists, announces the end of the Bavarian throne and creation of the "Bavarian Free State."

8 November 1918

Meuse-Argonne. The American Forty-second Division takes the Meuse River heights above Sedan, gaining control over the rail lines into the city. But the Americans halt, allowing the French Fourth Army to enter Sedan first.

Flanders. The British Fifth Army crosses the Scheldt River, and the First Army approaches Mons.

London and Paris. In a final effort to placate the Arabs, the British and French governments issue a joint declaration supporting "emancipation" of the peoples formerly ruled by Turkey and "establishment of national governments and administrations deriving their authority from the initiative and free choice of the indigenous populations."

United States. In the two months since 14 September, 316,089 men training at army bases fall ill with the flu, and another 53,449 develop pneumonia. At home and in Europe, the AEF's death toll from influenza during 1918 is 12,423.

Compiègne. At a railroad siding in the Forest of Compiègne, a German delegation meets with Marshal Foch to discuss terms of an armistice. Matthias Erzberger, leader of the Center Party in the *Reichstag* and author of the Peace Resolution of 1917, heads the German delegation. He has been instructed to achieve an armistice "at any price," but he will try to obtain concessions that preserve Germany's honor and integrity—a futile effort, as Foch is determined to dictate the terms.

9 November 1918
Berlin. The rebellion that began in Kiel flows into the capital. Prince Max of Baden, on his own authority without consulting the kaiser, announces Wilhelm II's abdication and Crown Prince Wilhelm's renunciation of the throne. After negotiations with Socialist leaders, Prince Max resigns as chancellor to be replaced in the post by Social Democratic Party leader Friedrich Ebert. In the afternoon, Kaiser Wilhelm II takes flight from Spa for exile in Holland.
Northern Rhodesia. Lettow-Vorbeck's advance guard captures Kasama, about a hundred miles southeast of Fife.
Romania. Units of General d'Esperey's army cross the Danube River into Wallachia.
Bucharest. For the second time, Romania, hoping to legitimize its claim to the territories promised by the alliance with the Allies (Transylvania, Bukovina, and Banat), declares war on Germany. At the same time, Romanian forces in these Romanian areas of Austria-Hungary take control of them.
Berlin. Ebert forms a coalition government and secures the support of the army high command through negotiations with Gen. Wilhelm Groner, the quartermaster. Their agreement will prevent yielding to the demands of far-left groups for such policies as nationalization of some industries and will secure a centrist government.

11 November 1918
Compiègne. Erzberger's efforts for some compromise on each of the clauses of the armistice has failed. He protests: "A people of 70 million men are suffering, but they are not dead." Foch responds, "Tres bien." At 5:10 A.M., the delegates sign the armistice that will end the war at exactly 11:00 A.M., when the guns fall silent. Other terms include evacuation of all German-occupied areas of France, Belgium, Luxembourg, and Alsace-Lorraine within fifteen days,

with the Allies occupying these areas as the Germans leave; repatriation of all inhabitants of the German-occupied areas within fifteen days; surrender of twenty-five hundred heavy guns, twenty-five hundred field guns, twenty-five thousand machine guns, three thousand *minenwerfer*, and seventeen hundred airplanes; evacuation of the left bank of the Rhine River, to be occupied by the Allies, who receive the right to build garrisons at Coblenz, Mainz, Cologne, and other strategic points, with a neutral zone of a little over six miles along this sector; assurances that no damages will be inflicted on people, structures, or communications facilities as the Germans evacuate occupied areas; revelation by the German army within two days of the locations of all mines; repatriation of all Allied prisoners; requisitions rights for the Allies in occupied areas, with the Germans paying costs of stationing Allied troops in these areas; and provision for German personnel to remain behind to tend the German sick and wounded. At 7:00 A.M., Foch leaves Compiègne to return to Paris. So the war ends. The British dead number 997,000; the French, 1.39 million; the Italian, 340,000; the American, 116,000. German dead total 1.85 million; Austro-Hungarian dead, 1.2 million; Turkish dead, 350,000.
Vienna. Emperor Karl abdicates the throne, bringing to an end the Habsburg Empire and dynasty.

12 November 1918
Northern Rhodesia. Lettow-Vorbeck's troops skirmish with British troops on the bank of the Chambeshi River.

13 November 1918
Northern Rhodesia. At Chambeshi a message from Gen. Louis van Deventer informs Lettow-Vorbeck of the armistice. It apprises him that the British commander has ordered a ceasefire and that he is expected to do the same. It states that "conditions of the armistice" will be sent as soon as they are received but gives no information on who was victorious in Europe. A second message instructs Lettow-Vorbeck to deliver up his troops and weapons at

American troops cheer the news of the Armistice on 11 November 1918 (Library of Congress)

Abercorn. Lettow-Vorbeck accepts van Deventer's terms.

17 November 1918
Russia. A convoy of twenty ships, led by one of the ships that had evacuated General Dunsterville's men from Baku, sails into Baku harbor bearing British troops and officers and Colonel Bicherakov and his Cossacks. They have come to take possession of Baku from the defeated Turks.

25 November 1918
Northern Rhodesia. The last of the *Schutztruppe,* led by Lettow-Vorbeck, march into Abercorn at noon. Before an honor guard and Brig. Gen. W.F.S. Edwards in the town's square, Lettow-Vorbeck forms his men into three ranks, salutes the British flag, and reads his surrender statement, first in German and then in English. The German commander surrenders an army of 155 Europeans and 1,168 askaris, along with 3,000 other Africans. After the surrender, British officers

and troops express their admiration to the indomitable Lettow-Vorbeck and his *Schutztruppe.*

28 November 1918
Bukovina. Romanians in this province of the Austro-Hungarian Empire vote to unite with Romania.

8 December 1918
German East Africa. Paul von Lettow-Vorbeck arrives in Dar es Salaam to await embarkation to Cape Town and Rotterdam.

18 December 1918
Damascus. Palestinians protest perceived Zionist ambitions to take Palestinian lands in messages sent to the Peace Conference convened at Paris and to the British Foreign Office.

31 December 1918
Germany. During the year the influenza epidemic has claimed 400,000 lives in

Germany. About 450,000 have died in the United States and 150,000 in Great Britain. Worst hit of all the nations is India, where 6 million have died. The epidemic had peaked in the fall months but continues to claim victims well into 1919.

Human Costs

A complete accounting of the horrendous human costs of World War I proved to be impossible, and all subsequent figures are only estimates based on the mind-numbing losses during the four years of conflict. Overall military and civilian deaths may have run as high as 13 million. The figures for military deaths are perhaps reasonably accurate, and estimates by various authorities usually come up with similar figures. The total of soldiers killed in the war is usually reckoned at more than 6 million.

Country	Killed	Wounded	Prisoners	Total
Gr. Britain	997,000	2.1 mil.	191,000	3.29 mil.
France	1.39 mil.	2 mil.	446,000	3.84 mil.
Italy	340,000	947,000	530,000	1.82 mil.
US	116,000	205,700	4,500	326,200
Russia	1.7 mil.	4.9 mil.	2.5 mil.	9.1 mil.
Germany	1.85 mil.	4.24 mil.	618,000	6.71 mil.
Austro/Hungary	1.2 mil.	3.62 mil.	2.2 mil.	7.02 mil.
Turkey	(specifics untabulated)			2.92 mil.

Aftermath

It seemed to later generations that the trouble had only begun when the rumble of guns on the Western Front ceased in the fall of 1918. The carnage on a grand scale was over, but little peace came to the nations that had fought the war.

The victors wrought miserably when they opted to fix blame for the war entirely on Germany. The resulting treaty (or series of treaties), signed during 1919 and 1920, stripped Germany of all her military power, imposed absurdly high war reparations, and provided a demilitarized buffer for France.

The Austro-Hungarian Empire ceased to exist after the war, and in its place the victors established a series of independent Balkan states, some of them incorporating several ethnic and "national" minorities. Almost nothing proved to be stable in these new nations except the propensity toward violence, dictatorship, and mutual ethnic hatred.

The victors in the war failed in the long run to reap much from their victory. France had been so devastated and had lost so many men on the Western Front that the grip of global depression nearly strangled the nation in the two decades following the end of World War I. Likewise, Great Britain never recovered the economic and military dominance she had enjoyed worldwide during the hundred years before the war. Italy, the most rapacious at the peace table, was the first to fall prey to fascism. Only the United States appeared to have gained from her war experience—the costs had been relatively light, and U.S. involvement allowed the nation eventually to assume a strong international role, although such was

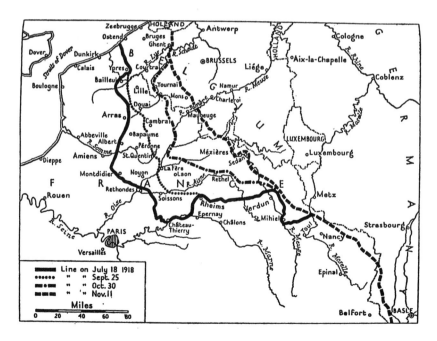

The Western Front (Armistice). From *A History of the Great War, 1914-1918*, by C.R.M.F. Cruttwell, published by Academy Chicago Publishers. All rights reserved.

shunned in the immediate postwar period. The Soviet empire that emerged directly from the war and the Russian civil war following it seemed to have been a permanent legacy of the times, but the Bolsheviks' state proved to be relatively short-lived.

The Literature of War

As ghastly as it was, World War I produced a remarkable flowering of the literature of war, probably surpassing any previous war in the quality of the subsequent writings by veterans. Perhaps the most famous were the British "war poets" including Siegfried Sassoon, Wilfred Owen, Robert Graves, and others who produced a considerable body of verse after the war that expressed in an evocative way the pain of combat and loss. Graves's classic *Goodbye to All That* was a vivid prose memoir of his experiences in France as a junior officer of the Royal Welch Fusiliers, his wounding at the front, and his consequent rejection of British life and values in light of the viciousness of the war. Frenchman Henri Barbusse's *Under Fire* (published in 1917 before the end of the war and at about the time of the great mutinies among the French regiments) detailed the grim realities of fighting on the Western Front in a way seldom before accomplished by a common soldier. After the war, the German experience was depicted by Erich Maria Remarque in *All Quiet on the Western Front*, which probably became the most widely read of all novels of World War I. While these works differ greatly in tone and method of execution, they all share an unremitting condemnation of war and a stark invocation of the horrors of modern fighting. There is nothing of the glorification of combat or the heroic that so characterized war literature from previous generations.

The dehumanization and demoralization of the war experience also influenced the new generation of American writers, nudging many into profound disillusionment with Western civilization. As Ezra Pound portrayed the war's legacy in his 1919 poem "Hugh Selwyn Mauberley": "There died a myriad,/ And of the best, among them,/For an old bitch gone in the teeth,/For a botched civilization." Of the survivors, F. Scott Fitzgerald, whose novels chronicled "the jazz age" of the war's aftermath, observed at the end of his first novel, *This Side of Paradise*, that they had "grown up to find all Gods dead, all wars fought, all faiths in man shaken." This disillusionment, together with an intensely antiwar stance tinged sometimes with bitterness, characterized such works about the war as John Dos Passos's *Three Soldiers* and Ernest Hemingway's *A Farewell to Arms*. Poet E.E. Cummings reflected similar views, with an ironic twist, in his autobiographical novel, *The Enormous Room*, based on his experiences as a prisoner. And of course this same war legacy formed the backdrop of the great seminal poem of the era, T.S. Eliot's *The Wasteland*.

Biographies

ALBERT I. 1875-1934. King of Belgium. Seen in the West as a courageous opponent of the German juggernaut, Albert insisted on strict neutrality for his tiny country during most of the war, which made him a more complex figure than his public image indicated. He was the nephew of King Leopold II and the son of a prince of the Germanic house of Saxe-Coburg. Albert's mother was a Hohenzollern. The royal family had been recruited in the early nineteenth century to supply a monarchy for the newly established country of Belgium, which was created after the Napoleonic Wars as a buffer state. Unfortunately for the Belgians, the buffer arrangement meant that they stood in the path of any thrust toward France by Germany (a nation far younger than Belgium). Albert was trained as a soldier, entering the army in 1892, a year after he became heir apparent on the death of his older brother. Not surprisingly, he was a lieutenant general by 1907, but he was more than a ceremonial figure. As events proved, he was a competent general, especially by World War I standards. He came to the throne in 1909 and was soon deeply involved in the events that led up to the onset of war. Belgium's traditional policy had been strict neutrality, backed by the military guarantees of other powers, principally France and Great Britain. The obvious military buildup of Germany and the increasing diplomatic tensions, however, prompted the Belgian government—headed by Baron Charles de Broqueville—to begin a program of military training that was intended to allow the nation to fend off invasion from either Germany or France. The German war plan meant crossing Belgium at a minimum and seizing the country if need be. When the kaiser's armies crossed the frontiers on 4 August 1914, Albert immediately took center stage with a speech to the parliament. He declared that Belgium would fight for its territory and neutrality against all comers, and he assumed the role of commander in chief of the small army. Showing con-siderable wisdom, Albert withdrew the Belgian army to Antwerp and then farther to the west to avoid annihilation by the Germans. While he seemed to be firmly on the side of the Allies as the war settled into a stalemate on the Western Front, in fact Albert continued to insist on neutrality. He fought with his army on the Yser in October and steadfastly refused to place himself or his troops under French or British command. His goals were to keep his army in being and to keep it fighting on Belgian soil. During the following two years, Albert succeeded in holding his government strictly to the neutral position, although Germany was clearly the enemy of France and Britain, the allies of Belgium. By 1916, Albert was in severe conflict with many of his ministers, some of whom began to regard him almost as a traitor for his refusal to formally join the Allies and for his continued attempts to find a compromise end to the war. Intense pressure built by 1918, however, finally convincing Albert to acquiesce, and he placed his army at the disposal of the Allied commander, Foch. Albert himself became commander of an Allied army group for the final offensive in Flanders. He emerged at the end of 1918 as a war hero, and he used the prestige to institute a series of political and social reforms after the war. He died in a mountain climbing accident.

ALBRECHT, Duke of Württemberg. 1865-1939. German field marshal. Albrecht was one of several royal field commanders in the German army during the war. He was the grandson of Archduke Albrecht of Austria and heir apparent to the childless Wilhelm II of Württemberg. Albrecht's military career began in 1885, and he spent the years leading up to the war as an increasingly elevated officer—few royal figures failed to shoot to the top of the military hierarchy. He commanded a full corps by shortly after the turn of the century and was inspector general in command of the Württemberg army with the rank of colonel general by 1914. Despite his social status, Albrecht was a competent soldier. He was given command of the Fourth Army, which formed one of the major components of the German right-wing force that was intended to sweep through Belgium and end the war within a few weeks in the fall of 1914. He was successful in his first engagements, most notably at Neufchâteau on 22 August against the French. He won again at Sedan a few days later, but his force had been turned inward to move south by a change in German strategy. By September, his Fourth Army was part of the German concentration on the Marne, where it was stymied by a desperate French counteroffensive. In October 1914, Albrecht was shifted northward and given command of a new Fourth Army with which he was to smash the British and win through to the Channel ports. The battles near Ypres resulted in a stalemate, and Albrecht had to settle for a position on the Yser that developed into the characteristic situation of trenches and territorial stasis. In April 1915, he tried a series of offensives against the British at Ypres but could not dislodge the BEF despite horrendous fighting and heavy casualties on both sides. Albrecht was promoted to field marshal and a few months later transferred to the command of a new army group in Alsace, where he remained for the rest of the war. In 1921, he became titular head of the house of Württemberg on the death of Wilhelm II.

ALEXEYEV, Mikhail Vasilivich. 1857-1918. Russian general. As the overall commander of Russian forces during 1916, Alexeyev presided over the increasingly futile efforts of Russia to continue to make war as the army and the empire crumbled. A career officer trained at the General Staff Academy, he served in the Russo-Japanese War as a major general and became chief of staff of the Kiev Military District after the Russian defeat in the East. Alexeyev was one of the prewar planners who urged that Russia concentrate its offensive power against the Austrians in Galicia instead of attempting an offensive thrust into East Prussia in the event of war with Germany.

When the conflict actually began in 1914, he was named chief of staff to Nikolai Ivanov, who commanded the Southwest Army Group in the initial campaign against the Austrians. The Russians found little success, of course, despite their numerical superiority, and it was soon apparent that the poor organization and logistics of the Russian army would seldom match those of the Germans or even the weaker Austrians in Galicia. In March 1915, Alexeyev was elevated to command of the Northern Front, and he was less than effective in opposing the Germans there. He also was slow to cooperate with his fellow commanders—a consistent failing among Russian commanders, who often hated each other. He effectively had command of most of Russia's field armies by mid-1915 when the Czar sacked Grand Duke Nicholas and took over as commander in chief, naming Alexeyev as his chief of staff. Alexeyev labored to reform the command structure of the Russian forces, but he was hampered by the same problems that had dogged his predecessors. He was also obliged to send troops to the Western Front in early 1916 and to launch an unlikely offensive against the Austrians in order to relieve pressure on Italy. He failed to sufficiently appreciate Busilov's rapid successes in June 1916 and was slow to support the latter's breakthrough, and this ultimately resulted in the nullification of the gains. Alexeyev suffered a heart attack in late 1916 and was out of the picture until February 1917. He then became embroiled in the political events leading to the Revolution. After urging the Czar to abdicate, Alexeyev allied himself with Kerensky in a commitment to continue the war. As the army in the field disintegrated, he was dismissed by the Kerensky government in May 1917 and fled to the Don region in October with the ascension of the Bolsheviks. He had begun organization of the White Army when he died.

ALLENBY, Edmund. 1861-1936. British field marshal. Although an indifferent commander on the Western Front early in the war, Allenby found his metier in the Middle East and became a legend for his campaigns against the Turks. He was born in Nottinghamshire and attended Sandhurst after failing to win entry in the Indian civil service. By the time of the Boer War, Allenby had reached the rank of brigadier general. He was a major general at the outbreak of World War I and commanded one of the cavalry divisions in the British Expeditionary Force in 1914. He was engaged in the battles at Ypres, thereafter receiving command of the newly formed Third Army in 1915. He did not get on with Sir Douglas Haig, however, and was not one of the leading British performers during 1916. There was, in fact, little to predict his immense success after he was posted to Egypt in June 1917. The British had tried to attack the Turkish Empire in the Middle East, at first giving the task to the Indian army. The Turks had proved surprisingly tough opponents, however, and despite relatively heavy fighting and casualties, the British had failed to dislodge their opposition from any of the key points on the Arabian peninsula. With a considerable force of infantry and cavalry, Allenby mounted a vigorous offensive in the fall of 1917, attacking toward Beersheba and then Gaza and Jaffa. The important objective of Jerusalem fell to Allenby in December, establishing his reputation as a successful fighter in an exotic theater. A subsequent campaign made slower headway but eventually drove on and culminated at Allenby's great cavalry victory at Megiddo in September. By the end of October, Allenby had taken Damascus, Tripoli, and Aleppo, and the Turks sued for an armistice, ending the war in the Middle East shortly after the final fighting on the Western Front in Europe. Allenby remained in Egypt after the war as British High Commissioner, and he exercised immense political power and influence in establishing the Arabian kingdoms and a sovereign Egyptian state. He was elevated to the rank of field marshal and made a peer. Allenby died in England.

ASQUITH, Herbert. 1852-1928. British prime minister. Asquith was the long-time leader of the dominant Liberal Party in Britain and the prime minister during the first years of World War I. He came from very humble beginnings and made his way to the pinnacle of political power in class-conscious Britain by sheer merit. (He was one of the first students to attend prestigious Balliol College at Oxford without first attending a public school.) He entered the House of Commons in 1886 and first took office as home secretary under Gladstone in 1891. Following more than a decade of Conservative Party governments, the Liberals came back into power in 1906 with Asquith as Chancellor of the Exchequer. He became prime minister in 1908. His government was preoccupied with several crises during his first six years in office, including a constitutional confrontation with the House of Lords over the power to reject the budget and, even more serious, the ever-divisive question of home rule for Ireland. The war swept aside these issues, and Asquith assumed responsibility for the civil direction of the war. Like most people in England and Europe, he assumed that the conflict would be a short one, but after the stalemate settled in during the fall of 1914, Asquith set about making arrangements for a long struggle. He was not a dynamic leader by any means, but he was an able and agile politician despite his boring public front. He numbered the mercurial Churchill and David Lloyd George as members of his cabinet, and they supplied all the color one might need. Asquith—like his counterparts in Europe—only slowly came to have a glimmering of the immense effort and cost the war would require. England was unable to produce rapidly the huge amounts of munitions called for by the hitherto-unheard-of bombardments that came to characterize the trench war in France. When coupled with the mind-numbing casualty lists of the BEF, the deficiencies rebounded on Asquith's head. He also had to take responsibility for the major failures of the Allies in the Dardanelles. In December 1916, Asquith was compelled to hand over the government to Lloyd George and move to the opposition. He lost his own seat in the Commons in December 1918 but returned in 1920. He took a peerage in 1925 and died three years later.

BAKER, Newton D. 1871-1937. American secretary of war. A native of West Virginia, Baker attended Johns Hopkins University and then graduated with a law degree from Washington and Lee. He moved to Cleveland to practice law but soon became interested in politics and public office, running successfully for mayor after serving as a city legal officer. He was also involved in national politics as a supporter of Woodrow Wilson (who had been one of Baker's undergraduate teachers) and had declined appointment to Wilson's first cabinet. By 1916, however, Baker was willing to accept service as Secretary of War with the strong likelihood that America would be drawn actively into the European conflict despite the formal policy of neutrality that was still in place. After the entrance of the United States on the side of the Allies in April 1917, Baker faced a huge task. America had traditionally distrusted the notion of a standing army, and with little to fear from its neighbors except border raids by people like Pancho Villa, the U.S. Army had been kept small and underequipped. The Germans assessed the American force—fewer than a hundred thousand men when war was declared by Congress—as roughly equivalent to one of the more minor European armies. Throughout the following months, Baker quite ably mobilized the nation's resources, including effecting a vast increase in military manpower through conscription, and put the United States on an effective war footing sooner than anyone could have expected. Patriotic fervor, once unleashed, demanded even more, however, and Baker was roundly criticized. He had a particularly difficult time in dealing with the entrenched officer corps and found it necessary to broker prolonged disagreements between the armchair generals and John J. Pershing, the American commander in France. Baker supported Pershing's notion of keeping the American Expeditionary Force as a distinct body and helped fend off the Allied demands to use the Americans as replacement cannon fodder in the trenches. Baker's performance must be judged as successful, although relatively unrewarded at the time. He returned to his law practice in Cleveland after the war and later served as a member of the international arbitration court at The Hague.

BALFOUR, Arthur. 1848-1930. British government official. Balfour was one of the principal British politicians and ministers before, during, and after the war. He was a Conservative who came from landed gentry and was educated at Eton and Cambridge. He was the nephew of Conservative leader Lord Salisbury and benefitted from Salisbury's political patronage. Balfour entered Parliament as a member for East Manchester in 1885 and immediately became embroiled in the question of home rule for Ireland—as an opponent. By 1891, he was leader of his party in the Commons and sat in the cabinet as Treasury Lord. He was a hard-liner during the Boer War. In 1902, Balfour succeeded Salisbury as prime minister, and he was the head of the British government while the entente with France was worked out. Since the Conservatives went out of office in 1906, Balfour was leader of the opposition during the first years of the war, although he was included as a member of Asquith's Committee of Imperial Defense and supported the government's early war efforts. He was not loath, however, to taking political advantage of the great hue and cry over the munitions shortages and the disasters in the Dardanelles. He helped form the coalition government that replaced Asquith in 1915, serving as first lord of the admiralty and thus head of the Royal Navy during the only great surface engagement of the war, the Battle of Jutland. Balfour was lackadaisical, however, in coming to grips with the German U-boat offensive that threatened to tip the balance during late 1916 and early 1917. He was finally removed from the admiralty in April 1917 and made head of the mission in the United States, where he was effective in urging the new belligerent up to speed in aiding the war effort. Balfour was one of the major players at the postwar peace conference and was responsible for much of the final settlement. His name was attached to the infamous declaration that nebulously declared Britain's approval of a homeland for the Jews in the Middle East—a particularly cynical diplomatic document. He left government in the early 1920s after serving as foreign secretary. Balfour was honored with a peerage in 1922.

BEATTY, David. 1871-1936. British admiral. Beatty was in the thick of the large-scale naval actions between the Royal Navy and the German High Seas Fleet. He was the son of a captain in the British army and entered the navy at age thirteen. Beatty had wide experience during his early career, serving with Kitchener in the Sudan and in China during the Boxer Rebellion. He was distinguished for the speed of his promotion up the ladder of rank, something very unusual in the conservative navy, a service that seldom allowed even the brightest talents to advance before the slow workings of seniority said they should. Beatty was posted captain at age twenty-nine (most officers reached this rank only in their forties) and in 1910 became the youngest admiral since the Napoleonic era. Beatty was a favorite of Winston Churchill, who controlled the Admiralty before the war, and became commander of the main battle-cruiser squadron in 1914. Beatty was therefore commander of the most flexible and speedy ships of the main British fleet, a circumstance that led him into combat with the reluctant Germans, especially his opposite number, Admiral Hipper. On 27 August 1914, Beatty's squadron engaged and defeated a force of German light cruisers off Heligoland Island, sinking four enemy ships. The victory, although not overwhelming, established Beatty as a naval hero. Five months later, Beatty fought Hipper's squadron off Dogger Bank. The German technical advantages came into play during the engagement: Beatty's flagship HMS *Lion* was knocked out of the fight early on, and poor British communications allowed most of the German ships to escape destruction. At the end of May 1916, Beatty and his squadron were the lead ships in what turned out to be the only large fleet engagement of the war—the Battle of Jutland. He found the entire German High Seas Fleet at sea (which had come out of port for the only time) and lured it within range of the British Grand Fleet. The subsequent battle, a curious, inconclusive affair during which the Germans managed to escape through deft maneuvers and in fact sank more tonnage than their opponents, did not achieve the effect the British had come to expect from centuries of sea domination, but Beatty emerged nonetheless as the foremost naval hero. In 1916, Beatty was promoted to full admiral and given command of the Grand Fleet, which never again fought. Following the war, he served as first lord of the admiralty, overseeing the dismantling of the wartime fleet. He was given a peerage in 1919.

BELOW, Otto von. 1857-1944. German general. A successful field commander on four different fronts during the war, Below was one of Germany's best generals, most famed for his overwhelming drive against the Italians at Caporetto. He was born in Danzig and was a soldier from early in his adult life. He advanced in grade steadily in the decades before the war, reaching the rank of lieutenant general when the war began. By August 1914, Below was in command of a corps of the Eighth Army facing the Russians. He effectively won at Gumbinnen in August and around the Masurian Lakes in September 1914. Promoted to full general, Below took over the entire Eighth Army in early 1915 and defeated the Russians again at the Masurian Lakes, taking a huge number of prisoners. Other victories followed during early 1916. In October 1916, he was transferred to the Balkans as commander of an entire army group (named after him) and given the task of stopping a nascent Allied thrust through Greece and Bulgaria. He was generally successful—winning a victory at Salonika—but less overwhelming than he had been in East Prussia. In April 1917, Below was moved to the Western Front to command the Sixth Army near Arras, but he was recalled in September and sent to the Italian front as head of a joint German-Austrian Fourteenth Army. In late October and early November, Below's forces attacked the Italian lines (which had remained basically stationary for nearly three years) and drove the Italians back behind the Piave River, inflicting more than half a million casualties. The prolonged drive, knows as the Battle of Caporetto, was one of the largest breakthroughs of the war, but in the end gained little for the Central Powers. Below was moved back to France in early 1918 and set to the task of helping launch the final great German offensive of the war. His Seventeenth Army was ultimately repulsed by the Allies, and Below was forced to retreat shortly before the final collapse of the German war effort. He served briefly after the armistice as head of an army corps but resigned in June 1919 due to political differences with the new German government. An Allied attempt to try him as a war criminal failed.

BERCHTOLD, Leopold von. 1863-1942. Austro-Hungarian foreign minister. Berchtold (whose full aristocratic title was Count von Berchtold von und zu Ungarschita, Fratting und Pullitz) was a weak diplomat who caused much mischief as head of Austrian foreign policy during 1914. He was born in Vienna and entered the diplomatic corps in 1894. He demonstrated few diplomatic skills during his early career—he served five years as the Empire's ambassador to Russia—but had the social graces and aristocratic pedigree to meet the demands of high government service in Vienna. Somewhat against his better judgment, Berchtold accepted the post of foreign minister in early 1912. It is hard to point to a single issue with which he dealt well during his tenure. He earned a reputation for vacillation during the Balkan War, and there was little to recommend him as the crisis with Serbia approached. When the archduke was assassinated in June 1914, Berchtold seemed bent on driving Austria-Hungary and Germany into war. He engineered the presentation of an ultimatum to Serbia that all knew in advance would never be accepted—this was less diplomacy than it was overt provocation. After the beginning of the war, whose consequences Berchtold could not even begin to imagine, he fumbled relations with Italy, ostensibly an

Austrian ally. He resigned in January 1915 and retired from public life.

BETHMANN HOLLWEG, Theobald von. 1856-1921. German chancellor. As head of Wilhelm's government for nearly the entire war, Bethmann demonstrated a consistent inability to cope with the raging forces unleashed by the conflict—a fate he shared with more European politicians. He was the son of a minor provincial official, but he managed a rapid rise to a series of progressively more influential posts in the Prussian state bureaucracy as a civil servant, beginning in 1879 when he was barely out of his teens. Throughout the latter decades of the nineteenth century, Bethmann showed his abilities as an administrator and government official, rising by 1907 to the post of secretary of the interior for the entire Reich. In 1909, he became chancellor. His domestic policies were not successful, and within a few years Bethmann had managed to alienate both ends of the political spectrum in Germany, although the elected government played such a minor role in the political structure of the nation that he suffered only small harm. Bethmann's main focus was on foreign policy, and here, too, he charted a course that ultimately led to failure. He tried during the years before the war to win assurances from Britain that Germany could have a free hand in Europe but could never gain much ground. He was intent on moving against Russia and the noisome Balkan states at some point, but the Austrian crisis after the assassination at Sarajevo forced Bethmann into a position of merely reacting to what other less-powerful nations decided to do. He essentially gave Austria a free hand to deal with Serbia and thus allowed the order of Europe to be sundered. Throughout the subsequent war, Bethmann clung to a set of goals that would have made Germany the complete master of Europe, and he never really turned aside from this fantastical blueprint. By 1916, his actual power had slipped in favor of the military, personified by Ludendorff and Hindenburg. When these two, who virtually took over the German state, demanded a new policy of unrestricted submarine warfare in January 1917, Bethmann went along despite his opinion that such a course would bring the United States into the conflict and ultimately destroy Germany's chances of victory. With the failure of the final German offensive in mid-1918, the state began to disintegrate, and in July Bethmann was forced to resign from office.

BLISS, Tasker H. 1853-1930. American general. Bliss was one of the chief diplomatic and administrative soldiers on the American side of the war. He was born in Pennsylvania and graduated from the U.S. Military Academy at West Point in 1875. His career before the involvement of the United States in the European conflict was dominated by appointments as a military educator. He returned to West Point soon after graduation to teach there and, in 1885, became an instructor at the Naval College in Newport, Rhode Island. He then moved into staff positions, first as an aide to Commanding General Schofield. In 1897, Bliss broadened his experience with an appointment as military attaché in Spain. He was with the small military action in Puerto Rico before moving to Cuba as an administrator after the Spanish-American War. Having reached the rank of brigadier general, Bliss became the first president of the new Army War College shortly after the turn of the century. By 1917, he was a major general and one of the nation's most experienced desk soldiers. He was named as chief of staff in September 1917 in the hope that he could smooth some of the conflicts between the American commander in France, John J. Pershing, and the command staff in Washington. Bliss worked closely with Secretary of War Newton Baker, and he demonstrated a good understanding of the relationship between Pershing and military headquarters in the United States, something his predecessors had failed to do. In November 1917, Bliss was appointed to the new Supreme War Council as Woodrow Wilson's representative. He walked the tightrope between supporting Pershing's resistance to Allied attempts to drain American manpower (Pershing insisted on keeping the American forces in France together as cohesive national units) and, on the other hand, supporting a unified Allied military command under Foch. Bliss got on well with Pershing, and the strategy of retaining American troops as distinct units finally paid off by mid-1918. Bliss was a moderate in relation to a defeated Germany, wanting an unconditional surrender but hoping to build a stable government in the ruins of defeat—he urged adoption of the League of Nations, for example. He served as a delegate to the Paris Peace Conference after the war, having left his post as chief of staff the previous year. Relegated, as were most American generals, to a minor role after the war, Bliss consistently wrote and spoke for world peace and a reduction in armaments.

BRUSILOV, Aleksey A. 1853-1926. Russian general. Brusilov was unquestionably the best Russian field commander of the war, showing the only glimmer of initiative and military sense in virtually the entire Russian army. He was born in the Caucasus at Tiflis to a noble family of military traditions (his father was a general). Brusilov's military education was privileged, and he rose in the officer ranks in accord with his aristocratic background. He distinguished himself in the war with Turkey in 1877 and then took further training as a cavalryman at the Officer's Cavalry School in Saint Petersburg. When he graduated, Brusilov joined the staff of the school, where he maintained a connection for more than twenty years, including a stint as commandant from 1902 to 1906. With a promotion to general, he moved from the Cavalry School to the field, serving in a succession of increasingly important commands before the beginning of the war. In 1914, he was in command of the XII Corps, and after the outbreak of hostilities, he was given charge of the Eighth Army in Galicia. The initial fighting was a disaster for the Russians, and Brusilov retreated along with his fellow commanders. However, at Luck, near the Pripet Marshes, he turned his forces and hit the pursuing Austrians hard, showing a streak of aggressiveness lacking in other Russian generals. He was given command of the entire Southwestern Front in March 1916 and planned a new offensive. Brusilov was nearly unique among World War I generals whose experience before the war had been in the cavalry. Most cavalrymen continued to think in hidebound terms and were bewildered to find that mounted troops had no place on the modern battlefield. Brusilov, on the other hand, attempted to develop tactics to counter the stasis that settled over most battles of the new war. In part motivated by a lack of manpower and supplies, which meant that he had to use small forces effectively, Brusilov designed a new approach to tactics for his 1916 offensive. Instead of a massive artillery bombardment followed by huge troop assaults on a broad front, Brusilov suggested a sharply focused attack by trained troops with hidden reserves ready to exploit local breakthroughs. This approach came to be knows as the "Hutier tactic" later in the war when exploited to the fullest by the Germans on the Western Front. In June 1916, Brusilov's new tactics paid handsomely. His well-coordinated attacks on the Austrians drove his enemies backward at a pell-mell pace, and the Russian armies in the Southwest achieved the clearest and deepest breakthrough of the war to date. Unfortunately, the Russian advance quickly outpaced the meager Russian supply and logistical system, and when fellow commanders refused to launch supporting attacks, Brusilov's advance came to a halt. In the end, little was gained—all the hard-won ground was returned to the enemy—but Brusilov's offensive had diverted strength from the Verdun and Trentino offensives to the West. By early 1917, the Russian state was altered forever, and the army began to disintegrate. Brusilov was named by the Kerensky government as commander in chief of the new army, and he began a new offensive in July that was successful at first. The effort soon collapsed, however, and the Bolshevik Revolution in the fall ended the active war on the Russian side, Brusilov having been earlier replaced by Kornilov. Somewhat surprisingly for an old aristocratic cavalry officer, Brusilov eventually embraced the new Soviet order. In 1920, he joined the Red Army, although he avoided taking the field against his former comrades who now led the armies of the Whites. He died in Moscow.

BÜLOW, Karl von. 1846-1921. German general. Bülow, one of the highest-ranking German officers at the beginning of the war, bore the brunt of the blame for the German defeat at the Marne. He was born in Berlin and fought as a Prussian officer in the wars against Austria and France that established the new German state. By the 1890s, Bülow was a senior officer with the rank of major general, having commanded the Fourth Foot Guards and served as head of the Prussian War Ministry. By 1904, he was a colonel general and commander of the IIIrd Corps. He was given a key role in the German war plan that was designed to sweep through Belgium and take Paris during the first weeks of the war. Bülow commanded the Second Army and also had at least nominal control of Kluck's First Army, holding the outer positions on the German right wing. Bülow himself took Liége and Namur during the first weeks of the German offensive and defeated the French at Sambre, moving swiftly toward Paris and crossing the Marne in the first week of September. Then the German plan began to come apart. Bülow settled into positions across the Marne but suddenly turned defensive and even pessimistic. He actually exerted little control over Kluck, who turned inward to the southwest toward the French armies rather than driving toward the enemy capital. A fatal gap opened between Kluck and Bülow, which the latter did nothing to repair. The German High Command decreed a new formation on the Marne that eventually led to a massive desperation counteroffensive by the French that stopped the Germans and essentially set off the prolonged stalemate on the Western Front. Bülow commanded the entire German right wing, consisting of three armies, but could not break out of the basic dispositions reached in September. He was promoted to field marshal in January 1916 but was removed from active command in March after a heart attack. He never again returned to a post of real importance.

CADORNA, Luigi. 1850-1928. Italian general. Cadorna was one of the more controversial military commanders of the war, responsible for creating a horrendous meat-grinder front in Italy into which he fed hundreds of thousands of soldiers. He came from an important military family—his father was a well-known general—and he began service in the artillery as a teenager. By 1898, after a thirty-year career in the army, Cadorna held the rank of major general. His military career was closely entwined with politics (not unusual in World War I commanders), and he spend much of his energies fending off civilian authorities, whom he distrusted and denigrated. He became Italian chief of staff in mid-1914, when Italy was still a formal member of the Central Alliance and expected to join Germany and Austria in the coming war, so Cadorna's first efforts were to organize his armies to fight against France. Italy, however, abandoned her alliance at the outset of hostilities and eventually entered the war on the side of the Entente in May 1915. Cadorna had mobilized massive manpower during the wait, but he lacked sufficient artillery—a constant problem during the ensuing three years—and the terrain was very much against him. The Austrians held the mountainous region that Cadorna would have to traverse in order to attack, and attack was his only idea. The battle line was established along the Isonzo River, and Cadorna threw offensive after offensive against the Austrians during the second half of 1915. All were completely futile, demonstrating the worst conditions typical of the war in the West. Hundreds of thousands of casualties over years and years of fighting along the Isonzo (encompassing a dozen major "battles") did nothing to dissuade Cadorna from his absurd ideas of massive assaults against the impregnable defenses. Only acute political weakness in the civilian government allowed Cadorna to retain his command, and he was just strong enough to hold on until 1917, when the Austrian breakthrough at Caporetto (which took Cadorna by surprise) destroyed his credibility and he was finally removed from command in November. A postwar investigation of the military blamed Cadorna for Italy's poor performance, but Mussolini, needing a military hero, resuscitated Cadorna in 1924 by promoting him to field marshal.

CASTELNAU, Édouard de. 1851-1944. French general. Castelnau, a native of Saint-Afrique, was one of France's principal generals. He was born into a military family and was a strong Roman Catholic supporter of the Clerical Party in French politics, a position that earned him the prolonged distrust of Republican politicians. After graduating from the military academy at Saint-Cyr in 1870, Castelnau fought in the disastrous Franco-Prussian War the following year. In the decades leading up to World War I, he became a seasoned officer with a high reputation for his impeccable staff work and strong command of logistics. In 1911, Castelnau was selected by Joffre as the deputy chief of staff of the army, and he thus became a primary architect of the French plan for an all-out offensive in the event of war with Germany. Castelnau personally discounted the threat of a German thrust from the north, and instead insisted that France could win a war within days by a spirited attack in Alsace. Of course, the first weeks of the actual war showed the defects of the French strategy. Castelnau himself was in command of the Second Army and was soundly defeated by the Germans in late August after having been drawn forward in what was essentially a trapping maneuver. Working with his subordinate, Foch, however, Castelnau managed to retreat in order and established a defensive line that became part of the stabilized and stalemated Western Front. However, he refused to give up the idea that massive attacks could succeed, and he continued to advocate to Joffre the plan of trying for a breakthrough during 1915. The result, of course, was the death or wounding of an entire generation of Frenchmen and the desolation of vast areas of the French countryside. Castelnau in early 1916 decided to shore up the defenses at Verdun, and he made the commitment to hold the French line there against the massive German offensive. The army did, indeed, hold, but at a terrible price. With the changes in French top command at the end of 1916, Castelnau was out of power, although he continued as an army commander under Pétain, who formerly had been his subordinate. He lived to a very old age, serving in the Chamber of Deputies after the war.

CHURCHILL, Winston. 1874-1965. British minister. Churchill was one of the titanic figures of the twentieth century, but his performance during World War I was essentially a disaster. Few would have predicted in 1916 that he would ever recover a place of power and import. He was born at Blenheim Palace, the seat of his illustrious ancestor, the Duke of Marlborough. Churchill's brilliant but erratic father, Lord Randolph Churchill, viewed the boy as poor material and decreed a military career—a second-class future. Churchill was never good at academics and barely managed entrance to Sandhurst, but he graduated, took a commission, and served adequately in India and Africa. He resigned to become a journalist, and he won considerable fame for his coverage of the Boer War (he was briefly captured by the Afrikaners). In 1900, he won a seat in the Commons as a Conservative but changed parties in 1904 and was first given office as undersecretary for the colonies. He served in increasingly important cabinet posts, and in 1911, he became first lord of the admiralty, the post through which he exerted his major influence on the war. As head of the Royal Navy, Churchill supervised and stimulated the continuing buildup of naval power, with the result that Britain still had a firm edge in traditional surface forces by the beginning of the conflict. The pugnacious Churchill seemed to welcome, even relish, the final outbreak; however, the performance of the Royal Navy—for generation upon generation the dominant naval power in the world—was less than sterling during the first months. The German cruisers in the Mediterranean eluded the British, Admiral Spee destroyed a British squadron in the Pacific and killed Admiral Cradock before finally succumbing in the Falklands, and three British cruisers were sunk by two German torpedoes.

The balance was redressed to a degree by the British "successes" at Heligoland and Dogger Bank, but Churchill had very little to crow about. His ultimate downfall was the Dardanelles campaign, which he enthusiastically supported and drove onward. The initial attempt to force the Dardanelles with naval power alone was a complete failure, resulting in the loss of ships and men on a scale scarcely imagined. When the army was added and a full-scale offensive launched by landings on the Gallipoli Peninsula, the result was one of the greatest disasters for the Allies of the war, with complete defeat and huge casualty lists the only fruits of the poorly executed campaign. Churchill paid the price of failure. He was ousted from the cabinet in mid-1915, and took up command of the Sixth Royal Fusiliers in France in early 1916 with the rank of lieutenant colonel. His field command was undistinguished, but Churchill made the beginnings of a comeback in 1918, when the war coalition government of Lloyd George made him minister of munitions. After the armistice, he held important offices, but essentially passed into a political wilderness for many years. His moment came in 1939, when he assumed the leadership of Great Britain at the eve of World War II. He subsequently helped lead the Western Allies to victory, was turned out of office in 1945 by a wave of political reaction, and returned as prime minister in 1951.

CLEMENCEAU, Georges. 1841-1929. French minister. Clemenceau became the dominant force in the French national government by the end of the war and was perhaps the major player at the postwar peace conference. He was born in the Vendee, studied medicine, lived in the United States for four years, and first entered the chamber of deputies in 1876. He was a leader of the Radical Party and as such held a strong position in French politics, which enabled him to manipulate coalitions during much of the final quarter of the century. He was out of the legislature for a long period, however, after 1893 and returned to the senate only in 1902. He formed a government in 1906 and developed the Entente with Britain during his tenure, which ended in 1909. He was already decades older than most of the prominent political and civilian leaders of Europe, but his most vigorous days were yet ahead. He declined office at the beginning of the war, instead devoting the first three years of the conflict to criticizing the way the French government and the military conducted the war. He developed, above all, a burning drive toward complete victory, and he severely handled the leaders who began to crack under the immense strain of the prolonged and costly war. Clemenceau thought Joffre's insistence on massed offensives to be insane, and as the French military appeared more and more ineffective by mid-1917, Clemenceau moved closer to power. He was called on to form a cabinet in November 1917 and assumed the role of primary French leader for the remainder of the war. He held the portfolio of minister of war and ruthlessly swept aside all opposition, focusing on doing whatever was necessary to win in the face of the renewed German offensives of 1918. Perhaps most important, Clemenceau asserted his dominance over the commanding generals—Pétain and Foch by this stage—but also gave them the final support needed to achieve triumph after the German collapse. At the peace table, he tried to secure the borders of France and pushed for fierce economic dismemberment of the German state. In these goals he was only partially successful. He retired from public life in 1920 at the age of seventy-nine.

CONRAD von HÖTZENDORF, Franz, Count. 1852-1925. Austrian field marshal. Although largely unsuccessful and under the shadow of his German counterparts, Conrad von Hötzendorf commanded the armies of the Austro-Hungarian Empire during most of the war. He was the son of an Austrian officer and attended the imperial military academy, graduating in 1871. He served on the general staff and fought in the minor campaigns in the Balkans in the late 1870s and early 1880s. Having reached the rank of major, he taught in the War Academy before taking command of an infantry regiment. By 1903, Conrad von Hötzendorf was a general and had formed a relationship with Archduke Franz Ferdinand, who promoted the soldier's career. He became chief of staff in 1906. He firmly believed that Austria-Hungary would benefit from a general war, especially in regard to the Serbians and the Italians, and he vigorously promoted the conflict that came to a head in the summer of 1914. When actually faced with fighting on a large scale, however, Conrad von Hötzendorf proved to be a less-than-adequate general. He appeared to be a good planner, but most of his plans worked only on paper. In the field his armies seldom matched his expectations, and time after time the Germans were called on to bail out Austrian offensives. Eventually, the Germans took virtual control of the armies of Austria. His first great offensive against the Russians in 1914 was unsuccessful, and Austria ended the year on the defensive, suffering additional humiliation at the hands of the Serbs. A renewed Austrian offensive in early 1915 was essentially controlled by the Germans, although Conrad von Hötzendorf was in nominal command. In 1916, Conrad von Hötzendorf launched his own independent attack on the Italians in the Trentino region, but he was stymied; and the transfer of troops needed for the campaign allowed the Russians under Brusilov to penetrate deeply from what had been relatively stable lines in the East. In September 1916, Conrad von Hötzendorf was compelled to formally turn over command of the Austrian forces to Hindenburg. He was removed as chief of staff the following spring and relegated to command of an army group in the southern Tyrol. For the final year of the war, he was colonel of the Imperial Guard.

De ROBECK, Sir John M. 1862-1928. British admiral. De Robeck was one of the few British naval commanders to emerge from the war with reputation intact. He was the son of a British subject who held a Swedish title, and he was born in Ireland—a rather exotic background. In the long tradition of the Royal Navy, de Robeck entered service as a boy (aged thirteen in his case) and saw duty in a wide range of places and on many ships during his first two decades as an officer. He was a rear admiral by the outbreak of World War I, but at the time had no active assignment. His first appointment was as commander of a cruiser squadron in the Atlantic, but in early 1915, he was made second in command of the naval part of the ill-fated Dardanelles expedition. He fought aboard the *Vengeance* during the first assaults against the Turkish forts, and when the naval commander, Admiral Carden, succumbed to stress and ill health, de Robeck assumed command. None of his subsequent attempts to move the campaign forward met with anything but failure, but his extremely skillful withdrawal of the British Imperial Forces—when most thought huge casualties would be the price, but few men were lost in the end—won him high marks anyway for his role in the Dardanelles. The Grand Fleet was reorganized after the Battle of Jutland in May 1916, and de Robeck got command of the Second Battle Squadron with a promotion to vice admiral. The Fleet, of course, never again fought. He was made a baronet after the war and appointed commander of the Mediterranean Fleet. He followed with a tour in command of the Atlantic Fleet before retiring as a full admiral in 1925.

DRUM, Hugh A. 1879-1951. American general. Drum was the chief planner and logistical brains behind the American Expeditionary Force that was sent to France in 1917. He was the son of an army officer and born at Fort Brady in Michigan. His father was killed in the Spanish-American War, and as a consequence the young Drum, after attending Boston College, received a commission directly from the president. Between 1910 and 1912, Drum trained at the Army School at Fort Leavenworth, and he served with the Vera Cruz expedition in 1914. He was a colonel when appointed by Pershing as a staff officer for the movement of American troops to France. The initially small American force faced serious obstacles, not the least of which was the intense desire of the French and British to break up American units and use the troops as replacements among the heavily depleted Allied units at the front. While appreciating the effort of the Americans, the old-world soldiers, by then veterans of three years of grinding war, thought the Yanks would require too long to train before becoming effective. Pershing (and Drum) had other ideas, however, and insisted on preserving the integrity of the AEF. Drum came to exert a high degree of influence on how and where the Americans fought. When the AEF had built itself up and proved its worth, a new First American Army was organized in 1918 with Drum as chief of staff. He planned and organized the major American offensives in the Saint-Mihiel salient and the Meuse-Argonne. He continued his army career after the war and seemed to be the heir apparent to the army chief of staff, but he quarreled with Franklin Roosevelt in 1939 and was shunted aside during World War II. He was forced into retirement in 1943.

DUBAIL, Auguste. 1851-1934. French general. One of the many political French generals, Dubail was a product of Saint-Cyr and a veteran of the Franco-Prussian War. His early career was stellar, and he enjoyed a reputation as a reliable soldier and an adroit politician. By 1904, Dubail had reached the rank of major general and was commander at Saint-Cyr and then of a division. In 1911, he was appointed as chief of staff, but was most important as a member of the Supreme War Council. He helped form the detailed joint plans with the British and the Russians in the event of a German attack. With the eruption of war in August 1914, Dubail took the field as commander of the First Army. He attempted to follow the French prewar plan with an attack through Alsace, but was halted by the German counterattack and pushed back, but he established a strong defensive that proved to be the basis for the French offensive along the Marne in September. As the war settled into a defensive stalemate along a strung-out front, Dubail assumed command of the relatively quiet central section. His main function was to hold his positions and provide troops for the massive French assaults elsewhere, and he was employed by Joffre as something of a political hatchet man to dispose of other generals. Dubail made the mistake of following Joffre's lead concerning Verdun, and he publicly stated before the German offensive in 1916 that the defenses were adequate. When the Germans brought huge numbers of guns and men to bear on the forts and scored initial successes, Dubail became one of the generals to take the fall. He was removed by Joffre in late March and transferred to Paris as a military governor. All of Dubail's previous political clout was to no effect, and his career was essentially at an end.

ENVER PASHA. 1881-1922. Turkish minister and general. Enver Pasha was the chief military figure in the Turkish government during the war, and he was one of the triumvirate of Young Turks who essentially ruled the Empire. He was born in Constantinople of Turkish-Macedonian parents, and his early military career was spend in Macedonia fighting guerrillas. He was a major in 1908, when he was forced to flee to the mountains as a result of his political activities, but he returned with the successful revolt of the Young Turks. He continued to hold military rank in the new regime, fighting in Libya against the Italians in 1911 and 1912. In January 1913, he led a military coup against the civilian government. Coupled with his victory at Adrianople, this established him as one of the rulers of Turkey, sharing power with Kemal Pasha and Talat. He was strongly pro-German in his views and actively worked to bring Turkey into the war on the side of the Central Powers, hoping to gain territory in the bargain. He also directed the main Turkish campaigns, although he turned out to be a poor strategist on the large scale. Enver Pasha assumed command of the armies with the post of war minister in 1914, but his attempt to attack the Russians in the Caucasus was a disaster. Growing from this campaign were the genocidal policies of the Turkish government against the Christian Armenians, a policy for which Enver was largely responsible. He was again

beaten by the Russians in 1916—he seemed unable to read a map that showed mountains between him and his intended objectives. He likewise came to grief in Mesopotamia in a planned campaign to retake Baghdad from the British. His policies during 1918 strained relations with Germany, and he pushed for renewed terror against the Armenians. British victories in Mesopotamia finally sounded the end for Enver and his colleagues. They resigned in October 1918 and fled the country with the help of the Germans. He drifted to the Turkish-speaking area of Uzbekistan and tried to assist the indigenous peoples there to resist the revolutionary reorganization of the Russian Empire under the Bolsheviks. He died there in a battle with Red Army troops.

FALKENHAYN, Erich von. 1861-1922. German general. As chief of staff of the German armies during a crucial stage of the war, Falkenhayn felt the tug of a two-front conflict and finally succumbed to his military and political critics. He was born in West Prussia to a family of the Junker, or land-owning class, that was nearly penniless by the time of Falkenhayn's birth. Nonetheless, for most of his life, Falkenhayn looked and acted the part of the Prussian aristocratic officer. He served in the Far East during his early career as an instructor at a Chinese military school and as an officer during the Boxer Rebellion. He rose through the officer ranks with the patronage of Wilhelm II, reaching the rank of colonel by 1908 and major general by 1912. In mid-1913, Falkenhayn was promoted to lieutenant general and made Prussian minister of war. When the German plan for quickly conquering France came to grief at the Marne, Falkenhayn was named as chief of the general staff: the conduct of the war was in his hands. He was faced with what proved to be insurmountable difficulties. No one quite knew what modern war was to be like, and many of Falkenhayn's generals—like commanders on both sides—insisted on adding more and more troops to make massive assaults that they believed would lead to a breakthrough and victory. He received demands from generals on the Western Front to give them stockpiles of bodies with which to attack in many different places. Moreover, the decision to attack the Russians in the East and the early victories there under Ludendorff and Hindenburg created a demand for more and more strength to be concentrated for what the duo believed would be a decisive drive against the disarrayed armies of Nicholas I. Falkenhayn found no solution to the tugging and pulling, and his response has been characterized as falling back on half measures that satisfied no one and failed to provide for victory on any front—although one is hard-pressed to see how the latter would have been possible in any event. In early 1916, Falkenhayn bet on the effectiveness of a huge offensive against Verdun that he thought would deplete the French and allow a victory. The gigantic series of battles there during the following weeks did in fact weaken the French to the point of collapse, but it also nearly destroyed the Germans. With Brusilov's astounding initial gains in the East at the same time, Falkenhayn's position deteriorated, and he was sacked under pressure from his political enemies and such strident voices as those of Ludendorff and Hindenburg. He took a command in Romania and proved to be a good field soldier, defeating his enemies and taking Bucharest in December. The following year, Falkenhayn went to Turkey and planned a campaign to retake the gains made by the British in Mesopotamia, but he was relieved before beginning his offensive. After a short assignment as commander of the Tenth Army in Lithuania, he retired at the end of the war.

FOCH, Ferdinand. 1851-1929. French and Allied marshal. Foch was, by the end of the war, the supreme Allied commander and the architect of the final victory. He was a native of southwestern France and had served as a private in the Franco-Prussian War of 1871. He became a lieutenant of artillery in 1874, after graduation from the École Polytechniqué. He moved up the ladder of rank and appointment rapidly during the latter decades of the nineteenth century, gaining a reputation as a good staff officer and planner. He contemplated war on a more abstract level than many of his contemporary officers, and he wrote his ideas down, publishing *The Principals of War* in 1903, a book in which he developed the ideas of offensive spirit that came to dominate French military strategy before the war. He was a wholehearted proponent of the attack under all circumstances at this stage of his development. He was promoted to brigadier general in 1907, to major general in 1911, and to command of the Lorraine sector in 1913. The first battles of the war in 1914, of course, disproved all the theories about the utility of the offensive, but Foch never completely abandoned his belief in the need to attack. He merely began to modify them to rule out a single, quick victory. Foch discovered that a grand attack was hopeless, but he used a series of smaller but no less vigorous counterattacks as his primary mode of defense. He exerted power during the first years of the war as the right-hand man to Joffre, who approved Foch's aggressive fighting at the Battle of the Marne. He became Joffre's chief aide in the fall of 1914, and in early 1915, he took command of the northern sector of the Western Front. One of his primary jobs was to coordinate the activities of the French and British armies in the North, and he was thus called on to be a military diplomat as well as a strategist. Foch retained power only so long as Joffre remained in command, and when the latter was forced out after the catastrophic losses at Verdun in 1916, Foch, too, fell from grace. He spent nearly all of 1917 in relatively meaningless jobs, but with the rise of Georges Clemenceau to political control late in the year, Foch's star began to shine again. Clemenceau pushed to establish a Supreme War Council for the Allies, and by April 1918, under pressure from a renewed German offensive on the Western Front, he succeeded. Foch became the generalissimo, with authority over all Allied armies in the West: the French, the British, the Americans, and the Belgians. He directed the final offensive of the war that began to push back the crumbling German armies by the fall of the year, leading to the armistice and the capitulation of the Central Powers in November 1918. He tried to influence the peace negotiations toward securing France's frontiers with Germany—he held out for permanent bridgeheads on the Rhine—but was not successful. Much honored as the ultimate victor of the war, he retired from active political and military life in 1920.

FRENCH, Sir John D. 1852-1925. British field marshal. French was the first British commander in France and the first to be broken by the realities of war. He was the son of a naval officer and entered the Royal Navy as a lad of fourteen but transferred to the army within a few years. He served in India, Egypt, and the Sudan—advancing in rank all the while—and was a major general by the time of the Boer War. His rise was even more spectacular during the first years of the new century: he was a full general by 1907, chief of the Imperial General Staff by 1912, and a field marshal by 1913. His career was in the midst of a blip in 1914, owing to his involvement in the aftermath of a mutiny among officers in Ireland, but with the entry into the war by Great Britain, French was selected as the commander in chief of the British Expeditionary Force. The original BEF was made up almost entirely of professional soldiers, who were expected to make up for their small numbers by the excellence of their training and experience. The actual nature of combat as revealed during the first months of the war in Europe caught French almost completely by surprise, as it did nearly all military leaders. Nothing in his long career prepared him for the horrors imposed on his troops by modern technology, and nearly all of his assumptions about what he could and could not do in war were rapidly proven false. The initial sweep of the German advance on the right wing met the tiny BEF at Mons in August 1914, and the British were nearly enveloped and destroyed. French thereafter never quite regained his equilibrium, growing increasingly uncooperative with the French commanders and vacillating between unwarranted optimist and dark pessimism. He failed to understand what was happening during the battles in the north, and he found himself too remotely placed with little control. Nonetheless, he pushed the BEF into an offensive in Flanders during late October 1914, at Ypres, that resulted in extensive trench warfare. Later repulses—with giant butcher's bills—at Artois and Loos resulted in a nearly completely loss of credibility for French, and he was forced to resign in December 1915. Given a title and relegated to command of the home front, French faced further crisis in Ireland with the Easter Rebellion of 1916. He retired in 1921.

GEORGE V. 1865-1936. King of Great Britain. George V was one of the last British monarchs to actually play even a minor role in national governance and politics, and he deftly assumed the wartime duty of building morale. He was the grandson of Queen Victoria and the second son of Edward VII, so he was third in line for the throne during his early life. This circumstance allowed him to pursue a military career, and he was trained as a sailor and held an active commission until the death of his elder brother in 1892, which made him a likely heir to the throne and ended any hope for a real life. He married a princess of the German house of Württemberg in 1893. Victoria died in 1901, making George the next in line for the throne after his father, the new king. Edward VII died in 1910, and George became king, the fifth of that name. Although the British monarchy had become little more than a figurehead under the reforms of the previous two centuries, one last large moment remained. When the House of Lords insisted on exercising veto power over a Commons budget in the fall of 1910, George was called upon to resolve the dispute by promising to create enough compliant new peers to pass the bill. The threat alone was enough, and the issue of Lords' veto power was laid to rest. George V also tried to influence the issue of home rule for Ireland, but was no more successful than others. With the outbreak of the war, he took up duties as the figurehead national leader, visiting the troops in France and the hospitals filled with casualties. He banished liquor from the royal household because he thought it might set a good example for his subjects. In 1917, George—who was the cousin of Germany's Wilhelm II and came from almost purely German stock on both sides—changed the names of the royal family from Hanover and Battenberg to Windsor and Mountbatten. After the war, he became the first monarch to call a Labor government.

HAIG, Sir Douglas. 1861-1928. British field marshal. Haig was the British commander in chief on the Western Front for most of the war and was the man most responsible for sending British soldiers to death and wounding in senseless battle after senseless battle. Despite his blind ineptness at modern war—he disdained the machine gun as a useless weapon even though all evidence pointed to the contrary—Haig was rewarded by Britain with a peerage and a prize of £100,000 after the war. One assumes the grateful nation failed to realize that the international power of Britain had been crushed by the costs of the war and that an entire generation lay dead in the fields of France. He was a Scot, born in Edinburgh. He attended Sandhurst and served in India and then with Kitchener in the Sudan and in the Boer War. By 1911, Haig had reached the rank of lieutenant general and assumed command of one of the two corps of the British Expeditionary Force sent to France in August 1914. Under the command of Sir John French, Haig did a relatively poor job of coordinating with his fellow corps commander, Smith-Dorrien, but performed well in cooperation with the French. He stood firm at the first Battle of Ypres in October, but failed miserably to learn anything from the first months of the war. He was given command of a reorganized First Army in early 1915 and launched a large attack, which was futile from the beginning, at Neuve-Chapelle in March. He resolutely refused to believe the evidence that infantry could not attack entrenched machine guns, despite the mind-boggling casualty rates. He repeated his performance again and again over the remainder of the war. At Loos in December 1915, the British suffered twice the casualties of the Germans by taking the

offensive. At the Somme in mid-1916, sixty thousand British soldiers were lost on the first day of fighting, and the total casualties—all for no gain—amounted to more than four hundred thousand. During 1917, with Haig's most hated political enemy, Lloyd George, in control of the government at home, Haig fought the third Battle of Ypres and lost another four hundred thousand men. He held out against the renewed German offensive in Flanders in 1918 and then pursued the decaying German army in the final weeks of the war. After commanding the home army, Haig retired a hero in 1921.

HAMILTON, Sir Ian. 1853-1947. British general. Hamilton was—with some justification—the scapegoat of the Dardanelles disaster. He was born on the island of Corfu to British parents. As a career soldier and a graduate of Sandhurst, he had an extremely varied and wide experience in the four decades before World War I. A charming man, he added considerable social clout and inter-army political influence to his talents as an officer. Hamilton (known as "Johnny") served in Ireland, India, Afghanistan, Natal, Egypt, Burma, South Africa, and Japan. He enjoyed the patronage of Lord Kitchener and Lord Roberts and, on the eve of the war, was an aide-de-camp to the king with the rank of full general. His initial assignment was command of the home forces that would repulse any German invasion of the home British Islands, but in March 1915, he was appointed as commander of land forces for the attempt to force the Dardanelles and attack Turkey. The planners of the operation believed that the ships of the Royal Navy alone could reduce the Turkish forts and force their way to Constantinople. They were badly mistaken, and the navy suffered grievous losses with no appreciable gain. It was then up to Hamilton to organize an invasion and landing on the Turkish coast on the Gallipoli Peninsula. He managed to assemble a force at Alexandria, and he got it onto the beaches at Gallipoli but with much fumbling and in some places horrible casualties from the well-sited and surprisingly hard-fighting

Turks. Hamilton and his peers imagined that the Turks would fold up when faced with the might of Britain. Nothing was further from the truth, and the Turks fought tenaciously and well. The British were terribly slow at the places where they landed unopposed and managed to dally away all the advantages gained. The conflict settled into one of the most miserable theaters of the war—trench warfare under the worst conditions. Hamilton could find no way to break the stalemate, despite reinforcements and new landings. When it became apparent that the Gallipoli adventure was a costly failure, the government sacked Hamilton in October. He never again was employed in command. Hamilton lived to a very old age, dying two years after the end of World War II.

HINDENBURG, Paul von. 1847-1934. German field marshal. Perhaps the most famous man in Germany at the end of the war, Hindenburg was a good soldier, although often manipulated by others and usually over his head in political matters. He was native of Posen and came from a military family that had been landowners in a more prosperous past. He began his military career at age eight as a cadet, fought in the wars with Austria and France, and had reached the rank of lieutenant general by 1900. Hindenburg enjoyed several significant commands between 1900 and the beginning of the war, but he was passed over for the offices of chief of the general staff and Prussian war minister, and he retired in 1911 with his career apparently at an end. He was called up in August 1914 as a full general and told to take command of the German armies in East Prussia, where the first advances of the Russians had threatened the German imperial heartland. He met his new chief of staff, Erich von Ludendorff, at the train station in Hanover, and the two began to plan as they traveled eastward, which was the first collaboration in a long association. Their first joint success was the smashing victory over the Russians at Tannenberg, followed by victory near the Masurian Lakes. These two triumphs established the Hindenburg-Ludendorff duo as the saviors and reign-

ing military geniuses of imperial Germany. They were less successful in the following months, however, although they continued to defeat the Russians on a regular basis. They were frustrated by army chief of staff Falkenhayn, who refused to release troops from the Western Front to fulfill Hindenburg and Ludendorff's plans in the East. When Falkenhayn's grand offensive in 1916 against Verdun failed, Hindenburg was elevated in his place as imperial chief of staff with Ludendorff as his immediate subordinate. In fact, Ludendorff soon came to dominate the relationship, using Hindenburg as a front. Between them, they established a virtual military dictatorship in Germany, with the elected politicians and the kaiser moving further and further into the background and further and further from real power. Throughout the last two years of the war, Hindenburg and Ludendorff controlled the military, the economy, and the civilian population in Germany. Hindenburg made several errors of grand policy, however, notably allowing the unrestricted submarine warfare that ultimately brought the United States into the war on the side of the Allies, and making outrageous demands for postwar German hegemony over nearly all of Europe, which discouraged the Allies from negotiating peace. They launched a final massive offensive in the West in 1918, but when it failed, the end was inevitable. Ludendorff fled to Sweden, but Hindenburg remained behind, retiring after the signing of the peace treaty. When he ran for president of the new Weimar Republic in 1925, he was easily elected, although he was completely at sea in the political atmosphere of the times. Perhaps his greatest disservice to his country was to embrace Adolph Hitler and appoint the Nazi as chancellor in 1933.

HIPPER, Franz von. 1863-1932. German admiral. The leading German sailor of the war, Hipper fought well against the British but failed to win decisive victories. He was of humble origins, coming from a family of Bavarian brewers, but won rank and command in the navy during the years before the war. In 1912, he was promoted to rear admiral and commanded the battle-cruiser squadrons of the High Seas Fleet in August 1914. Since his ships were the most mobile of the German Fleet, they became the focus of the few naval engagements since they were often out in harm's way while the capital ships remained safe and snug in harbor. At Heligoland in August 1914, three of Hipper's cruisers were sunk by the British, but he retaliated with quick shelling raids against the main British island in November and December—raids that did little real damage but asserted a German naval presence. At the running battle off the Dogger Bank in January 1915, Hipper outmaneuvered the British cruisers and demonstrated the superiority of German fire control that essentially had to run away. The only large-scale engagement of the war came in May 1916, when the High Seas Fleet came out with Hipper in the van, assigned to draw the British battle cruisers into a trap. Hipper was surprised to discover that the British Grand Fleet and Beatty's cruisers were in the water with a similar mission. The ensuing Battle of Jutland was inconclusive, although the Germans sank the greater tonnage. Hipper performed very well during the action, but was able to have little effect against the British dreadnoughts without stronger support from his own large ships. He was rewarded with a Bavarian title, but there was not much during the remainder of the war for him to celebrate. The condition of the fleet began to deteriorate, and when he was promoted to full admiral and made commander of the High Seas Fleet in August 1918, his main task was to suppress mutinies aboard the German ships. He attempted a final "death or glory" sortie by the Fleet in late October, but his crews refused to sail. He retired in December 1918 after surrendering his fleet to the British.

HOFFMANN, Max. 1869-1927. German general. Hoffmann was one of the brightest generals on the German side but was often overlooked or merely exploited by his superiors. His early career established him as an expert in Eastern affairs, and he learned much about the Russian military as an official observer of the Russo-Japa-

nese War—specifically that Russian generals hated each other and could be relied on to quarrel among themselves. Hoffmann was a mere lieutenant colonel at the beginning of World War I, but he held a key position as the head of the staff of Gen. Max von Prittwitz in East Prussia. Hoffmann planned in detail an offensive to take back the initial gains made by the Russians during the first weeks of the war, but Prittwitz was sacked and the duo of Hindenburg and Ludendorff took his place and proceeded to usurp Hoffmann's plan. The result was the great triumph at Tannenberg, for which, of course, Hindenburg and Ludendorff took credit. Hoffmann also planned the German success at the winter battle at the Masurian Lakes in February 1915, but again received little credit: he was not promoted to full colonel until August of that year. He then moved to an assignment as chief of staff for the new commander in the East and personally managed the drive that sent the Russian general Brusilov reeling back after immense initial gains in mid-1917. Hoffmann was elevated to the rank of major general in October 1917 and two months later was entrusted with the negotiations at Brest-Litovsk with the new Bolshevik government of Russia. Although personally opposed to the iron demands of Hindenburg and Ludendorff, Hoffmann pressed the weak Russians for draconian concessions and renewed the war in early 1918 until they capitulated in humiliation. He remained in the Eastern theater until the final German surrender in late 1918.

JELLICOE, Sir John R. 1859-1935. British admiral. Jellicoe was, in the words of Winston Churchill, the only man on either side of the conflict who could have lost the war in an afternoon. He commanded the British Grand Fleet for the first two years of the war. He was aboard his flagship, *Iron Duke*, at the Battle of Jutland when the two great dreadnought fleets met in their only engagement, and a British loss would have spelled disaster. Jellicoe was born of a seafaring family in Southampton and joined the Royal Navy at a typically early age: thirteen. His career was in the Mediterranean and in the Far East (he was badly wounded during the Boxer Rebellion). However, he was most talented as a planner and builder of the navy. He became a protégé of Sir John Fisher, serving in the admiralty as director of naval ordnance and successively as third and second sea lord. Jellicoe had much of the responsibility for developing the new class of super battleships—including the original dreadnought—that came to dominate the balance of naval power before World War I. By August 1914, he was a vice admiral and commander in chief of the Grand Fleet. Jellicoe was therefore in control of a huge naval force that was in theory counterbalanced by a weaker but still potent German High Seas Fleet. The long history of British naval power led to the expectation that the nation's sailors would once again triumph at the first opportunity. However, the opportunity was long denied since the Germans (particularly the kaiser) so feared losing their hideously expensive dreadnought fleet that they refused to leave port. Jellicoe and the Grand Fleet settled into a position of distant blockade, guarding the approaches to the North Sea from bases at Scapa Flow, Rosyth, and Cromarty. Only the respective battle-cruiser squadrons roamed the waters for the first year and a half of the war. At the end of May 1916, the German command finally decided to bring its fleet out, and Admiral Hipper was sent ahead with the battle cruisers to bait a trap for the British light squadron. Ironically, Jellicoe had the same plan, and the Grand Fleet was on the water with Admiral Beatty sent on to draw the Germans into the maw of the British dreadnoughts. The two fleets met off Jutland on 31 May. Jellicoe had a greater weight of firepower and ships, but he lacked the Germans' better fire control systems and their speed of maneuver and communication. Despite twice approaching the line of German ships in an advantageous position, Jellicoe could not deliver a heavy enough blow, for the most part frustrated by swift German maneuvers. At the end of the day, the High Seas Fleet had escaped, leaving several British ships sunk or disabled—an inconclusive result from the British point of view, although one Jellicoe could scarcely

have prevented given the German unwillingness to fight it out. Six months later, Jellicoe was removed from fleet command and made first lord of the admiralty (Fisher had resigned over the Dardanelles debacle). In his new position, Jellicoe ran into trouble over the issue of convoys—he was slow to accept this solution to the German U-boat menace—and he was turned out of office at the end of 1917. He was elevated to the peerage and in 1919 went to New Zealand where he became governor general the following year.

JOFFRE, Joseph. 1852-1931. French marshal. The first French commander in chief of World War I and hailed as his nation's savior after the Battle of the Marne, Joffre ultimately failed to understand the rigidity of the stalemate on the Western Front and sacrificed hundreds of thousands of French soldiers to futile massed offensives. He arrived at high command through an unusual route. His family background was far from glittering—he was the son of a provincial barrel maker, and he was by training an engineer. He graduated from the École Polytechnique after serving in the Franco-Prussian War and then spent most of his early career in the Colonial Service. Joffre was clearly a good engineering officer, but his activities over fifteen years in Indochina, Africa, and Madagascar seemed to have removed him from the obvious lines of advancement in the French army. These things may have turned out to his advantage, however, since he was free of political or social entanglements when appointed in 1911 as chief of the general staff, holding the rank of major general. He was, however, short on administrative experience and had to rely on subordinates (primarily Castelnau) for much of the day-to-day work. Joffre was largely responsible for putting the infamous Plan 17 into place as the essence of French military theory and planning. He absorbed the prevailing ideas of aggressive attack and established these principles as the guiding force behind all French planning to meet a German onslaught. He was not unaware of the threat of an invasion through Belgium, but he preferred, as did nearly all the French military, to concentrate on a planned massive offensive in the region of Alsace-Lorraine as a counterpoise to the German threat. The rapid events of August 1914 showed the fragility of this set of ideas. The German sweep brushed aside the weak French left wing, and the vaunted French offensive failed miserably. Joffre did, however, manage to stabilize his forces on the Marne and—with the help of subordinates, notably Galliéni—to stop the Germans and, indeed, give them a bloody repulse. Despite the fundamental weaknesses of Joffre's military ideas when faced with the circumstances of August 1914, his characteristic imperturbability was vital to redeeming the situation and averting an even worse catastrophe. He was unable thereafter to overcome the ingrained idea that prolonged, massive offenses might win a breakthrough, however, and throughout 1915 he commanded that such hugely costly enterprises go forth again and again. His ultimate folly was to have removed most of the armaments and troops from the Verdun region in order to feed his grand offensives elsewhere. When the largest German offensive to date fell on Verdun in early 1916, Joffre's weaknesses as a commander were exposed, and his subsequent costly offensive on the Somme sealed his fate. He was dismissed by a restive civil government at the end of the year. Joffre was assuaged with promotion to marshal, but he was completely out of the command loop for the rest of the war.

KEMAL PASHA, Mustapha (Ataturk). 1881-1938. Turkish general. Kemal was the best Turkish general of World War I and subsequently the political father of modern Turkey. He was born in Salonika and began a military education at age twelve. He was marked early as a brilliant student and strong personality, but because he was also a political intriguer, he was shunted to remote posts early in his army career as a way of keeping him away from the centers of power. Despite being posted to faraway Damascus in 1905, Kemal formed a revolutionary group and tried to organize a second cell in his native Salonika. He was too slow, however, and

the rival Young Turks usurped the role of revolutionaries, establishing themselves in 1908 as the effective rulers of the empire. Sealed off from politics, Kemal poured his energies into his military career. He gained valuable experience fighting the Italians in Libya in 1911 and 1912, and he developed ideas about how to resist amphibious landings. At the outbreak of the war in Europe in 1914, Kemal was a military attaché in Bulgaria. He was not in favor of Turkey's entry into the war on the side of the Central Powers, but once Enver Pasha had pushed his country into the conflict, Kemal fought brilliantly. He was in command of the main Turkish reserve forces on the Gallipoli Peninsula and correctly foresaw that the British would try to land there. Kemal deftly organized his defenses and ruthlessly counterattacked when the British forces came ashore in 1915. Far from the easy landings and quick victory they expected, the British army (made up to a large extent of Anzac troops) found that the Turks were well placed, quick to respond, and fierce fighters. The British hardly got off the beachheads and in several places were nearly destroyed. The ignominious British withdrawal made Kemal—justly—a national military hero. Advanced to the rank of general, Kemal in 1916 led Turkish armies in offensives in Anatolia against the Russians; but the terrain and the circumstances were against him (he thought the enterprise foolish), and little came of the effort. He was then transferred to the Middle Eastern theater, but the British were essentially already in control. The end of the war brought the dissolution of the Young Turk regime, and Kemal was free to assume a major political role in postwar Turkey. He skillfully fended off the calls to break up the empire completely and guided the nation toward a complete reorganization. He took office as the first president of a new Turkish republic in 1924. Known after 1934 as Ataturk, he remained in office until the year of his death.

KITCHENER, Horatio Herbert, Earl. 1850-1916. British field marshal. One of the great British military heroes of the late nineteenth century, Kitchener was British secretary of state for war during the first years of World War I. He was the son of an officer and was trained at the Royal Military Academy. Most of his illustrious career was spent in the far reaches of the empire, particularly the Middle East and Northern Africa. He was commander in Egypt (technically as an Egyptian official, but in truth as a British general) during most of the 1890s, and he won lasting fame and glory for his defeat of the forces of the Mahdi at Omdurman in 1897. Elevated to the peerage in reward, Kitchener (known usually thereafter as "Kitchener of Khartoum") subsequently served as governor of the Sudan, chief of staff at Gibraltar, second in command during the Boer War, and commander in chief of India. He became the first Earl of Kitchener and a field marshal by 1914, and he was the obvious choice as secretary of state for war when the conflict with the Central Powers began. His performance during the war was mixed, with his greatest accomplishment the raising of an entirely new army nearly three times the size of the British Expeditionary Force—the recruiting poster with his visage became a classic. Unfortunately, Kitchener's new armies were destroyed on the battlefields of the Western Front. Kitchener himself had few illusions about the nature of the conflict in France. Unlike most of his contemporaries, Kitchener realized early on that the line of trenches from the sea to Switzerland comprised a mutually unbreakable barrier, but he had little effect on changing the overall Allied strategy of trying to achieve a breakthrough by means of huge man-eating offensives. He was brisk with his civilian colleagues and hard on his commanders, notably Sir John French, all of which did little to endear him. He was more or less sucked into supporting the Dardanelles campaign. Despite his efforts to improvise a new command structure when things went awry, he personally bore much of the blame for the humiliating and costly failure of the campaign. He accepted an invitation to visit Russia in 1916, sailing aboard a cruiser in early June. His ship hit a mine and went down with all hands.

KLUCK, Alexander von. 1846-1934. German general. Commander of the German right wing in August 1914, Kluck is usually blamed for a fatal mistake during the first weeks of the war. He was a career officer, entering the army at age nineteen, and a veteran of the Austrian and French wars of 1866 and 1870-71. He was a major general by 1899 and continued to advance in rank and appointment until the eve of the war, which found him a colonel general in command of the First Army, assigned to form the far right-hand element of the planned German sweep through Belgium into France. His task was to move as rapidly as possible to a position west of Paris. The first efforts went well, despite surprisingly stubborn Belgian resistance, and by late August von Kluck had defeated the tiny British army twice and seemed to have nothing in his way between his army and his objectives. He was seduced, however, by the prospect of a vulnerable French army to the east of Paris. Kluck altered his route of march to swing inward to the south with the hope of enveloping the main French force in a grand double encirclement. Unfortunately for the Germans, the movement was ill-coordinated and opened a wide gap between Kluck's First Army and the Second Army of Bülow. Having crossed the Marne in the first days of September, Kluck was nevertheless open to a flanking attack, which the French managed to bring on by tapping the last resources at their command. At this stage, despite local success, Kluck was ordered to pull back to defensive positions. The result of the subsequent Battle of the Marne was the beginning of the massive stalemate along the intended trench lines in Eastern France. Kluck bore the brunt of much blame for the failed German grand plan. He was badly wounded in March 1915, and coupled with his advanced age, the lingering injury prompted the German high command to retire Kluck in October 1916. He lived for nearly two more decades, however, and never ceased to blame the German general staff for the failure to beat France in September 1914.

LANREZAC, Charles. 1852-1925. French general. Lanrezac was born in the

French overseas possession of Guadeloupe and attended the military academy at Saint-Cyr before fighting as a young officer in the Franco-Prussian War of 1870-71. He became one of the bright stars of the French army, revered as an intellectual as well as a capable officer. By 1906, he was a brigadier general and the protégé of Joffre, who was just coming to the heights of power in the French military establishment. Lanrezac was assigned in the event of war to command the Fifth Army on the far left wing, and it would be his responsibility to stop any German assault from that quarter. The infamous French Plan 17, in which Joffre and others placed such faith, assumed that the Germans would be weak on their right and that Lanrezac should be able not only to stop an offensive from Belgium, but to then turn and add weight to the main planned French offensive through Alsace and Lorraine. Lanrezac, when he saw the details of Plan 17 in the spring of 1914, was dubious. His fears were realized during the first weeks of the war, when it became increasingly obvious that the main German thrust was through Belgium and massive forces were bent on sweeping Lanrezac (and the British army) aside before advancing on Paris. Lanrezac was a poor one at coordinating with the British. In fact, he showed disdain for his ally. The defeats inflicted on the British prompted Lanrezac to rapidly withdraw southward. At the last minute, he turned on the Germans and gave them a nasty repulse at Guise, but thereafter his Fifth Army began to fall apart under the strain of prolonged movement and fighting. Joffre removed Lanrezac from command just as the crucial Battle of the Marne began. The sacked general—who had grown more vocally pessimistic as the Germans pressed southward—never again held command. His reputation was revived to a large degree by Pétain after the war.

LANSING, Robert. 1864-1928. American secretary of state. Lansing was the wartime American secretary of state and had a major role in drawing up the eventual peace treaty. He was born in New York and became a lawyer after study at Amherst College in Massachusetts. For two decades before World War I, Lansing served as an increasingly important counsel to the federal government on matters of international law, and he also worked for several foreign governments in Washington, D.C. He was appointed to the State Department in spring 1914 under Secretary of State William Jennings Bryan. When Bryan resigned in protest over Pres. Woodrow Wilson's handling of the *Lusitania* affair, Lansing was advanced to the secretaryship. He found Wilson a difficult master most of the time. The president conducted much of the nation's foreign affairs from his own office and seldom was Lansing at center stage in the three years before America entered the European war. Lansing favored American involvement, however, and supported the war effort vigorously after April 1917. His greatest role was at the Paris Peace Conference, where he was again somewhat at odds with Wilson. Lansing saw Wilson's idealism as naive, and his ideology more resembled some of the veteran European diplomats than that of his own president. Lansing was responsible for inserting the war guilt clause in the final treaty—a clause that eventually aided the Nazi mischief by establishing a smoldering German resentment. Lansing, like other American officials, was placed in a difficult position by the onset of Wilson's debilitating illness. After calling a cabinet meeting in Wilson's absence (the president was in fact not functional) in early 1920, Lansing was forced out of office. He returned to the practice of law in Washington, a time-honored employment for former officeholders.

LAWRENCE, T.E. ("Lawrence of Arabia"). 1888-1935. One of the most colorful and controversial figures of World War I and widely known today as a subject of popular films, Lawrence genuinely accomplished a good deal among the Arabs of the Persian Gulf against the Turks. He was the illegitimate son of an Irish family, whose real name was Chapman (Lawrence fostered obscurity about his identity throughout his life). He was well educated at Oxford and became interested in Middle Eastern archaeology and culture, traveling to Egypt, Palestine, Syria, and Turkey, and learning the region's languages. He joined the geographical division of the War Office in 1914, having proved too short for regular army duty. He soon joined the Arab Department headquartered in Cairo and by 1916 had cultivated relationships among the Arab tribes. He was named as liaison to Faisal (third son of Grand Sherif Hussein) late in that year. In the following months, Lawrence helped organize the Arab forces as guerrilla fighters against the Turks, raiding the rail lines and hemming in the garrison-bound enemy. In August 1917, he took the city of Aqaba in Faisal's name. With the support of British commander Allenby, Lawrence brought even better organization and supplies to the Arabs during 1917. He was captured and tortured by the Turks, but they failed to recognize him before he escaped. He and Faisal led a victorious Arab army into Damascus just ahead of Allenby in October 1918. Back in England after the armistice, Lawrence was embittered by the cynical British partition of the Middle East, in which he believed the Arabs to have gotten the short end, and he withdrew from official life, despite a wave of romantic journalism that had made him famous. He eventually published classic accounts of the war in *Revolt in the Desert* and *Seven Pillars of Wisdom,* books with great literary merit but short on veracity. He enlisted in the Royal Flying Corps and then the Royal Tank Corps under pseudonyms, although he maintained contact with many of his powerful literary and political friends. He died from injuries suffered in a motorcycle accident. Much energy has been expended in attempting to explain Lawrence's complex character and behavior.

LENIN, Vladimir or Nicolai (Ulianov). 1870-1924. Russian revolutionary. Among the most dramatic characters of the twentieth century, once the secular saint of the modern communist Soviet Union, and now discredited as the founder of a failed ideological state, Lenin was born in a provincial town on the Volga with the family name Ulianov (he assumed "Lenin" as a revolu-

tionary name later in life). Embittered by the execution of his elder brother for a treasonous murder conspiracy, Lenin became a radical revolutionary devoted to the theories of Karl Marx. During the long decades before the war, Lenin seemed unlikely to ever have a major role in history. He spent five years as a prisoner in Siberia and then moved into exile from his homeland. He was a brilliant writer and orator, but between 1900 and 1917 seemed to be little more than one among many contentious exiled Russian revolutionaries. The Russian Revolution of 1905 passed him by, although it brought a rival, Leon Trotsky, to prominence. Lenin believed that the massive dislocations of the war would so disrupt Russia that revolution would be inevitable. Therefore, having survived on subsidies from the Germans during the first years of the war when he lived in Switzerland, Lenin accepted German transportation to Russia in March 1917 when the abdication of the czar and the breakdown of most of Russian society seemed to present his great opportunity. His triumph was not swift or easy, however, and not until November when the city of Saint Petersburg led the way did his small party of Bolsheviks manage to gain control. He proved a ruthless and skillful politician once the reins of power were within his grasp. Using the Peoples' Councils ("soviets") that sprang up among the peasants, soldiers, sailors, and industrial workers as his organizational basis, Lenin took over the Russian state, sharing power with Trotsky. His first order of business was to conclude a peace agreement with the Germans, a necessity in any event since the Russian army had disintegrated in the field. He tried to bargain with the German military dictatorship that by then controlled Berlin, but the Germans refused to budge from their extreme demands. After they renewed fighting, Lenin was forced to capitulate and agree to the humiliating treaty of Brest-Litovsk in March 1918. The following years saw civil war between the new Communist state and the dissident ethnic republics and the White supporters of the older regime, with armies and supplies from the western powers complicating the issue. By late 1920, Lenin and his Communist state had the upper hand. Within two years, however, he began to suffer a series of strokes and died in 1924 before his new government had been fully developed. His body was embalmed and placed on display at the Kremlin in Moscow.

LETTOW-VORBECK, Paul von. 1870-1964. German general. Fighting nearly in isolation in Africa, Lettow-Vorbeck displayed consummate skill as a soldier, eluding defeat by the vastly superior numbers of the British and South Africans. He was born in Pomerania and began his overseas duty in 1904 as a member of a China expedition. In 1907, he went to Africa to help put down a black uprising in German South-West Africa, receiving promotion to major at the end of the conflict. He was given command of the small German forces—around three thousand white troops—in East Africa in January 1914 with the rank of lieutenant colonel. Germany had been as eager as other European nations to grab parts of black Africa for itself during the late nineteenth century, making territorial acquisitions a matter of national prestige. However, unlike Great Britain, Germany had no way to support governments or military forces in the new possessions once a fighting war began in Europe. German transports could not reach African colonies during World War I in any appreciable numbers, so Lettow-Vorbeck was on his own to fight a war with a handful of white troops and black askaris. He probably never commanded more than thirteen or fourteen thousand men at any one time during the war, although the British and the South Africans had armies numbering in the hundreds of thousands. During the first months of the conflict, Lettow-Vorbeck actually won a few battles, notably at Tanga, but by the end of 1915, he could do little except conduct a skillful, elusive series of retreats. The main British effort to crush Lettow-Vorbeck was headed by South African General Jan Smuts, who had to contend with rebellion among his own Afrikaner officers. Smuts chased Lettow-Vorbeck during most of 1916, but could never quite bring his superior num-

bers to bear. After a victory against a far larger enemy at Lindi in October 1917, Lettow-Vorbeck had to abandon organized resistance and fall back on guerrilla warfare. He was still at it in late 1918 when the armistice in Europe brought an end to the war and his surrender. He returned to Germany and became one of the chief military supporters of the right wing against the radical German revolutionaries. He was forced to resign in 1920 after lending his troops to a right-wing coup attempt. He lived to a very old age, being one of the longest surviving major figures of World War I.

LIGGETT, Hunter. 1857-1935. American general. Liggett was born in Pennsylvania and graduated from West Point in 1879. His first duties were on the western frontier, but he moved through the usual peacetime army staff posts and schools. By 1912 he served as president of the Army War College with the rank of colonel. He received his major generalship only a month before the United States entered World War I. He took command of the Forty-first Division in France in October 1917 and was promoted to command of the Ist Army Corps four months later. Liggett was an immensely fat man but clearly one of considerable intelligence and courage: his famous *bon mot* was to tell his critics that fat was most serious if it was above the collar. Liggett commanded the American fighting at Château-Thierry in July 1918, a successful action that established the Americans as competent and able to hold the trench line and participate fully in offensives. He also commanded four divisions during the American advance against the Saint-Mihiel salient in mid-September, and he was the primary field commander at the American offensive in the Argonne Forest. In mid-October, Liggett was given command of the million man First Army and launched the American portion of the final offensive that drove Germany to surrender. After brief postwar service in Europe, Liggett returned to a command in California. He retired from the army in 1921.

LIMAN von SANDERS, Otto. 1855-1929. German and Turkish general. Although a German general, most of Liman von Sanders's service during the war was as a field marshal of the Turkish Empire. He was born in Pomerania and trained as a cavalryman. He had reached the rank of major general by 1906 and was promoted to lieutenant general in 1911. He added his wife's name, Sanders, to his own when raised to the nobility in 1913. Late in the same year, he went to Turkey as head of the German military mission, and he received full rank as a Turkish field marshal. The Germans had immense influence in Turkish affairs even before the formal entry of Turkey into the war on the side of the Central Powers, and Liman von Sanders was essentially commander of the Turkish armies. He was in overall command of the Turkish defenses during the British attempt to force the Dardanelles Straits and the subsequent landings at Gallipoli. He skillfully used his forces to hem the British landings on the beachheads and received a great deal of justifiable credit for the Turkish triumph, although he was criticized for allowing the British to eventually evacuate unscathed. Affairs did not go so well in 1918, when Liman von Sanders was sent to command the failing Turkish fortunes in Mesopotamia. Despite a long struggle that had at times been successful, the Turks had been pushed slowly backward. Liman von Sanders found few reliable troops left and suffered severely from a lack of supplies and reinforcements. He could do little to stem the tide, and the Turkish effort more or less collapsed in the fall of 1918 under pressure from British General Allenby. Liman von Sanders stayed in Constantinople until January 1919 and was taken into custody by the British at Malta when he tried to return to Germany. He retired later in the year.

LLOYD GEORGE, David. 1863-1945. British prime minister. Unlike most of the government and military leaders of Great Britain, Lloyd George was from humble social origins and identified during most of his career with the lower and middle classes of the kingdom. His Welshness and his pugnacious public persona (especially on the speaking platform) set him distinctly

apart. He was the son of an impoverished Welsh schoolmaster and enjoyed none of the advantages of financial security or an easy path to education. By his late twenties, however, Lloyd George had become a lawyer and was on his way to the top of the political heap as a member of the Liberal Party. In 1890, he took a seat in the House of Commons. He was a vocal opponent of national policy in South Africa but had little effect on the Boer War. He took national office in 1905 as president of the Board of Trade, and in 1908 Lloyd George became chancellor of the Exchequer, a position that earned him great attention when he introduced the "People's Budget" that established the outlines of the modern welfare state and set off a major constitutional crisis when the House of Lords rejected Lloyd George's plan. Soon after the coming of the war in Europe in 1914, Lloyd George became one of the more vociferous proponents of an aggressive policy of all-out prosecution of the conflict. He saw the long-range implications of the war far more quickly than most of his government colleagues, and his understanding was considerably in advance of the generals, a group he came into conflict with during the rest of the war. Lloyd George's main strategic scheme was to strike at the Triple Alliance through Greece, and he argued long (but futilely) for a major effort from Salonika. The major political crisis of 1915, when the failure of the Dardanelles Campaign and the shortage of munitions brought down the Asquith government and humbled Kitchener, elevated Lloyd George to the key post of minister of munitions, and he became secretary of war when Kitchener was lost at sea in 1916. In December of that year, Lloyd George engineered the fall of the final Asquith coalition, and he assumed the prime minister's post himself. He exhibited his direct and vigorous approach to matters almost immediately by paring down the War Cabinet and entering into a prolonged fight with the army command. He had a difficult time dislodging the idea of massive attacks from the minds of the generals—nearly half a million casualties came during the ill-conceived new offenses during the late summer of 1917—but the horrible butcher's bills finally gave Lloyd George the upper hand, and he forced out Robertson as head of the Imperial General Staff and managed to have Haig (Lloyd George's special foe) finally subordinated to a new supreme allied commander, Foch. Lloyd George remained in office after the war as head of the coalition, but increasing problems, especially after the establishment of the Irish Free State, forced him to resign in 1922. He remained out of power for the rest of his life.

LUDENDORFF, Erich. 1865-1937. German general. Arguably the finest tactician of the war on either side of the conflict, Ludendorff's early brilliant successes in the field led to his eventual assumption of almost dictatorial political power during the final years of the war. Along with his alter ego, Paul von Hindenburg, Ludendorff symbolized the German war effort and virtually the entire German state by 1918. He was not, like most of his fellow German generals, an aristocrat but was the son of a merchant family from the Polish section of Prussia. His early military career was marked by relatively slow advancement but initiative and brilliance of thought that scared his superiors. After serving as a junior officer on the general staff and as a humble company commander, Ludendorff finally won an important post in 1908 as the officer responsible for mobilization and deployment under the Schlieffen Plan. Once again, however, his boldness and vision were too much for his more cautious seniors, and he was removed from his post in 1913 after proposing massive increases in spending for munitions and men. When the war began in August 1914, Ludendorff was rescued from obscurity and given the spot as deputy chief of staff to Bülow's Second Army. He won undying fame with his lightning seizure of Liége a few days later. Within another two weeks, Ludendorff was snatched from the Western Front and appointed chief of staff of the Eighth Army in the East. He joined Hindenburg on their famous train ride from Hanover to East Prussia during the last weeks of August 1914. The duo took control of the

German forces and executed the brilliant maneuvers that brought the overwhelming victories at Tannenberg and the Masurian Lakes. In effect these victories destroyed the potential of the huge Russian armies to ever seriously threaten the Eastern Front, although huge campaigns remained over the subsequent three years. Ludendorff's flame burned incandescently, even though conflicts with Falkenhayn prevented a full and decisive blow in the East. When Falkenhayn fell from grace in mid-1916, Ludendorff became quartermaster general of the entire German army with Hindenburg the chief of the general staff. In truth, the older man was more and more a figurehead, and Ludendorff came to virtually rule the nation from late 1916 on. He not only assumed an iron control over the military in the field, but he also directed domestic economical and political affairs with complete authority. During 1917, Ludendorff's plan to defeat the Allies through unrestricted submarine warfare came to naught, and the eventual entry of the United States into the European conflict threatened the German position. Ludendorff effectively mobilized the civilian population and economy to sustain the massive war effort, but he was unable to follow up on the great victory at Caporetto on the Italian front in the fall of the year. Perhaps his greatest mistake was in forcing the new revolutionary government in Russia into the humiliating treaty of Brest-Litovsk that stripped Russia of most of her previous territory in Eastern Europe. Ludendorff and Hindenburg apparently saw few limits to German expansion in the East, but in fact, they claimed far more than the nation could practically control. Turning to the Western Front in 1918, Ludendorff decided to gamble on a massive attack that would either achieve the long-sought breakthrough or so bleed the Allies that they would capitulate. The horrendous offensives (employing the new assault tactics developed on the Eastern Front) launched in the spring and early summer created deep bulges in the Allied front but did not quite burst through. The effort was the last the German nation could sustain, and collapse began. Ludendorff then lost his nerve entirely and asked for peace on any terms. He resigned in October 1918, a few weeks before the armistice, and fled the country for the safety of neutral Sweden. After the war, he returned to Germany and became a right-wing politician, supporting the Nazi putsch in 1923 and eventually running for president of the Weiman Republic on the Nazi ticket in 1925. His final years were spent as a shrill voice of anti-Semitism.

MACKENSEN, August von. 1849-1945. German field marshal. Mackensen was one of the most successful of all German field commanders, going from triumph to triumph in the East during almost the entire war. Much of his reputation may have been built on the talents of his subordinates, but selecting staff skillfully is one of the requisites of good generalship. Mackensen was born in Saxony. He entered the army as a twenty-year-old, left service briefly for a stretch of schooling, and returned in 1873. He rose steadily in the Imperial military establishment in the four decades between the Franco-Prussian War and the beginning of World War I. He was ennobled in 1899 and served as adjutant to the kaiser. Mackensen's most conspicuous posts were in command of cavalry, and he acquired a reputation as a dashing horseman, resplendent in the cavalry uniforms of the day. Beneath the glitter, however, was a very capable soldier. He commanded the Eighth Army on the Eastern Front in August 1914 and was forced to withdraw in the face of unexpectedly strong Russian attacks during the first days of the conflict under the orders of Prittwitz. When Hindenburg and Ludendorff took control of the East, however, Mackensen moved to the offensive against the Russians with great success. His stunning victory at the Masurian Lakes in early September and his even more impressive triumph at Lodz in December (following a temporary repulse by the Russians) more or less sealed the general issue on the Eastern Front—Russia might threaten but would never again pose a serious challenge. In early 1915, Mackensen took command of a new army that included Austro-Hungarian units and in early May broke through the opposition at Gorlice in one of the greatest victories of the war. He followed up with victory after victory over the retreating Russians. He was made a field marshal in June as a consequence of his string of successes. By the end of the summer, Mackensen had pushed the Russians as far as the Pripet Marshes. He then assumed command of a mixed force of German, Austro-Hungarian, and Bulgarian troops and turned to attack Serbia. Within three weeks, he had taken the enemy capital and within four had chased the entire Serbian army from its own country. The following year, after Romania entered the war on the side of the Allies, Mackensen led another mixed Central Powers force in an invasion of the new foe, seizing the capital of Bucharest after a three-month campaign. For the balance of the war, Mackensen remained in Romania. He was arrested by the Hungarians after the armistice in November 1918 but was allowed to return home and retire. During the 1930s, Mackensen actively supported the Nazis and lent his name and presence to Hitler's regime. He died at a great age at the end of the second war.

MILNE, Sir Archibald Berkeley. Born 1855. British admiral. Milne's career was based on personal charm, high birth, and support from the British court—all factors that failed to provide sufficient fighting qualities when the war broke out in 1914. He had actually been born on the premises of the Royal Navy at the admiralty (his father was an admiral of the fleet) and began his career with the naval equivalent of a silver spoon in his mouth. He entered the navy at age fifteen and set the course of his life in 1882 when he was assigned to the royal yacht. Henceforth, Milne enjoyed the direct patronage of the court. His rise up the grades was relatively swift thereafter, and by 1904 he flew his flag as an admiral. His notable commands include a term as second of the Atlantic Fleet and as head of the Channel and home fleets. When the war broke out, Milne was commander of the fleet in the Mediterranean, where a confused set of circumstances confounded the British. No one was quite certain what Italy would do in the case of war (she was theoretically tied to Germany and Austria-Hungary by treaty) or if Turkey would remain neutral. Milne's role initially was to support the French Fleet in guarding transports from North Africa, but more important was the presence in the Mediterranean of two German cruisers, the *Goeben* and the *Breslau*. Milne had a greatly superior force and should have been able to take or sink the Germans, but he dithered and allowed the two German warships to escape to Turkey, where they were formally interned and taken into the Turkish service—a circumstance that helped push Turkey into the arms of the enemy alliance. Milne was recalled and, although officially absolved of blame, not again employed by the admiralty.

MOLTKE, Helmuth von. 1848-1916. German general. Widely viewed after the war as a lesser heir of great German military minds, the "younger" Moltke (as he was known) was the nephew of the illustrious German victor in the Franco-Prussian War. He had entered the army in 1869, in time to fight under his uncle in the lightning victories against France. He served as an adjutant to the elder Moltke and then was attached to the staff of the kaiser. Moltke had reached the rank of major general by the turn of the century. In 1906, he became chief of the general staff, taking over the reins from the legendary Schlieffen. Moltke was by no means an inept or incompetent soldier, and he saw the possibilities of war in Europe with a much clearer vision than many, especially Wilhelm II. The general was, nonetheless, not in command of the strongest will or nerves, and this may have led to his undoing of the grand German plan for quick victory in the West. While it is debatable that the Schlieffen Plan would have worked as envisioned if carried out flawlessly, Moltke's alterations to the concept of a massive right-hand sweep through Belgium, Holland, and northeastern France clearly were responsible for letting the French off the hook insofar as the French and British armies remained intact after the first weeks of the war and Paris remained unoccupied. Moltke insisted that his right-wing commanders pause to take Liége, and he detached key elements from the right wing and sent them to the Eastern Front when massive Russian movements threatened East Prussia. He acquiesced in allowing a strong offensive on the left of the French—enticed perhaps by the possibility of a double envelopment in the classic mode—which weakened the right. He then appeared to give up close observation of the western campaign, allowing his field commanders to turn inside Paris and set up on the Marne with no comment or direction from general headquarters. By the time Moltke dispatched an emissary to the front with orders to rearrange the armies, it was too late. The French counterattacks along the Marne had stymied the possibility of German movements. The course of the war as a stalemate had been set. Moltke resigned as chief of staff in mid-September, turning over command to Falkenhayn. He attempted an unsuccessful comeback in early 1915 and died of a heart attack in June 1916.

MONRO, Sir Charles C. 1860-1929. British general. A capable although not brilliant soldier, Monro showed more common sense than most British generals during the war, preferring to view hopeless situations with clear eyes and to run the risk of opprobrium rather than throw away thousands (or hundreds of thousands) of lives fruitlessly, as was the habit of his colleague commanders. He was a Scot who attended Sandhurst and first served in 1879 in the Second Regiment of Foot. His career before the beginning of World War I was not unusual for a rising British officer. In addition to tours of duty at Malta and in India, he commanded a division in South Africa during the Boer War. Several of his subsequent assignments—to the musketry school and as commander of London Territorials—were less than fashionable, but he nonetheless was advanced to significant command when the British Expeditionary Force was sent to France in August 1914. Monro headed a division under Haig in the Ist Corps, and in October, he commanded his division at the first battle of Ypres. By the end of the year, Monro took command of Ist Corps after the government's juggling of commanders advanced Haig to overall control of the BEF. Following the summer offensives, Monro was appointed as commander of the new Third Army, but very shortly thereafter was ordered to the Dardanelles to take command of the faltering Gallipoli Expedition. Here he demonstrated better judgment than almost all his fellow general officers. The situation was hopeless, the Allies having frittered away their early opportunities and settled into a series of impossible positions along the coastline. Tens of thousands of casualties from disease, the strong Turkish resistance, and inept supply and strategy had drained all possibility of a breakout. Monro recognized the futility of the Allies' position, and he immediately recommended a withdrawal. The idea was politically unacceptable to the war government, but eventually—after Kitchener himself came out to view the scene—Monro was allowed to evacuate the troops, a move he carried out skillfully with a minimum of further loss of life. During the first months of 1916, Monro returned to command in France but was content to keep most of his troops out of the horrendous offensives in Somme. In October, he was transferred to India as commander in chief, and he remained on the subcontinent for the rest of the war. During the 1920s, he served as governor of Gibraltar.

NICHOLAS II. 1869-1918. Russian czar. The cousin of both George V of Great Britain and Wilhelm II of Germany, Nicholas was a weak incompetent who was called on to face historic problems only a genius could have mastered. In the end, he and his family paid the ultimate price for the forces unleashed by the war. He was the eldest son of Alexander III and was married to a German princess, Alix of Hesse-Darmstadt. Nicholas came to the throne in Russia in 1894, inheriting a complex, cumbersome imperial system that placed him at the apex of virtually all civil, military, and political institutions with theoretically unfettered autocratic power. In fact, his vast nation was in creaky disrepair, despite vast natural resources and a numberless population. Nicholas apparently perceived reality only dimly during most of his reign. He appointed a succession of poor ministers and seemed to take interest in his responsibilities only when it was too late to make a difference. The first great series of crises came in 1904 and 1905, when Russia was ignominiously defeated in a foreign war by the Japanese, and a subsequent domestic near-revolution came close to toppling the state. A measure of reforms—including the establishment of a token representative body, the Duma—assuaged the political and civil unrest for a decade, but the fundamental instabilities of the Russian Imperial system, especially when all power was vested in a person of such slim resources, remained. By the beginning of the war in 1914, Nicholas had turned more and more inward. The birth of a male heir to the throne in 1904 had proved a bitter disappointment—the young prince bore the defective family gene that caused hemophilia and was subject to a precarious life of painful illness. The czarina, who strongly influenced Nicholas, was under the thrall of the malevolent Rasputin. The result was a nation with a political system that relied on an autocrat who in this case was incapable of ruling. For example, Nicholas refused in 1914 to take command of the armies, relinquishing this role to his uncle, the Grand Duke Nicholas. While the Grand Duke was far and away a better choice, the Russian system made it impossible to organize, coordinate, and control the army without the direct authority of the czar at the head. The fatal disorganization of the Russian war effort was to a degree the result of the vacuum at the top. At the same time, Nicholas refused to make meaningful political appointments or reforms that would have diminished his power in any way. By mid-1915, the war had nearly eroded all the essential structures of the Russian state. Nicholas fired his uncle and took direct control of the army, but not only was he incapable of performing adequately, it was too late. The following year and a half witnessed the final deterioration of the nation in the face of the horrendous costs of the war—and a rising tide of civil unrest. Nicholas became more and more isolated from reality and continued to resist reforms that involved diminution of his divine right to absolute power. By spring 1917, the situation had reached a critical point. Seemingly simple bread riots in Saint Petersburg could not be repressed, and the army commanders refused to support the czar. Nicholas was forced to abdicate in March. He and his family were arrested by the new provincial government and packed off to Ekaterinburg in Siberia where they remained while the Bolshevik Revolution took place. On the orders of Lenin, Nicholas and his entire family were shot to death in a basement in July 1918. Their bodies were crudely buried in a nearby wood and only positively identified in 1992 after the dissolution of the Soviet Communist state.

NICHOLAS, Grand Duke. 1856-1929. Russian commander. The uncle of Nicholas II and brother of Alexander II, the Grand Duke was one of the more talented members of the imperial family. A man of impressive personal bearing—at six feet eight inches he towered over most of his associates—he showed competence during his military career, although he lacked the brilliance that might have meant better fortunes for Russian arms. He was trained as a soldier, attending both the army engineering school and the general staff academy. By the turn of the century, Nicholas was inspector general of the cavalry. He also played an important political role in Russia. During the "revolution" of 1905, he urged constitutional reforms on his nephew the czar (to no avail) and continued periodically during the remainder of the time of imperial rule to suggest a loosening of the autocratic stranglehold on political power. It came as something of a surprise when the Grand Duke was named commander in chief of the Russian forces in August 1914. The command should have been held by the czar under the Russian system, but the young ruler insisted that his uncle take control in his place. Nicholas had little success during his year as head of the large but uncoordinated Russian army. He could do little to direct or coordinate the two separate fronts that faced

Germany and Austria-Hungary. The initial success of Russian offensives into East Prussia was wiped away by the disasters at Tannenberg and the Masurian Lakes. The final blows were delivered by Mackensen in the breakthrough at Gorlice in May 1915. Grand Duke Nicholas was relieved of command by his nephew in August and given a post as commander of the Caucasus. He supported other field commanders in March 1917 and pressured the czar to abdicate. After a brief residence in the Crimea, Nicholas fled Russia and the Bolsheviks in 1919. He died in France ten years later as the Romanov pretender to the imperial throne.

NIVELLE, Robert. 1856-1924. French general. Nivelle was the most disastrous of the French commanders in chief during World War I. He was half French and half British (he spoke perfect, unaccented English), born in Tulle. His prewar career was not spectacular, since he was only a colonel in 1914 when the fighting began. His training and field command experience was in the artillery, and he was a master of the small-scale engagement where he used his guns with great imagination and skill, showing himself especially adept at the first battles on the Marne in September 1914. He advanced rapidly up the ladder of promotion and responsibility thereafter. He commanded a corps as a major general by the time he was sent to defend the fortresses at Verdun, which had been left open to a massive German attack. His very strong will and considerable abilities helped the French hold on to part of the fortress system and eventually—over the better part of a year—to win back much that had been lost in the initial German assault, but the cost to both sides was astronomical. By the end of the prolonged battles over Verdun, Nivelle had assumed a heroic glow in the minds of the public and the politicians. He was named in late 1916 to replace Joffre as commander in chief, mostly on the strength of his loud, confident assertions that he could win the war in one glorious offensive. Nivelle's ideas turned out to be no better than any of his predecessors—he clung to the increasingly absurd notion that a spirited offense could somehow batter through the defensive trench lines and turn a static war into an open-ground free-for-all. Fighting off critics who foretold the doom of his plan, Nivelle forced agreement by the government to a massive assault against the German lines at Chemin des Dames. The result of his April attack was a slaughter for the French troops and scarcely any ground won from the Germans. Nivelle's brainless reversion to the ideal of the all-out offensive led to widespread mutinies among the French army, which had had all humans can take. Nivelle was replaced by Pétain a month after his offensive and relegated to a meaningless post in Africa.

PERSHING, John J. 1860-1948. American general. The strong-willed commander of the American Expeditionary Force in Europe in 1917 and 1918, Pershing had graduated from the U.S. Military Academy at West Point and served in the cavalry. After a hiatus as a college professor, he saw duty in the Philippines and in the Spanish-American War in Cuba as an officer of black troops (hence his nickname "Black-Jack"). He caught the eye of Pres. Teddy Roosevelt and was promoted over the heads of several hundred senior officers in 1906, becoming a brigadier general. After another tour in the Philippines, he was given the task of chasing Mexican bandit Pancho Villa in 1916. He spent a year in a futile series of small operations on and across the border. When the United States finally resolved to enter the European war in the spring of 1917, Pershing was the choice to head American divisions that would sail for France. He was a hard-headed man and clung tightly to the principle that American doughboys would not be separated and used to replace dead British or French soldiers in existing armies. The Americans were full of vigor but had practically no logistical system and nothing in the way of artillery, tanks, or planes, the three elements that had assumed the most important roles in the war along the Western Front by 1917. Despite the pleas of Foch and Haig, Pershing kept his American army—eventually numbering more than

half a million men—together. Finally placed in the line, some of the American infantry gained enough experience to be entrusted with an offensive in September 1918 against the Saint-Mihiel salient. They fought well and pushed out the disintegrating German units. Pershing followed up in a second offensive at the Argonne Forest a few days later. At the end of the war, Pershing was a hero to the public and returned home to high reward—he was named to the rarely awarded rank of general of the army and was appointed as chief of staff.

PÉTAIN, Henri Philippe. 1856-1851. French marshal. Although his name was indelibly sullied by his actions during the subsequent war in 1940, Pétain was one of the great French heroes during the 1914-1918 conflict, but he began the war as an obscure officer. He was an orphan, raised by an uncle and educated in Catholic schools. He attended Saint-Cyr, graduating in 1878, and became a specialist in infantry tactics. By 1900, he was still only a major. Between the turn of the century and the outbreak of the war, Pétain was embroiled in the drawn-out debates in the French military establishment over the proper theory of war: he advocated caution, meticulous preparation, reliance on massive artillery, and avoidance of headlong assaults. The prevailing view, of course, as embodied finally in Plan 17, held just the opposite. Pétain was on his way out of the army in 1914 as an object of derision among his peers, even though he proved in the end to be one of the few Allied generals who grasped the nature of modern industrial warfare. He commanded infantry during the crucial days of August 1914 and was promoted to brigadier on the strength of his leadership. Thereafter he rose steadily in rank and responsibility, despite the fact that his views were still in the minority. In May 1915, one of his carefully prepared offensives took Vimy Ridge. He continued as the year drew to a close to advise the high command to use men sparingly and artillery in profusion. When Falkenhayn unleashed his giant attack on the fortress area of Verdun, hoping to bleed the French army to death, Pétain was rushed in to take command. He performed magnificently in organizing the nonstop supply of the front along the single road left open to the French. He also rotated troops in and out of the front lines, preserving their fighting qualities. Despite his success, Pétain was passed over in favor of Nivelle when Joffre was finally ousted in late 1916. Nivelle's spectacular failure the following spring brought the army to mutiny and finally elevated Pétain to the top spot of command. His personal efforts helped restore order to the mutinous troops within a few weeks, and the Germans failed to take advantage of the lapse in discipline. Pétain was passed over again, however, in April 1918 when his arch-rival, Foch, was named as the Supreme Allied Generalissimo. Following the war, Pétain remained in the army, and in the 1930s turned to political office. When the Germans overran France at the beginning of the next war, Pétain (by then in his eighties) consented to head the collaborationist government of "unoccupied" France at Vichy. He was tried and convicted as a traitor after the war, but his death sentence was suspended in favor of life imprisonment.

POINCARÉ, Raymond. 1860-1934. French president. As the most consistent political officeholder in France during the war, Poincaré wielded great influence while holding a post that seemed to be mostly ceremonial. He was a native of Lorraine and as a child had seen the Germans occupy his home after the Franco-Prussian War, a memory that seemed to drive his anti-German stance of later years with a particular, personal fury. He was elected to the Chamber of Deputies in 1887, first taking government office five years later as minister for public education. He seemed destined for early political brilliance after a term as minister of finance, but in 1896 Poincaré withdrew from office and politics in favor of a private (and lucrative) practice of law. After making a fortune as a lawyer, he returned to political life and became prime minister in 1912. During the months immediately before the war, Poincaré appeared to work both publicly and behind the scenes to increase tensions and to push the nations of Europe toward armed conflict. In 1913, he ran for the hitherto meaningless office of president of the French Republic, winning easily and assuming the post he was to hold during the entire war. He was the only major French political official to remain for the duration without changing posts. By virtue of his consistency and his own personality, Poincaré came to influence mightily the course of the war. He manipulated the selection of prime ministers, sometimes without recourse to public elections or a vote of no confidence in the national assembly, and he became the chief diplomat for the nation. He was never able to exert much control over the military, however, and at crucial junctures was basically ignored by the first commander in chief, Joffre. Poincaré provided strong backing for the appointment of Nivelle as French commander in 1917, this allowing Nivelle the political power needed to launch the disastrous offensive campaigns that nearly broke the French army. Late in the war, Poincaré's power was diminished by the assertive Clemenceau after the latter became premier. An advocate of harsh measures against Germany after the war, Poincaré continued in high office throughout the 1920s.

POTIOREK, Oskar. 1853-1933. Austro-Hungarian general. Potiorek was a measure of the incompetence of much of the Austro-Hungarian high command at the beginning of the war. He was a general with great political clout because of his high standing with the imperial family, but his actual military skills were slim and his deficiencies in the field cost the empire mightily in men and material. At the turn of the century, Potiorek was a rival of Conrad von Hötzendorf for the post of chief of the Imperial Staff, but lost in 1906 and was consoled with being named commander and governor of Bosnia-Herzegovina. He was directly responsible for the security arrangements for the visit to Sarajevo in June 1914 of the Austrian heir, but—typical of Potiorek's vision of life—he refused to bring additional troops into the city despite warnings of terrorists because no troops had suitable dress uniforms. It would have marred the occasion to have them appear in unfashionable costume. As it turned out, the damage was much more than to the stylish image of the governor, yet Potiorek was never blamed for the lapses that led to the assassination of Franz Ferdinand and his wife. When the war began in August 1914, Potiorek wanted to invade Serbia and take Serbian territory. This should have been simple for the Austrians, since they vastly outnumbered and outgunned the relatively small Serbian forces. Potiorek, however, lost badly at Jadar in his first attempt to invade. He regrouped, begged more troops from the emperor, and tried again in September. He was again repulsed by the Serbs. A third invasion in November began more promisingly—he actually took the Serbian capital of Belgrade for a few days—but he was again decisively defeated by the doughty Serbs under their talented general Putnik. During his last campaign, Potiorek managed to suffer two hundred thousand casualties and to severely damage the Austro-Hungarian forces in the East. He was dumped from command in December. The Central Powers finally crushed Serbia a year later under the command of German generals.

PUTNIK, Radomir. 1847-1917. Serbian general. Although not accorded much fame, Putnik was one of the most able field commanders of the war. He was an artillery officer and fought in the wars against Turkey in the 1870s before becoming a general staff member. He rose to the rank of colonel and seemed fated for further promotion when he was summarily halted in career advancement due to the complex politics of Serbia in the late 1890s. When a group of military commanders butchered the king in 1903 and put Peter Karadjordjevic in his place, Putnik was returned to grace (he had been dismissed from active service for eight years) and assumed the post of chief of the Serbian general staff with the rank of general. He proved to be a vigorous and intelligent planner, modernizing the Serbian army and building up resources and experience during the series

of Balkan wars that preceded the outbreak of the general conflict. Putnik decisively defeated the Turks and the Bulgarians in the two years before the assassination of Austro-Hungarian Archduke Franz Ferdinand by Serbian-inspired terrorists in June 1914. After Austria-Hungary's declaration of war on Serbia (the actual flash point of World War I), Putnik faced an invasion by a superior force under Austrian general Potiorek. Fortunately for Serbia, Putnik was a much better general. He screened off the border until he saw Potiorek's point of attack, and then the Serb concentrated his mobile infantry and defeated the Austrians. In the following weeks, Putnik even managed significant raids into Bosnia before withdrawing to prepare for a second Austrian invasion in October. The result was much the same as the first attempt by Potiorek: the Serbs under Putnik beat up on the Austrians. A third invasion was even more decisively defeated by Putnik in December 1914, and the Austro-Hungarian army was severely damaged and chased completely out of Serbia. Unfortunately, Putnik's success could not be sustained in the face of the better generalship of the German Mackensen, who was given a mixed force of German, Bulgarian, and Austro-Hungarian troops to invade Serbia in the fall of 1915. Despite a tactically skilled retreat into and over the rugged Serbian mountains, Putnik had no chance at victory. His army barely survived the retreat, and he grew too ill to continue. He was evacuated to France where he died before the end of the war.

RAWLINSON, Henry S. 1864-1925. British general. A relatively able general who had the misfortune to be in command at the Somme on the worst single day of British military history, Rawlinson was born and bred to the life of a soldier. His father was a major general, and the young Rawlinson graduated from the military academy at Sandhurst after attending Eton. He followed a suitable course of overseas service in India, Burma, and Egypt, and he served in the socially elite Coldstream Guards. Rawlinson was one of Roberts's chief subordinates during the Boer War, and he returned to increased responsibility and promotion during the decade before the beginning of World War I. With the outbreak of hostilities, Rawlinson was given command of a small force designed to relieve the Belgians at Antwerp. The gesture was far too little too late in the face of the massive German advance, and the best Rawlinson could do was to help cover the Belgian army's retreat. He then joined the BEF in Flanders and became commander of the IVth Corps. He was promoted to lieutenant general in 1915 and given command of the entire Fourth Army. He was not a strikingly enlightened general—almost none of that description existed on the Western Front—but he was far more realistic in his appraisal of trench warfare than many of his fellow "Chateau" commanders. By 1916, Rawlinson had come to believe that a general breakthrough was unlikely if not impossible and that the Allies should amend their tactics to concentrate on limited front assaults. Unfortunately, the exactly opposite philosophy directed Rawlinson's superior, Haig, who ordered Rawlinson's army to make a vast frontal assault along the Somme River in July 1916. The troops were fed into a slaughter of immense proportions: sixty thousand were wiped from the field on the first day, and at least three hundred thousand became casualties before the assault was called off four months later. Despite the carnage and lack of achievement, Rawlinson was promoted again and continued as a full army commander throughout the remainder of the war. He died in India while serving as commander in chief.

RENNENKAMPF, Pavel K. 1854-1918. Russian general. One among many disastrously poor Russian generals, Rennenkampf was an aristocrat from an originally German family. Nothing in his pre-World War I career could have given hope to a clear-eyed observer that Rennenkampf would prove to be anything more than a nonentity in the field. His advancement in rank and responsibility before 1914 was due primarily to his court connections and his family's social standing. He led troops in the Russo-Japanese War, but he led them

to defeat. His major service was to put down the civil unrest in Siberia. At the beginning of World War I, Rennenkampf was commander of the Vilna district and given command of the Russian First Army. He was to advance into East Prussia in coordination with the Second Army, which was to move up from Poland. As in nearly all major campaigns on the Eastern Front, the Russian advance began well and then collapsed under the weight of the totally deficient Russian military system. Commanders, including Rennenkampf, nearly always refused to cooperate with fellow commanders. Given the choice of supporting a rival general or allowing the Germans an easy victory with immense losses to the motherland, nearly all Russian generals chose the latter. Rennenkampf was no exception. After moving rather boldly into East Prussia and scaring the daylights out of the German high command, he stopped his advance and failed to coordinate with the other Russian army moving from Warsaw. Moreover, his organization and equipment were terrible. His staff communicated over their radio net in clear language—they simply lacked the elementary skill to use codes—giving the eavesdropping Germans full knowledge of Russian plans and movements. The result was a smashing German victory over Rennenkampf at the Masurian Lakes. The rest of his active career was spent in retreat and hesitation, although he continued in command until the end of the year. He was removed from the field and subjected to an inquiry as to his corrupt practices—he most likely stole his men's supplies for personal profit—but he escaped censure or punishment. He came to an unexpected end: he was requested by the Bolsheviks to take up command of the Red Army force in Southern Russia in 1918, and when he refused, the new rulers of Russia had him shot.

RICHTHOFEN, Manfred, Baron von. 1892-1918. German flying ace. The most famous flier of the war, Richthofen was known as the "Red Baron" or the "Red Knight" due to the color of his plane. He began the war inauspiciously as a junior cavalry officer on the Eastern Front. He abandoned the cavalry for an infantry assignment in late 1914, but discovered that he was impatient with all land-based efforts. He transferred to the fledgling Air Corps in 1915. Surprisingly, he was not an apt pupil and had a difficult time learning to fly—Richthofen failed on his first attempt to pass the examination for a pilot's license. His performance during assignments at Verdun on the Western Front did little to make observers suppose he would be an outstanding pilot. However, after he was assigned to a fighter squadron under Oswald Boelcke in mid-1916, Richthofen's flair for single-plane combat became apparent. He soon began to ring up victory after victory over his British opponents. As time wore on and his total number of victories climbed higher and higher, he became a public figure with much propaganda value to the German high command. By January 1917, Richthofen claimed seventeen kills and was given command of his own fighter squadron. Consequently, his life was arranged to provide maximum glamor and maximum opportunity for him to claim kills. His famous "flying circus" was a mobile unit, housed in circus-like tents, that could move rapidly from place to place in search of easy targets. He also developed the tactic of staying high above the pell-mell of mass dogfights until he identified a vulnerable opponent, then sweeping down with machine guns blazing. The baron met his end in April 1918, when he was shot down behind enemy lines. The British buried him with all honors of war.

ROBERTSON, William R. 1860-1933. British field marshal. Robertson had the distinction of being the only British general to have begun his career as an enlisted man. However, the fact of his humble social origins probably influenced his habit of deferring to the aristocratic generals who were nominally under his direction. He was born in a small Lincolnshire village and enlisted at age seventeen. In 1887, Robertson won a commission by virtue of examination and was posted to India. He eventually managed to attend the Staff College—no mean feat for a former "ranker"—and by sheer merit began to advance rapidly up the ladder of promotion. He served in South Africa as an intelligence officer during the Boer War and returned to England to receive his brigadier's appointment in 1907. By the outbreak of World War I, Robertson was a major general and commandant of the Staff College. His first wartime duty was as quartermaster general of the BEF. His social origins hampered him, however, since the class-conscious commander in chief, Sir John French, refused to have anything to do with the lowly Robertson and even barred Robertson from eating in his mess. French's chief of staff collapsed under the stress of the first months of the war, however, and French had to appoint Robertson in his place in January 1915. During the following year, Robertson formed a strong attachment to the idea of winning the war on the Western Front, and he viewed the campaigns planned for the Dardanelles, the Middle East, and Greece as resource-sapping diversions. In December 1915, the entire British high command was reorganized: French was out, Haig was in (Robertson was not appointed commander in chief because he was not a gentleman), and Robertson was recalled to Britain to become chief of the imperial general staff, placing him, on paper at least, over Haig and all field commanders. In practice, Robertson deferred to Haig and did all he could to throw support behind the commander in France. Robertson ordered the immediate evacuation of the disastrous expedition at Gallipoli and tried to stall a large campaign in Mesopotamia. He completely supported Haig's plan for a massive offensive on the Somme—one of the costliest ideas of the entire war. Robertson's tenure as chief of the imperial staff seemed in danger when the old coalition government of Asquith left office in late 1916. The new prime minister, David Lloyd George, was not in agreement with Robertson and Haig. The two sides disagreed during the following months, with Lloyd George pushing for campaigns away from the Western Front. By early 1918, it was clear that Robertson could no longer work peacefully with the prime minister, and he was forced from his office in February. He accepted meaningless commands thereafter until his retirement in 1921 with the rank of field marshal.

RUPPRECHT, Crown Prince of Bavaria. 1869-1951. German field marshal. Despite his high-sounding title and elevated social position, Rupprecht was a fine soldier who earned his reputation by achievement rather than by birth. He was the son of Ludwig III of Bavaria and, as such, moved early in life into the Bavarian military hierarchy. He also studied law at one stage of his training. He moved upward in rank and responsibility in a manner expected of a royal soldier, and by the eve of World War I, Rupprecht was a colonel general. He was given command of the German Sixth Army, which, under the grand plan of Schlieffen, was to hold fast in Lorraine while the mighty right wing swept down from Belgium. As the German offensive developed, Rupprecht was given responsibility for several assaults that he carried out with skill. At the end of the first weeks of the war, however, Rupprecht found himself enmeshed in static trench warfare—a fate that was to persist during the balance of the war. For most of 1915, Rupprecht commanded the part of the front in Flanders that opposed the British. In mid-1916, however, he was promoted to field marshal and given charge of a new army group on the Somme. After retreating to defensive positions behind the Hindenburg Line in 1917, Rupprecht began to harbor serious reservations about the course of the war and the prospects for ultimate German victory. Thereafter he grew more and more pessimistic, although he continued to lead his troops skillfully, lamenting their sacrifices all the while. He directed one of the spearheads of the final great German offensive in 1918, but it was ultimately repulsed by a joint Franco-American force. As the final months of the war eroded German strength, Rupprecht came to regard Ludendorff as the chief problem for Germany. With the defeat and surrender in the fall of 1918, Rupprecht retired to a private estate in Bavaria. He refused to take part in the right-wing politics of the 1920s and 1930s, and he withdrew to Italy during World War II. He returned to Bavaria after 1945.

SALANDRA, Antonio. 1853-1931. Italian prime minister. Salandra led Italy's government before the war and during Italy's first year of participation. His weak performance illustrated the vacillation and incompetence of most Italian politicians of the day. He was born in southern Italy, trained as a lawyer, and worked for a while as a teacher in Rome. He was elected to the Italian parliament in 1886, and he took office as minister of agriculture thirteen years later. He was finance minister twice between 1906 and 1909. As the outbreak of a general war in Europe approached, Salandra was not the most prominent member of the majority party in Italy but rather a subordinate to Giovanni Giolitti. Nonetheless, Salandra became prime minister in the spring of 1914 when Giolitti left office for what most in Italy believed would be a short respite. As it turned out, Salandra held center stage of the government for the next two years. Italy was nominally a member of the Triple Alliance and pledged to go to war to support Germany and Austria-Hungary in the event of a general conflict. However, Austria-Hungary was the chief object of nationalist hatred among Italians, who lusted after Trieste and territorial gains in the Trentino. It was clear to most that Italy had no intention of honoring her treaty when the Austrians dragged Germany into war over Serbia. Salandra equivocated and back-pedaled during the fall of 1914 and found a pretext to stay out of the conflagration. He then proceeded on a hazardous path to strike the best deal with one of the two sides. British naval power was a major threat to Italian security, and there was still the desire to wrest land away from the hated Austrians, so Salandra tilted toward joining the Allies and signed a treaty to that effect in April 1915. British reverses in the Dardanelles and Austrian victories, however, nearly persuaded the Chamber of Deputies to stay a declaration of war, and Salandra was forced to resign briefly in May. He returned to office within three days, and Italy formally declared war by the end of the month. Salandra discovered that the actual conduct of war was fraught with difficulty. The Italian front froze at the line of the Isonzo River, and nothing in the way of bloody campaigning could move it. When the Austrians pushed into the Trentino passes in mid-1916, Salandra's government came to an end. He served as a delegate to the Peace Conference in Paris after the war and supported the rise of Mussolini.

SAMSONOV, Alexander. 1859-1914. Russian general. One of the many incompetent generals commanding Russian armies at the beginning of the war, Samsonov failed to survive his first test in August 1914. He was a veteran imperial officer, a graduate of the general staff academy who had seen service in both the war against the Turks in 1877 and the Russo-Japanese War. He was a general by the end of the conflict with the Japanese. He returned from the defeat in the East to become chief of staff of the Warsaw district and then governor general of Turkestan. When World War I began in the late summer of 1914, Samsonov was recalled from Turkestan and given command of the Second Army. He was to form the southern half of a two-part pincer movement against the Germans in East Prussia, with Rennenkampf advancing from the north. The plan dissolved in a complete muddle within a few days. At first Samsonov moved briskly into Germany, but he bogged down and soon found himself under attack by overwhelming numbers of German troops. His opponents had stopped Rennenkampf, and because the Russians conducted all radio traffic in the clear (they couldn't manage the technicalities of encoding), the Germans knew that it was safe to turn all available forces against Samsonov. He was helpless to prevent the disintegration of his entire army with massive casualties and capture of prisoners. He rode into a wooded area and committed suicide when the scale of the disaster became apparent.

SARRAIL, Maurice. 1856-1929. French general. A controversial figure during much of the war, Sarrail was born in the southern region of France. He was trained at the military academy at Saint-Cyr and served his first duties in North Africa. He was swept up in the great political earthquake of the Dreyfuss Affair in the 1890s and became, surprisingly for a serving officer, a political Radical. He was thus at odds with most of his fellow officers. The Radicals' political strength waxed and waned in the national Chamber of Deputies, but since Sarrail was one of the few important officers with close Radical ties, he benefited from the connection. He held important posts between 1900 and the beginning of the war, which found him a major general in command of a corps. During the first confused days of the war in August 1914, Sarrail showed courage and determination. He was named to command the Third Army when his previous commander appeared to waver under the fierce German offensive. Sarrail tenaciously held on to the fortresses at Verdun and thus protected the French flank during the crucial battles on the Marne. The next months passed relatively uneventfully for Sarrail, but in July 1915 the Germans attacked his sector and won a quick victory that damaged Sarrail's reputation in the army. His political connections remained strong, however, and although he was removed from command on the Western Front, he managed to have himself appointed as head of the so-called Army of the Orient, a multinational force operating in the Balkans, principally from Salonika in Greece. Sarrail became the focus of a long controversy among Allied high command councils. Some wanted to reinforce Sarrail and make the Balkans a major theater; others—notably Joffre—wanted to concentrate on victory on the Western Front. Sarrail himself meddled deeply and often in domestic Greek affairs, engineering a virtual coup that brought most of Greece into the Allied camp. He solidified his position with victories in the field during the fall of 1916, and for a time Sarrail enjoyed nearly complete independence of command. The following year he was given even more power and more troops from all of the Allied powers. However, by the end of the year he had tumbled from the heights. A series of mutinies among his disparate troops weakened his position. He attempted new offensives, but failed. When Georges Clemenceau came to power in Paris, Sarrail's fate was sealed. He was removed from command in December 1917 and played no role in the remaining months of the war. After a six-year hiatus, he returned to active duty in 1924 when the party of the left took power, but his service in Syria and the Middle East was undistinguished and he retired permanently in 1925.

SMITH-DORRIEN, Horace L. 1858-1930. British general. Smith-Dorrien commanded one of the two British corps in the initial month of the BEF presence in France. He had been born into a military family and educated at Harrow and Sandhurst. His tours of duty before World War I included most of the high spots of the British Empire: he fought the Zulus, served in Egypt, spent ten years in India, was with Kitchener at Omdurman, and took part in the Boer War. He was a major general by the end of the conflict in South Africa. When the British Expeditionary Force was organized and sent to France in August 1914, Smith-Dorrien was given charge of the IInd Corps under the overall command of Sir John French. Smith-Dorrien showed considerably more sense than his commander in chief and his fellow corps commander, Douglas Haig. Both of the latter generals insisted on ignoring the realities of the situation in Northern Europe and demanded brave but futile and costly stands by their outnumbered and outgunned troops. The BEF had unwittingly placed itself squarely in the path of the German right-wing juggernaut, so it bore the full blow of the German advance. Sir John French lost touch with what was happening but continued to order Smith-Dorrien to stand fast no matter what the cost. The IInd Corps was separated from Haig's corps and nearly crushed at Mons. A heroic stand at Le Château by Smith-Dorrien preserved the BEF as a force and helped weaken the German sweep toward Paris, but his efforts were little appreciated by Sir John French. Subsequently, Smith-Dorrien took command of

the reorganized Second Army and faced the Germans at Ypres in April 1915 when the enemy broke the Allied lines with the first effective gas attack of the war. Despite Smith-Dorrien's pleas to be allowed to withdraw to better positions, Sir John French ordered a stand that resulted in huge casualties. When Smith-Dorrien vigorously objected to the senseless losses, he was abruptly relieved of command by French and sent home. After a brief command in England, Smith-Dorrien withdrew from active service due to a severe bout with pneumonia. He died from injuries suffered in a car accident.

SMUTS, Jan. 1870-1950. British general. Smuts was the most important of the non-English British generals from the Empire. He was a South African Boer, born in what was then Cape Colony. Smuts was sent to England, however, for education and graduated from Cambridge. On his return to South Africa, Smuts took up the practice of law, but the conflict between the Boers and Great Britain impinged on his civilian career. He fought in the Boer War as a general, enjoying considerable success as a raider. Following the war, Smuts entered politics. He was a political ally of Louis Botha and served in several key government posts during the decade between the end of the Boer War and the beginning of World War I. In 1914, he was given command in the field and ordered to invade German South-West Africa. Many of the South African Boer troops had mutinied and in effect gone over to the Germans, so Smuts and Botha (who shared command) spent the early months of 1915 restoring order and reorganizing their forces. Eventually Smuts forced the surrender of large numbers of German forces, but he was never successful in tracking down or defeating the elusive Lettow-Vorbeck, despite nearly two years of trying to do so. Nonetheless, Smuts had won the confidence and respect of the government in London, and in early 1917 he was called to England to join the new War Cabinet of David Lloyd George. Over the following months, Smuts was a sort of roving military adviser and diplomat, dispatched to all corners to make assessments and report back to the central government. In 1918, he volunteered to take command of all the American troops being sent to Europe, an offer declined by the Americans. Following the war, Smuts returned to politics and took office as prime minister of South Africa in mid-1919. He remained the principal figure of South African government and politics for the following twenty years and then resumed his military career during World War II as a British field marshal.

SPEE, Maximilian von. 1861-1914. German admiral. Spee was a member of an aristocratic German family, although actually born in Denmark. He entered the Imperial Navy in 1878 and held the rank of rear admiral by 1914. At the beginning of the war, he was stationed in the Far East as commander of the small German squadron. He had two cruisers, the *Scharnhorst* and the *Gneisenau,* at his disposal as well as lighter craft. He steamed toward the Coromandel coast of Chile when he learned of the declaration of war, and there he achieved the brightest triumph of the naval war for the Germans, albeit a victory that in the long run had very little significance. Spee found a British squadron under Adm. Christopher Cradock waiting off the Chilean coast. The German ships enjoyed the advantages of superior speed and firepower, and after a brief engagement at long range, the two main British warships were destroyed. Cradock died in the battle. While this loss was a stunner to the British Admiralty and public, Spee realized he could do little more as an isolated naval force, so he set sail for Europe, hoping to pause at the Falkland Islands to destroy a British radio station. Unfortunately for him, the British had sent a strong force to the South Atlantic in hopes of catching Spee. A greatly superior British flotilla found Spee's ships off Port Stanley in December 1914 and proceeded to sink all but one. Spee died in the engagement.

TIRPITZ, Alfred von. 1849-1930. German admiral. The architect of Germany's prewar naval buildup, Tirpitz proved to be less than a dynamic leader when the conflict actually began. He had begun his career as an officer of the Prussian navy in 1865. After the unification of the German Empire, Tirpitz rose rapidly in the ranks and had reached the status of rear admiral just before the turn of the century. Thereafter, he moved even more rapidly in promotion—he was the first "grand admiral" in the German navy—but more importantly, Tirpitz gained a large measure of political power. He decided that the fate of the German Empire depended on countering the might of Britain's navy, the force that had dominated world military affairs for two centuries. Tirpitz therefore set out to push Germany into a long-range program of massive naval building that was calculated to give it superiority by 1920. He engineered a Navy Bill in 1900 that poured huge sums into building battleships and cruisers. When Britain upped the stakes with the introduction of the dreadnought class of ships, Tirpitz's plans began to unravel. Although he failed to realize it at the time, the naval race would cost more than Germany could afford, and when the war began in 1914, the kaiser's navy was still badly outnumbered and outgunned by the British. However, Tirpitz and other German naval commanders found themselves in a silly but desperate position: the German fleet was too valuable and had cost too much money to be risked in battle, but without a battle it was a worthless commodity. The High Seas Fleet remained in port during the first year and three-quarters of the war, while the British Fleet conducted a successful long-distance blockade. Belatedly, Tirpitz came to favor unrestricted submarine warfare, but his time had passed. He was more or less forced to resign in March 1916. (When the Germans finally risked a battle off Jutland in mid-1916, the results were inconclusive, and the High Seas Fleet returned to the safety of its harbors.) Tirpitz then became a right-wing politician, a role he maintained after the German defeat.

TROTSKY, Leon. 1879-1940. Russian revolutionary. One of the two principal revolutionaries who overturned the Russian state in 1917, Trotsky was both the colleague and rival of Lenin. Born into a Russian Jewish peasant family, Trotsky early espoused a revolutionary philosophy and suffered at the hands of the czarist authorities for his beliefs and activities. He was sent to Siberian imprisonment at age nineteen, but he escaped four years later and traveled to London where he met Lenin. For the ensuing years until the Bolshevik triumph, Trotsky and Lenin enjoyed an uneasy relationship, sometimes as rivals and sometimes as allies in the swirling world of the European revolutionary underground. Trotsky was a keen writer and a fervent speaker. He returned to Russia during the heady days of the 1905 "revolution." When that movement failed, he was again arrested and sent to Siberia where he again managed an escape. He worked in the West as a journalist thereafter, learning much about military affairs by means of covering wars for newspapers. He spent the first years of the war in Paris but was in New York when the March 1917 revolution deposed the czar. He arrived in Saint Petersburg two months later, allied himself finally to Lenin, and assisted in the maneuvers that led to the Bolshevik victory in the fall. He assumed office under the new communist government as Foreign Minister, and he attempted to negotiate a peace with the Germans. Unfortunately, Ludendorff was in complete command of the situation and forced Trotsky to accept the humiliating treaty of Brest-Litovsk as the price for an end to hostilities. Trotsky's most enduring legacy to the new Soviet state was the creation of the Red Army, which proved to be the main instrument of state policy during the ensuing civil wars. Trotsky himself, however, lost influence as new leaders—especially Stalin—came to center stage. He was ousted from power and exiled to Mexico in 1927. He was assassinated by a Stalinist agent who drove an ice axe through his skull in 1940.

WILHELM II. 1859–1941. German emperor. The royal blood of British Queen Victoria ran thin in her grandson Wilhelm (as it did in her nephew, Nicholas II). Despite being made the object of intense Allied hate propaganda, Wilhelm was a rather silly man who seldom showed much more than a surface understanding of issues. Although he had to bear some of the blame for the beginning and subsequent conduct of the war, he was for the most part the tool of others, despite his resplendent uniforms and high sounding title of "Supreme War Lord." He was Victoria's grandson on his mother's side and in line for both the Prussian crown and the new German imperial throne on his father's side. His spotty education and practical experience of life was almost all ceremonial and military. Wilhelm suffered a severely withered arm as a result of a birth defect, an affliction that many have made the focal point of psychological analysis as to his overly belligerent behavior as an adult. He ascended to the throne in 1888, ill-prepared to rule. Within two years, he dispensed with the services of the great minister Bismarck, and Wilhelm never replaced him with much more than mediocrities. Wilhelm enjoyed much formal power. However, he was forced on occasion to share authority with an elected assembly and, in fact, seldom initiated much in the way of policy, despite appearances. He was adept at public displays, however, and during the fifteen years before the outbreak of the war, he repeatedly took center stage—usually dressed in one of his comic opera uniforms, and on occasion literally riding a white charger—in forcing conflicts with the French and the Russians. Wilhelm was more or less maneuvered into giving Austria carte blanche to begin a general war after the assassination of Franz Ferdinand in the summer of 1914. During the war, Wilhelm's role went from weak to weaker. He provided virtually no personal or official leadership during the struggle other than to approve changes in command. Once Ludendorff and Hindenburg came on the scene, Wilhelm was reduced to little more than a puppet, a fact tactfully hidden from the publics of Europe and the United States. In the fall of 1918, with the German armies in retreat and the war effort in ruin, Wilhelm twisted and turned and refused to accept the end of his reign. His abdication was declared unilaterally by his ministers and against his will, and he was forced to flee to refuge in neutral Holland, where he lived out the remainder of his life.

WILSON, Henry H. 1864-1922. British general. A strange character to have stood so high in the ranks of British war leaders, Wilson was Protestant Irish by birth and had a very unprepossessing start as a soldier, being twice turned down for admission to the training school at Woolwich and three times to the military academy at Sandhurst. The best Wilson could manage was a direct militia commission. However, he soon parlayed this humble start into a strong career, based more on his political acumen than his military abilities. After a variety of staff and field assignments, he was chief of military operations for the British and a major general during the years just before World War I. He was also an unabashed and vociferous Francophile who believed completely that the French (and Ferdinand Foch in particular) were the founts of all military knowledge. He wanted to subordinate any British force to French control in case of war. A few months before the war actually began in Europe, Wilson and a group of fellow Irish Protestants staged what amounted to a minor mutiny rather than allow North Ireland to be included in a new Irish State under home rule proposals. He was not, however, penalized for his actions. With the outbreak of the conflict in France, Wilson became deputy chief of staff under Sir John French. He performed rather poorly during the first weeks of the fighting but again escaped the consequences of his actions and became the chief liaison with the French army. In late 1915, Wilson was given field command of the IVth Corps but did little of note while commanding a quiet sector of the front. He was restored briefly in 1917 as liaison officer, but the ascension of Pétain, who hated Wilson, squelched that role. By the end of the year, however, Wilson's star began to rise to the heights. As a close political supporter of David Lloyd George, Wilson was on hand when the Allies revamped their command system. As a reward for his help, he was named as chief of the British Imperial Staff in February 1918. He was thus the nominal head of the British army during the last months of the war. He lost political favor soon after the armistice and withdrew from active service to stand for parliament for Northern Ireland. He was assassinated by Irish terrorists in 1922.

WILSON, Woodrow. 1856-1924. American president. Born in rural Virginia, Wilson was the son of a Presbyterian minister and had a distinguished academic career before entering politics. He graduated from Princeton in 1879 and went on to the University of Virginia and Johns Hopkins for law and doctoral degrees. He taught at Princeton and then became the school's president in 1902. Eight years later, Wilson ran successfully for the governorship of New Jersey. In 1912, after only a few years on the national political scene, Wilson won the Democratic nomination for president and defeated the Republican Taft and the third-party candidate, Teddy Roosevelt. Wilson was a great idealist (his enemies, especially in Europe, called him a hypocrite) and stood strongly for the rights of neutrals on the high seas, criticizing both Britain and Germany. The German use of submarines against commercial liners and shipping, however, caused him the greatest pain, and he forced Germany to abandon submarine warfare after the *Lusitania* affair in 1915. Running on a platform of neutrality, Wilson was reelected in 1916, but soon after his second inauguration he was faced with a renewal of unrestricted submarine warfare by the Germans, who were gambling that they could defeat Britain before America would enter the war. Ironically for a man who ran on the slogan "He kept us out of war," Wilson pushed the United States into a declaration on the side of the Allies in April 1917. Thereafter he was a strong wartime president, although his idealism led him to propagate the famous Fourteen Points, which he hoped would form the basis for a postwar settlement. He was a complete failure as a peacemaker, however. His European allies found him to be a self-righteous prig who failed to see the realities of dealing with a defeated enemy, and he lost most of his political clout at home in the midst of the peace conference. When he returned from Versailles, he suffered a severe stroke that left him paralyzed and virtually incompetent. His wife manipulated the powers of government for several months. Moreover, his political enemies in the U.S. Congress rejected the treaty and the League of Nations, which had been his brainchild. He died in 1924.

Selected Bibliography

Ahmad Amin. *Turkey in the Great War.* New Haven: Yale Univ. Press, 1930.

Asprey, Robert B. *The First Battle of the Marne.* London: Weidenfeld & Nicolson, 1962.

———. *The German High Command at War: Hindenburg and Ludendorff Conduct World War I.* New York: William Morrow, 1991.

Banting, D.R., and G.A. Embleton. *The Western Front, 1914-1918.* London: Almark, 1974.

Barbeau, Arthur E. *The Unknown Soldiers: African American Troops in World War I.* New York: De Capo Press, 1996 (1974).

Barker, A.J. *The Basard War: Mesopotamia, 1914-1918.* New York: Dial Press, 1967.

Bean, C.E.W. *Anzac to Amiens: A Shorter History of the Australian Fighting Forces in the Western and Eastern Theatres of War, 1914-1918.* Canberra: Australian War Memorial, 1946.

Bennett, Geoffrey. *The Battle of Jutland.* London: Batsford, 1964.

Bradley, John F.N. *Allied Intervention in Russia, 1917-1920.* London: Weidenfeld & Nicolson, 1968.

Churchill, Winston S. *The World Crisis.* 5 vols. London: Thornton Butterworth, 1923-31.

Clark, Alan. *Aces High: The War in the Air over the Western Front, 1914-1918.* New York: Ballantine, 1973.

Coffman, Edward M. *The War to End All Wars: The American Military Experience in World War I.* Madison: Univ. of Wisconsin Press, 1986.

Cowles, Virginia, *The Last Tsar and Tsarina.* London: Weidenfeld & Nicolson, 1977.

Cruttwell, C.R.M.F. *A History of the Great War, 1914-1918.* 1936. 2d ed. Chicago: Academy Chicago, 1991.

Dupuy, Trevor N. *The Military History of World War I.* New York: Watts, 1967.

Falls, Cyril B. *Marshall Foch.* Dehru Dun, India: Natraz Publishers, 1975.

Farwell, Byron. *The Great War in Africa, 1914-1918.* New York: W.W. Norton, 1986.

Feldman, Gerald D. *German Imperialism, 1914-1918.* New York: Wiley, 1972.

Fischer, Fritz. *Germany's Aims in the First World War.* London: Chatto & Windus, 1967.

Fitzsimons, Bernard, ed. *Tanks and Weapons, of World War I.* London: Phoebus, 1973.

Freidel, Frank B. *Over There: The Story of America's First Great Overseas Crusade.* Boston: Little, Brown, 1964.

Fussell, Paul. *The Great War and Modern Memory.* New York: Oxford Univ. Press, 1975.

Gardner, Brian. *The Big Push: A Portrait of the Battle of the Somme.* London: Cassell, 1961.

———. *German East Africa: The Story of the First World War in East Africa.* London: Cassell, 1963.

Gilbert, Martin. *Atlas of World War I.* New York: Dorset Press, 1970.

———. *The First World War: A Complete History.* New York: Henry Holt, 1994.

Giles, John. *The Somme: Then and Now.* Folkestone, England: Bailey, 1977.

———. *The Ypres Salient.* London: Cooper, 1970.

Gilford, Henry. *The Black Hand at Sarajevo.* Indianapolis: Bobbs-Merrill, 1975.

Goldberg, George. *The Peace to End Peace: The Paris Peace Conference of 1919.* New York: Harcourt, 1969.

Goodspeed, Donald J. *The Road Past Vimy: The Canadian Corps, 1914-1918.* Toronto: Macmillan, 1969.

Gray, Randal, and Christopher Argyl, eds., *Chronicle of the First World War.* 2 vols. New York: Facts on File, 1990, 1991.

Greger, Rene. *The Russian Fleet, 1914-1917*. London: Ian Allan, 1972.

Haste, Cate. *Keep the Home Fires Burning: Propaganda in the First World War.* London: Lane, 1977.

Hazlehurst, Cameron. *Politicians at War: A Prologue to the Triumph of Lloyd George.* London: Cape, 1971.

Heisser, D.C.R. *The Impact of the Great War on French Imperialism, 1914-1924.* Ann Arbor: University Microfilms International, 1981.

Hoehling, Adolph A. *The Great War at Sea: A History of Naval Action, 1914-1918.* London: Barker, 1965.

Horn, Daniel. *The German Naval Mutinies of World War I.* New Brunswick: Rutgers Univ. Press, 1969.

Horne, Alistair. *Death of a Generation: From Neuve Chapelle to Verdun and the Somme.* London: Macdonald, 1970.

———. *The Price of Glory: Verdun, 1916.* London: Macmillan, 1962.

Hough, Richard. *The Great War at Sea, 1914-1918.* Oxford: Oxford Univ. Press, 1983.

———. *The Pursuit of Admiral von Spee.* London: Allen & Unwin, 1969.

Hoyt, Edwin Palmer. *Disaster at the Dardanelles.* London: Barker, 1976.

Hudson, James J. *Hostile Skies: A Combat History of the American Air Service in World War I.* Syracuse: Syracuse Univ. Press, 1968.

James, Robert Rhodes. *Gallipoli.* London: B.T. Batsford, 1965.

Jameson, William. *The Most Formidable Thing: The Story of the Submarine from Its Earliest Days to the End of World War I.* London: Hart-Davis, 1965.

Jukes, Geoffrey. *Carpathian Disaster: Death of an Army.* London: Ballantine, 1973.

Kearsey, A.H.C. *The Operations in Egypt and Palestine, 1914 to June 1917.* Aldershot, England: Gale & Polden, 1932.

Keegan, John. *Opening Moves.* New York: Ballantine, 1971.

Keep, J.L.H. *The Russian Revolution: A Study in Mass Mobilization.* London: Weidenfeld & Nicolson, 1976.

Kennedy, David M. *Over Here: The First World War and American Society.* New York: Oxford Univ. Press, 1982.

Kennett, Lee. *The First Air War, 1914-1918.* New York: Free Press, 1991.

Kettle, Michael. *The Allies and the Russian Collapse, March 1917-March 1918.* London: Andre Deutsch, 1981.

Kitchen, Martin. *The Silent Dictatorship: The Politics of the German High Command under Hindenburg and Ludendorff, 1916-1918.* New York: Holmes & Meier, 1976.

Langer, William L. *Gas and Flame in World War I.* New York: Knopf, 1965.

Liddell Hart, Basil. *History of the World War, 1914-1918.* London: Faber, 1934.

Liddle, Peter H. *The 1916 Battle of the Somme: A Reappraisal.* London: Leo Cooper, 1992.

Link, Arthur S. *Woodrow Wilson and the Progressive Era, 1910-1917.* New York: Harper & Row, 1954.

MacDonald, Lyn. *1915: The Death of Innocence.* London: Headline, 1993.

———. *They Called It Passchendaele: The Story of the Third Battle of Ypres and of the Men Who Fought in It* . New York: Atheneum, 1989.

Macksey, Kenneth. *Vimy Ridge.* New York: Ballantine, 1972.

Marshall, S.L.A. *World War I.* New York: American Heritage, 1964.

Marshall-Cornwall, James H. *Haig as Military Commander.* London: Batsford, 1973.

Martin, Laurence W. *Peace without Victory: Woodrow Wilson and the British Liberals.* New Haven: Yale Univ. Press, 1958.

May, A.J. *The Passing of the Habsburg Monarchy, 1914-1918.* London: Oxford Univ. Press, 1966.

May, Ernest R. *The World War and American Isolation, 1914-1917.* Cambridge: Harvard Univ. Press, 1959.

Mayer, Arno J. *Politics and Diplomacy of Peacemaking: Containment and Counter-Revolution at Versailles, 1918-1919.* New York: Knopf, 1967.

McLaughlin, Redmond. *The Escape of the Goeben: Prelude to Gallipoli.* London: Seeley, 1974.

Messenger, Charles. *Trench Fighting, 1914-1918.* New York: Ballantine, 1972.

Moorehead, Alan. *Gallipoli.* New York: Ballantine Books, 1956.

Morrow, John H., Jr. *German Air Power in World War I.* Lincoln: Univ. of Nebraska Press, 1982.

Norman, Terry. *The Hell They Called High Wood: Somme 16.* London: W. Kimber, 1984.

Norris, Geoffrey. *The Royal Flying Corps: A History.* London: Mueller, 1965.

Palmer, Alan. *The Gardeners of Salonika.* London: Andre Deutsch, 1965.

———. *The Kaiser: Warlord of the Second Reich.* London: Weidenfeld & Nicolson, 1978.

Paschall, Rod. *The Defeat of Imperial Germany, 1917-1918.* Chapel Hill, N.C.: Algonquin Books, 1989.

Rimell, Raymond Laurence. *Zeppelin! A Battle for Air Supremacy in World War I.* London: Conway Maritime Press, 1984.

Robbins, Keith. *The First World War.* Oxford: Oxford Univ. Press, 1984.

Rutherford, Ward. *The Russian Army in World War I.* London: Gordon & Cremonesi, 1975.

Silberstein, Gerard E. *The Troubled Alliance: German-Austrian Relations, 1914-1917.* Lexington: Univ. Press of Kentucky, 1970.

Smith, Daniel Malloy. *The Great Departure: The United States and World War I, 1914-1920.* New York: Wiley, 1965.

Smythe, Donald. *Pershing: General of the Armies.* Bloomington: Indiana Univ. Press, 1986.

Snyder, Louis L. *Historic Documents of World War I.* Princeton, N.J.: Van Nostrand, 1958.

Stallings, Laurance. *The Doughboys: The Story of the A.E.F., 1917-1918.* New York: Harper, 1963.

Steiner, Zara S. *Britain and the Origins of the First World War.* London: Macmillan, 1977.

Stone, Norman. *The Eastern Front, 1914-1917.* London: Hodder & Stoughton, 1975.

Tauber, Eliezer. *The Arab Movements in World War I.* London: Frank Cass, 1993.

Taylor, A.J.P. *The First World War: An Illustrated History.* London: Hamilton, 1963.

Terraine, John. *Mons: The Retreat to Victory.* London: Batsford, 1960.

———. *The Great War, 1914-1918: A Pictorial History.* London: Hutchinson, 1965.

———. *The Road to Passchendaele, the Flanders Offensive: A Study in Inevitability.* London: Cooper, 1977.

———. *The Western Front, 1914-1918.* London: Hutchinson, 1964.

Toland, John. *No Man's Land: 1918, the Last Year of the Great War.* New York: Doubleday, 1980.

Tuchman, Barbara W. *The Guns of August.* London: Constable, 1962.

———. *The Zimmerman Telegram.* New York: Viking, 1958.

Turner, John. *British Politics and the Great War: Coalition and Conflict, 1915-1918.* New Haven: Yale Univ. Press, 1992.

Van der Vat, Dan. *The Grand Scuttle: The Sinking of the German Fleet at Scapa Flow in 1919.* London: Hodder & Stoughton, 1982.

Vaughan, Edwin Campion. *Some Desperate Glory: The World War I Diary of a British Officer, 1917.* New York: Simon & Schuster, 1981.

Walworth, Arthur. *Woodrow Wilson.* 3d ed. New York: W.W. Norton, 1978.

Warner, Philip. *The Battle of Loos.* London: Kimber, 1976.

———. *The Zeebrugge Raid.* London: Kimber, 1978.

Watson, D.R. *Georges Clemenceau: A Political Biography.* London: Eyre Methuen, 1974.

Weintraub, Stanley. *A Stillness Heard Around the World: The End of the Great War, November 1918.* London: Allen & Unwin, 1985.

Whitehouse, Arthur George. *Decisive Air Battles of the First World War.* New York: Duell, 1963.

Williams, John. *The Home Fronts: Britain, France and Germany, 1914-1918.* London: Constable, 1972.

Williamson, Samuel R., Jr. *Austria-Hungary and the Origins of the First World War.* London: Macmillan, 1991.

Woodward, Llewellyn. *Great Britain and the War of 1914-1918.* London: Methuen, 1967.

Woolcombe, Robert. *The First Tank Battle: Cambrai 1917.* London: Barker, 1967.

Young, Peter, editor-in-chief. *The Marshall Cavendish Illustrated Encyclopedia of World War I.* 11 vols. New York: Marshall Cavendish, 1986.

Zeman, Z.A.B. *A Diplomatic History of the First World War.* London: Weidenfeld & Nicolson, 1971.

Index